Discovering the Western Past

A LOOK AT THE EVIDENCE

THIRD EDITION

Discovering the Western Past

A LOOK AT THE EVIDENCE

VOLUME II
SINCE 1500

THIRD EDITION

Merry E. Wiesner
University of Wisconsin—Milwaukee

Julius R. Ruff
Marquette University

William Bruce Wheeler
University of Tennessee, Knoxville

HOUGHTON MIFFLIN COMPANY   Boston   New York

Sponsoring Editor: Patricia A. Coryell
Senior Associate Editor: Jeffrey Greene
Project Editor: Christina Horn
Senior Production/Design Coordinator: Carol Merrigan
Manufacturing Manager: Florence Cadran
Marketing Manager: Clint Crockett

Cover Design: Sandra Burch, NYC
Cover Image: Maximilien Luce (1858–1941), *Le Quai St. Michel and Notre Dame.* Musée D'Orsay, Paris/Giraudon/Bridgeman Art Gallery

Printed in the U.S.A.
Library of Congress Catalog Card Number: 96-76975
ISBN Student Text: 0-395-79670-9
ISBN Examination Copy: 0-395-84401-0
3456789-DH-00 99 98 97

CONTENTS

CHAPTER SEVEN
Two Programs for Social and Political Change: Liberalism and Socialism   171

CHAPTER EIGHT
Vienna and Paris, 1850–1930: The Development of the Modern City   202

CHAPTER FOURTEEN
The Perils of Prosperity: The Unrest of Youth in the 1960s   387

CHAPTER FIFTEEN
Ethnic Nationalism and the Challenge to the State: The Example of the Former Soviet Union   419

Republics.   Census data from the former USSR.   Articles and photos from
the underground press of Ukraine and Lithuania.   Photographs of the Hill
of Crosses and of the human chain in the Baltic States, 1989.   The basic
principles of the Estonian National Independence Party.   The treaty among
Belarus, the Russian Federation, and Ukraine establishing the
Commonwealth of Independent States.   A portion of the language
law of Latvia and a radio editorial on the language laws of
Kyrgyzstan.   Refugee data from the republics of the former Soviet Union.

PREFACE

The first two editions of *Discovering the Western Past: A Look at the Evidence* elicited a very positive response from instructors and students alike, and that response encouraged us to proceed with this Third Edition. As authors, we were particularly gratified by the widespread acceptance of the central goal of *Discovering the Western Past*, that of making students active analysts of the past and not merely passive recipients of its factual record.

The title of this book begins with a verb, a choice that reflects our basic philosophy about history. History is not simply something one learns about; it is something one does. One discovers the past, and what makes this pursuit exciting is not only the past that is discovered but the process of discovery itself. This process can be simultaneously exhilarating and frustrating, enlightening and confusing, but it is always challenging enough to convince those of us who are professional historians to spend our lives at it. And our own students, as well as many other students, have caught this infectious excitement.

The recognition that history involves discovery as much as physics or astronomy does is often not shared by students, whose classroom experience of history frequently does not extend beyond listening to lectures and reading textbooks. The primary goal of *Discovering the Western Past: A Look at the Evidence* is to allow students enrolled in the Western Civilization course to *do* history in the same way we as historians do—to examine a group of original sources in order to answer questions about the past. We feel that contact with original sources is an excellent means of communicating the excitement of doing history, but incorporating complete works or a collection of documents into a Western Civilization course can be problematic for many instructors.

The evidence in this book thus differs from that in most source collections in its variety. We have included visual evidence such as coins, paintings, aerial photographs, cartoons, buildings, architectural plans, maps, and political posters. In choosing written evidence we again have tried to offer a broad sample—songs, plays, poems, novels, court records, notarial contracts, statistical data, and work regulations all supplement letters, newspapers, speeches, autobiographies, and other more traditional sources.

For students to learn history the way we as historians do, they must not only be confronted with the evidence; they must also learn how to use that evidence to arrive at a conclusion. In other words, they must learn historical methodology. Too often methodology (or even the notion that historians *have* a methodology) is reserved for upper-level majors or graduate students; beginning students are simply presented with historical facts and interpretations without being shown how these were unearthed or formulated. Students may learn that historians hold different interpretations of the significance of an event or individual or different ideas about causation, but they are not informed of how historians come to such conclusions.

Thus, along with evidence, we have provided explicit suggestions about how one might analyze that evidence, guiding students as they reach their own conclusions. As they work through the various chapters, students will discover not only that the sources of historical information are wide-ranging, but that the methodologies appropriate to understanding and using them are equally diverse. By doing history themselves, students will learn how intellectual historians handle philosophical treatises, economic historians quantitative data, social historians court records, and political and diplomatic historians theoretical treatises and memoirs. They will also be asked to consider the limitations of their evidence, to explore what historical questions it cannot answer as well as those it can. Instead of passive observers, students become active participants.

Following an approach that we have found successful in many different classroom situations, we have divided each chapter into five parts: The Problem, Sources and Method, the Evidence, Questions to Consider, and Epilogue. The section called "The Problem" presents the general historical background and context for the evidence offered and concludes with the central question or questions explored in the chapter. The section titled "Sources and Method" provides specific information about the sources and suggests ways in which students might best study and analyze this primary evidence. It also discusses how previous historians have evaluated such sources and mentions any major disputes about methodology or interpretation. "The Evidence" forms the core of each chapter, presenting a variety of original sources for students to use in completing the central task. In "Questions to Consider," suggestions are offered about connections among the sources, and students are guided to draw deductions from the evidence. The final section, "Epilogue," traces both the immediate effects of the issue under discussion and its impact on later developments.

Within this framework, we have tried to present a series of historical issues and events of significance to the instructor as well as of interest to the student. We have also aimed to provide a balance among political, social, diplomatic, intellectual, and cultural history. In other words, we have attempted to create a kind of historical sampler that we believe will help students learn the methods and skills used by historians. These skills—analyzing arguments, developing hypotheses, comparing evidence, testing conclusions, and reevaluating material—will not only enable students to master historical content; they will also provide the necessary foundation for critical thinking in other college courses and after college as well.

Discovering the Western Past is designed to accommodate any format of the Western Civilization course, from the small lecture/discussion class of a liberal arts or community college to the large lecture with discussions led by teaching assistants at a sizable university. The chapters may be used for individual assignments, team projects, class discussions, papers, and exams. Each is self-contained, so that any combination may be assigned. The book is not intended to replace a standard textbook, and it was written to accompany any Western Civilization text the instructor chooses. The Instructor's Resource Manual, written by the authors of the text, offers further suggestions for class discussions as well as a variety of ways in which students' learning may be evaluated and annotated lists of suggestions for further reading.

New to the Third Edition

The Third Edition of *Discovering the Western Past* incorporates the responses to the book that we have received from our own students, as well as from student and faculty users of the book around the country. Every chapter in the two volumes has received some reworking, and three new chapters are included in each volume.

Volume I includes new chapters on the medieval village, the medieval cloth trade, and peasant violence in the period 1300–1789. Volume II offers readers new chapters on the liberator-hero in Western revolutions, feminism and the peace movement, and ethnic nationalism in the former Soviet Union.

Acknowledgments

In the completion of this book, the authors received assistance from a number of people. Our colleagues and students at the University of Wisconsin—Milwaukee, Marquette University, and the University of Tennessee, Knoxville, have been generous with their ideas and time. Merry E. Wiesner (-Hanks) wishes especially to thank Judith Bennett, Martha Carlin, Michael Gordon, Ian Harris, Laura Roskos, and Marci Sortor for their critiques and suggestions, and Neil Wiesner-Hanks and Kai and Tyr Wiesner-Hanks for their help in maintaining the author's perspective. Julius Ruff acknowledges the assistance of two valued colleagues who aided in preparing all three editions of this work: the Reverend John Patrick Donnelly, S.J., of Marquette University and Michael D. Sibalis of Wilfrid Laurier University. He also wishes to thank Laura, Julia, and Charles Ruff for their continued support. William Bruce Wheeler wishes to thank Owen Bradley and Todd Diacon for their valuable assistance.

We wish to acknowledge particularly the following historians who read and commented on the manuscript of this Third Edition as it developed:

Virginia Aksan, *McMaster University*
Arthur Auten, *University of Hartford*

Linda T. Darling, *University of Arizona*
Luci Fortunato DeLisle, *Bridgewater State University*
Alison Futrell, *University of Arizona*
Michael Honhart, *University of Rhode Island*
Laird Jones, *Lock Haven University*
Caroline Litzenberger, *West Virginia University*
James Parry, *Seattle University*
Marjorie Plummer, *College of Charleston*
Richard Wagner, *Des Moines Area Community College*

Finally, the authors extend their thanks to the staff of Houghton Mifflin Company for their enthusiastic support.

M.E.W.
J.R.R.
W.B.W.

Discovering the Western Past

A LOOK AT THE EVIDENCE

THIRD EDITION

CHAPTER ONE

THE SPREAD

OF THE REFORMATION

In 1517, an Augustinian monk in the German province of Saxony named Martin Luther (1483–1546) began preaching and writing against papal *indulgences*, those letters from the pope that substituted for earthly penance or time in Purgatory for Christians who earned or purchased them. Luther called for an end to the sale of indulgences because this practice encouraged people to believe that sins did not have to be taken seriously but could be atoned for simply by buying a piece of paper. In taking this position he was repeating the ideas expressed more than one hundred years earlier by John Hus (1369?–1415), a Czech theologian and preacher. Many of Luther's other ideas had also been previously expressed by Hus, and even earlier by John Wyclif (1328–1384), an English philosopher and theologian. All three objected to the wealth of the Church and to the pope's claims to earthly power; called for an end to pilgrimages and the veneration of saints;

said that priests were no better than other people, and that in fact all believers were priests; and believed that the Bible should be available for all people to read for themselves in their own language.

Though Luther's beliefs were quite similar to those of Wyclif and Hus, their impact was not. Wyclif had gained a large following and died peacefully in his bed; less than twenty years after his death, however, English rulers ordered anyone espousing his beliefs to be burned at the stake as a heretic and so the movement he started was more or less wiped out. Hus himself was burned at the stake in 1415 at the Council of Constance, which ordered the bones of Wyclif to be dug up and burned as well. Hus's followers were not as easily steered back to the fold or stamped out as Wyclif's had been, but his ideas never spread beyond Bohemia (modern-day Czech Republic). Martin Luther's actions, on the other hand, led to a permanent split in Western Christianity, dividing an institution that had existed as a unified body for almost 1,500 years.

Within only a few years, Luther gained a huge number of followers in Germany and other countries, inspiring other religious reformers to break with the Catholic church in developing their own ideas. This movement has come to be known collectively as the "Protestant Reformation," though perhaps *Revolution* might be a more accurate term.

To understand why Luther's impact was so much greater than that of his predecessors, we need to examine a number of factors besides his basic set of beliefs. As with any revolution, social and economic grievances also played a role. Many different groups in early-sixteenth-century German society were disturbed by the changes they saw around them. Peasants, wanting the right to hunt and fish as they had in earlier times, objected to new taxes their landlords imposed on them. Bitter at the wealth of the Church, they believed the clergy were more interested in collecting money from them than in providing spiritual leadership. Landlords, watching the price of manufactured goods rise even faster than they could raise taxes or rents, blamed urban merchants and bankers, calling them greedy and avaricious. Those with only small landholdings were especially caught in an inflationary squeeze and often had to sell off their lands. This was particularly the case for the free imperial knights, a group of about 3,000 individuals in Germany who owed allegiance directly to the emperor but whose landholdings were often less than one square mile. The knights were also losing their reason for exis-

tence because military campaigns increasingly relied on infantry and artillery forces rather than mounted cavalry. All these groups were becoming nationalistic and objected to their church taxes and tithes going to the pope, whom they regarded as primarily an Italian prince rather than an international religious leader.

Political factors were also important in the Protestant Revolution. Germany was not a centralized monarchy like France, Spain, and England, but a collection of hundreds of semi-independent territories loosely combined into a political unit called the Holy Roman Empire, under the leadership of an elected emperor. Some of these territories were ruled by nobles such as princes, dukes, or counts; some were independent cities; some were ecclesiastical principalities ruled by archbishops or bishops; and some were ruled by free imperial knights. Each territory was jealous of the power of its neighbors and was equally unwilling to allow the emperor any strong centralized authority. This effect usually worked to the benefit of the individual territories, but it could also work to their detriment. For example, the emperor's weakness prevented him from enforcing such laws against alleged heretics as the one the English king had used against Wyclif's followers, with the result that each territory was relatively independent in matters of religion. On the other hand, he was unable to place limits on papal legal authority or tax collection in the way the stronger kings of western Europe could, with the result that Germany supported many more indulgence peddlers than England or Spain.

The decentralization of the Holy Roman Empire also left each territory more vulnerable than before to external military threats, the most significant of which in the early sixteenth century was the Ottoman Turks. Originating in central Asia, the Turks had adopted the Muslim religion and begun a campaign of conquest westward. In 1453 they took Constantinople and by 1500 were nearing Vienna, arousing fear in many German rulers. The Turkish threat combined with social and economic grievances among many sectors of society to make western Europeans feel the end of the world was near or to look for a charismatic leader who would solve their problems.

Technological factors also played a role in the Protestant Revolution. The printing press was developed in Germany around 1450, and by Luther's time there were printers in most of the major cities in Europe. The spread of printing was accompanied by a rise in literacy, so that many more people were able to read than in the time of Wyclif or Hus. They were also more able to buy books and pamphlets, for the rag paper used by printers was much cheaper than the parchment or vellum used by copyists in earlier centuries. Owning a Bible or part of a Bible to read in one's own language was now a realistic possibility.

In many ways, then, the early sixteenth century was a favorable time for a major religious change in west-ern Europe. Your task in this chapter will be to assess how that change occurred. How were the ideas of Luther disseminated so widely and so quickly? How were they made attractive to various groups within German society?

SOURCES AND METHOD

Before you look at the evidence in this chapter, think about how ideas are spread in modern American society. What would be the best ways to reach the greatest number of people if you wanted to discuss a new issue or present a new concept? You might want to use health issues as an example, for these often involve totally new ideas and information on one hand and are regarded as vitally important on the other. Think, for example, about the means by which the dangers of cigarette smoking or information about the spread of AIDS are communicated. To answer the first question, we will need to examine the sixteenth-century equivalents of these forms of communication. Health is an appropriate parallel because the most important such issue for many people in the sixteenth century was the health of their souls, a problem directly addressed by Luther and the other reformers.

The spread of the Reformation was perhaps the first example of a successful multimedia campaign; in consequence, as you might imagine, we will be using a wide variety of sources. As you read the written sources and look at the visual evidence, keep in mind that people were seeing, hearing, and reading all these materials at once. As in any successful advertising or propaganda campaign, certain ideas were reinforced over and over again to make sure the message was thoroughly communicated. You will need to pay particular attention, then, to those points that come up in more than one type of source.

Though they were seeing, hearing, or reading the same message, different groups within German society interpreted Protestant ideas differently. They latched on to certain concepts which had relevance for their own situations and often attached Protestant ideas to existing social, political, or economic grievances. Artists and authors spreading the Protestant message often conveyed their ideas in ways they knew would be attractive to various social groups. In answering the second question, it is important to note the portrayal of various social groups and pay attention to the frequency with which these portrayals appear. Thus as you look at the visual sources and read the written ones, jot down one list of the ideas expressed and another of the ways in which various types of people are depicted. In this way you will begin to see which ideas are central and perceived as popular, and which might be interpreted differently by different people.

Source 1 is a sermon delivered in 1521 by Martin Luther in Erfurt on his way to the Diet of Worms, a meeting of the leaders of the territories in the Holy Roman Empire. It is not based on Luther's own notes but was written down by a person in the audience who then gave the transcript to a local printer. This sermon is thus a record of both how the Reformation message was spread orally—so many people wanted to hear him that the church where Luther preached could not hold them all—and how it was spread in written form, for seven editions of the sermon appeared in 1521 alone. What teachings of the Catholic church did Luther criticize, and what ideas of his own did he emphasize? In assessing how ideas are spread, we have to pay attention not only to the content of the message but also to the form. In what sorts of words and images did Luther convey his ideas to his large audience?

The next sources—three hymns—also serve as both oral and written evidence. Martin Luther believed congregational hymn singing was an important part of a church service and an effective way to teach people about theology. In this tactic he anticipated modern advertisers, who recognize the power of a song or jingle in influencing people's choices. The first two hymns were written by Luther and the third by Paul Speratus, an early follower. As you read them, pay attention both to their content and their images. What ideas from Luther's sermon are reinforced in the hymns? What sorts of mental pictures do the words produce? (Keep in mind that you are reading these simply as poetry, whereas sixteenth-century people sang them. You may know the tune of "A Mighty Fortress," which is still sung in many Protestant congregations today, and can use your knowledge of its musical setting to help your assessment of the impact of the hymn and its message.)

The Lutheran message would certainly not have spread as widely as it did if church services were its only forum. The remaining sources are those people might have encountered anywhere. The woodcuts all come from Protestant pamphlets—small, inexpensive paperbound booklets written in German that were readily available in any city with a printer— or *broadsheets*—single-sheet posters that were often sold alone or as a series. These documents are extremely complex visually and need to be examined with great care. Most of the images used would have been familiar to any sixteenth-century person, but they may not be to you. Here, then, are some clues to help guide your analysis.

In Source 5, the person on the right wearing the triple crown with money on the table in front of him is the pope. The devils in front of the table are wearing the flat hats worn by cardinals; the pieces of paper with seals attached that they are handing out are indulgences. At the bottom are the flames of hell; at the top, heaven with a preacher and people participating in the two Church sacraments that the Protestants retained, baptism and communion.

Source 6, another heaven and hell image, shows Christ at the top deciding who will stay in heaven and two linked devils at the bottom dragging various people to hell. The right-hand devil wears the triple-crowned papal tiara, the left-hand the rolled turban worn by Turks. Included in the hell-bound group on the right are men wearing the flat cardinal's hat, the pointed hat of bishops, and the distinctive haircut of monks.

Source 7 comes from a series of woodcut contrasts. The left pictures show biblical scenes and the right the contemporary Church. The top left picture shows Christ with his disciples; the top right, the pope. From their hats and haircuts you can recognize some of the people gathered in front of the pope; those kneeling are wearing crowns, which in the sixteenth century were worn only by rulers. The bottom left picture shows Christ and the moneylenders at the temple at Jerusalem; the bottom right, the pope and indulgences.

Source 8 is the cover of a pamphlet called "The Wolf's Song." By now you recognize the hats and haircuts of the wolves at the top and sides; some of the geese wear crowns, and many carry jeweled necklaces. The choice of animals is intentional. Wolves were still a threat to livestock in sixteenth-century Europe, and geese were regarded as foolish, silly creatures willing to follow their leader blindly into dangerous situations.

Source 9 is a woodcut by the well-known German artist Lucas Cranach whom Luther commissioned to illustrate his pamphlet "Against the Papacy at Rome, Founded by the Devil" (1545). It shows two men defecating into the papal triple crown.

Taking all of the images into account, what message do the woodcuts convey about the pope and other Catholic clergy? About the Protestant clergy?

[5]

Which images and ideas are frequently repeated? How do these fit in with what was preached or sung in church?

The last source is a pamphlet by an unknown author printed in 1523. It is written in the form of a dialogue, a very common form for these Reformation printed materials. Read it, as you did the sermon and the hymns, for both content and tone. Why do you think the author chose these two characters to convey his message? What do they criticize about Catholic practices? How do the ideas expressed here compare with those in Luther's sermon? Which of the woodcuts might have served as an illustration for this pamphlet?

THE EVIDENCE

Source 1 from John W. Doberstein, editor, Luther's Works, *vol. 51 (Philadelphia: Fortress, 1959), pp. 61–66.*

1. Sermon Preached by Martin Luther in Erfurt (Germany), 1521

Dear friends, I shall pass over the story of St. Thomas this time and leave it for another occasion, and instead consider the brief words uttered by Christ: "Peace be with you" [John 20:19] and "Behold my hands and my side" [John 20:27], and "as the Father has sent me, even so I send you" [John 20:21]. Now, it is clear and manifest that every person likes to think that he will be saved and attain to eternal salvation. This is what I propose to discuss now.

You also know that all philosophers, doctors and writers have studiously endeavored to teach and write what attitude man should take to piety. They have gone to great trouble, but, as is evident, to little avail. Now genuine and true piety consists of two kinds of works: those done for others, which are the right kind, and those done for ourselves, which are unimportant. In order to find a foundation, one man builds churches; another goes on a pilgrimage to St. James'[1] or St. Peter's;[2] a third fasts or prays, wears a cowl, goes barefoot, or does something else of the kind. Such works are nothing whatever and must be completely destroyed. Mark these words: none of our works have any power whatsoever. For God has chosen a man, the Lord Christ Jesus, to crush death, destroy sin, and shatter hell, since there was no one before he came who did not inevitably belong to the devil. The devil therefore thought he would get a hold upon the Lord when he hung between the two thieves and

1. St. James of Compostella, a cathedral in northern Spain.
2. A cathedral in Rome.

was suffering the most contemptible and disgraceful of deaths, which was cursed both by God and by men [cf. Deut. 21:23; Gal. 3:13]. But the Godhead was so strong that death, sin, and even hell were destroyed.

Therefore you should note well the words which Paul writes to the Romans [Rom. 5:12–21]. Our sins have their source in Adam, and because Adam ate the apple, we have inherited sin from him. But Christ has shattered death for our sake, in order that we might be saved by his works, which are alien to us, and not by our works.

But the papal dominion treats us altogether differently. It makes rules about fasting, praying, and butter-eating, so that whoever keeps the commandments of the pope will be saved and whoever does not keep them belongs to the devil. It thus seduces the people with the delusion that goodness and salvation lies in their own works. But I say that none of the saints, no matter how holy they were, attained salvation by their works. Even the holy mother of God did not become good, was not saved, by her virginity or her motherhood, but rather by the will of faith and the works of God, and not by her purity, or her own works. Therefore, mark me well: this is the reason why salvation does not lie in our own works, no matter what they are; it cannot and will not be effected without faith.

Now, someone may say: Look, my friend, you are saying a lot about faith, and claiming that our salvation depends solely upon it; now, I ask you, how does one come to faith? I will tell you. Our Lord Christ said, "Peace be with you. Behold my hands, etc." [John 20:26–27]. [In other words, he is saying:] Look, man, I am the only one who has taken away your sins and redeemed you, etc.; now be at peace. Just as you inherited sin from Adam—not that you committed it, for I did not eat the apple, any more than you did, and yet this is how we came to be in sin—so we have not suffered [as Christ did], and therefore we were made free from death and sin by God's work, not by our works. Therefore God says: Behold, man, I am your redemption [cf. Isa. 43:3], just as Paul said to the Corinthians: Christ is our justification and redemption, etc. [I Cor 1:30]. Christ is our justification and redemption, as Paul says in this passage. And here our [Roman] masters say: Yes, *Redemptor*, Redeemer; this is true, but it is not enough.

Therefore, I say again: Alien works, these make us good! Our Lord Christ says: I am your justification. I have destroyed the sins you have upon you. Therefore only believe in me; believe that I am he who has done this; then you will be justified. For it is written, *Justicia est fides*, righteousness is identical with faith and comes through faith. Therefore, if we want to have faith, we should believe the gospel, Paul, etc., and not the papal breves,[3] or the decretals,[4] but rather guard ourselves against them as against fire. For everything that comes from the pope cries out: Give, give; and if you refuse, you are of

3. **breve:** letter of authority.
4. **decretal:** decree on matters of doctrine.

the devil. It would be a small matter if they were only exploiting the people. But, unfortunately, it is the greatest evil in the world to lead the people to believe that outward works can save or make a man good.

At this time the world is so full of wickedness that it is overflowing, and is therefore now under a terrible judgment and punishment, which God has inflicted, so that the people are perverting and deceiving themselves in their own minds. For to build churches, and to fast and pray and so on has the appearance of good works, but in our heads we are deluding ourselves. We should not give way to greed, desire for temporal honor, and other vices and rather be helpful to our poor neighbor. Then God will arise in us and we in him, and this means a new birth. What does it matter if we commit a fresh sin? If we do not immediately despair, but rather say within ourselves, "O God, thou livest still! Christ my Lord is the destroyer of sin," then at once the sin is gone. And also the wise man says: *Septies in die cadit iustus et resurgit."* "A righteous man falls seven times, and rises again" [Prov. 24:16].

The reason why the world is so utterly perverted and in error is that for a long time there have been no genuine preachers. There are perhaps three thousand priests, among whom one cannot find four good ones—God have mercy on us in this crying shame! And when you do get a good preacher, he runs through the gospel superficially and then follows it up with a fable . . . or he mixes in something of the pagan teachers, Aristotle, Plato, Socrates, and others, who are all quite contrary to the gospel, and also contrary to God, for they did not have the knowledge of the light which we possess. Aye, if you come to me and say: The Philosopher says: Do many good works, then you will acquire the habit, and finally you will become godly; then I say to you: Do not perform good works in order to become godly; but if you are already godly, then do good works, though without affectation and with faith. There you see how contrary these two points of view are.

In former times the devil made great attacks upon the people and from these attacks they took refuge in faith and clung to the Head, which is Christ; and so he was unable to accomplish anything. So now he has invented another device; he whispers into the ears of our Junkers[5] that they should make exactions from people and give them laws. This way it looks well on the outside; but inside it is full of poison. So the young children grow up in a delusion; they go to church thinking that salvation consists in praying, fasting, and attending mass. Thus it is the preacher's fault. But still there would be no need, if only we had right preachers.

The Lord said three times to St. Peter: *"Petre, amas me? etc.; pasce oves meas"* [John 21:15–17]. "Peter, feed, feed, feed my sheep." What is the meaning of *pascere*? It means to feed. How should one feed the sheep? Only by preaching the Word of God, only by preaching faith. Then our Junkers come along and

5. **junker:** member of the landowning nobility.

say: *Pascere* means *leges dare,* to enact laws, but with deception. Yes, they are well fed! They feed the sheep as the butchers do on Easter eve. Whereas one should speak the Word of God plainly to guide the poor and weak in faith, they mix in their beloved Aristotle, who is contrary to God, despite the fact that Paul says in Col. [2:8]: Beware of laws and philosophy. What does "philosophy" mean? If we knew Greek, Latin, and German, we would see clearly what the Apostle is saying.

Is not this the truth? I know very well that you don't like to hear this and that I am annoying many of you; nevertheless, I shall say it. I will also advise you, no matter who you are: If you have preaching in mind or are able to help it along, then do not become a priest or a monk, for there is a passage in the thirty-third and thirty-fourth chapters of the prophet Ezekiel, unfortunately a terrifying passage, which reads: If you forsake your neighbor, see him going astray, and do not help him, do not preach to him, I will call you to account for his soul [Ezek. 33:8; 34:10]. This is a passage which is not often read. But I say, you become a priest or a monk in order to pray your seven canonical hours and say mass, and you think you want to be godly. Alas, you're a fine fellow! It [i.e., being a priest or monk] will fail you. You say the Psalter, you pray the rosary, you pray all kinds of other prayers, and say a lot of words; you say mass, you kneel before the altar, you read confession, you go on mumbling and maundering; and all the while you think you are free from sin. And yet in your heart you have such great envy that, if you could choke your neighbor and get away with it creditably, you would do it; and that's the way you say mass. It would be no wonder if a thunderbolt struck you to the ground. But if you have eaten three grains of sugar or some other seasoning, no one could drag you to the altar with red-hot tongs.[6] You have scruples! And that means to go to heaven with the devil. I know very well that you don't like to hear this. Nevertheless, I will tell the truth, I must tell the truth, even though it cost me my neck twenty times over, that the verdict may not be pronounced against me [i.e., at the last judgment].

Yes, you say, there were learned people a hundred or fifty years ago too. That is true; but I am not concerned with the length of time or the number of persons. For even though they knew something of it then, the devil has always been a mixer, who preferred the pagan writers to the holy gospel. I will tell the truth and must tell the truth; that's why I'm standing here, and not taking any money for it either. Therefore, we should not build upon human law or works, but rather have true faith in the One who is the destroyer of sin; then we shall find ourselves growing in Him. Then everything that was bitter before is sweet. Then our hearts will recognize God. And when that happens we shall be despised, and we shall pay no regard to human law, and then the

---

6. Because of the rule that the priest must say mass fasting.

pope will come and excommunicate us. But then we shall be so united with God that we shall pay no heed whatsoever to any hardship, ban, or law.

Then someone may go on and ask: Should we not keep the man-made laws at all? Or, can we not continue to pray, fast, and so on, as long as the right way is present? My answer is that if there is present a right Christian love and faith, then everything a man does is meritorious; and each may do what he wills [cf. Rom. 14:22], so long as he has no regard for works, since they cannot save him.

In conclusion, then, every single person should reflect and remember that we cannot help ourselves, but only God, and also that our works are utterly worthless. So shall we have the peace of God. And every person should so perform his work that it benefits not only himself alone, but also another, his neighbor. If he is rich, his wealth should benefit the poor. If he is poor, his service should benefit the rich. When persons are servants or maidservants, their work should benefit their master. Thus no one's work should benefit him alone; for when you note that you are serving only your own advantage, then your service is false. I am not troubled; I know very well what man-made laws are. Let the pope issue as many laws as he likes, I will keep them all so far as I please.

Therefore, dear friends, remember that God has risen up for our sakes. Therefore let us also arise to be helpful to the weak in faith, and so direct our work that God may be pleased with it. So shall we receive the peace he has given to us today. May God grant us this every day. Amen.

Source 2 from Ulrich Leupold, editor, Luther's Works, *vol. 53 (Philadelphia: Fortress, 1965), p. 305.*

2. Luther, *Lord, Keep Us Steadfast in Thy Word*, hymn, 1541–1542

1. Lord, keep us steadfast in thy Word,
And curb the pope's and Turk's vile sword,
Who seek to topple from the throne
Jesus Christ, thine only Son.

2. Proof of thy might, Lord Christ, afford,
For thou of all the lords art Lord;
Thine own poor Christendom defend,
That it may praise thee without end.

3. God Holy Ghost, who comfort art,
Give to thy folk on earth one heart;

Stand by us breathing our last breath,
Lead us to life straight out of death.

Sources 3 and 4 from Lutheran Book of Worship *(Minneapolis: Augsburg, 1978), hymn 229; hymn 297.*

3. Luther, *A Mighty Fortress Is Our God*, hymn, 1527–1528

1. A mighty fortress is our God,
A sword and shield victorious;
He breaks the cruel oppressor's rod
And wins salvation glorious.
The old satanic foe
Has sworn to work us woe!
With craft and dreadful might
He arms himself to fight.
On earth he has no equal.

2. No strength of ours can match his might!
We would be lost, rejected.
But now a champion comes to fight,
Whom God himself elected.
You ask who this may be?
The Lord of hosts is he!
Christ Jesus, mighty Lord,
God's only Son, adored.
He holds the field victorious.

3. Though hordes of devils fill the land
All threat'ning to devour us,
We tremble not, unmoved we stand;
They cannot overpow'r us,
Let this world's tyrant rage;
In battle we'll engage!
His might is doomed to fail;
God's judgment must prevail!
One little word subdues him.

4. God's Word forever shall abide,
No thanks to foes, who fear it;
For God himself fights by our side
With weapons of the Spirit.
Were they to take our house,

Goods, honor, child, or spouse,
Though life be wrenched away,
They cannot win the day.
The Kingdom's ours forever!

4. Paul Speratus, *Salvation unto Us Has Come*, hymn, 1524

1. Salvation unto us has come
By God's free grace and favor;
Good works cannot avert our doom,
They help and save us never.
Faith looks to Jesus Christ alone,
Who did for all the world atone;
He is our mediator.

2. Theirs was a false, misleading dream
Who thought God's law was given
That sinners might themselves redeem
And by their works gain heaven.
The Law is but a mirror bright
To bring the inbred sin to light
That lurks within our nature.

3. And yet the Law fulfilled must be,
Or we were lost forever;
Therefore God sent his Son that he
Might us from death deliver.
He all the Law for us fulfilled,
And thus his Father's anger stilled
Which over us impended.

4. Faith clings to Jesus' cross alone
And rests in him unceasing;
And by its fruits true faith is known,
With love and hope unceasing.
For faith alone can justify;
Works serve our neighbor and supply
The proof that faith is living.

5.   All blessing, honor, thanks, and praise
To Father, Son, and Spirit,
The God who saved us by his grace;
All glory to his merit.
O triune God in heav'n above,
You have revealed your saving love;
Your blessed name we hallow.

Source 5 from Kupferstichkabinett Staatliche Museen zu Berlin, Preussischer Kulturbesitz, Berlin. Photograph by Jorg P. Anders.

5. Matthias Gerung, Broadsheet, Lauingen (Germany), 1546

Source 6 from the Mitchell Collection, London.

6. Matthias Gerung, Broadsheet, Lauingen, 1546

7. Lucas Cranach, Pamphlet, Wittenberg (Germany), 1521

Source 9 from Brieg Gymnasialbibliothek.

9. Lucas Cranach, Pamphlet, Wittenberg, 1545[7]

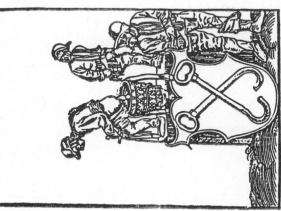

Bapst hat dem reich Christi gethon
Wie man hie handelt seine Cron.
Machts jr zweifelig: spricht der geist
Schendt getrost ein: Gott ists des heist.
Mart. Luth.

7. The lines below the woodcut read, "The pope has done to the king-dom of Christ / What is here being done to his own crown.

Source 8 from Herzog August Bibliothek, Wolfenbüttel.

8. Unknown Artist, Pamphlet, Augsburg (Germany), 1522

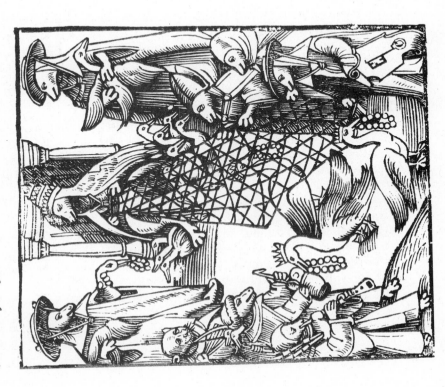

Source 10 from Oskar Schade, Satiren und Pasquille aus der Reformationszeit, *vol. 2, no. 15 (Hannover: 1863). Selection translated by Merry E. Wiesner.*

10. Anonymous German Pamphlet, 1523

A dialogue between two good friends named Hans Tholl and Claus Lamp, talking about the Antichrist[8] and his followers.

They are in a good mood while drinking wine and sit and discuss some ideas from the letters of Paul.

PREFACE

Dear Christians and brothers, if we want to recognize and know the Antichrist, we have to go to the brothers who can read, so that they will read us the second chapter of the second letter of Paul to the Thessalonians. There we will clearly find him, with his gestures and manners, how he acted and still acts, how he is now revealed so that we do not have to wait any longer but can know him despite his masks. How the devil sends his followers to knock us down, and how the old women and bath maids see him. We have long been blind to the lies and deceits of Satan, the devil. Because we have not paid attention to the divine warnings from Daniel, Paul, Christ, Peter, and the apocalypse of John, God has tormented us with ghosts and apparitions who will take us all with them to hell. Why should this cause God to suffer when He has offered you His holy word? If you don't want it, then go to the devil, for he is here now. He sees, finds, and possesses.

It happened that Hans Tholl and Claus Lamp were looking for each other and finally found each other in the evening.

CLAUS: My friend Hans, where have you been all day? I've been looking for you. The innkeeper has a good wine for two cents, and I wanted to drink a glass of wine with you.

HANS: Dear friend, I've been in a place that I wouldn't take six glasses of wine for.

CLAUS: So tell me where you have been.

HANS: I've got exciting news.

CLAUS: Well, what is it then? Tell me!

HANS: I was in a place where a friend read to four of us from the Bible. He read in the second chapter of the second letter of Paul to the Thessalonians about the Antichrist and how one is to recognize him.

CLAUS: Oh I would have given a penny to have been there.

8. **Antichrist:** the devil.

HANS: I want you to believe that I haven't heard anything like this in my whole life; I wouldn't have given three pennies to miss it.

CLAUS: Can't you remember anything, Hans? Can you tell me something about it?

HANS: I think I can tell you about almost the whole chapter, and only leave a little out.

CLAUS: So tell me! But let's get some wine first. I'll pay for yours.

HANS: Here's to your money!

CLAUS: Innkeeper, bring some wine.

HANS: What does he get for it?

CLAUS: He gets two cents. Now, tell me! I really want to hear what you will say about the Antichrist.

HANS: I'll tell you, but it will seem strange to you.

CLAUS: Why?

HANS: It seemed strange and odd to me, too, that people or states are the Antichrist.

CLAUS: Go ahead, then, you're boring me.

HANS: Stop that. All right, here's what the chapter says: "Dear brothers," Paul writes to the Thessalonians, "We ask you in the name of the coming of Christ and our coming together for the same, that you not be moved in your senses (or from your senses), or frightened by the spirit or the word or by letters supposedly coming from us, saying that the day of the Lord has come or will be coming soon. Let no one deceive you in any way, it will come only when there is disagreement and disunity (even though they all say they are preaching and believing nothing but the Gospel and Christianity) and the man of lawlessness will be disclosed, the son of damnation, who is against the gospel. Then he will be raised up (here Claus Lamp began to understand) above everything that is called a god (or is worshipped as a god) until he sits in the temple of God and lets himself be prayed to as if he were God." Claus, what are you thinking about? Do you know this man of lawlessness?

CLAUS: Now all the devils will come for you! He is no other beast than the Pope and his realm. I would never in my whole life have realized that if you hadn't been there [to hear it]. I'll buy you a second glass of wine!

HANS: Be quiet! I want to tell you more.

CLAUS: My dear friend, still more?

HANS: Of course. First I'll tell you the reason why I was talked to for so long.

CLAUS: My friend, for God's sake keep talking!

HANS: So listen! Here is the text: Paul says: "Don't you remember the things that I told you when I was with you? And now you know what is holding him (or what you should pay attention to), and that he will be revealed in his time. I tell you, that now he is doing so many evil and underhanded things, that only those who stop it now will stop it when his time comes fully. And then he will be revealed, the lawless one"—listen here, Claus—"who the lord Jesus Christ will slay with the breath of His mouth and will totally destroy with the light of His coming. But the coming of the Antichrist is through the activity of Satan, the devil, with great power and supposed signs and wonders, and with misguided celebration of the evil of those who will be destroyed. Because they would not accept the love of truth" (this clearly refers to the Gospel) "and be saved, God sends them the results of their errors, a great delusion, so that they believe the lies and are all condemned who did not believe the truth but agreed to the evil (and took it on themselves)." See that, Claus! Now you have heard why God has allowed error. Even though we have long wanted not to do wrong, we still hard-headedly keep doing it.

CLAUS: That says a lot. I would set my life on it, if it were only half as important. Now I hear and see that God allows very little understanding.

HANS: Yes, and why? People don't want to know very much and don't go to the Bible. God has hardened them and we are so godless. God will make us suffer because we don't ask about the truth. If we only had half as much concern about the health of our souls as we have about material goods, we wouldn't have come so far from the right path. As you have just heard, it isn't God who sent the so-called preachers [to lead us astray]. Here, I'll say it to you straight: Paul goes on to say: "Dear brothers, we should give thanks to God at all times because he chose you from the beginning, and he called you through the Gospel" (and not through other fairy-stories, as people are now saying).

CLAUS: Unfortunately you are right. Right now I hear strange things about the beast of the Antichrist from priests and monks. God help us!

HANS: Yes, we need to pray earnestly to God to send us good preachers, that preach the pure Gospel and leave the fairy-stories at home.

CLAUS: My friend, I am still thinking about the Antichrist, that he has begun so many devilish things and made the whole world to be his fool.

HANS: That astonishes me, too. But you have now heard from Paul, when he says: "God has allowed them to be deluded because they have not accepted the truth." We haven't noticed this, and the priests have hidden it from us.

CLAUS: I believe that the devil has possessed them all so that they haven't preached to us about these things.

HANS: They are afraid that people would recognize that their God, the Pope, is the Antichrist. People are supposed to honor and pray to him, just like Paul says about the Antichrist. So they are afraid.

CLAUS: That's really true. They've thought: If we tell the lay people this, they will notice and think about how they have to kiss the Pope's foot and call him "most holy." And some know-it-alls even say: The Pope can't do any wrong; he can't sin.

HANS: It's amazing that God has allowed this to happen for so long, that it hasn't been made clear that we have been so blind. What really matters is that we have deserted the truth, my dear Claus. Let's ask God for the true faith! I see clearly that everything will soon be over, that the Last Judgment stands right before the door!

CLAUS: My dear brother Hans, I've thought that for a long time. Shall we go home?

HANS: Yes, let's drink up and go.

CLAUS: I don't want to drink any more, because I have been so seized by pity and compassion. I see that things will end soon. My dear Hans, I want to take this thing to its end with you, so I have to ask: what do you think about the fact that there is such a commotion now about Luther and his writings?

HANS: I think it's because he has discovered the Antichrist. He can't stand it, and I believe he will make many martyrs. I've heard that it has already started in some places; in Antwerp three people have been burnt because of his teachings. And I've heard that in some places they are imprisoning people and hunting them down.

CLAUS: If that's true, that's what's supposed to happen. I have always heard that the Antichrist will make martyrs and will pay money so that people will kill those who do not believe in him but instead preach the word of God.

HANS: I've heard that, too. Now to the next thing: when I want to hear more things read, I'll tell you.

CLAUS: My dear friend, I'll let everything be open to you, because I see clearly what will come out of it. I see clearly, if I want to be saved, I have to come back to the true faith, from which without a doubt the Antichrist and his horde have led us. God give you a good night!

HANS: Same to you! See that you don't forget what I've said.

CLAUS: I won't for the rest of my life. God be praised.

QUESTIONS TO CONSIDER

In exploring how the Reformation movement grew and took root throughout Europe, many scholars point to the printing press as the key factor in explaining why Luther's reforms had a much greater impact than those of Wyclif and Hus. After examining the sources, would you agree? What difference did it make that Luther's sermons were not only delivered but also printed? That hymns were not simply taught to choirs of monks or clergymen but to congregations of laypeople, out of hymnals that were printed and might be purchased by any fairly well-to-do member? That small pamphlets such as the one reproduced here were written in German and appeared in paperback?

Several historians have also pointed to the opposite effect, that the Protestant emphasis on individual reading of the Bible dramatically increased the demand for books. Judging by the language, what sort of person might have bought Luther's sermon or the pamphlet? What effects would you expect the Protestant Reformation to have had on literacy? The religious conflict itself was also a spur to book production and book buying, and religious works were the best sellers of the sixteenth century. What techniques did the pamphlet writer use to make his work more appealing to a buyer? How might including some of the woodcuts have affected sales?

Of course, the great majority of people in the sixteenth century could not read, so it may be wrong to overemphasize written sources of communication. As you noticed in the dialogue, however, people who could not read often turned to their neighbors who could, so that printed pamphlets were often heard by many who could not read them themselves. This dialogue itself was probably read out loud and may even have been acted out, which we know was the case with more elaborate dialogues containing stage directions and a whole cast of characters. Do you think this dialogue would have been effective read aloud rather than silently? The printing press also increased the circulation of visual images; woodcuts such as those reproduced here often became best sellers. Why did so many people purchase these woodcuts? If a person's only contact with Protestant thinking were images such as these, how would his or her beliefs have differed from those of a person who could read Luther's words as well?

To answer the second question—how the Protestant message was made attractive to people—look at your list of frequently repeated ideas and images. Which seem directed to all Christians? For example, what do the sources say about the role of good works in helping a person achieve salvation? The role of faith? Why might these ideas have been appealing? What was wrong with the Catholic clergy? In contrast, what did "good preachers" do and emphasize? Why might the contrast have made Luther's ideas attractive?

Though ideas and images were often repeated, not everyone understood them in the same way nor was attracted to them for the same reasons. Groups within German society responded to different parts of the Protestant message and must be examined separately. Begin with the peasants. How are they depicted in the various sources? Why did the pamphlet writer and the artist of Source 9 choose to make their characters peasants? In the heaven and hell woodcuts, where are peasants and poor people? Why would peasants have been particularly attracted to the criticism of indulgences? Why would Luther's ideas about the value of good works have appealed to them? Source 5 shows nobles in fancy feathered hats near hell and Source 8 depicts rulers as geese; how would peasants have responded to these images? In the dialogue, Claus and Hans both agree that the Last Judgment is near. Why might sixteenth-century peasants have accepted this idea of the imminence of the end of the world?

Now consider the nobles and rulers. We have already noted that several of the woodcuts portray them negatively. How did Luther portray them in his sermon? Though hostility to nobles and rulers is evident in the Protestant message, many of the movement's ideas and images appealed to this class. Look, for example, at the upper right picture in Source 7. How does this scene reflect the hostility of rulers to the papacy? The noble class was primarily responsible for military actions in sixteenth-century Germany. How would they have responded to the language of the hymns? What effect might linking the Turks and the pope in the second hymn and the woodcut of Source 6 have had? Luther's sermon, the second and third hymns, Source 6, and the final dialogue all include devils attacking people or dragging them to hell at the Last Judgment. Why might nobles have been attracted to such imagery? What message would they have gotten from imagery linking such devils with the pope? In what ways did the reasons why Luther's

ideas appealed to nobles contradict the reasons they appealed to peasants?

Other groups in German society appear only rarely in the sources given here, so you will not be able to discover as much about the ways in which the Protestant message attracted them as you can in the case of peasants and nobles. You may, however, want to review the sources for evidence relating to the middle class, which you can find most easily in the woodcuts. Which of your answers about the reasons certain ideas were appealing to peasants or nobles would also apply to middle-class people?

You are now ready to answer both questions posed in this chapter. How were the basic concepts of the Reformation communicated to a wide range of the population? How were these concepts made attractive to different groups?

EPILOGUE

Though Luther's initial message was one of religious reform, people quickly saw its social, economic, and political implications. The free imperial knights used Luther's attack on the wealth of the Church and his ideas about the spiritual equality of all Christians to justify their rebellion in 1521. Quickly suppressed, this uprising was followed by a more serious rebellion by peasants in 1525. Peasants in south Germany added religious demands, such as a call for "good pastors" and an end to church

taxes, to their long-standing economic grievances and took up arms. The Peasants' War spread eastward and northward but was never unified militarily, and it was brutally put down by imperial and noble armies later the same year.

Given some of Luther's remarks about rulers and human laws (as you read in the sermon), the peasants expected him to support them. He did not and urged them instead to obey their rulers, for in his opinion religion was not a valid justification for political revolution or social upheaval. When the peasants did not listen and continued their rebellion, Luther turned against them, calling them "murdering and thieving hordes." He supported the rulers in their slaughter of peasant armies, and his later writings became much more conservative than the sermon you read here.

The nobles and rulers who accepted Luther's message continued to receive his support, however. Many of the German states abolished the Catholic church and established their own Protestant churches under their individual ruler's control. This expulsion led to a series of religious wars between Protestants and Catholics that were finally ended by the Peace of Augsburg in 1555. The terms of the peace treaty allowed rulers to choose between Catholicism and Lutheran Protestantism; they were further given the right to enforce religious uniformity within their territories. By the middle of the sixteenth century, then, the only people who could respond as they chose to the Protestant message were rulers.

Achieving religious uniformity was not as simple a task as it had been earlier, however. Though rulers attempted to ban materials they did not agree with and prevent their subjects from reading or printing forbidden materials, religious literature was regularly smuggled from city to city. Because printing presses could produce thousands of copies of anything fairly quickly, ideas of all types spread much more quickly than they did earlier. Once people can read, it is much more difficult to control the information they take in; though rulers could control their subjects' outward religious activities, they could not control their thoughts.

Rulers were not the only ones who could not control thinking and the exchange of ideas during the sixteenth century. As Luther discovered to his dismay, once ideas are printed and widely disseminated, they take on a life of their own; no matter how much one might wish, they cannot be called back nor be made to conform to their original meaning. Not only did German knights and peasants interpret Luther's message in their own way, but other religious reformers, building on what he had written, developed their own interpretations of the Christian message. They used the same variety of methods that had been so successful in spreading Luther's ideas to communicate their own, and the Protestant Reformation became a multifaceted movement with many different leaders and numerous plans for action.

The Catholic church, learning from Protestant successes, began to publish its own illustrated pamphlets with negative images of Luther and other Protestant leaders along with explanations of its theology in easy-to-understand language. In this chapter we have looked exclusively at Lutheran propaganda, but the oral, written, and visual techniques of communication presented here were employed by all sides in the sixteenth-century religious conflict. Later they would be adapted for other political and intellectual debates.

CHAPTER TWO

STAGING ABSOLUTISM

The "Age of Absolutism" is the label historians often apply to the history of Europe in the seventeenth and eighteenth centuries. In many ways it is an appropriate description because, with the exception of England where the Civil War (1642–1648) and the Glorious Revolution (1688) severely limited royal power and created parliamentary government, most European states had monarchs in this era who aspired to absolute authority in their realms.

The royal absolutism that evolved in seventeenth-century Europe represents an important step in governmental development. In constructing absolutist states, monarchs and their ministers both created new organs of administration and built on existing institutions of government to supplant the regional authorities of the medieval state with more centralized state power. In principle, this centralized authority was subject to the absolute authority of the monarch; in practice, royal authority was nowhere as encompassing as that of a modern dictator. Poor communication systems, the persistence of traditional privileges that exempted whole regions or social groups from full royal authority, and other factors all set limits on royal power. Nevertheless, monarchs of the era strove for the ideal of absolute royal power, and France was the model in their work of state building.

French monarchs of the seventeenth and early eighteenth centuries more fully developed the system of absolute monarchy. In these rulers' efforts to overcome impediments to royal authority we can learn much about the creation of absolutism in Europe. Rulers in Prussia, Austria, Russia, and many smaller states sought not only the real power of the French kings but also the elaborate court ceremony and dazzling palaces that symbolized that power.

Absolutism in France was the work of Henry IV (r. 1589–1610), Louis XIII (r. 1610–1643) and his minister Cardinal Richelieu, and Louis XIV (r. 1643–1715). These rulers established a system of centralized royal political authority that destroyed many remnants of the feudal monarchy. The reward for their endeavors was great: with Europe's largest population and immense wealth, France was potentially the mightiest country on the continent in 1600 and its natural leader, if only these national strengths could be unified and directed by a strong government. Creation of such a government around an absolute monarch was the aim of French rulers, but they confronted formidable problems, common to many early modern states, in achieving their goal. Nobles everywhere still held considerable power, in part a legacy of the system of feudal monarchy. In France they possessed military power, which they used in the religious civil wars of the sixteenth century and in their Fronde revolt against growing royal power in the mid-seventeenth century. Nobles also exercised considerable political power through such representative bodies as the Estates General and provincial assemblies, which gave form to their claims for a voice in government. Moreover, nobles served as the judges of the great law courts, the *parlements*, that had to register all royal edicts before they could take effect.

A second obstacle to national unity and royal authority in many states, in an age that equated national unity with religious uniformity, was the presence of a large and influential religious minority. In France the Protestant minority was known as the Huguenots. Not only did they forswear the Catholic religion of the king and the majority of his subjects, but they possessed military power in their rights, under the Edict of Nantes,[1] to fortify their cities.

A third and major impediment to unifying a country under absolute royal authority lay in regional differences. The medieval monarchy of France had been built province by province over several centuries, and the kingdom was not well integrated. Some provinces, like Brittany in the north, retained local estates or assemblies with which the monarch actually had to bargain for taxes. Many provinces had their own cultural heritage that separated them from the king's government centered in Paris. These differences might be as simple as matters of local custom, but also as complex as unique systems of civil law. A particular problem was the persistence of local dialects, which made the French of royal officials a foreign and incomprehensible tongue in large portions of the kingdom.

The only unifying principle that could overcome all these centrifugal forces was royal authority. The task in the seventeenth century was to build a theoretical basis for a truly powerful monarch, to endow the king with tangible power that gave substance to theory, and to place the sovereign in a setting that would never permit the country to forget his new power.

To establish an abstract basis for absolutism, royal authority had to be strengthened and reinforced by a veritable cult of kingship. Seventeenth-

1. **Edict of Nantes:** In this 1598 decree, King Henry IV sought to end the civil warfare between French Catholics and Huguenots. He granted the Protestants basic protection, in the event of renewed fighting, by allowing them to fortify some 200 of their cities. The edict also accorded the Protestants freedom of belief with some restrictions and civil rights equal to those of Catholic Frenchmen.

century French statesmen built on medieval foundations in this task. Medieval kings had possessed limited tangible authority but substantial religious prestige; their vassals had rendered them religious oaths of loyalty. French monarchs since Pepin the Short had been anointed in a biblically inspired coronation ceremony in which they received not only the communion bread the Catholic church administered to all believers, but also the wine normally reserved for clerics; once crowned, they claimed to possess mystical religious powers to heal with the royal touch. All these trappings served to endow the monarch with almost divine powers, separating him from and raising him above his subjects. Many seventeenth-century thinkers emphasized this traditional divine dimension of royal power. Others, as you will see, found more practical grounds for great royal power.

To achieve greater royal power, Henry IV reestablished peace after the religious civil warfare of the late sixteenth century and Cardinal Richelieu curbed the military power of the nobility. With the creation of loyal provincial administrators, the *intendants,* and a system of political patronage that he directed, the cardinal also established firmer central control in the name of Louis XIII. Richelieu, moreover, ended Huguenot political power by crushing their revolt in 1628, and he intervened in the Thirty Years' War to establish France as a chief European power.

The reign of Louis XIV completed the process of consolidating royal authority in France. Louis XIV created much of the administrative apparatus necessary to centralize the state. The king brought the nobility under even greater control, building in Europe's largest army a force that could defeat any aristocratic revolt and creating in Versailles a court life that drew nobles near to the king, away from provincial plotting, where their actions could be observed. The king also sought to extend royal authority by expanding France's borders through a series of wars and to eliminate completely the Huguenot minority by revoking their religious freedoms embodied in the Edict of Nantes.

The king supplemented his military and political work of state building with other projects to integrate France more completely as one nation. With royal patronage, authors and scholars flourished and, by the example of their often excellent works, extended the French dialect in the country at the expense of provincial tongues. In the king's name, his finance minister, Jean-Baptiste Colbert (1619–1683) sought to realize a vision of a unified French economy. He designed mercantilist policies to favor French trade and to build French industry, and he improved transportation to bind the country together as one unit. The result of Louis's policies, therefore, was not only a stronger king and a more powerful France but a more unified country as well.

Far more than previous French monarchs, Louis XIV addressed the third task in establishing absolutism. In modern terms it consisted of effective public relations, which required visible evidence of the new royal authority. The stage setting for the royal display of the symbols of absolute authority was Versailles, the site of a new royal palace. Built between 1661 and 1682, the palace itself was massive, with a façade one-quarter mile long pierced by 2,143 windows. It was set in a park of 37,000 acres, of which 6,000 acres were embellished with formal gardens. These gardens contained 1,400 fountains that required massive hydraulic works to supply them with water, an artificial lake one mile long for royal boating parties, and 200 statues. The palace grounds contained various smaller palaces as well, including Marly, where the king could entertain small, select groups, away from the main palace that was the center of a court life embracing almost 20,000 persons (9,000 soldiers billeted in the town; and 5,000 royal servants, 1,000 nobles and their 4,000 servants, plus the royal family, all housed in the main palace). Because the royal ministers and their secretaries also were in residence, Versailles was much more than a palace: it was the capital of France.

Royal architects deliberately designed the palace to impart a message to all who entered. As a guidebook of 1681 by Laurent Morellet noted regarding the palace's art:

The subjects of painting which complete the decorations of the ceilings are of heroes and illustrious men, taken from history and fable, who have deserved the titles of Magnanimous, of Great, of Fathers of the People, of Liberal, of Just, of August and Victorious, and who have possessed all the Virtues which we have seen appear in the Per-

son of our Great Monarch during the fortunate course of his reign; so that everything remarkable which one sees in the Château and in the garden always has some relationship with the great actions of His Majesty.[2]

The court ritual and etiquette enacted in this setting departed markedly from the simpler court life of Louis XIII and were designed to complement the physical presence of the palace itself in teaching the lesson of a new royal power.

In this chapter we will analyze royal absolutism in France. What was the theoretical basis for absolute royal authority? What was traditional and what was new in the justification of royal power as expressed in late sixteenth- and seventeenth-century France? How did such early modern kings as Louis XIV communicate their absolute power in the various ceremonies and symbols of royal authority presented in the evidence that follows?

SOURCES AND METHOD

This chapter assembles several kinds of sources, each demanding a different kind of historical analysis. Two works of political theory that were influential in the formation of abso-

2. Laurent Morellet, *Explication historique de ce qu'il y a de plus remarquable dans la maison royale de Versailles et en celle de Monsieur à Saint-Cloud* (Paris, 1681), quoted in Robert W. Hartle, "Louis XIV and the Mirror of Antiquity" in Steven G. Reinhardt and Vaughn L. Glasgow, eds., *The Sun King: Louis XIV and the New World* (New Orleans: Louisiana State Museum Foundation, 1984), p. 111.

lutism open the evidence. To analyze these works effectively, you will need some brief background information on their authors and on the problems these thinkers discussed.

Jean Bodin (1530–1596) was a law professor, an attorney, and a legal official. His interests transcended his legal education, however. He brought a wide reading in Hebrew, Greek, Italian, and German to the central problem addressed in his major work, *The Six Books of the Republic* (1576), that of establishing the well-ordered state. Writing during the religious wars of the sixteenth century when government in France all but broke down, Bodin offered answers to this crisis. Especially novel for the sixteenth century was his call for religious toleration. Although he was at least formally a Catholic[3] and recognized unity in religion as a strong unifying factor for a country, Bodin was unwilling to advocate force in eliminating Protestantism from France. He believed that acceptance was by far the better policy.

Bodin's political thought was also significant, and his *Republic* immediately was recognized as an important work. Published in several editions and translated into Latin, Italian, Spanish, and German, the *Republic* influenced a circle of men, the *Politiques*, who advised Henry IV. Through the process of seeking to explain how to establish the well-ordered state, Bodin contributed much to Western political theory. Perhaps his most important idea was that there was nothing divine about governing power. Men created governments solely to ensure their physical and material security; to meet those needs, the ruling power had to exercise a sovereignty on which Bodin placed few limits.[4] Indeed, Bodin's concept of the ruler's power is his most important contribution to political thought. In the brief selection from Jean Bodin's complex work, examine his conception of the sovereign power required to establish a well-ordered state in France and contrast this conception with the feudal state still partially existing in his time.

The second work of political theory was written by Jacques Bénigne Bossuet (1627–1704), Bishop of Meaux. A great orator who preached at the court of Louis XIV, Bossuet was entrusted with the education of the king's son and heir, the Dauphin. He wrote three works for that prince's instruction, including the one excerpted in this chapter, *Politics Drawn from the Very Words of the Holy Scripture* (1678).

As tutor to the Dauphin and royal preacher, Bossuet expressed what has been called the *divine right* theory of kingship: that is, the king was God's deputy on earth, and to oppose him was to oppose divine law. Here, of

3. Bodin's religious thought evolved in the course of his life. Although he was brought up a Catholic and was briefly a Carmelite friar, his knowledge of Hebrew and early regard for the Old Testament led some to suspect he was a Jew. Writings of his middle years indicate some Calvinist leanings. Later in life, his thought seems to have moved beyond traditional Catholic and Protestant Christianity. He was nevertheless deeply religious.

4. Bodin saw the sovereign power limited by natural law and the need to respect property (which meant that the ruler could not tax without his subjects' consent) and the family.

course, the bishop was drawing on those medieval beliefs and practices imputing certain divine powers to the king. Because Bossuet was an influential member of the court of Louis XIV, his ideas on royal authority carried considerable weight. Trained as a theologian, he buttressed his political theories with scriptural authority. In this selection, determine the extent of the royal link to God. Why might such a theory be particularly useful to Louis XIV?

Source 3 is a selection from the *Memoirs* of Louis de Rouvroy, Duke of Saint-Simon (1675–1755). Saint-Simon's memoirs of court life are extensive, comprising forty-one volumes in the main French edition. They constitute both a remarkable record of life at Versailles and, because of their style, an important example of French literature. As useful and important as the *Memoirs* are, however, they must be read with care. All of us, consciously or unconsciously, have biases and opinions, and memoirists are no exception. In fact, memoir literature illustrates problems of which students of history should be aware in all they read. The way in which authors present events, even what they choose to include or omit from their accounts, reflects their opinions. Because memoir writers often recount events in which they participated, they may have especially strong views about what they relate. Thus, to use Saint-Simon's work profitably, it is essential to understand his point of view. We must also ask if the memoir writer was in a position to know firsthand what he or she is relating or is

simply recounting less reliable rumors.

Saint-Simon came from an old noble family recently risen to prominence when his father became a royal favorite. Ironically, no one was more deeply opposed to the policies of Louis XIV, which aimed at destroying the traditional feudal power of the nobility in the name of royal authority, than this man whose position rested on that very authority. Saint-Simon was, quite simply, a defender of the older style of kingship in which sovereignty was limited by the monarch's need to consult with his vassals. His memoirs reflect this view and are often critical of the king. But even with his critical view of the king and his court, Saint-Simon was an important figure there, an individual privy to state business and court gossip, who gives us a remarkable picture of life at Versailles. Analyze the court etiquette and ritual Saint-Simon describes as a nonverbal message from the king to his most powerful subjects. For example, what message did the royal waking and dressing ceremony convey to the most powerful and privileged persons in France, who crowded the royal bedroom and vied for the privilege of helping the king dress? What message did their very presence convey in turn to Louis XIV? Recall Bossuet's ideas of kingship. Why might public religious ritual such as that attending the royal rising be part of the agenda of a king not particularly noted for his piety during the first half of his life?

Studied closely, the three different kinds of written evidence presented— the work of a sixteenth-century political theorist, the writings of a contemporary supporter, and the memoirs of one of the king's opponents—reveal much about the growing power of the French monarchy. What common themes do you find in these works? What were the sources of the king's political authority? From these written sources we move on to pictorial evidence of the symbols of royal authority. Symbols are concrete objects possessing a meaning beyond what is immediately apparent. We are all aware of the power of symbols, particularly in our age of electronic media, and we all, perhaps unconsciously, analyze them to some extent. Take a simple example drawn from modern advertising: the lion appears frequently as an image in advertisements for banks and other financial institutions. The lion's presence is intended to convey to us the strength of the financial institution, to inspire our faith in the latter's ability to protect our funds. Using this kind of analysis, you can determine the total meaning of the symbols associated with Louis XIV.

Consider the painting presented as the fourth piece of evidence, *Louis XIV Taking Up Personal Government in 1661.* Louis XIV had been king in name since the age of five after his father's death in 1643, but only in 1661, as an adult, did he assume full power. Remember that such art was generally commissioned by the king and often had an instructional purpose. What do the following elements symbolize: the portrayal of Louis XIV as a Roman emperor; the positioning of a figure representing France on his right; the crowning of the king with a wreath of flowers; the figure of Time (note the hourglass and scythe) holding a tapestry over the royal head; and the presence of herald angels hovering above?

Now go on to the other pictures and perform the same kind of analysis, always trying to identify the symbolic message the painter or architect wished to convey. For Source 5 study the royal pose and such seemingly superficial elements in the picture as the king's dress and the background details. Ask yourself what ideas these were intended to convey. Source 6 presents the insignia Louis XIV chose as his personal symbol, which decorated much of Versailles. Reflect on Louis's reasons for this choice in reading his explanation:

The symbol that I have adopted and that you see all around you represents the duties of a Prince and inspires me always to fulfill them. I chose for an emblem the Sun which, according to the rules of this art [heraldry], is the noblest of all, and which, by the brightness that surrounds it, by the light it lends to the other stars that constitute, after a fashion, its court, by the universal good it does, endlessly promoting life, joy, and growth, by its perpetual and regular movement, by its constant and invariable course, is assuredly the most dazzling and most beautiful image of the monarch.[5]

With Sources 8 through 13, we turn to analysis of architecture, which of course also served to symbolize royal power. You must ask yourself how great that concept of royal power was

5. Quoted in Reinhardt and Glasgow, *The Sun King,* p. 181.

as you look at the pictures of Versailles. The palace, after all, was not only the royal residence but also the setting for the conduct of government, including the king's reception of foreign ambassadors. At the most basic level, notice the scale of the palace. What impression might its size have been intended to convey? At a second level, examine decorative details of the palace. Why might the balustrade at the palace entry have been decorated with statuary symbolizing Magnificence, Justice, Wisdom, Prudence, Diligence, Peace, Europe, Asia, Renown, Abundance, Force, Generosity, Wealth, Authority, Fame, America, Africa, and Victory?

Observe the views of the palace's interior, considering the functions of the rooms and their details. Source 10 offers a view of the royal chapel at Versailles. Richly decorated in marble and complemented with ceiling paintings such as that depicting the Trinity, the chapel was the site of daily masses as well as of royal marriages and celebrations of victories. Note that the king attended mass in the royal gallery, joining the rest of the court on the main floor only when the mass celebrant was a bishop. Why might such a magnificent setting be part of the palace? More important, what significance do you place on the position the king chose for himself in this grand setting?

Sources 11 and 12 present the sites of the royal rising ceremony described by Saint-Simon. The royal bedroom, Source 11, was richly decorated in gilt, red, and white, and was complemented by paintings of biblical scenes. Notice the rich decoration of the Bull's Eye Window Antechamber, just outside the bedroom, where the courtiers daily awaited the king's arising. Why were the rooms decorated in such a fashion?

Source 13 offers an artist's view of Marly. Again, notice the scale of this palace, reflecting that it was, according to Saint-Simon, a weekend getaway spot for Louis XIV and selected favorites. How might the king have used invitations to this château with the closeness to the royal person they entailed? Examine details of the palace. The central château had twelve apartments, four of which were reserved for the royal family, the others for its guests. The twelve pavilions around the lake in the center of the château's grounds each housed two guest apartments and represented the twelve signs of the zodiac. What symbolic importance might you attach to this?

Finally, return to Source 7, which recreates the pageant known as the Carousel of 1662, one of many such entertainments at court. The scale of such festivals could be huge. In 1662, 12,197 costumed people took part in a celebration that included a parade through the streets of Paris and games. Costumed as ancient Romans, Persians, and others, the participants must have made quite an impression on their audience. What kind of impression do you think it was?

What common message runs through the art and architecture you have analyzed? As you unravel the message woven into this visual evidence, combine it with the evidence you derived from Saint-Simon's portrayal of court life and the political theory of absolutism. Remember, too, the unstated message: that the monarchy of Louis XIV possessed in Europe's largest army the ultimate means for persuading its subjects to accept the divine powers of the king.

You should be able to determine from all this material what was new in this conception of royal authority and the ways in which the new authority was expressed.

Source 1 from Francis William Coker, editor, Readings in Political Philosophy *(New York: Macmillan, 1926), pp. 235–236.*

1. From Jean Bodin, *The Six Books of the Republic*, **Book I, 1576**

The first and principal function of sovereignty is to give laws to the citizens generally and individually, and, it must be added, not necessarily with the consent of superiors, equals, or inferiors. If the consent of superiors is required, then the prince is clearly a subject; if he must have the consent of equals, then others share his authority; if the consent of inferiors—the people or the senate—is necessary, then he lacks supreme authority. . . .

It may be objected that custom does not get its power from the judgment or command of the prince, and yet has almost the force of law, so that it would seem that the prince is master of law, the people of custom. Custom, insensibly, yet with the full compliance of all, passes gradually into the character of men, and acquires force with the lapse of time. Law, on the other hand, comes forth in one moment at the order of him who has the power to command, and often in opposition to the desire and approval of those whom it governs. Wherefore, Chrysostom[6] likens law to a tyrant and custom to a king. Moreover, the power of law is far greater than that of custom, for customs may be superseded by laws, but laws are not supplanted by customs; it is within the power and function of magistrates to restore the operation of laws which by custom are obsolescent. Custom proposes neither rewards nor penalties; laws carry one or the other, unless it be a permissive law which nullifies the penalty of some other law. In short, a custom has compelling force only as long as the prince, by adding his endorsement and sanction to the custom, makes it a law.

It is thus clear that laws and customs depend for their force upon the will of those who hold supreme power in the state. This first and chief mark of sovereignty is, therefore, of such sort that it cannot be transferred to subjects,

6. **Chrysostom:** Saint John Chrysostom (ca 347–407), an early Father of the Greek church whose religion led him into conflict with the Eastern Roman emperor.

though the prince or people sometimes confer upon one of the citizens the power to frame laws (*legum condendarum*), which then have the same force as if they had been framed by the prince himself. The Lacedæmonians bestowed such power upon Lycurgus, the Athenians upon Solon;[7] each stood as deputy for his state, and the fulfillment of his function depended upon the pleasure not of himself but of the people; his legislation had no force save as the people confirmed it by their assent. The former composed and wrote the laws, the people enacted and commanded them.

Under this supreme power of ordaining and abrogating laws, it is clear that all other functions of sovereignty are included; that it may be truly said that supreme authority in the state is comprised in this one thing—namely, to give laws to all and each of the citizens, and to receive none from them. For to declare war or make peace, though seeming to involve what is alien to the term law, is yet accomplished by law, that is by decree of the supreme power. It is also the prerogative of sovereignty to receive appeals from the highest magistrates, to confer authority upon the greater magistrates and to withdraw it from them, to allow exemption from taxes, to bestow other immunities, to grant dispensations from the laws, to exercise power of life and death, to fix the value, name and form of money, to compel all citizens to observe their oaths: all of these attributes are derived from the supreme power of commanding and forbidding—that is, from the authority to give law to the citizens collectively and individually, and to receive law from no one save immortal God. A duke, therefore, who gives laws to all his subjects, but receives law from the emperor, Pope, or king, or has a co-partner in authority, lacks sovereignty.

Source 2 from Richard H. Powers, editor and translator, Readings in European Civilization Since 1500 *(Boston: Houghton Mifflin, 1961), pp. 129–130.*

2. From Jacques Bénigne Bossuet, *Politics Drawn from the Very Words of the Holy Scriptures,* 1678

TO MONSEIGNEUR LE DAUPHIN

God is the King of kings. It is for Him to instruct and direct kings as His ministers. Heed then, Monseigneur, the lessons which He gives them in His Scriptures, and learn . . . the rules and examples on which they ought to base their conduct. . . .

7. **Lacedæmonians:** the Spartans of ancient Greece. **Lycurgus:** traditional author of the Spartan constitution. **Solon:** sixth-century B.C. Athenian lawgiver.

BOOK II: OR AUTHORITY . . .

CONCLUSION: Accordingly we have established by means of Scriptures that monarchical government comes from God. . . . That when government was established among men He chose hereditary monarchy as the most natural and most durable form. That excluding the sex born to obey[8] from the sovereign power was only natural. . . .

BOOK III: THE NATURE OF ROYAL AUTHORITY . . .

FIRST ARTICLE: Its essential characteristics. . . . First, royal authority is sacred; Second, it is paternal; Third, it is absolute; Fourth, it is subject to reason. . . .

SECOND ARTICLE: Royal authority is sacred.

FIRST PROPOSITION: God establishes kings as his ministers and reigns over people through them.—We have already seen that all power comes from God. . . .

Therefore princes act as ministers of God and as His lieutenants on earth. It is through them that he exercises His empire. . . .

Thus we have seen that the royal throne is not the throne of a man, but the throne of God himself. So in Scriptures we find "God has chosen my son Solomon to sit upon the throne of the kingdom of Jehovah over Israel." And further, "Solomon sat on the throne of Jehovah as king."

And in order that we should not think that to have kings established by God is peculiar to the Israelites, here is what Ecclesiastes says: "God gives each people its governor; and Israel is manifestly reserved to Him.". . .

SECOND PROPOSITION: The person of the king is sacred.—It follows from all the above that the person of kings is sacred. . . . God has had them anointed by His prophets with a sacred ointment, as He has had His pontiffs and His altars anointed.

But even before actually being anointed, they are sacred by virtue of their charge, as representatives of His divine majesty, delegated by His providence to execute His design. . . .

The title of *christ* is given to kings, one sees them called *christs* or the Lord's *anointed* everywhere.

Bearing this venerable name, even the prophets revered them, and looked upon them as associated with the sovereign empire of God, whose authority they exercise on earth. . . .

THIRD PROPOSITION: Religion and conscience demand that we obey the prince.—After having said that the prince is the minister of God Saint Paul concluded: "Accordingly it is necessary that you subject yourself to him out of fear of his anger, but also because of the obligation of your conscience. . . ."

And furthermore: "Servants, obey your temporal masters in all things. . . ." Saint Peter said: "Therefore submit yourselves to the order established among

---

8. **Sex born to obey:** women. The Salic Law, mistakenly attributed to the medieval Salian Franks, precluded women from inheriting the crown of France.

men for the love of God; be subjected to the king as to God . . . be subjected to those to whom He gives His authority and who are sent by Him to reward good deeds and to punish evil ones."

Even if kings fail in this duty, their charge and their ministry must be respected. For Scriptures tell us: "Obey your masters, not only those who are mild and good, but also those who are peevish and unjust."

Thus there is something religious in the respect which one renders the prince. Service to God and respect for kings are one thing. . . .

Thus it is in the spirit of Christianity for kings to be paid a kind of religious respect. . . .

BOOK IV: CONTINUATION OF THE CHARACTERISTICS OF ROYALTY

FIRST ARTICLE: Royal authority is absolute.

FIRST PROPOSITION: The prince need render account to no one for what he orders. . . .

SECOND PROPOSITION: When the prince has judged there is no other judgment. . . . Princes are gods.

Source 3 from Bayle St. John, translator, The Memoirs of the Duke of Saint-Simon on the Reign of Louis XIV and the Regency, *8th ed. (London: George Allen, 1913), vol. 2, pp. 363–365, vol. 3, pp. 221–227.*

3. The Duke of Saint-Simon on the Reign of Louis XIV

[*On the creation of Versailles and the nature of its court life*]

He [Louis XIV] early showed a disinclination for Paris. The troubles that had taken place there during the minority made him regard the place as dangerous;[9] he wished, too, to render himself venerable by hiding himself from the eyes of the multitude; all these considerations fixed him at St. Germains[10] soon after the death of the Queen, his mother. It was to that place he began to attract the world by fêtes and gallantries, and by making it felt that he wished to be often seen.

9. During the Fronde revolt of 1648–1653, the royal government lost control of Paris to the crowds and the royal family was forced to flee the city. Because Louis XIV was a minor (only ten years of age) when the revolt erupted, the government was administered by his mother, Anne of Austria, and her chief minister, Cardinal Mazarin.

10. **St. Germain-en-Laye:** site of a royal château, overlooking the Seine and dating from the twelfth century, where Louis XIV was born. The court fled there in 1649 during the Fronde.

His love for Madame de la Vallière,[11] which was at first kept secret, occasioned frequent excursions to Versailles, then a little card castle, which had been built by Louis XIII—annoyed, and his suite still more so, at being frequently obliged to sleep in a wretched inn there, after he had been out hunting in the forest of Saint Leger. That monarch rarely slept at Versailles more than one night, and then from necessity; the King, his son, slept there, so that he might be more in private with his mistress; pleasures unknown to the hero and just man, worthy son of Saint Louis, who built the little château.[12]

These excursions of Louis XIV by degrees gave birth to those immense buildings he erected at Versailles; and their convenience for a numerous court, so different from the apartments at St. Germains, led him to take up his abode there entirely shortly after the death of the Queen.[13] He built an infinite number of apartments, which were asked for by those who wished to pay their court to him; whereas at St. Germains nearly everybody was obliged to lodge in the town, and the few who found accommodation at the château were strangely inconvenienced.

The frequent fêtes, the private promenades at Versailles, the journeys, were means on which the King seized in order to distinguish or mortify the courtiers, and thus render them more assiduous in pleasing him. He felt that of real favours he had not enough to bestow; in order to keep up the spirit of devotion, he therefore unceasingly invented all sorts of ideal ones, little preferences and petty distinctions, which answered his purpose as well.

He was exceedingly jealous of the attention paid him. Not only did he notice the presence of the most distinguished courtiers, but those of inferior degree also. He looked to the right and to the left, not only upon rising but upon going to bed, at his meals, in passing through his apartments, or his gardens of Versailles, where alone the courtiers were allowed to follow him; he saw and noticed everybody; not one escaped him, not even those who hoped to remain unnoticed. He marked well all absentees from the court, found out the reason of their absence, and never lost an opportunity of acting towards them as the occasion might seem to justify. With some of the courtiers (the most distinguished), it was a demerit not to make the court their ordinary abode; with others 'twas a fault to come but rarely; for those who never or scarcely ever came it was certain disgrace. When their names were in any way mentioned, "I do not know them," the King would reply haughtily. Those who presented themselves but seldom were thus characterized: "They are people I never see;" these decrees were irrevocable. . . .

11. **Madame de la Vallière:** Louise de la Baume le Blanc, Duchesse de la Vallière (1644–1710), the king's first mistress.

12. Saint-Simon greatly admired Louis XIII, whom he had never met, and for over half a century attended annual memorial services for the king at the royal tombs in the basilica of St. Denis.

13. Anne of Austria (1601–1666), the mother of Louis XIV.

Louis XIV took great pains to be well informed of all that passed everywhere; in the public places, in the private houses, in society and familiar intercourse. His spies and tell-tales were infinite. He had them of all species; many who were ignorant that their information reached him; others who knew it; others who wrote to him direct, sending their letters through channels he indicated; and all these letters were seen by him alone, and always before everything else; others who sometimes spoke to him secretly in his cabinet, entering by the back stairs. These unknown means ruined an infinite number of people of all classes, who never could discover the cause; often ruined them very unjustly; for the King, once prejudiced, never altered his opinion or so rarely, that nothing was more rare.

[*On the royal day and court etiquette*]

[*The royal day begins*]

At eight o'clock the chief valet de chambre on duty, who alone had slept in the royal chamber, and who had dressed himself, awoke the King. The chief physician, the chief surgeon, and the nurse (as long as she lived), entered at the same time. The latter kissed the King; the others rubbed and often changed his shirt, because he was in the habit of sweating a great deal. At the quarter, the grand chamberlain was called (or, in his absence, the first gentleman of the chamber), and those who had, what was called the *grandes entrées*. The chamberlain (or chief gentleman) drew back the curtains which had been closed again, and presented the holy water from the vase, at the head of the bed. These gentlemen stayed but a moment, and that was the time to speak to the King, if any one had anything to ask of him; in which case the rest stood aside. When, contrary to custom, nobody had aught to say, they were there but for a few moments. He who had opened the curtains and presented the holy water, presented also a prayer-book. Then all passed into the cabinet of the council. A very short religious service being over, the King called, they re-entered. The same officer gave him his dressing-gown; immediately after, other privileged courtiers entered, and then everybody, in time to find the King putting on his shoes and stockings, for he did almost everything himself and with address and grace. Every other day we saw him shave himself; and he had a little short wig in which he always appeared, even in bed, and on medicine days. He often spoke of the chase, and sometimes said a word to somebody. No toilette table was near him; he had simply a mirror held before him.

As soon as he was dressed, he prayed to God, at the side of his bed, where all the clergy present knelt, the cardinals without cushions, all the laity remaining standing; and the captain of the guards came to the balustrade during the prayer, after which the King passed into his cabinet.

He found there, or was followed by all who had the entrée, a very numerous company, for it included everybody in any office. He gave orders to each for the day; thus within a half a quarter of an hour it was known what he meant to do; and then all this crowd left directly. The bastards, a few favourites, and the valets alone were left. It was then a good opportunity for talking with the King; for example, about plans of gardens and buildings; and conversation lasted more or less according to the person engaged in it.

All the Court meantime waited for the King in the gallery, the captain of the guard being alone in the chamber seated at the door of the cabinet.

[*The business of government*]

On Sunday, and often on Monday, there was a council of state; on Tuesday a finance council; on Wednesday council of state; on Saturday finance council. Rarely were two held in one day or any on Thursday or Friday. Once or twice a month there was a council of despatches[14] on Monday morning; but the order that the Secretaries of State took every morning between the King's rising and his mass, much abridged this kind of business. All the ministers were seated according to rank, except at the council of despatches, where all stood except the sons of France, the Chancellor, and the Duc de Beauvilliers.[15]

[*The royal luncheon*]

The dinner was always *au petit couvert*,[16] that is, the King ate by himself in his chamber upon a square table in front of the middle window. It was more or less abundant, for he ordered in the morning whether it was to be "a little," or "very little" service. But even at this last, there were always many dishes, and three courses without counting the fruit. The dinner being ready, the principal courtiers entered; then all who were known; and the first gentlemen of the chamber on duty, informed the King.

I have seen, but very rarely, Monseigneur[17] and his sons standing at their dinners, the King not offering them a seat. I have continually seen there the Princes of the blood and the cardinals. I have often seen there also Monsieur,[18] either on arriving from St. Cloud to see the King, or arriving from the council of despatches (the only one he entered), give the King his napkin and remain standing. A little while afterwards, the King, seeing that he did not go away, asked him if he would not sit down; he bowed, and the King ordered a seat to be brought for him. A stool was put behind him. Some moments after the

---

14. **Council of Despatches:** the royal council in which ministers discussed the letters from the provincial administrators of France, the *intendants.*

15. **Duc de Beauvilliers:** Paul de Beauvilliers, Duc de St. Aignan (1648–1714), friend of Saint-Simon and tutor of Louis XIV's grandsons, the dukes of Burgundy, Anjou, and Berry.

16. **Au petit couvert:** a simple table setting with a light meal.

17. **Monseigneur:** Louis, Dauphin de France (1661–1711), son of Louis XIV and heir to the throne.

18. **Monsieur:** Philippe, Duc d'Orléans (1640–1701), Louis XIV's only sibling. His permanent residence was at the Château of St. Cloud near Paris.

King said, "Nay then, sit down, my brother." Monsieur bowed and seated himself until the end of the dinner, when he presented the napkin.

[*The day ends*]

At ten o'clock his supper was served. The captain of the guard announced this to him. A quarter of an hour after the King came to supper, and from the antechamber of Madame de Maintenon[19] to the table again, any one spoke to him who wished. This supper was always on a grand scale, the royal household (that is, the sons and daughters of France), at table, and a large number of courtiers and ladies present, sitting or standing, and on the evening before the journey to Marly all those ladies who wished to take part in it. That was called presenting yourself for Marly. Men asked in the morning, simply saying to the King, "Sire, Marly." In later years the King grew tired of this, and a valet wrote up in the gallery the names of those who asked. The ladies continued to present themselves.

After supper the King stood some moments, his back to the balustrade of the foot of his bed, encircled by all his Court; then, with bows to the ladies, passed into his cabinet, where on arriving, he gave his orders. He passed a little less than an hour there, seated in an arm-chair, with his legitimate children and bastards, his grandchildren, legitimate and otherwise, and their husbands or wives. Monsieur in another arm-chair; the princesses upon stools, Monseigneur and all the other princes standing.

The King, wishing to retire, went and fed his dogs; then said good night, passed into his chamber to the *ruelle*[20] of his bed, where he said his prayers, as in the morning, then undressed. He said good night with an inclination of the head, and whilst everybody was leaving the room stood at the corner of the mantelpiece, where he gave the order to the colonel of the guards alone. Then commenced what was called the *petit coucher,* at which only the specially privileged remained. That was short. They did not leave until he got into bed. It was a moment to speak to him. Then all left if they saw any one buckle to the King. For ten or twelve years before he died the *petit coucher* ceased, in consequence of a long attack of gout he had had; so that the Court was finished at the rising from supper.

19. **Madame de Maintenon:** Françoise d'Aubigné, Marquise de Maintenon (1635–1719), married Louis XIV after the death of his first wife, Marie Thérèse of Spain.

20. **ruelle:** the area in the bedchamber in which the bed was located and in which the king received persons of high rank.

4. **Charles Le Brun, *Louis XIV Taking Up Personal Government,* ca 1680, from the Ceiling of the Hall of Mirrors at Versailles**

5. **Hyacinthe-François-Honoré-Pierre-André Rigaud,** *Louis XIV, King of France and Navarre,* **1701**

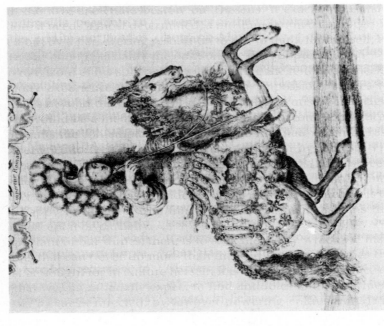

Source 7 from Charles Perrault, Festiva ad captia, 1670. British Library, London.

7. Rousselet, Louis XIV as "Roman Emperor" in an engraving from the Carousel of 1662

Source 6 from Musée de la Marine, Photographic Service.

6. Mask of Apollo, God of Light, 17th century

[43]

Sources 8 and 9 from French Government Tourist Office.

8. Garden Façade of Versailles

9. Aerial View of Versailles

Sources 10 through 13 from Château de Versailles/Cliché des Musées Nationaux—Paris.

10. The Royal Chapel at Versailles

11. Reconstruction of the King's Chamber at Versailles, after 1701

12. Antechamber of the Bull's Eye Window at Versailles

13. Pierre Denis Martin, *Château of Marly,* **1724**

QUESTIONS TO CONSIDER

Louis XIV is reputed to have said, "I am the state." Whether the king actually uttered those words is immaterial for our purpose; they neatly summarize the unifying theme in all this chapter's evidence, which demonstrates how royal power was defined as absolute and how that authority was expressed in deeds, art, and architecture.

Consider first the theories of royal authority, comparing the political ideas of Bodin and Bossuet. What are the origins of sovereignty for Bodin and Bossuet? How do they differ? Why can Bodin be said to have justified absolutism on the basis of expediency, that is, that absolute royal power was the only way to ensure order? Do the two thinkers ultimately arrive at the same conclusions? What is the difference between Bodin's conclusion that the royal power permitted the king to hand down laws to his subjects and receive them from no one and Bossuet's definition of the king as virtually a god on earth?

Royal ceremony and etiquette enforced this view of the king. Consider Saint-Simon's *Memoirs* again. The selection describes only limited aspects of court etiquette, but it conveys to us a vivid image of court life. Who was the center of this court made up of the country's most prominent nobles? Analyze individual elements of court ceremony. How does each contribute to a consistent message? Consider the royal dining ritual. To reinforce the lesson of royal power,

who was kept standing during the king's luncheon? Who had the task, for most commoners performed by an ordinary waiter, of handing the king his napkin? A message of royal power is being expressed here in a way that is almost theatrical.

Indeed, the image of theater can be useful in further structuring your analysis. The stage setting for this royal display, the palace of Versailles, shows the work of a skilled director in creating a remarkably uniform message in landscape and architecture alike. Who do you suppose that director was? Examine his statement at Versailles. Look first at the exterior views of both Versailles (Sources 8 and 9) and Marly (Source 13). How do the grounds add to the expression of royal power? What view of nature might they suggest to a visitor? How did the stage set enhance the play described by Saint-Simon? How did it encourage the French to accept the authority of Louis XIV?

Look next at the interior of the palace. It was, of course, a royal residence. But do you find much evidence of its function as a place to live in? Examine the royal bedroom and its outer room (Sources 11 and 12). Modern bedrooms are generally intimate in size and decoration; how does the king's differ? Why? Notice, too, the art and use of symbols in the palace. Why might the king's artists and architects have decorated the palace so richly with biblical and classical heroes and themes (Sources 8, 9, 10, 11, 12)?

Finally, consider the principal actor, Louis XIV. Notice how his self-presentation is consistent with the trappings of the stage set. We find him consciously acting a role in Source 7, portraying an emperor in the Carousel of 1662. That engraving embodies a great deal of indirect information. What details reinforce the aura of royal power? Why should the king be mounted and in Roman costume? What strikes you about the king's attitude atop the prancing horse? Compare this picture with the Le Brun (Source 4) and Rigaud (Source 5) paintings. What elements do you find these pictures to have in common? How does the royal emblem of the sun (Source 6) contribute to the common message?

With these considerations in mind, return now to the central questions of this chapter. What was the theoretical explanation of royal power expressed in late sixteenth- and seventeenth-century France? How did such early modern kings as Louis XIV communicate their absolute power in the various ceremonies, displays, and symbols of royal authority presented in the evidence?

EPILOGUE

We all know that any successful act produces imitators. In the seventeenth century the monarchy of Louis XIV for a long time looked like the most successful regime in Europe. Royal absolutism had seemingly unified France. Out of that unity came a military power that threatened to overwhelm Europe; an economic strength, based on mercantilism, that increased French wealth; and an intellectual life that gave the culture of seventeenth-and eighteenth-century Europe a distinctly French accent. Imitators of Louis XIV's work were therefore numerous. At the very least, kings sought physically to express the unifying and centralizing monarchical principle of government in palaces recreating Versailles.[21]

But the work of such monarchs as Louis XIV involved far more than the construction of elaborate palaces in which to stage the theater of their court lives. The act of focusing the state on the figure of the monarch began the transition to the centralized modern style of government and marked the beginning of the end of the decentralized medieval state that bound subjects in an almost contractual relationship to their ruler. The king now emerged as theoretically all-powerful and also as a symbol of national unity.

The monarchs of the age did their work of state building so effectively that the unity and centralization they created often survived the monarchy itself. The French monarchy, for example, succumbed to a revolution in 1789 that in large part stemmed from the bankruptcy of the royal government after too many years of overspending on wars and court life in

21. Palaces consciously modeled on Versailles multiplied in the late seventeenth and early eighteenth centuries. They included the Schönbrunn Palace in Vienna (1694), the Royal Palace in Berlin (begun in 1698), Ludwigsburg Palace in Württemberg, Germany (1704–1733), the Würzburg Residenz in Franconia, Germany (1719–1744), and the Stupinigi Palace (1729–1733) near Turin, Italy.

the name of royal glory. But the unified state endured, strong enough to retain its sense of unity despite challenges in war and changes of government that introduced a new politics of mass participation.

The methods employed by Louis XIV and other monarchs also transcended their age. Modern governments understand the importance of ritual, symbolism, and display in creating the sense of national unity that was part of the absolute monarch's goal. Ritual may now be centered on important national observances. The parades on such days as July 4 in the United States, July 14 in France (commemorating one of the earliest victories of the Revolution of 1789), and the anniversary of the October 1917 Revolution as it was celebrated until 1990 in the former Soviet Union all differ in form from the rituals of Louis XIV. They are designed for a new political age, one of mass participation in politics, in which the loyalty of the whole people, not just an elite group, must be won. But their purpose remains the same: to win loyalty to the existing political order.

Modern states also use symbolism to build political loyalty. Artwork on public buildings in Washington, D.C., and the capital cities of other republics, for example, often employs classical themes. The purpose of such artwork is to suggest to citizens that their government perpetuates the republican rectitude of Athens and Rome. Display also is part of the political agenda of modern governments, even among governments of new arrivals in the community of nations. This is why newly independent, developing nations of the twentieth century expend large portions of their meager resources on such things as grand new capital cities, the most sophisticated military weaponry, and the latest aircraft for the national airline. These are symbols of their government's successes and thus the basis for these regimes' claims on their peoples' loyalty. These modern rituals, symbols, and displays perform the same function for modern rulers as Versailles did for the Sun King.

CHAPTER THREE

THE MIND OF AN AGE:

SCIENCE AND RELIGION

CONFRONT EIGHTEENTH-CENTURY

NATURAL DISASTER

THE PROBLEM

Because of the tremendous loss of life and damage to property that great natural disasters, like earthquakes and floods, inflict on their victims, such events require some explanation for their survivors. What was the reason for the disaster? Why did it occur where it did? In the answers that the thinkers of an age propose for such questions we may find indications of the general thought patterns that characterize a particular era in history.

In the late twentieth century, for example, most of us would understand earthquakes scientifically, as the result of pressures along geological faults that occasionally produce cataclysmic movements of the earth's surface. Earlier ages often understood earthquakes in terms of supernatural action. The eighteenth cen-

tury, the focus of this chapter, is an age whose intellectual life we may investigate with particularly rewarding results. We will find that the intellectual life of this century illustrates the persistence of traditional thought patterns increasingly challenged by a new, scientific vision of the physical world.

By the middle of the eighteenth century, Europe approached the culmination of an intellectual revolution that had been underway since the sixteenth century. Scientific discoveries of the sixteenth and seventeenth centuries, which your textbook describes as the Scientific Revolution, produced a wholly new outlook on the physical world that gained increasing acceptance among educated Europeans. The result of the sixteenth- and seventeenth-century work of Nicholas Copernicus, Johannes Kepler, Galileo Galilei, René Descartes, Sir Isaac Newton, and others was a growing certainty that the physical world could be understood through the ability of human reason to discern immutable mathematical laws that governed it. No longer did intellectuals explain the world in terms of supernatural action. The physical world increasingly appeared to be a great machine, and many eighteenth-century thinkers, called Deists in their religious outlook, posited a novel relationship between God and the physical world. The movements of the world-machine might have been created by God, but Deists believed that they could not be interrupted by Him. Some thinkers also had faith that a divine plan governed the world, affirming that all would be well. But all agreed that nothing happened in such a world without sufficient cause or reason. This was a true revolution in thought, espoused by intellectuals called *philosophes,* who sought to apply their faith in the existence of reasonable and comprehensible natural laws to all aspects of the human experience. Their efforts in this regard constitute the intellectual milieu that historians call the Enlightenment of the eighteenth century.

The Enlightenment's concept of a machine-like universe contradicted much in the traditional Judeo-Christian concept of God. Most important, perhaps, Enlightenment thought precluded any belief in divine intervention in the physical world. Miracles or divinely ordained disasters, for example, simply were impossible for the *philosophes* because they violated natural laws of cause and effect. Traditional religious beliefs, however, were not without their defenders. Often these defenders were clergymen who, using the same tools of reason employed by the Enlightenment's exponents, strongly disagreed with the *philosophes*. In Catholic Europe, members of the Society of Jesus, or Jesuits, were important defenders of traditional beliefs; in France they even published an influential monthly journal for their cause, the *Journal de Trevoux.* Clergymen in Protestant countries also espoused traditional beliefs concerning a divine presence in the world.

Debate between the proponents of these differing visions of the world's relationship to God had been underway for years before a major earthquake in Lisbon, Portugal, in 1755 forced Western thinkers to focus closely on the problem of explaining the causes of natural disasters. The Lisbon earthquake particularly captured the attention of Western thinkers because it struck a major political capital and international trading center close to Europe's heart.[1] It, moreover, was quite destructive.[2] The earthquake struck the Portuguese

1. Other earthquakes of the period either struck on the fringes of the West, as in Jamaica in 1692 and Peru in 1746, or in isolated parts of Europe, as in Sicily in 1693. The few that had occurred in major cities—like London's quakes of 1750—had been slight in comparison to Lisbon's.

2. A number of twentieth-century earthquakes, for which we have accurate casualty counts, have clearly been more devastating. For example, the quake that struck Yokohama, Japan, on September 1, 1923, took about 200,000 lives; another in Tangshan, China, on July 28, 1976, killed about 242,000 persons.

Chapter 3

The Mind of an

Age: Science

and Religion

Confront

Eighteenth-

Century

Natural Disaster

capital on November 1, 1755, All Saints' Day. At 9:30 A.M. on that holy day, which obligates Roman Catholics like the inhabitants of Lisbon to attend mass in commemoration of all of the church's saints, a loud rumbling disturbed a peaceful morning marked by religious observance or preparation for church attendance. Then three great seismic shocks rocked the city and ended its citizens' religious devotions. Churches and homes alike tumbled during this earthquake whose shocks were felt as far away as Switzerland and northern France, and many persons perished. Other disasters resulting from the earthquake soon increased the loss of life. Fires spread from the hearths of the damaged city and burned for almost a week before they could be extinguished. The trembling of the earth created ocean waves fifteen to twenty feet high that swept up the Tagus River on which Lisbon is situated and broke over the city's waterfront. The combined destruction of earthquake, fires, and tidal waves left about 10,000 to 15,000 dead on that holy day of November 1.[3]

Natural disasters like that at Lisbon elicited explanations from theologians who sought the work of God's hand in the Portuguese capital. The *philosophes*, however, differed

markedly among themselves on the earthquake's significance. By reading selections on the exchange of ideas quickened by the Lisbon earthquake, the background on how some of these ideas developed, and the later implications of these thoughts, you will gain a deeper understanding of eighteenth-century thought about God and His relationship to the world. This was a key issue for the age, and one that was widely debated. Examining it allows us to learn a great deal about the Enlightenment by posing basic questions to the sources presented in this chapter: Why did the Lisbon earthquake present such an intellectual crisis for eighteenth-century thinkers? How did theologians explain the disaster within the framework of their beliefs? How did Enlightenment thinkers explain it? In what direction was their thought on the physical world and its relationship to divine forces leading them?

SOURCES AND METHOD

The problem at hand presents you with questions in the history of ideas, or what historians call "intellectual history." For generations, intellectual historians wrote about the ideas of the past without asking a question that seems central to historians today: "Who, in a certain period, held a particular set of ideas?". More precisely, "How representative were these ideas of the society as a whole?" In other words, "How broad

3. Estimates on the earthquake toll vary greatly, ranging as high as 60,000 persons. T. D. Kendrick, the author of a modern study, *The Lisbon Earthquake* (Philadelphia: J. B. Lippincott, 1957), accepts 10,000–15,000 as the probable number of dead, and, indeed, as the city's population was only about 275,000, the figure of 60,000 dead is difficult to accept.

was the impact of these ideas in their own time?"

As your text probably notes, literacy was not widespread in eighteenth-century Europe, so that the majority of the continent's population never had access to the ideas of the Scientific Revolution or the Enlightenment. Indeed, historians in recent years have come to recognize the persistence of a culture of the people, a popular culture, sometimes pre-Christian in its roots, that coexisted with the ideas of the *philosophes*. The intellectual world of the unlettered was one inhabited by witches and warlocks, in which people readily accepted supernatural explanations for physical phenomena. Such people might be frightened almost to death by an earthquake, but they took little part in the discussion of its philosophical ramifications presented here.

If the majority of the population of eighteenth-century Europe had little or no access to the ideas we will examine, are those ideas still relevant to our study of the past? The answer is certainly yes, though we must take care not to attribute the ideas to all persons. We are discussing ideas that were current among the small, educated elite of the eighteenth century. We must recognize, however, that this privileged group had tremendous influence in a societal and governmental system that accorded little role to anyone born outside that class. Moreover, such persons were the opinionmakers of their age. Their ideas would have had considerable influence among those with some education among the middle classes. Thus the thought of this minority of Europe's total population had an impact well outside the boundaries of the social group from which it arose and thus is quite worthy of study.

The evidence that follows has been chosen to present you with a broad sample of the thought of Europe's eighteenth-century intellectual elite and the background of its development. The Lisbon earthquake raised the immediate problem of explaining the disaster. This question involved large issues, chief among them the relationship of the physical world to God. Did God intervene in the world's daily operation, as theologians argued? Was He, as Deists said, like a watchmaker who created a world-machine and then stood back, letting it operate on its own? Or was no divine hand at work in the world at all? In reading these selections, you should gain an understanding of why the Lisbon disaster preoccupied so many eighteenth-century thinkers.

Sources 1 and 2 represent a tendency perhaps as old as humankind, that is, the attempt to explain natural phenomena in terms of supernatural or divine forces. Source 1, "An Opinion on the True Cause of the Earthquake," was a pamphlet written by a Roman Catholic priest, the Jesuit Gabriel Malagrida (1689–1761). Born in Italy, Malagrida spent much of his life in missionary work in Portugal's Brazilian colony and lived in Lisbon after 1754. It is not insignificant that he was a Jesuit; the Society of Jesus was one of the most influential orders in the early modern Roman Catholic church. The absolute loyalty of the

Chapter 3

The Mind of an

Age: Science

and Religion

Confront

Eighteenth-

Century

Natural Disaster

Jesuits to the papacy, combined with their energy and preaching ability, had done much to stem the spread of sixteenth-century European Protestantism. In subsequent centuries the order's excellent schools had strengthened Catholicism, as had the influence its members wielded as spiritual advisers to monarchs. Malagrida in every way typified his order. He was an excellent preacher, well connected at court, and consequently his attempt to justify the earthquake in theological terms had an impact in Catholic Portugal. How did he account for the earthquake?

Source 2 is a sermon by John Wesley (1703–1791), one of the most influential English Protestant leaders of the eighteenth century. Ordained a priest of the Church of England, Wesley experienced a religious conversion in 1738 that led him to found a new Protestant faith, Methodism. In the eighteenth century Methodism represented a dynamic new faith, espousing an emotional and personal kind of religion, that contrasted with the practices of both Catholics and traditional Protestant groups.

Wesley preached widely in the cause of his faith; he is estimated to have journeyed 250,000 miles in the course of delivering 40,000 sermons, often to large audiences. Because many of his sermons were published in pamphlet form, he reached an even larger public than only those able to attend his sermons. According to this influential Protestant clergyman, what was the cause of the Lisbon earthquake? How might future earthquakes be avoided?

With Source 3 we encounter the thought of the Enlightenment. Voltaire was the pen name of François-Marie Arouet (1694–1778), one of the greatest of the *philosophes* and the author of Source 3. Born the son of a Parisian notary, Voltaire received a traditional education from French Jesuits but early developed an independence of thought and an irreverence toward established creeds and institutions that plunged him into difficulties. In 1717 the royal government imprisoned him for eleven months for alleged insults to the regent of France. In 1726 his writings provoked the authorities once again, and he avoided a second, lengthy imprisonment by agreeing to leave France for an extended stay in England. Voltaire remained in England more than two years.

The lack of official tolerance for Voltaire's early writings defined the theme that became a constant in his writings: the cause of toleration. In England, he believed he found a much freer and more tolerant society than that in France, and his *Letters Concerning the English Nation* (published 1733) contrasted France very unfavorably with England. The book also reflected the deep impact of the ideas of the English thinkers Newton and Locke on Voltaire. He would go on to write an extensive popular version of Newtonian physics, *Elements of the Philosophy of Newton* (1736), but in the earlier work on England, excerpted in Source 3, we find a brief summary of Newton's thought. What sort of world did Newton describe? What was the relationship of God to this world? In what ways does Voltaire express a Deistic interpretation of God's relationship to the physical world?

Source 4 is a passage from the poem "An Essay on Man" by Alexander Pope (1688–1744), an English poet whose acquaintance Voltaire made during his English sojourn. As a member of England's Roman Catholic minority, Pope was excluded from educational opportunities open to Protestants, and he was largely self-taught. "An Essay on Man," published in 1734, is therefore remarkable as a summary of philosophical speculation of the day on God's relationship to the world described by Newton. What is that relationship, according to Pope? Why does Pope tell his readers to accept the world as they find it?

Source 5 is an excerpt from the *Encyclopedia: The Rational Dictionary of the Sciences, the Arts, and the Crafts*, edited by Denis Diderot. Conceived as an attempt to summarize the knowledge of the eighteenth century and especially the results of the Scientific Revolution, the *Encyclopedia* also served to recapitulate Enlightenment thought. Many of the chief *philosophes*, including Voltaire, wrote its articles and brought to the work their criticism of institutions of their age. Immediate controversy was the result. Church authorities sought to stop publication of the *Encyclopedia*, but slowly, over the years 1751 to 1772, the work appeared in seventeen volumes of text and eleven volumes of illustrations. The entry reproduced here as Source 5 is on the subject

"Observation." What methods of research did its anonymous author urge scientific researchers to adopt? How does this article reflect the Scientific Revolution? Is there any role for the intervention of God in this method of amassing knowledge?

In Source 6 we have evidence of the effort to apply these methods of research. This selection is the work of Georges Louis Leclerc, Comte de Buffon (1707–1788), a nobleman and scientist who served as director of the French royal botanical gardens in Paris. In addition, he devoted himself for forty years to writing a forty-four-volume *Natural History*, his attempt to summarize and popularize the results of the Scientific Revolution. Although Buffon may not have been a particularly original thinker and his observation of earthquakes clearly was confined to their above-ground effects, his work was a great success, becoming something of a best seller that greatly influenced his age. Certainly we cannot scientifically accept Buffon's explanation of earthquakes today. But what approach to the physical world does his work represent? Would he in any way be able to accept the ideas of Malagrida or Wesley? Does Buffon see any evidence of divine design? How does his concept of the world grow out of Newton's science?

In Source 7 we encounter a rather different Voltaire from the man who discussed Newton. In his "Poem on the Lisbon Disaster, or An Examination of that Axiom 'All Is Well' " published twenty years after *Letters*, we have the work of an older Voltaire,

Chapter 3

The Mind of an
Age: Science
and Religion
Confront
Eighteenth-
Century
Natural Disaster

whose words reflect a growing doubt about the ideas of the early Enlightenment on the relationship of the physical world to God. What is Voltaire's view of God's role in the physical world in this poem he wrote on receiving the news of the Lisbon disaster? Why can Voltaire accept neither a theological explanation of the event nor the faith of some Deists that a divine plan dictated that all would work out for the best? What possible implications for the later Enlightenment's views on God do you find in this work of the influential Voltaire?

Voltaire's Lisbon poem, Source 8, elicited a forceful response in the form of a letter from Jean-Jacques Rousseau (1712–1778). Born in Geneva, Switzerland, Rousseau was the child of a mother who died shortly after his birth, and his subsequent haphazard upbringing was followed by a wandering life that permitted few lasting relationships. His works, including *The Social Contract*, a work of political theory, and *Emile*, a work of educational philosophy, rank Rousseau among the eighteenth century's greatest thinkers. But he was not part of the company of the *philosophes* and ultimately disassociated himself from them. Rousseau's works glorify the simplicity to be found in nature, and in many ways he was a precursor of the Romantic movement in early-nineteenth-century literature, which consciously sought to negate the Enlightenment.

It was only natural for Rousseau, therefore, to have intellectual differences with Voltaire. When he wrote his letter in 1755, however, Rousseau's great work was still in the future and he was as yet relatively unknown. His letter to Voltaire, already an internationally known thinker, was thus rather audacious. What does Rousseau find wrong in Voltaire's view of the Lisbon earthquake? What relationship between God and humans does Rousseau express?

The author of Source 9, "The Essay on Miracles," was David Hume (1711–1776), a Scottish philosopher who lived for a time in France and who briefly befriended Rousseau. (Hume offered Rousseau a home when the latter was expelled from Bern, Switzerland, for his ideas. Rousseau soon quarreled with Hume, however, as he did with many persons.) Hume's thought reflects the Enlightenment search for hard, observable facts to justify conclusions, whether historical, philosophical, or theological. Could Hume find evidence of the God of Malagrida and Wesley on one hand or of the God of Newton and the early Voltaire on the other? According to Hume, is any divine scheme at work in the world?

If Hume represents the skepticism of the Enlightenment, Baron d'Holbach, a German-born nobleman who passed much of his life in France, perhaps reflects a logical culmination of Enlightenment thought about the physical world. Source 10 presents an expression of Holbach's views in a selection from his most important work, *The System of Nature*. What room is there for a divinity in Holbach's view, which sees the world as an "uninterrupted succession of causes and effects" in which "matter always existed"? Why do you think Holbach's contemporaries, including Voltaire, criticized his position as atheistic?

As you read these selections, you should be able to answer the central questions of this chapter: Why did the Lisbon earthquake pose an intellectual crisis for eighteenth-century thinkers? How did theologians explain the disaster? How did Enlightenment thinkers explain it? In what direction was their thought on the physical world and its relationship to divine forces leading them?

<hr>

THE EVIDENCE

<hr>

Source 1 from T. D. Kendrick, The Lisbon Earthquake *(Philadelphia: Lippincott, 1957), pp. 137–138. Translated by T. D. Kendrick.*

1. Gabriel Malagrida, "An Opinion on the True Cause of the Earthquake," 1756

Learn, O Lisbon, that the destroyers of our houses, palaces, churches, and convents, the cause of the death of so many people and of the flames that devoured such vast treasures, are your abominable sins, and not comets, stars, vapours and exhalations, and similar natural phenomena. Tragic Lisbon is now a mound of ruins. Would that it were less difficult to think of some method of restoring the place; but it has been abandoned, and the refugees from the city live in despair. As for the dead, what a great harvest of sinful souls such disasters send to Hell! It is scandalous to pretend the earthquake was just a natural event, for if that be true, there is no need to repent and to try to avert the wrath of God, and not even the Devil himself could invent a false idea more likely to lead us all to irreparable ruin. Holy people had prophesied the earthquake was coming, yet the city continued in its sinful ways without a care for the future. Now, indeed, the case of Lisbon is desperate. It is necessary to devote all our strength and purpose to the task of repentance. Would to God we could see as much determination and fervour for this necessary exercise as are devoted to the erection of huts and new buildings! Does being billeted in the country outside the city areas put us outside the jurisdiction of God?[4] God undoubtedly desires to exercise His love and mercy, but be sure that wherever we are, He is watching us, scourge in hand.

<hr>

4. Many of Lisbon's citizens fled the danger of the city for the countryside and remained there in shacks and tents until the earthquake danger passed.

Chapter 3

The Mind of an

Age: Science

and Religion

Confront

Eighteenth-

Century

Natural Disaster

Source 2 from The Works of John Wesley, *vol. 11 (Grand Rapids, Mich.: Zondervan, 1958), pp. 1–2, 6–7, 8, 11.*

2. John Wesley, "Some Serious Thoughts Occasioned by the Late Earthquake at Lisbon," 1755

Tua res agitur, paries quum proximus ardet.[5]

Thinking men generally allow that the greater part of modern Christians are not more virtuous than the ancient Heathens; perhaps less so; since public spirit, love of our country, generous honesty, and simple truth, are scarce anywhere to be found. On the contrary, covetousness, ambition, various injustice, luxury, and falsehood in every kind, have infected every rank and denomination of people, the Clergy themselves not excepted. Now, they who believe there is a God are apt to believe he is not well pleased with this. Nay, they think, he has intimated it very plainly, in many parts of the Christian world. How many hundred thousand men have been swept away by war, in Europe only, within half a century![6] How many thousands, within little more than this, hath the earth opened her mouth and swallowed up! Numbers sunk at Port-Royal, and rose no more! Many thousands went quick into the pit at Lima! The whole city of Catanea, in Sicily, and every inhabitant of it, perished together.[7] Nothing but heaps of ashes and cinders show where it stood. Not so much as one Lot escaped out of Sodom![8]

And what shall we say of the late accounts from Portugal? That some thousand houses, and many thousand persons, are no more! that a fair city is now

5. From the Roman poet Horace: "'Tis your own interest that calls, when flames invade your neighbor's walls."

6. Intense warfare did mark the half-century preceding the earthquake. The great Northern War (1700–1716) pitted Sweden against Russia. In the War of the Spanish Succession (1702–1714), France and Spain fought against England, Holland, the armies of the Holy Roman Emperor, and most of the German states. In the War of the Polish Succession (1733–1735), Spain and France confronted Russia and the forces of the Holy Roman Emperor. Almost all of Europe was involved in the War of the Austrian Succession (1740–1748) in which France, Spain, Prussia, and a number of the German states fought England and Austria. At the time Wesley wrote, fighting between English and French forces had already broken out in North America that would lead to the Seven Years War of 1756–1763. And these were only the major wars! Minor conflicts also raged. One historian reckoned that all of Europe was at peace for only two years in the century spanning 1700–1800.

7. Wesley refers here to the earthquakes of 1692, 1693, and 1746 mentioned in note 1.

8. In the Bible's book of Genesis, chapters 11–14 and 19, God destroyed Sodom and Gomorrah with fire because of their wickedness. Abraham's nephew, Lot, a resident of Sodom, was warned of the destruction and escaped.

in ruinous heaps! Is there indeed a God that judges the world? And is he now making inquisition for blood? If so, it is not surprising, he should begin there, where so much blood has been poured on the ground like water! where so many brave men have been murdered, in the most base and cowardly as well as barbarous manner, almost every day, as well as every night, while none regarded or laid it to heart.[9] "Let them hunt and destroy the precious life, so we may secure our stores of gold and precious stones."[10] How long has their blood been crying from the earth! Yea, how long has that bloody *House of Mercy*,[11] the scandal not only of all religion, but even of human nature, stood to insult both heaven and earth! "And shall I not visit for these things, saith the Lord? Shall not my soul be avenged on such a city as this?". . .

But alas! why should we not be convinced sooner, while that conviction may avail, that it is not chance which governs the world? Why should we not now, before London is as Lisbon, Lima, or Catanea, acknowledge the hand of the Almighty, arising to maintain his own cause? Why, we have a general answer always ready, to screen us from any such conviction: "All these things are purely natural and accidental; the result of natural causes." But there are two objections to this answer: First, it is untrue: Secondly, it is uncomfortable.

First. If by affirming, "All this is purely natural," you mean, it is not providential, or that God has nothing to do with it, this is not true, that is, supposing the Bible to be true. For supposing this, you may descant ever so long on the natural causes of murrain, winds, thunder, lightning, and yet you are altogether wide of the mark, you prove nothing at all, unless you can prove that God never works in or by natural causes. But this you cannot prove; nay, none can doubt of his so working, who allows the Scripture to be of God. For this asserts, in the clearest and strongest terms, that "all things" (in nature) "serve him;" that (by or without a train of natural causes) He "sendeth his rain on the earth;" that He "bringeth the winds out of his treasures," and "maketh a way for the lightning and the thunder;" in general, that "fire and hail, snow and

---

9. In this sentence Wesley is referring to the executions resulting from trials by the Portuguese Inquisition. The Inquisition was a system of Roman Catholic courts created to identify and judge heretics. Like all continental European courts of the day, these courts could torture the defendant to gather evidence against him or her. Civil, not church, authorities, however, executed sentences.

10. **precious stones:** "Merchants who have lived in Portugal inform us that the King has a large building filled with diamonds; and more gold stored up, coined and uncoined, than all the other monarchs of Europe." [Wesley's note] This may or may not have been true, but Lisbon certainly received gold from New World mines and diamonds from mines discovered in the Portuguese colony of Brazil in the 1730s.

11. **House of Mercy:** "The title which the Inquisition of Portugal (if not in other countries also) takes to itself." [Wesley's note]

Chapter 3

The Mind of an

Age: Science

and Religion

Confront

Eighteenth-

Century

Natural Disaster

vapour, wind and storm, fulfil his word." Therefore, allowing there are natural causes of all these, they are still under the direction of the Lord of nature: Nay, what is nature itself, but the art of God, or God's method of acting in the material world? . . .

A Second objection to your answer is, It is extremely uncomfortable. For if things really be as you affirm; if all these afflictive incidents entirely depend on the fortuitous concourse and agency of blind, material causes; what hope, what help, what resource is left for the poor sufferers by them? . . .

What defence do you find from thousands of gold and silver? You cannot fly; for you cannot quit the earth, unless you will leave your dear body behind you. And while you are on the earth, you know not where to flee to, neither where to flee from. You may buy intelligence, where the shock was yesterday, but not where it will be to-morrow,—to-day. It comes! The roof trembles! The beams crack! The ground rocks to and fro! Hoarse thunder resounds from the bowels of the earth! And all these are but the beginning of sorrows. Now, what help? What wisdom can prevent, what strength resist, the blow? What money can purchase, I will not say deliverance, but an hour's reprieve? Poor honourable fool, where are now thy titles? Wealthy fool, where is now thy golden god? If any thing can help, it must be prayer. But what wilt thou pray to? Not to the God of heaven; you suppose him to have nothing to do with earthquakes. . . .

But how shall we secure the favour of this great God? How, but by worshipping him in spirit and in truth; by uniformly imitating Him we worship, in all his imitable perfections? without which the most accurate systems of opinions, all external modes of religion, are idle cobwebs of the brain, dull farce and empty show. Now, God is love: Love God then, and you are a true worshipper. Love mankind, and God is your God, your Father, and your Friend. But see that you deceive not your own soul; for this is not a point of small importance. And by this you may know: If you love God, then you are happy in God; if you love God, riches, honours, and the pleasures of sense are no more to you than bubbles on the water: You look on dress and equipage, as the tassels of a fool's cap; diversions, as the bells on a fool's coat. If you love God, God is in all your thoughts, and your whole life is a sacrifice to him. And if you love mankind, it is your own design, desire, and endeavour, to spread virtue and happiness all around you; to lessen the present sorrows, and increase the joys, of every child of man; and, if it be possible, to bring them with you to the rivers of pleasure that are at God's right hand for evermore.

Source 3 from Voltaire, Letters Concerning the English Nation *(New York: Burt Franklin Reprints, 1974), pp. 65–66, 96–97, 100, 103, 105–106.*

3. Voltaire on Newtonian Physics, 1733

Not long since, the trite and frivolous Question following was debated in a very polite and learned Company, *viz.* (namely) who was the greatest Man, *Cæsar, Alexander, Tamerlane, Cromwell,* & *c.*[12]

Some Body answer'd, that Sir *Isaac Newton* excell'd them all. The Gentleman's Assertion was very just; for if true Greatness consists in having receiv'd from Heaven a mighty Genius, and in having employ'd it to enlighten our own Minds and that of others; a Man like Sir *Isaac Newton,* whose equal is hardly found in a thousand Years, is the truly great Man. And those Politicians and Conquerors, (and all ages produce some) were generally so many illustrious wicked Men. That Man claims our Respect, who commands over the Minds of the rest of the World by the Force of Truth, not those who enslave their Fellow Creatures; He who is acquainted with the Universe, not They who deface it. . . .

The Discoveries which gain'd Sir *Isaac Newton* so universal a Reputation, relate to the System of the World, to Light, to Geometrical Infinites; and lastly to Chronology, with which he us'd to amuse himself after the Fatigue of his severer Studies.

I will now acquaint you (without Prolixity if possible) with the few Things I have been able to comprehend of all these sublime Ideas. With Regard to the System of our World, Disputes were a long Time maintain'd, on the Cause that turns the Planets, and keeps them in their Orbits; and on those Causes which make all Bodies here below descend towards the Surface of the Earth.

Having . . . destroy'd the *Cartesian* Vortices,[13] he despair'd of ever being able to discover, whether there is a secret Principle in Nature which, at the same Time, is the Cause of the Motion of all celestial Bodies, and that of Gravity on the Earth. But being retir'd in 1666, upon Account of the Plague, to a Solitude near *Cambridge*; as he was walking one Day in his Garden, and saw

12. **Julius Caesar** (102–44 B.C.) dominated Rome during the last years of the republic. **Alexander the Great** (356–323 B.C.) was the king of Macedonia who led the Greeks on wars of conquest to create an empire including modern Greece, Turkey, Egypt, and much of the Middle East to the borders of India. **Tamerlane** (ca 1336–1405) was a Turkish chieftain who created an empire embracing parts of southern Russia, Turkey, the Middle East, Afghanistan, Pakistan and northern India. **Oliver Cromwell** (1599–1658) led Parliament's armies against the king in the English Civil War. After the king's defeat and execution, he ruled England as virtual dictator.

13. **Cartesian vortices:** René Descartes (1546–1650), a French philosopher and mathematician, accounted for planetary motion in terms of vortices, that is, a rapid movement of cosmic bodies in a fluid or ether around an axis. Newtonian physics with its law of gravity dispensed with such theories.

Chapter 3

The Mind of an

Age: Science

and Religion

Confront

Eighteenth-

Century

Natural Disaster

some Fruits fall from a Tree, he fell into a profound Meditation on that Gravity, the Cause of which had so long been sought, but in vain, by all the Philosophers, whilst the Vulgar think there is nothing mysterious in it. He said to himself, that from what height soever, in our Hemisphere, those Bodies might descend, their Fall wou'd certainly be in the Progression discover'd by *Galileo*;[14] and the Spaces they run thro' would be as the Square of the Times. Why may not this Power which causes heavy Bodies to descend, and is the same without any sensible Diminution at the remotest Distance from the Center of the Earth, or on the Summits of the highest Mountains; Why, said Sir *Isaac,* may not this Power extend as high as the Moon? And in Case, its Influence reaches so far, is it not very probable that this Power retains it in its Orbit, and determines its Motion? But in case the Moon obeys this Principle (whatever it be) may we not conclude very naturally, that the rest of the Planets are equally subject to it? In case this Power exists (which besides is prov'd) it must increase in an inverse *Ratio* of the Squares of the Distances. All therefore that remains is, to examine how far a heavy Body, which should fall upon the Earth from a moderate height, would go; and how far in the same time, a Body which should fall from the Orbit of the Moon, would descend. To find this, nothing is wanted but the Measure of the Earth, and the Distance of the Moon from it.

This is Attraction, the great Spring by which all Nature is mov'd. Sir *Isaac Newton* after having demonstrated the Existence of this Principle, plainly foresaw that its very Name wou'd offend; and therefore this Philosopher in more Places than one of his Books, gives the Reader some Caution about it. He bids him beware of confounding this Name with what the Ancients call'd occult Qualities; but to be satisfied with knowing that there is in all Bodies a central Force which acts to the utmost Limits of the Universe, according to the invariable Laws of Mechanicks.

Give me Leave once more to introduce Sir *Isaac* speaking: . . . "The Spring that I discover'd was more hidden and more universal, and for that very Reason Mankind ought to thank me the more. I have discover'd a new Property of Matter, one of the Secrets of the Creator; and have calculated and discover'd the Effects of it. After this shall People quarrel with me about the Name I give it."

Vortices may be call'd an occult Quality because their Existence was never prov'd; Attraction on the contrary is a real Thing, because its Effects are demonstrated, and the Proportions of it are calculated. The Cause of this Cause is among the *Arcana*[15] of the Almighty.

Procedes huc, & non amplius.
Hither thou shalt go, and no farther.

14. **Galileo Galilei:** Italian astronomer, mathematician, and physicist (1564–1642) whose work was an important contribution to the Scientific Revolution. He developed the mathematical explanation of the rates at which bodies fall to earth in his law of falling bodies.

15. **Arcana:** secrets or mysteries.

Source 4 from A. W. Ward, editor, The Poetical Works of Alexander Pope *(London: Macmillan, 1879), pp. 199–200.*

4. From Alexander Pope, "An Essay on Man," 1734

All are but parts of one stupendous whole,
Whose body Nature is, and God the soul;
That, chang'd thro' all, and yet in all the same;
Great in the earth, as in th' ethereal[16] frame;
Warms in the sun, refreshes in the breeze,
Glows in the stars, and blossoms in the trees,
Lives thro' all life, extends thro' all extent,
Spreads undivided, operates unspent;
Breathes in our soul, informs our mortal part,
As full, as perfect, in a hair as heart:
As full, as perfect, in vile Man that mourns,
As the rapt Seraph[17] that adores and burns:
To him no high, no low, no great, no small;
He fills, he bounds, connects, and equals all.

Cease then, nor Order Imperfection name:
Our proper bliss depends on what we blame.
Know thy own point: This kind, this due degree
Of blindness, weakness, Heav'n bestows on thee;
Submit.—In this, or any other sphere,
Secure to be as blest as thou canst bear:
Safe in the hand of one disposing Pow'r,
Or in the natal, or the mortal hour.
All Nature is but Art, unknown to thee;
All Chance, Direction, which thou canst not see;
All Discord, Harmony not understood;
All partial Evil, universal Good:
And, spite of Pride, in erring Reason's spite,
One truth is clear, WHATEVER IS, IS RIGHT.

16. **ethereal:** heavenly.
17. **Seraph:** one of the heavenly creatures hovering around the throne of God described in Isaiah 6.

Chapter 3
The Mind of an
Age: Science
and Religion
Confront
Eighteenth-
Century
Natural Disaster

Source 5 from Denis Diderot, The Encyclopedia: Selections, *edited and translated by Stephen J. Gendzier (New York: Harper & Row, 1967), pp. 175–177.*

5. From the *Encyclopedia,* Anonymous Entry on "Observation," ca 1765

OBSERVATION (*Gram. Physic. Med.*) is the attention of the soul focused on objects offered by nature. An experiment is the result of this same attention directed toward phenomena produced by the labors of man. We must, therefore, include within the meaning of the generic noun *observation* the examination of all natural effects, not only of those that present themselves at once and without intermediary to our sight but also those we would not be able to discover without the hand of a worker, provided that this hand has not changed, altered, or disfigured them. The work necessary to reach a mine does not prevent the examination that is made of the metal's distribution, position, quantity, and color from being a simple *observation.* It is also by *observation* that we know the interior geography, that we estimate the number, position, and nature of the layers of earth, although we are obliged to resort to instruments for the excavation that allows us to see the mine. We must not consider as an *experiment* the opening of cadavers, the dissection of plants or animals, and certain analyses or mechanical sorting of mineral matter that scientists are obliged to do in order to be able to *observe* the parts that enter into their composition. The telescope of astronomers, the magnifying glass of the naturalist, and the microscope of the physicist do not prevent the knowledge acquired by these means from being the exact product of *observation.* All these preparations, these instruments only serve to render the different objects of *observation* more concrete, to remove the obstacles that prevent us from perceiving them, or to pierce the veil that hides them. But no change results from this, and there is not the slightest alteration in the nature of the *observed* object. It appears, nevertheless, such as it is; and this is the main difference between an *observation* and an *experiment* which decomposes, combines, and thereby gives use to rather different phenomena from those which nature presents. . . .

Observation is the primary foundation of all the sciences, the most reliable way to arrive at one's goal, the principal means of extending the periphery of scientific knowledge and of illuminating all its points. The facts, whatever they are, constitute the true wealth of the philosopher and the subject of *observation:* the historian collects them, the theoretical physicist combines them, and the experimenter verifies the results of their synthesis. Several facts taken separately appear dry, sterile, and unfruitful. The moment we compare them, they acquire a certain power, assume a vitality that everywhere results from the mutual harmony, from the reciprocal support, and from a chain that binds them together. The connection of these facts and the general cause that links them together are some of the objects of reasoning, theories, and systems, while the facts are the materials. The moment a certain number of them have been gathered, some people hasten to construct; and the building is the more solid as the materials are more numerous and each one of them finds a more appropriate place.

Source 6 from Georges Louis Leclerc, Comte de Buffon, Histoire naturelle, générale et particulière, avec description du cabinet du roi, *vol. 1 (Paris: De l'Imprimerie Royale, 1749), pp. 526–529. Translated by Julius R. Ruff.*

6. From Georges Louis Leclerc, Comte de Buffon, *Natural History, General and Specific*, ca 1750

There are two kinds of earthquakes. One type is caused by the action of subterranean fires and by the explosion of volcanoes and is only felt over small distances when volcanoes are active or when they erupt. When the materials which make up subterranean fires begin to ferment, to heat up, and to ignite, the fire expands on all sides and, if it does not naturally find outlets, it heaves up the ground and makes a passage by throwing out the earth in its way. This produces a volcano, the effects of which repeat themselves and endure in proportion to the inflammable materials.

But there is another kind of earthquake, very different as regards its effects and perhaps as regards its causes. These are the earthquakes which are felt over long distances and which shake a large area of terrain without the appearance of a new volcano or an eruption. We have examples of earthquakes which are felt at the same time in England, France, Germany, and as far away as Hungary. These earthquake always extend over an area much longer than it is wide. They shake a band or zone of the earth with varying force in different locations. They are almost always accompanied by a muffled sound, similar to that of a large, quickly rolling coach.

To understand more fully the causes of this kind of earthquake, it is necessary to remember that all inflammable and explosive materials produce . . . a great deal of air in igniting.[18] This air produced by the fire is in a very highly rarefied state and, because of its state of compression in the depths of the earth, it must produce very violent effects. Let us therefore suppose that at a very great depth, say 600 to 1200 feet, there are found pyrites and other sulphurous materials and that by the fermentation produced by the filtration of water or by other causes, these materials ignite. Let us see what must hap-

---

18. Buffon advanced this description of combustion a quarter of a century before the great French chemist Antoine Laurent Lavoisier (1743–1794) accurately described combustion and the role of oxygen in this process.

Chapter 3

The Mind of an

Age: Science

and Religion

Confront

Eighteenth-

Century

Natural Disaster

pen. These materials are not regularly arranged in horizontal strata . . . they are, on the contrary, in perpendicular clefts in the caverns . . . where water can penetrate and have an effect. These materials ignite, producing a large quantity of air, the force of which, compressed in a small space like a cavern, not only will shake the terrain above but will look for routes of escape. . . . The routes which are available are caverns and cuts by water and subterranean streams. The rarefied air will rush violently through all of these passages which are open to it. It will form a raging wind in its subterranean paths, the noise of which will be heard on the earth's surface, and it will be accompanied by shock and concussions. This subterranean wind produced by the fire will extend as far as the subterranean cavities and cuts, and will cause a tremor the violence of which will depend on the distance from the source and the narrowness of the passages through which the wind passes. . . . This air will produce no eruption or volcano because it will have found enough space in which to expand or indeed because it will have found escapes and will have left the earth in the form of wind or vapor.[19]

Source 7 from Oeuvres complètes de Voltaire, *nouvelle edition, vol. 9 (Paris: Garnier frères, 1877), p. 470. Translated by Julius R. Ruff.*

7. From Voltaire, "Poem on the Lisbon Disaster, or An Examination of that Axiom 'All Is Well,' " 1755

Oh, miserable mortals! Oh wretched earth!
Oh, dreadful assembly of all mankind!
Eternal sermon of useless sufferings!
Deluded philosophers who cry, "All is well,"
Hasten, contemplate these frightful ruins,
This wreck, these shreds, these wretched ashes of the dead;
These women and children heaped on one another,
These scattered members under broken marble;
One-hundred thousand unfortunates devoured by the earth,[20]

19. The article on "Earthquakes" in the *Encyclopedia* edited by Diderot also explains this phenomenon with a theory of subterranean fire. Modern geologists have shown earthquakes to be the result of stresses in the earth's crust. Interestingly, however, modern research also has shown that the eighteenth-century theories of subterranean fire were not entirely incorrect: the earth does have a liquid core of practically molten rock.

20. Voltaire wrote this poem on hearing the first news of the disaster. Those first reports grossly exaggerated the number of deaths, as does the poem.

Who, bleeding, lacerated, and still alive,
Buried under their roofs without aid in their anguish,
End their sad days!
In answer to the half-formed cries of their dying voices,
At the frightful sight of their smoking ashes,
Will you say: "This is the result of eternal laws
Directing the acts of a free and good God!"
Will you say, in seeing this mass of victims:
"God is revenged, their death is the price for their crimes?"
What crime, what error did these children,
Crushed and bloody on their mothers' breasts, commit?
Did Lisbon, which is no more, have more vices
Than London and Paris immersed in their pleasures?
Lisbon is destroyed, and they dance in Paris!

Source 8 from Theodore Bestermann, editor, Voltaire's Correspondence, *vol. 30 (Geneva: Institut et Musée Voltaire, 1958), pp. 102–115. Translated by Julius R. Ruff.*

8. From Jean-Jacques Rousseau's Letter to Voltaire Regarding the Poem on the Lisbon Earthquake, August 18, 1756

All my complaints are . . . against your poem on the Lisbon disaster, because I expected from it evidence more worthy of the humanity which apparently inspired you to write it. You reproach Pope[21] and Leibnitz[22] with belittling our misfortunes by affirming that all is well, but you so burden the list of our miseries that you further disparage our condition. Instead of the consolations that I expected, you only vex me. It might be said that you fear that I don't feel my unhappiness enough, and that you are trying to soothe me by proving that all is bad.

Do not be mistaken, Monsieur, it happens that everything is contrary to what you propose. This optimism which you find so cruel consoles me still in

---

21. Alexander Pope, whose "An Essay on Man" is Source 4 in this chapter.
22. **Gottfried Wilhelm von Leibnitz:** a German mathematician and philosopher (1646–1716), the author of *Essays on Theodicy,* in which he examined the origins of evil in the world. Leibnitz saw the universe operating according to a divine plan and therefore this was the best of all possible worlds. He was not a total optimist, however, because he recognized the existence of evil. Incompletely understanding the thought of Leibnitz, Voltaire satirized him as a blind optimist in his novel *Candide* (1759).

Chapter 3

The Mind of an

Age: Science

and Religion

Confront

Eighteenth-

Century

Natural Disaster

the same woes that you force on me as unbearable. Pope's poem[23] alleviates my difficulties and inclines me to patience; yours makes my afflictions worse, prompts me to grumble, and, leading me beyond a shattered hope, reduces me to despair. . . .

"Have patience, man," Pope and Leibnitz tell me, "your woes are a necessary effect of your nature and of the constitution of the universe. The eternal and beneficent Being who governs the universe wished to protect you. Of all the possible plans, he chose that combining the minimum evil and the maximum good. If it is necessary to say the same thing more bluntly, God has done no better for mankind because (He) can do no better."

Now what does your poem tell me? "Suffer forever unfortunate one. If a God created you, He is doubtlessly all powerful and could have prevented all your woes. Don't ever hope that your woes will end, because you would never know why you exist, if it is not to suffer and die. . . ."

I do not see how one can search for the source of moral evil anywhere but in man. . . . Moreover . . . the majority of our physical misfortunes are also our work. Without leaving your Lisbon subject, concede, for example, that it was hardly nature that there brought together twenty-thousand houses of six or seven stories. If the residents of this large city had been more evenly dispersed and less densely housed, the losses would have been fewer or perhaps none at all. Everyone would have fled at the first shock. But many obstinately remained . . . to expose themselves to additional earth tremors because what they would have had to leave behind was worth more than what they could carry away. How many unfortunates perished in this disaster through the desire to fetch their clothing, papers, or money? . . .

There are often events that afflict us . . . that lose a lot of their horror when we examine them closely. I learned in *Zadig*,[24] and nature daily confirms my lesson, that a rapid death is not always a true misfortune, and that it can sometimes be considered a relative blessing. Of the many persons crushed under Lisbon's ruins, some without doubt escaped greater misfortunes, and . . . it is not certain that a single one of these unfortunates suffered more than if, in the normal course of events, he had awaited [a more normal] death to overtake him after long agonies. Was death [in the ruins] a sadder end than that of a dying person overburdened with useless treatments, whose notary[25] and heirs do not allow him a respite, whom the doctors kill in his own bed at

23. **Pope's poem:** "An Essay on Man."

24. **Zadig:** a story published by Voltaire in 1747 that still reflected some faith on his part that a divine order for the world assured that all would work out for the best. In the story, Zadig, the main character, endures a lengthy series of misfortunes.

25. **notary:** in France and other Continental countries, a professional person specializing in drafting wills and inventorying the property involved in them as well as drawing up other property arrangements.

their leisure, and whom the barbarous priests artfully try to make relish death? For me, I see everywhere that the misfortunes nature imposes upon us are less cruel than those which we add to them. . . .

I cannot prevent myself, Monsieur, from noting . . . a strange contrast between you and me as regards the subject of this letter. Satiated with glory . . . you live free in the midst of affluence.[26] Certain of your immortality, you peacefully philosophize on the nature of the soul, and, if your body or heart suffer, you have Tronchin[27] as doctor and friend. You however find only evil on earth. And I, an obscure and poor man tormented with an incurable illness, meditate with pleasure in my seclusion and find that all is well. What is the source of this apparent contradiction? You explained it yourself: you revel but I hope, and hope beautifies everything.

. . . I have suffered too much in this life not to look forward to another. No metaphysical subtleties cause me to doubt a time of immortality for the soul and a beneficent providence. I sense it, I believe it, I wish it, I hope for it, I will uphold it until my last gasp. . . .

I am, with respect, Monsieur,

Jean-Jacques Rousseau

Source 9 from David Hume, Essays: Moral, Political and Literary *(Oxford: Oxford University Press, 1963), pp. 519–521, 524–526, 540–541.*

9. David Hume, "The Essay on Miracles," 1748

There is, in Dr. Tillotson's[28] writings, an argument against the *real presence*,[29] which is as concise, and elegant, and strong, as any argument can possibly be supposed against a doctrine so little worthy of a serious refutation. It is acknowledged on all hands, says that learned prelate, that the authority, either of the Scripture or of tradition, is founded merely on the testimony; of the Apostles, who were eye-witnesses to those miracles of our Saviour, by which he proved his divine mission. Our evidence, then, for the truth of the *Christian* religion, is less than the evidence for the truth of our senses; because, even in

26. Voltaire had prospered from his publishings and also had invested well. He owned property in Geneva, Switzerland, and a large estate at Ferney, France, on the Swiss border.

27. **Theodore Tronchin:** a physician (1709–1781) of Geneva, Switzerland. A pioneer in smallpox inoculation in Switzerland, he was a member of Voltaire's circle.

28. **Dr. John Tillotson:** Archbishop of Canterbury (1630–1694), that is, spiritual leader of the Church of England.

29. **real presence:** the presence of Jesus Christ in the sacramental bread and wine of Christian Communion.

Chapter 3

The Mind of an

Age: Science

and Religion

Confront

Eighteenth-

Century

Natural Disaster

the first authors of our religion, it was no greater; and it is evident it must diminish in passing from them to their disciples; nor can any one rest such confidence in their testimony as in the immediate object of his senses. But a weaker evidence can never destroy a stronger; and therefore, were the doctrine of the real presence ever so clearly revealed in Scripture, it were directly contrary to the rules of just reasoning to give our assent to it. It contradicts sense, though both the Scripture and tradition, on which it is supposed to be built, carry not such evidence with them as sense, when they are considered merely as external evidences, and are not brought home to every one's breast by the immediate operation of the Holy Spirit.

Nothing is so convenient as a decisive argument of this kind, which must at least *silence* the most arrogant bigotry and superstition, and free us from their impertinent solicitations. I flatter myself that I have discovered an argument of a like nature, which, if just, will, with the wise and learned, be an everlasting check to all kinds of superstitious delusion, and consequently will be useful as long as the world endures; for so long, I presume, will the accounts of miracles and prodigies be found in all history, sacred and profane.

Though experience be our only guide in reasoning concerning matters of fact, it must be acknowledged, that this guide is not altogether infallible, but in some cases is apt to lead us into errors. One who in our climate should expect better weather in any week of June than in one of December, would reason justly and conformably to experience; but it is certain that he may happen, in the event, to find himself mistaken. However, we may observe that, in such a case, he would have no cause to complain of experience, because it commonly informs us beforehand of the uncertainty, by that contrariety of events which we may learn from a diligent observation. All effects follow not with like certainty from their supposed causes. Some events are found, in all countries and all ages, to have been constantly conjoined together: others are found to have been more variable, and sometimes to disappoint our expectations; so that in our reasonings concerning matter of fact, there are all imaginable degrees of assurance, from the highest certainty to the lowest species of moral evidence.

A wise man, therefore, proportions his belief to the evidence. In such conclusions as are founded on an infallible experience, he expects the event with the last degree of assurance, and regards his past experience as a full *proof* of the future existence of that event. In other cases he proceeds with more caution: he weighs the opposite experiments: he considers which side is supported by the greater number of experiments: to that side he inclines with doubt and hesitation; and when at last he fixes his judgment, the evidence exceeds not what we properly call *probability*. All probability, then, supposes an opposition of experiments and observations, where the one side is found to overbalance the other, and to produce a degree of evidence proportioned to the superiority. A hundred instances or experiments on one side, and fifty on another, afford a doubtful expectation of any event; though a hundred uniform experiments, with only one that is contradictory, reasonably beget a pretty strong degree of assurance. In all cases, we must balance the opposite experiments, where they are opposite, and deduct the smaller number from the greater, in order to know the exact force of the superior evidence. . . . ·

A miracle is a violation of the laws of nature; and as a firm and unalterable experience has established these laws, the proof against a miracle, from the very nature of the fact, is as entire as any argument from experience can possibly be imagined. Why is it more than probable that all men must die; that lead cannot, of itself, remain suspended in the air; that fire consumes wood, and is extinguished by water; unless it be that these events are found agreeable to the laws of nature, and there is required a violation of these laws, or, in other words, a miracle to prevent them? Nothing is esteemed a miracle, if it ever happen in the common course of nature. It is no miracle that a man, seemingly in good health, should die on a sudden; because such a kind of death, though more unusual than any other, has yet been frequently observed to happen. But it is a miracle that a dead man should come to life; because that has never been observed in any age or country. There must, therefore, be an uniform experience against every miraculous event, otherwise the event would not merit that appellation. And as an uniform experience amounts to a proof, there is here a direct and full *proof*, from the nature of the fact, against the existence of any miracle. . . .

The plain consequence is (and it is a general maxim worthy of our attention), "That no testimony is sufficient to establish a miracle, unless the testimony be of such a kind, that its falsehood would be more miraculous than the fact which it endeavours to establish: and even in that case there is a mutual destruction of arguments, and the superior only gives us an assurance suitable to that degree of force which remains after deducting the inferior." When any one tells me that he saw a dead man restored to life, I immediately consider with myself whether it be more probable that this person should either deceive or be deceived, or that the fact which he relates should really have happened. I weigh the one miracle against the other; and according to the superiority which I discover, I pronounce my decision, and always reject the greater miracle. If the falsehood of his testimony would be more miraculous than the event which he relates, then, and not till then, can he pretend to command my belief or opinion.

Upon the whole, then, it appears, that no testimony for any kind of miracle has ever amounted to a probability, much less to a proof; and that, even supposing it amounted to a proof, it would be opposed by another proof, derived from the very nature of the fact which it would endeavour to establish. It is experience only which gives authority to human testimony; and it is the same experience which assures us of the laws of nature. When, therefore, these two kinds of experience are contrary, we have nothing to do but to subtract the one from the other, and embrace an opinion either on one side or the other, with that assurance which arises from the remainder. But according to the

Chapter 3

The Mind of an

Age: Science

and Religion

Confront

Eighteenth-

Century

Natural Disaster

principle here explained, this subtraction with regard to all popular religions amounts to an entire annihilation; and therefore we may establish it as a maxim, that no human testimony can have such force as to prove a miracle, and make it a just foundation for any such system of religion. . . .

What we have said of miracles, may be applied without any variation to prophecies; and, indeed, all prophecies are real miracles, and as such, only can be admitted as proofs of any revelation. If it did not exceed the capacity of human nature to foretell future events, it would be absurd to employ any prophecy as an argument for a divine mission or authority from heaven. So that, upon the whole, we may conclude, that the *Christian Religion* not only was at first attended with miracles, but even at this day cannot be believed by any reasonable person without one. Mere reason is insufficient to convince us of its veracity: and whoever is moved by *Faith* to assent to it, is conscious of a continued miracle in his own person, which subverts all the principles of his understanding, and gives him a determination to believe what is most contrary to custom and experience.

Source 10 from Paul-Henry Thiry, Baron d'Holbach, The System of Nature, *translated by H. D. Robinson (Boston: J. P. Mendum, 1853), pp. viii–ix, 12–13, 15, 19–23.*

10. From Paul-Henry Thiry, Baron d'Holbach, *The System of Nature*, 1770

Preface

The source of man's unhappiness is his ignorance of Nature. The pertinacity with which he clings to blind opinions imbibed in his infancy, which interweave themselves with his existence, the consequent prejudice that warps his mind, that prevents its expansion, that renders him the slave of fiction, appears to doom him to continual errour. He resembles a child destitute of experience, full of idle notions: a dangerous leaven mixes itself with all his knowledge: it is of necessity obscure, it is vacillating and false:—He takes the tone of his ideas on the authority of others, who are themselves in errour, or else have an interest in deceiving him. To remove this Cimmerian darkness,[30] these barriers to the improvement of his condition; to disentangle him from the clouds of errour that envelop him, that obscure the path he ought to tread; to guide him out of the Cretan labyrinth,[31] requires the clue of Ari-

30. **Cimmerian darkness:** in Greek mythology, the Cimmerians were a people inhabiting a land of perpetual darkness.
31. **Cretan labyrinth:** according to Greek mythology, there existed on the island of Crete a structure of winding passages leading to a monster with the body of a man and the head of a bull, the Minotaur. This monster was annually fed seven young men and seven young women from Athens as that city's tribute to the rulers of Crete.

adne,[32] with all the love she could bestow on Theseus. It exacts more than common exertion; it needs a most determined, a most undaunted courage—it is never effected but by a persevering resolution to act, to think for himself; to examine with rigour and impartiality the opinions he has adopted. . . .

Man seeks to range out of his sphere: notwithstanding the reiterated checks his ambitious folly experiences, he still attempts the impossible; strives to carry his researches beyond the visible world; and hunts out misery in imaginary regions. He would be a metaphysician before he has become a practical philosopher. He quits the contemplation of realities to meditate on chimeras. He neglects experience to feed on conjecture, to indulge in hypothesis. He dares not cultivate his reason, because from his earliest days he has been taught to consider it criminal. He pretends to know his fate in the indistinct abodes of another life, before he has considered of the means by which he is to render himself happy in the world he inhabits: in short, man disdains the study of Nature, except it be partially. . . .

The most important of our duties, then, is to seek means by which we may destroy delusions that can never do more than mislead us. The remedies for these evils must be sought for in Nature herself; it is only in the abundance of her resources, that we can rationally expect to find antidotes to the mischiefs brought upon us by an ill-directed, by an over-powering enthusiasm. It is time these remedies were sought; it is time to look the evil boldly in the face, to examine its foundations, to scrutinize its super-structure: reason, with its faithful guide experience, must attack in their entrenchments those prejudices to which the human race has but too long been the victim. For this purpose reason must be restored to its proper rank,—it must be rescued from the evil company with which it is associated. . . .

Truth speaks not to these perverse beings [the enemies of the human race]:—her voice can only be heard by generous minds accustomed to reflection, whose sensibilities make them lament the numberless calamities showered on the earth by political and religious tyranny—whose enlightened minds contemplate with horrour the immensity, the ponderosity of that series of misfortunes with which errour has in all ages overwhelmed mankind. . . .

Of Nature

. . . The *civilized man*, is he whom experience and social life have enabled to draw from nature the means of his own happiness; because he has learned to oppose resistance to those impulses he receives from exterior beings, when experience has taught him they would be injurious to his welfare.

The *enlightened man*, is man in his maturity, in his perfection; who is capable of pursuing his own happiness; because he has learned to examine, to think

---

32. **Ariadne:** daughter of the King of Crete, fell in love with Theseus, an Athenian hero and one of the youths sent by Athens to be offered to the Minotaur. Ariadne gave Theseus a ball of thread which he unwound as he penetrated the labyrinth and there killed the Minotaur. He then followed the thread back out of the labyrinth.

Chapter 3
The Mind of an
Age: Science
and Religion
Confront
Eighteenth-
Century
Natural Disaster

for himself, and not to take that for truth upon the authority of others, which experience has taught him examination will frequently prove erroneous. . . .

It necessarily results, that man in his researches ought always to fall back on experience, and natural philosophy: These are what he should consult in his religion—in his morals—in his legislation—in his political government—in the arts—in the sciences—in his pleasures—in his misfortunes. Experience teaches that Nature acts by simple, uniform, and invariable laws. It is by his senses man is bound to this universal Nature; it is by his senses he must penetrate her secrets; it is from his senses he must draw experience of her laws. Whenever, therefore, he either fails to acquire experience or quits its path, he stumbles into an abyss, his imagination leads him astray. . . .

Man did not understand that Nature, equal in her distributions, entirely destitute of goodness or malice, follows only necessary and immutable laws, when she either produces beings or destroys them, when she causes those to suffer, whose organization creates sensibility; when she scatters among them good and evil; when she subjects them to incessant change—he did not perceive it was in the bosom of Nature herself, that it was in her abundance he ought to seek to satisfy his wants; for remedies against his pains; for the means of rendering himself happy: he expected to derive these benefits from imaginary beings, whom he erroneously imagined to be the authors of his pleasures, the cause of his misfortunes. From hence it is clear that to his ignorance of Nature, man owes the creation of those illusive powers under which he has so long trembled with fear; that superstitious worship, which has been the source of all his misery. . . .

The universe, that vast assemblage of every thing that exists, presents only matter and motion: the whole offers to our contemplation nothing but an immense, an uninterrupted succession of causes and effects; some of these causes are known to us, because they strike immediately on our senses; others are unknown to us, because they act upon us by effects, frequently very remote from their original cause. . . .

Of Motion and Its Origin

. . . Observation and reflection ought to convince us, that every thing in Nature is in continual motion. . . . Thus, the idea of Nature necessarily includes that of motion. But, it will be asked, from whence did she receive her motion? Our reply is, from herself, since she is the great whole, out of which, consequently, nothing can exist. . . .

If they [natural philosophers] had viewed Nature uninfluenced by prejudice, they must have been long since convinced, that matter acts by its own peculiar energy, and needs not any exterior impulse to set it in motion. They would have perceived, that whenever mixed bodies were placed in a capacity to act on each other, motion was instantly engendered, and that these mixtures acted with a force capable of producing the most surprising effects. If filings of iron, sulphur and water be mixed together, these bodies thus capacitated to act on each other, are heated by degrees, and ultimately produce a violent combustion. If flour be wetted with water, and the mixture closed up, it will be found, after some little lapse of time, by the aid of a microscope, to have produced organized beings that enjoy life, of which the water and the flour were believed incapable: it is thus that inanimate matter can pass into life, or animate matter, which is in itself only an assemblage of motion. Reasoning from analogy, the production of a man, independent of the ordinary means, would not be more marvellous than that of an insect with flour and water. . . .

Those who admit a cause exterior to matter, are obliged to suppose, that this cause produced all the motion by which matter is agitated in giving it existence. This supposition rests on another, namely, that matter could begin to exist; a hypothesis that, until this moment, has never been demonstrated by any thing like solid proof. To produce from nothing, or the *Creation,* is a term that cannot give us the most slender idea of the formation of the universe; it presents no sense, upon which the mind can fasten itself.

Motion becomes still more obscure, when creation, or the formation of matter, is attributed to a *spiritual* being, that is to say, to a being which has no analogy, no point of contact, with it; to a being which has neither extent, nor parts, and cannot, therefore, be susceptible of motion, as we understand the term; this being only the change of one body relatively to another body, in which the body moved, presents successively different parts to different points of space. Moreover, as all the world are nearly agreed that matter can never be totally annihilated, or cease to exist, how can we understand, that that which cannot cease to be, could ever have had a beginning?

If, therefore, it be asked, whence came matter? it is a very reasonable reply to say, it has always existed. . . .

Let us, therefore, content ourselves with saying *that* which is supported by our experience, and by all the evidence we are capable of understanding; against the truth of which, not a shadow of proof such as our reason can admit, has ever been adduced; which has been maintained by philosophers in every age; which theologians themselves have not denied, but which many of them have upheld; namely, that *matter always existed; that it moves by virtue of its essence; that all the phenomena of Nature is ascribable to the diversified motion of the variety of matter she contains; and which, like the phenix,*[33] *is continually regenerating out of her own ashes.*

---

33. **phenix:** the common modern spelling is "phoenix." In Egyptian mythology, the phoenix was a large bird, living a life span of 500 to 600 years in the Arabian desert. At the end of its life the phoenix was consumed in fire and from its ashes a new phoenix arose.

Chapter 3

The Mind of an

Age: Science

and Religion

Confront

Eighteenth-

Century

Natural Disaster

QUESTIONS TO CONSIDER

The selections that you have read allow you to trace one of the major issues raised by the *philosophes* as they sought to use the discoveries of the Scientific Revolution to comprehend the physical world more completely. Your consideration of this issue—the relationship of God to the physical world—should give you some clear understanding of the thought of the *philosophes* and its implications.

Consider first the traditional views expressed by Catholic and Protestant theologians. What caused the Lisbon earthquake, according to Malagrida? Did he foresee further disaster overtaking the city? Can you find in his pamphlet possible remedies for the city's misery from which Lisbon residents might have derived comfort? Contrast Malagrida's view of the plight of Lisbon with that of John Wesley, bearing in mind, of course, the latter's Protestantism. What cause did Wesley ascribe to the earthquake? Did he see any way to avoid such disasters? Despite their obvious differences, do you find any similarity in outlook in Malagrida and Wesley?

Now move on to Enlightenment sources, which are arranged to permit you to trace the development of the *philosophes'* responses to the disaster and the implications of their thought. Voltaire's distillation of Newton's physics in Source 3 is fundamental to understanding the Enlightenment because Newton's work provided the basis for the *philosophes'* understanding of the world in which

they lived. Through what method did Newton propose to understand the physical world? What relationships did he find governing the physical world? In what way did Newton's ideas provide a governing theory to explain much of that physical world? Why might you expect those influenced by Newton to describe the physical world as a machine?

Source 4, Alexander Pope's "An Essay on Man," represents an early-eighteenth-century attempt to balance a belief in God with the new scientific discoveries of Newton and others. How does Pope reflect traditional religion? What elements of sixteenth- and seventeenth-century scientific thought do you find in Pope? Most important, what role does God play in the world, according to Pope? What effect does that divine role have on humankind?

Reconsider the entry on "Observation" from the *Encyclopedia*. What view of reason does the article offer to its readers? How does Buffon attempt to apply this vision in his selection on earthquakes? What sort of causal pattern does he find for earthquakes? Despite his explanation of earthquakes, which is recognized today as incorrect, is there any room for a divine role in Buffon's explanation of these disasters? With whose view do you more closely identify, that of Buffon or Malagrida?

Voltaire's "Poem on the Lisbon Disaster" is the reaction of the Enlightenment's most celebrated thinker to the earthquake. Contrast it with the account he had written earlier of Newton's science. How had Voltaire's point of view changed during this interval? How does Voltaire respond to the views of his friend Alexander Pope? What response does he have to the theological explanation of the quake? Do you detect a growing skepticism in the thought of the older Voltaire? If so, in what ways? What response to Voltaire does Jean-Jacques Rousseau make in his letter? What similarities in thinking with earlier selections do you find in Rousseau?

Next examine Source 9, the selection by David Hume. Compare Voltaire's skepticism about a divine role in the world with the position Hume takes in "The Essay on Miracles." Also contrast Hume with Rousseau; how might intellectual differences have helped to cause their break? Where had Enlightenment skepticism, evident in Voltaire's later thought, led Hume? What religious implications of the Enlightenment's search to apply human reason to all issues do you find in Hume's work? Is any room left here for a divine role in the natural order? Trace this tendency in the thought of Baron d'Holbach, whose ideas shocked even some *philosophes*. Where have the principles of the Enlightenment led in Holbach's *System of Nature*? As we noted earlier, some of Holbach's contemporaries called him an atheist. How else might you describe his thought?

Your answers in carefully considering these questions should provide you with the basis for responding to the main questions in this chapter: Why did the Lisbon earthquake pose such an intellectual crisis for eighteenth-century thinkers? How did theologians explain the disaster? How did Enlightenment thinkers explain it? In what direction was their thought on the physical world and its relationship to divine forces leading them?

EPILOGUE

The difference in outlook between Malagrida and Wesley on one hand and the older and skeptical Voltaire and the Baron d'Holbach on the other is immense, and it represents a long intellectual journey for eighteenth-century thinkers. The culmination of this journey represented the success of the Scientific Revolution in modeling for the Western mind a method of searching for reasonable, scientific explanations of natural phenomena as well as imparting its faith in human ability to find these answers.

The Enlightenment, however, meant much more than even this. The implications of a movement ultimately unprepared, as we have seen, to accept traditional religion were tremendous beyond the fields of theology and natural science. Enlightenment skepticism in matters religious is controversial even to the present day. Its search for reasonable and comprehensible natural laws to govern all aspects of the human experience helped to change the Western world. Though a new and grander Lisbon arose out of the old city's ruins, much else did not long survive the intellectual crisis of mid-century that

Chapter 3
The Mind of an
Age: Science
and Religion
Confront
Eighteenth-
Century
Natural Disaster

earthquake embodied. The *philosophes'* search failed to uncover rational, natural laws to justify many human institutions of the eighteenth century. As a result, they called for sweeping changes of such existing institutions as divine right monarchy (see Chapter 2). In his *Social Contract,* for example, Rousseau argued for a new governing principle in which the general will of the people should govern. In the criminal justice practiced by governments of the day, the *philosophes* found a brutal system in which courts might employ torture to force defendants to testify against themselves and in which capital punishment was common. Many *philosophes* argued against the barbarism of such a system. In the work of the Italian thinker Cesare Bonesana, Marchese di Beccaria (1738–1794), the Enlightenment produced a strong statement against the death penalty and in favor of punishments based on prison terms graduated to fit the offense.

In religious matters, *philosophes* everywhere found an intolerance that to them seemed irrational, and Voltaire led their call for toleration and freedom of thought. Not even economic affairs escaped the attention of the *philosophes.* Eighteenth-century economic life was still dominated by guilds that set prices and government mercantilist policies that regulated trade. Adam Smith (1723–1790), a Scottish economist, led many Enlightenment thinkers in calling for a free economy. Let the natural laws of the economy work unimpeded and unregulated and the needs of all would be met, they argued. Everywhere the *philosophes* looked, they saw the need for reform. The exis-

tence today in the modern West of much of what they called for testifies to the wide-ranging influence of their thought.

A further casualty of the earthquake in Portugal was the Society of Jesus, one of the great opponents of much of Enlightenment thought. The disaster enhanced the power of the Marquis of Pombal, chief minister of Portugal's weak-willed monarch, Joseph I, because he led the relief and rebuilding efforts in the devastated city. The Portuguese version of that eighteenth-century phenomenon described in your text as the "enlightened despot," Pombal wielded more and more royal power even though he never wore the crown.

Your text recounts the careers of a number of enlightened despots, including Frederick the Great of Prussia and Joseph II of Austria. Like these rulers, Pombal had a vision of a government that was first of all absolute in power and only secondarily reforming in its policies. He found the great power of the Catholic church in Portugal a formidable obstacle to his hopes of building the secular strength of the state. Armed with greater prestige after the earthquake, Pombal attacked the greatest bastion of clerical power, the Society of Jesus, and expelled almost all of Portugal's Jesuits on September 1, 1759. In 1761 he ordered the execution of Gabriel Malagrida, the Society's most visible Portuguese spokesman. Malagrida's ideas stood in the way of reconstruction because he preached a need for spiritual regeneration and focused people's attentions on the next life. Pombal, in contrast, required all of Portugal's energies for rebuilding in the here and now. Other Catholic countries duplicated the Portuguese expulsion of the Jesuits. Local political or theological issues were often at the root of such expulsions, but they resulted in the worldwide abolition of the Society of Jesus from 1773 to 1814.[34]

The postearthquake Western world, thanks to the natural forces of the Lisbon disaster and the intellectual forces of the Enlightenment, would b considerably transformed on a number of levels. The fruits of Enlightenment thought are still with us in many forms.

34. On the French experience, see Dale Van Kley, *The Jansenists and the Expulsion of the Jesuits from France* (New Haven: Yale University Press, 1974).

CHAPTER FOUR

A STATISTICAL VIEW

OF EUROPEAN RURAL LIFE,

1600–1800

THE PROBLEM

Chapter 3 gave us a glimpse into the intellectual currents circulating among the educated upper classes of eighteenth-century Europe. Such groups have left historians ample evidence of their intellectual milieu in the works of figures like Voltaire as well as copious records of their lives and activities in correspondence, autobiographies, and other written sources. As a consequence, historians have been able to describe in great detail both the thought and the daily routine of Europe's opinion molders and governing classes. No matter how much influence these groups wielded, however, ultimately they represented only a small minority of the total population of their countries.

Most Europeans in the seventeenth and eighteenth centuries were illiterate, or barely literate, and they left none of the conventional written records that have long provided historians their raw material in recon-

structing the world of the privileged classes. Moreover, the majority of the population was rural, earning its living from the land, far from London, Paris, Venice, Vienna, and the other great urban centers that traditionally have attracted the research efforts of historians. Consequently we know a great deal about Voltaire as a member of the European elite, for example, but very little about the many peasants who worked his estate at Ferney—or about any other peasants, for that matter.

Only relatively recently have historians developed the methodological skills to penetrate the world of the majority of early modern Europe, the nonelites who left no written records of their own. Twentieth-century French scholars led the way in research in this area, and consequently the largest body of materials now available is devoted to France. Here two groups of French scholars have advanced our knowledge. One school, associated with the historical journal *Annales: Economies, sociétés, civilisations,* attempts to write "total history." Their search to understand the entirety of human existence, not just the actions of generals and kings and the thought of the great philosophers, has led them into many interesting lines of research, including studies of climatic changes and of literacy.[1] Because the ability to read and write largely defines the relationships an individual or a group forms with the wider world, the presence or absence of literacy is a fundamental issue in studying historic populations. Based on the frequency with which persons were able to sign their names to such documents as marital registers and court records, these historians have reconstructed the literacy pattern of western Europe during the seventeenth and eighteenth centuries. A more literate north and a less literate south characterized western Europe at this time, a regional difference that can be attributed partially to religious factors: northern European countries like England and Sweden were Protestant and emphasized individual reading of the Bible as an integral part of religious practice. Throughout Europe a direct relationship existed between the ability to read and write on the one hand and personal wealth and social class on the other.

A second school of French researchers has focused attention on historical demography, that is, the historical study of population.[2] Because regular census data on populations is largely a nineteenth-century development, these historians have reconstructed the past by means of other data, as you will see.

English and other historians followed the French lead, with the result that our knowledge of Europe's unlettered majority has grown immensely over the past four decades. Whatever their nationalities, however, historians examining Europe's ill-educated majority have adopted a common approach in reconstructing the past. Because little information exists for any given seventeenth- or eighteenth-century individual, historians have employed the technique of *collective biography*: they attempt to reconstruct the life of a community or social group and often express the results of their studies statistically.

The picture that emerges from these statistical studies is one of deep poverty for Europe's farming majority, a poverty that left them utterly at the mercy of nature. This is how the French demographic historian, Pierre Goubert, draws on his many years of study to describe the lifestyle of poorer French peasants in the late seventeenth century:

> The humble day-labourer, with a garden, a plot of land, a couple of sheep, working seasonally for other people, spinning or woodworking at home, would live in the classic cottage, the *chaumine enfumée* (smoky cottage) spec-

---

1. The journal *Annales* espoused this approach to history from its founding in 1929 by the French historians Marc Bloch and Lucien Febvre. The influence of this approach to historical study grew immensely after World War II.

2. Historical demography is a relatively new field of study, too. The major early works of the French pioneers in the field date only from the 1950s.

Chapter 4

A Statistical

View of

European

Rural Life,

1600–1800

ified by La Fontaine,[3] and these would certainly have been the commonest dwellings in France at that time. Made of stone or daub, depending on the region, but always with a solid chimney, stone surrounds for door and windows, it would be built around a simple frame of local wood, and roofed with reeds, rye straw, heather, or fern, topped with some large stones to protect the thatch from the wind. Inside there would be a single room, square or elongated (sometimes with a stable at one end). Beneath its occupants' bare feet (they put clogs on to go out) would be a floor of trodden earth, sometimes strewn with reeds or branches, all pretty well soaked with rain, damp from the walls, and chicken urine and droppings. The "hearth," the heart of the house, usually had a hook and a pot; there they warmed themselves, when the door was not open to make the chimney draw. Wind, rain, small animals, and every sort of parasite—creeping, scratching, jumping—came in all the time. Apart from cold (which they could protect themselves from by means of old cloaks, flea-ridden blankets, and *poches* [sacks]), their chief enemy was *arsin*, fire.[4]

The methodology that allows historians to portray the details of a vanished way of life in this manner consists of two basic operations: first compiling their statistical data and then analyzing it, that is, asking the right questions of their figures. Their goal is to understand the life of rural farming poor, to learn if any change

3. **Jean de La Fontaine** (1621–1695): a French poet and author of fables often describing rural life.

4. Pierre Goubert, *The French Peasantry in the Seventeenth Century*, trans. Ian Patterson (New York: Cambridge University Press, 1986), p. 37.

in that life occurred over time, and to attempt to explain changes through other sets of data. Your objective in this chapter is to ask and respond to the kinds of questions of statistical data that historians pose to understand better the lifestyle of Europe's majority from 1600 to 1800. What were the natural forces that affected these people? How can we measure the effects of these forces on Europe's farming population? Can we discern any changes that might have allowed Europe's illiterate, rural majority to escape the grip of these natural forces?

SOURCES AND METHOD

The evidence in this chapter has been selected to present you with a wide variety of the forms in which historians advance the statistical results of their research: tables and graphs. Analyzing these materials jointly will allow you to understand more fully the lives led by seventeenth- and eighteenth-century Europeans.

Source 1 presents data on European agricultural productivity for the grains wheat, rye, and barley, the mainstays of European diet during the period 1600–1800. The data are arranged by regions and expressed in terms of yield ratios. *Yield ratios* are a basic statistical tool employed by historians of agriculture that express the number of bushels harvested from one bushel of seed. Thus, from 1600 to 1649 in Zone I, 1 bushel of grain seed produced 6.7 bushels at harvest. To put this data in perspective, you need to understand that modern farming methods on amply watered wheat fields in the U.S. Midwest produce yield rations of at least 40:1 and often much higher. What do you conclude about the productivity of agriculture in the period that is the subject of this chapter? Which areas of Europe were most and least productive? Which areas showed the greatest advance toward a more productive farming? Given such an agriculture, why would you not be surprised to find the majority of the population occupied with farming?

Source 2 presents the dietary consequences of this primitive agriculture and also illustrates how the historian uses old sources and new scientific methods to reconstruct the past. Source 2 is a "Nutritional Balance Sheet" drawn from the records of a notary in the Gévaudan region of southern France in the eighteenth century. Notaries were legal specialists, found even in the most isolated villages of France, who dealt with property matters. They drafted wills, inventories of the property of deceased persons, and marital agreements that specified property arrangements. Most important for the historian, notaries kept their documents for many years, preserving them until they came to be housed in modern archives funded by the French government that opened them as important sources for historians. From notarial records historians can determine marital patterns and individual and collective wealth within a community.

The table in Source 2 is drawn from a particular kind of notarial concern: often the notary recorded arrangements for the care of aged parents or a disabled sibling when, for example, an aging father transferred the family farm's ownership to his son. In order to avoid later conflict within the family, notarial documents often spelled out quite precisely what the aging parent or sibling was to be provided with in food by the person taking control of the family property. The result is a kind of record, rarely found, that tells us what people ate. Each of the eleven entries on the table represents one family's arrangements for the feeding of one of its members.

In order to adequately interpret Source 2, you need to know something of human dietary needs because the historian who assembled these data has interpreted food allotments in terms of their nutritional content. Most of the recipients of these food allotments were expected to work, and a daily food intake of about 2,400 calories is necessary to sustain moderate labor (1,500 calories per day is necessary simply to sustain life). But modern nutritionists know that diet must also be analyzed to determine if it is sufficiently rich in certain energy-producing substances. Proteins supply the body with essential nitrogens and amino acids, and about one gram of protein per kilogram of body weight is necessary daily. Assume an average male weight of 65 kilograms (143 lbs.). Are there sufficient proteins in these diets? Ideally, too, 40 percent of daily proteins should be of animal origin. What is the source of most of the proteins in Source 2? What role does meat assume in these diets?

Chapter 4

A Statistical

View of

European

Rural Life,

1600–1800

Lipids, or fats, are essential in maintaining body temperature, and about 40 grams daily are necessary. What do you find these diets provide in lipids? Combine this with your findings on proteins. What impact do you think such diets would have on an individual's ability to sustain physical labor in sometimes rigorous weather?

Glucides, or sugars, provide muscle energy, and an adult requires a minimum of 40 grams of these per day. What do the diets in Source 2 provide in sugars? Why do you find this the only source of energy provided in sufficient amount?

Various minerals also are essential to good nutrition. Minerals like calcium and phosphorus are necessary for skeletal development and sound teeth, and they must be present in the diet in certain proportions. Ideally, an adult's calcium consumption should be between 60 and 80 percent of his or her phosphorus consumption. Pregnant women and children require even more calcium. Consult Source 2 to determine whether the Gévaudan residents were getting sufficient calcium by simply dividing calcium consumption by phosphorus consumption. Why would you not be surprised to find calcium deficiency-related problems like poor teeth, bow legs, and scoliosis (abnormal curvature of the spine) in this population?

Consider the diets now as a group. What foods would you find missing? What food type, based on the calories it represents in daily consumption, seems to dominate the diet of the peasant farmers who consumed these rations? What do you think the health consequences of such a diet, more or less generalized in this population, would have been?

We must understand, too, that the diet presented in Source 2 represents the ideal, not the norm. Weather factors often affected European farming, resulting in diminished agricultural yields. Insufficient or excessive rainfall, abnormally low temperatures, and other climatological phenomena all influenced the harvest. The graphs in Source 3 represent some of the most interesting research of modern historians—the study of weather and its consequences. The work of such historians is showing the climatic differences that have affected the West over the last millennium. The diagrams in Source 3 illustrate the impact of weather changes over the period 1699–1789. The diagrams are designed to be read together. Diagram 1 presents temperature data in England in the eighteenth century as evidence of general European temperature trends. Note the scale of temperatures on this diagram has been inverted so that the temperature graph goes up for colder temperatures and down for higher ones. This has been done to allow you to correlate more readily increases in food prices with abnormally low temperatures. In what years do the data in Diagram 1 show abnormally cool spring and summer temperatures? What effect would such temperatures have had on agricultural products such as grapes and wheat? Diagram 2 presents the effects of temperature trends by showing simultaneously the dates of grape harvests and the advance of glaciers in the Alps. An especially extended period of glacial advance indicates a period of cool weather, as does an unusually late grape harvest. Diagram 3 draws on the data kept by the French along with other early modern European governments on the price of food, the ultimate consequence of weather trends. How do seasonal temperatures correlate with wheat prices? In what years did weather adversely affect agriculture and drive up prices?

The data presented in Source 4 may seem abstract to twentieth-century readers, who, after all, live in a society in which social welfare agencies prevent actual starvation among the poor despite price increases for dietary essentials. We must remember that such agencies are relatively recent additions to Western life; two centuries ago they did not exist. The graph in Source 4 presents the consequences of periodic food price increases for a French wagoner. You should understand that the graph assigns a value of 100 to wages and prices in the period 1726–1735, establishing that period as the base "index" for the graph. An index of 155 for the price of wheat in Arles in the late 1740s thus represents a 55 percent increase over wheat prices of the base period. What do you observe in long-term salary trends? What do you note about the long-term trends in the price of the wheat essential in making bread, the dietary staple of the poor? What sorts of conditions did the wagoners of Bas-Provence experience in the 1730s, the late 1740s, and especially from the 1760s into the late 1780s?

Poverty and dietary insufficiencies breed a multitude of maladies. But many epidemic diseases struck even well-fed populations. None of these was more feared in medieval and early modern Europe than the bubonic plague. Physicians knew no cure for this fatal disease that had ravaged Europe since its first appearance there in the fourteenth century. By the eighteenth century, Europeans at least understood somewhat the importance of quarantining districts afflicted by the plague as a means of stemming its spread. The table in Source 5 represents plague mortalities in southern France in 1720–1721 as the disease spread. Plague broke out first in the large port of Marseilles and spread to much of the surrounding region, grievously afflicting some towns and not others. Quarantines restricted the disease to the southern part of France, and the Marseilles epidemic was the last great outbreak of the plague in the modern West to date. In what towns did the greatest portion of the population die? What impact would such losses have had on the towns?

Disease was common in early modern Europe, as were famine conditions. When disease coincided with agricultural failure, the result could be what historians call a *demographic* or *population crisis,* a period when deaths exceed births and the population declines. Information on such crises in the population history of Europe has been amassed laboriously by historians using records left by the literate members of early modern society about the largely illiterate majority. Priests, for example, kept parish

Chapter 4

A Statistical

View of

European

Rural Life,

1600–1800

registers of baptisms, marriages, and burials, which, in the hands of skilled historical demographers, permit the scholarly reconstitution of the history of past populations. Sources 6 through 12 are assembled to reflect the combined effects of the agricultural cycle and disease on population.

The data presented in Source 6 offer evidence of the last great demographic crisis to afflict all of Europe, which occurred in the 1740s. The data illustrate trends in deaths, births, and marriages in the period 1735–1744. As in the graph in Source 4, the researchers have established values around a base period to which a value of 100 is assigned. Thus, for example, in the first table in Source 6, 100 represents the average number of deaths annually in 1735–1744. An index number of 106 for deaths in England during the year 1740 indicates simply that deaths that year were 6 percent higher than the average. Similarly, in the second table in Source 6, an index of 91 for 1742 indicates births were 91 percent of the base period total.

Was Europe's population growing rapidly prior to the 1740s? What reasons might account for this trend? In what years, as revealed in an abnormally high death rate, did demographic crises strike the various European countries? Consult the data on births and marriages. Did the crisis have a greater, more lasting effect than simply the deaths resulting from it? What happened to marriage and birth rates in the wake of the crisis? How might these developments affect a society's ability to replace its losses?

Inadequate means of transportation also affected the conditions of the population in early modern Europe. An area experiencing poor harvests might confront outright starvation simply because of the impossibility of moving food supplies to it from prosperous neighboring areas. Source 7 presents demographic data from Bresles-en-Beauvaisis, a town in northern France, for the seventeenth and early eighteenth centuries. Compare the graphs of food prices and births and burials. In what years were food prices high? In what years did burials exceed births? What do you think caused the excessive burials? How often, over the period 1655–1745, did burials exceed births? Do you think this population grew much in this period?

Our data thus far suggest that a very high death rate affected early modern Europeans. But death did not claim all equally. Examine Source 8, which presents data on infant and child mortality in several parts of France. Approximately what percentage of eighteenth-century French children might hope to live to age ten?

Source 9 employs the statistical tool of average life expectancy to show living conditions in Colyton, England. Average life expectancy is a statistical construct in which the life spans of all persons born at a given point in time are averaged together. In deriving such averages, historians of population as well as public health specialists average the life spans of the infant dying within minutes or hours of birth and the old person who reaches the age of eighty or ninety. The resulting figure offers a perspective on how well a given society provides for the health and welfare of its members. For purposes of comparison, the average life expectancy in modern England in the 1980s was 70.2 years for males and 76.2 years for females, whereas in some impoverished Third World countries today life expectancy is roughly 43 years for both men and women.

The Colyton figures show average life expectancy for years of high, low, and average death rates. How do such life expectancies compare with those of modern England and the modern Third World? What role do you think infant mortality had in keeping average life expectancy low?

The lives of early modern Europeans clearly were affected by the fortunes of agriculture. But even in non-crisis years the regular rhythm of the agricultural year ruled early modern rural Europeans' lives. The rural French experience was probably typical of Europe as a whole: the year opened with January and February, cold months when agricultural labor was light because of weather conditions. Food reserves, however, were beginning to shrink at this time, and farmers often slaughtered pigs and other livestock because fodder for the animals was running low. By March, April and May the fruits of the previous autumn's harvests were dwindling for humans, too, as agricultural labor resumed with plowing and planting. Late May and June, after the crops were planted, might bring a slight respite from work. But late summer and early autumn brought the more taxing labor of the harvest. In these months epidemics of disease as well as health problems resulting from the drinking of impure water and the eating of partially ripened fruits and vegetables made necessary by summer shortages affected the health of the rural population. Once the harvest was in, of course, winter's rigors resumed.

Source 10 presents the seasonal incidence of death in four areas in France. How does the death rate reflect the impact of the agricultural year and climatic conditions on French people? Note that the graph for Morannes distinguishes the deaths of the young from the old. When did children die? Why? In Sources 11 and 12, you find data on marriages and conceptions in rural France. To analyze the marriage data, you must remember that France is largely a Catholic country and you should understand that the Church forbade marriages during Advent (the period in late November and December for four Sundays before Christmas on December 25) and Lent (the period, usually in March and early April, of the forty weekdays before Easter. Lent begins on Ash Wednesday). Bearing in mind these religious strictures and the agricultural cycle, determine when rural Frenchmen married and why they chose the months they did. Why would these months in the agricultural cycle be propitious times for wedding feasts? When did French rural couples conceive their children? How might the agricultural cycle affect reproduction?

Your task in this chapter is to reconstruct the lifestyle of Europe's

Chapter 4

A Statistical

View of

European

Rural Life,

1600–1800

majority using the statistical sets provided. Use the mode of analysis suggested in this section, taking care to: (1) Study each data set, observing changes over time—for instance, increased agricultural productivity in some areas. (2) Once you have identified a change, seek an explanation in the other data sets. For example, what weather trends affected areas with improved agricultural output? How might they help to account for increased productivity? What role might diet have played? (3) Pose basic questions of your data. What trends were affecting the population?

Making use of this methodology, you should be able to answer the central questions of this chapter: What were the natural forces that affected these people? How can we measure the effects of these forces on Europe's farming population? Can we discern any changes that might have allowed Europe's illiterate, rural majority to escape the grip of these natural forces?

THE EVIDENCE

Source 1 from E. E. Rich and C. H. Wilson, editors, The Cambridge Economic History of Europe, *vol. 5*, The Economic Organization of Early Modern Europe *(New York: Cambridge University Press, 1977), p. 81.*

1. Combined Yield Ratios of Wheat, Rye, and Barley, 1500–1820

Period	Zone I[a]	Zone II[b]	Zone III[c]	Zone IV[d]
1600–1649	6.7:1	—	4.5:1	4.0:1
1650–1699	9.3	6.2:1	4.1	3.8
1700–1749	—	6.3	4.1	3.5
1750–1799	10.1	7.0	5.1	4.7
1800–1820	11.1	6.2	5.4	—

a. Zone I: England, Low Countries.
b. Zone II: France, Spain, Italy.
c. Zone III: Germany, Switzerland, Scandinavia.
d. Zone IV: Russia, Poland, Czechoslovakia, Hungary.

Source 2 adapted from R.-J. Bernard, "Peasant Diet in Eighteenth-Century Gévaudan" in Robert and Elborg Forster, eds., European Diet from Pre-Industrial to Modern Times (New York: Harper and Row, 1975), p. 38.

2. A Nutritional Balance Sheet

	Protein (in grams)			Lipids (in grams)					Glucides (in grams)			Trace Elements (milligrams)			Calories	
	Bread	Cheese	Total	Bread	Butter	Cheese	Salt Lard	Total	Bread	Cheese	Total	Phosphorus	Calcium	Iron	Total	% from Bread
1.	45.93	1.64	47.57	5.74	4.99	1.76	10.14	22.63	287.01	0.02	287.03	1,070.62	386.26	17.26	1,576.07	89.80
2.	48.00	5.01	53.01	6.00	10.14	5.37	15.21	36.72	300.00	0.71	300.71	1,171.28	486.49	18.10	1,665.51	83.20
3.	67.19	4.17	71.36	8.40	12.49	4.47	30.43	55.79	420.00	0.59	420.59	1,521.65	609.79	26.15	2,359.04	82.10
4.	36.55	1.97	38.52	4.55	5.99	2.11	8.11	20.76	227.83	0.02	227.85	860.10	324.65	14.20	1,195.20	88.10
5.	36.77	1.97	38.74	4.59	5.99	2.11	5.99	18.68	279.87	0.02	279.89	863.85	325.90	14.34	1,386.00	80.25
6.	54.30	2.05	56.35	6.78	7.60	2.21	20.28	36.87	339.43	0.03	339.46	1,230.45	418.22	20.45	1,861.28	84.10
7.	61.44	1.97	63.41	7.68	5.99	2.11	12.17	27.95	384.00	0.02	384.02	1,418.70	510.85	23.09	1,955.60	90.81
8.	68.08	6.82	74.90	8.51	20.28	7.30	20.28	56.37	425.50	0.97	426.47	1,607.18	683.35	26.12	2,487.01	83.04
9.	63.36	1.97	65.33	6.33	10.14	2.11	20.28	38.86	396.04	0.02	396.06	1,052.79	389.12	17.86	2,163.69	86.92
10.	84.75	3.94	88.69	10.59	10.14	4.22	15.21	40.76	529.71	0.04	529.75	1,979.25	735.54	32.68	2,816.25	90.60
11.	61.43	2.50	63.93	7.67	7.60	2.68	15.21	33.16	383.96	0.04	384.00	1,438.39	527.66	23.71	1,998.75	93.70

Sources 3 and 4 adapted from Ernest Labrousse, et al., Histoire économique et sociale de la France, *vol. II,* Des derniers temps de l'âge seigneurial aux préludes de l'âge industriel (1660–1789) *(Paris: Presses Universitaires de la France, 1970), pp. 392, 537.*

3. Wheat Prices and Weather, France, 1699–1789

1

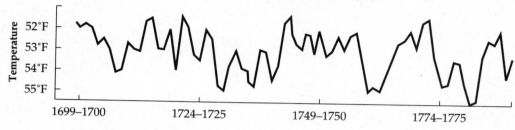

1. Spring and summer temperatures for England (two-year moving averages; temperature scale in Fahrenheit; graph of temperatures inverted for better comparison with the graph of grape harvests).

2

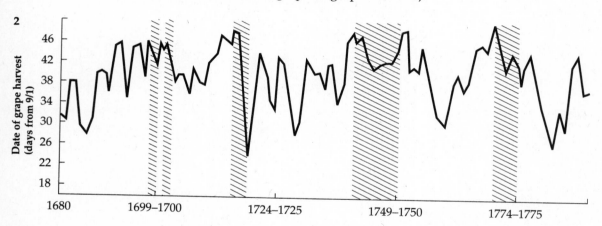

2. Dates of grape harvests (counted in days from September 1, in moving two-year averages); glacial maximums in the Alps shown in shading.

3

3. Price of wheat per *setier* of Paris in *livres tournois* (French currency of eighteenth century).

4. Contrast Between Fixed Salary of a Typical Agricultural Worker and Price of Wheat in Basse-Provence, France, 1726–1789

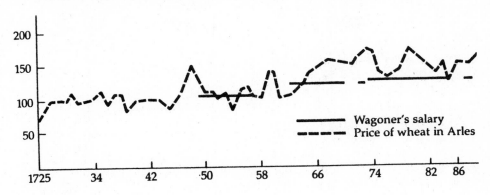

Source 5 from Jean-Noël Biraben, "Certain Demographic Characteristics of the Plague Epidemic in France, 1720–1722," Daedalus, Spring 1968, pp. 541–542.

5. Epidemics: The Plague in Southern France, 1720–1721

Place	Approximate Preplague Population	Date of First Appearance of Plague	Number of Plague Deaths	Percentage of Population Killed
Marseilles and environs	90,000	20 June 1720	39,334	43.7
Vitrolles	770	2 August	210	27.3
Gignac	470	15 August	42	8.9
Septèmes	940	26 August	200	21.3
Gaubert	500	4 September	29	5.8
Nans	500	27 September	125	25.0
Auriol	3,200	3 October	1,319	41.2
Villars Brancas	300	9 October	12	4.0
Martigues	6,000	1 November	2,200	36.7
Arles	22,000	26 November	9,400	42.7
Orgon	1,700	29 December	105	6.2
La Valette	1,600	20 February 1721	1,068	64.3
Trinquetaille les Arles	1,157	11 June	80	6.9
St. Nazaire (Sanary)	1,200	1 July	51	4.2
La Roquebrussane	997	14 August	201	20.1

Chapter 4

A Statistical

View of

European

Rural Life,

1600–1800

Source 6 from John D. Post, "Climatic Variability and the European Mortality Wave of the Early 1740s," The Journal of Interdisciplinary History, vol. 15 (1984), no. 10 (table 1) and Food Shortage, Climatic Variability, and Epidemic Disease in Preindustrial Europe: The Mortality Peak in the Early 1740s (Ithaca, N.Y.: Cornell University Press, 1985), pp. 46, 48 (tables 2 and 3).

6. Europewide Population Crisis of 1740–1742

INDEXES OF ANNUAL NUMBER OF DEATHS IN EUROPE, 1735–1744 (1735–1744 = 100)

Location	1735	1736	1737	1738	1739	1740	1741	1742	1743	1744
England	89	94	102	92	93	106	118	124	98	85
Scotland	88	96	109	88	93	122	116	107	90	91
Ireland (Dublin)	93	89	94	106	93	140	119	99	93	72
France	80	93	93	96	109	123	116	111	94	83
Low Countries	83	95	102	93	97	99	149	98	98	84
Germany	84	116	114	99	98	112	110	96	92	78
Austria (Vienna)	88	112	108	118	98	111	105	105	87	69
Switzerland	86	100	115	84	85	108	100	123	112	87
Italy	94	115	96	87	86	100	107	112	108	95
Sweden[a]	70[b]	82	102	92	93	108	98	118	131	76
Finland	64	75	104	85	97	157	95	136	112	74
Norway	68	74	88	83	83	92	149	187	100	76
Denmark	81	102	114	100	96	114	112	103	95	83
Unweighted average	82	96	103	94	94	115	115	117	101	81

a. Base period 1736–1744.
b. Index number derived from Stockholm and nine Swedish counties.

INDEXES OF ANNUAL NUMBER OF BIRTHS IN EUROPE, 1735–1744
(1735–1744 = 100)

Location	1735	1736	1737	1738	1739	1740	1741	1742	1743	1744
England	105	103	101	103	105	100	93	91	99	100
France	100	101	106	100	105	99	99	95	96	99
Low Countries	106	105	106	105	102	97	88	94	101	95
Germany	103	100	93	97	104	96	91	99	108	109
Austria (Vienna)	114	110	111	109	120	106	81	78	84	88
Switzerland	106	99	106	103	102	97	100	94	96	97
Italy	99	93	100	101	102	101	99	103	98	103
Sweden[a]	99[b]	92	94	104	113	100	99	98	92	107
Finland	105	111	110	113	112	104	98	74	78	96
Norway	100	105	105	97	108	103	95	90	95	102
Denmark	101	99	96	102	102	99	94	97	103	106
Unweighted average	103	102	103	103	107	100	94	92	95	100

a. Base period 1736–1744.
b. Index number derived from Stockholm and nine Swedish counties.

INDEXES OF ANNUAL NUMBER OF MARRIAGES IN EUROPE, 1735–1744
(1735–1744 = 100)

Location	1735	1736	1737	1738	1739	1740	1741	1742	1743	1744
England	104	95	100	100	103	98	88	97	107	107
France	93	94	99	101	97	96	96	101	122	101
Low Countries	108	107	101	99	103	86	90	107	102	99
Germany	97	93	97	99	104	88	101	115	109	97
Switzerland	102	99	102	105	96	99	88	97	114	98
Italy	99	93	101	104	101	99	97	92	104	111
Finland	105	106	105	103	95	93	78	75	101	140
Unweighted average	101	98	101	102	100	94	91	98	108	108

Source 7 adapted from Pierre Goubert and Daniel Roche, Les français et l'Ancien Régime, *vol. I (Paris: Armand Colin, 1984), p. 45.*

7. Local Crises at Bresles-en-Beauvaisis, France, late 17th and early 18th centuries

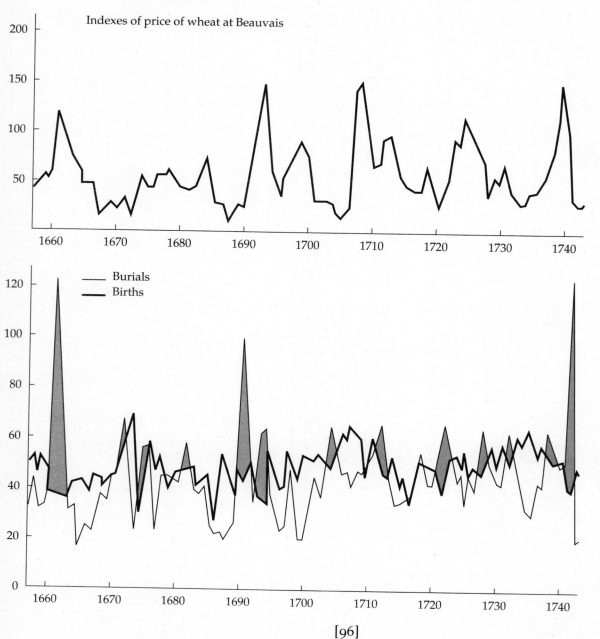

Source 8 from Pierre Goubert, "Legitimate Fecundity and Infant Mortality in France During the Eighteenth Century: A Comparison," Daedalus, Spring 1968, pp. 599–600.

8. Infant and Child Mortality in France: Children Living to the Age of 10 Years

Brittany:

Saint-Aubin (1748–1789)	580 of 1,000
La Guerche (1720–1790)	510 of 1,000
Saint-Méen (1720–1792)	463 of 1,000

Elsewhere (Southwest and Normandy):

Thézels (1747–1782)	645 of 1,000
Azereix (18th century)	639 of 1,000
Crulai (1674–1742)	672 of 1,000

Source 9 from E. A. Wrigley, "Mortality in Pre-Industrial England: The Example of Colyton, Devon, Over Three Centuries." Daedalus, Spring 1968, p. 574.

9. Life Expectancy in Colyton, England, in Years

Period	High Mortality	Low Mortality	Midpoint
1538–1624	40.6	45.8	43.2
1625–1699	34.9	38.9	36.9
1700–1774	38.4	45.1	41.8

Chapter 4

A Statistical

View of

European

Rural Life,

1600–1800

Source 10 from François Lebrun, Les hommes et la morte en Anjou aux 17ᵉ et 18ᵉ siècles. Essai de démographie et de psychologie historiques *(Paris and The Hague: Mouton, 1971), p. 190.*

10. Seasonal Incidence of Mortality in Several Rural Areas of France, 17th and 18th centuries

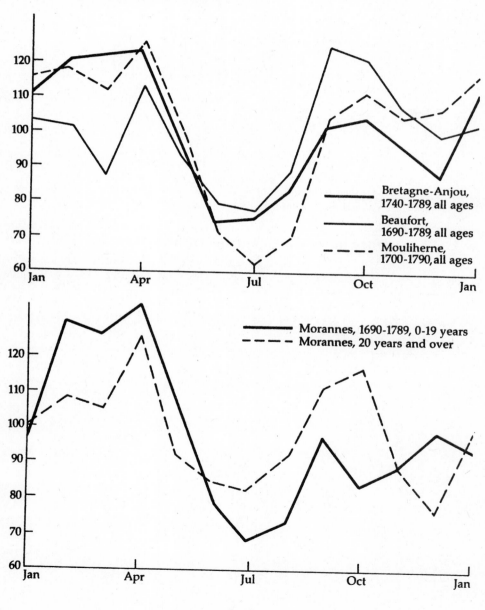

Sources 11 and 12 from Pierre Guillaume and Jean-Pierre Poussou, Demographie historique *(Paris: Armand Colin, 1970), p. 184; p. 172.*

11. Seasonal Incidence of Marriage in France, Showing the Three Most Common Months (1–3) and the Three Least Common Months (10–12), by Location

Parishes	Period of Observation	1	2	3	10	11	12
Thézels-Saint-Sernin (Lot)	1700–1792	Feb.	Nov.	June	Sept.	Aug.	Dec.
Castelnau-de-Montratier (Lot)	1716–1789	Feb.	Nov.	Jan.	Aug.	March	Dec.
La Rochelle, Saint-Barthélemy parish	1677–1685	Feb.	Jan.	July	April	March	Dec.
Chef-Boutonne (Deux-Sèvres)	1722–1792	Feb.	Jan.	Nov.	Aug.	March	Dec.
Avits (Tarn)	1692–1717	Feb.	June	Jan.	Aug.	March	Dec.
Lyon	1750–1774	Feb.	Jan.	Nov.	April	March	Dec.
Saint-Romain-d'Urfé (Loire)	1740–1749	Nov.	Feb.	Jan.	April	March	Dec.
Bonneuil-sur-Marne (Seine)	1680–1790	Nov.	Jan.	Feb.	Aug.	March	Dec.
Bagneux (Seine)	1691–1789	Feb.	Nov.	Jan.	April	Dec.	March
Paris	{ 1728–1737	Feb.	Nov.	Jan.	April	March	Dec.
	1778–1787	Feb.	Nov.	Jan.	Aug.	March	Dec.
Crulai (Orne)	1675–1798	Nov.	Feb.	Jan.	April	March	Dec.

12. Seasonal Incidence of Conceptions in France, Showing the Three Most Common Months (1–3) and the Three Least Common Months (10–12), by Location

Parishes	Period of Observation	1	2	3	10	11	12
Thézels-Saint-Sernin (Lot)	1700–1792	June	May	July	Oct.	March	Sept.
Castelnau-de-Montratier (Lot)	1716–1789	June	May	April	Aug.	Sept.	March
Divillac (Lot)	1671–1692	June	May	April	Aug.	March	Nov.
Ile de Ré, 8 parishes	1764–1773	June	Jan.	April	Aug.	Sept.	Oct.
La Rochelle, Saint-Barthélemy parish	1677–1685	Feb.	June	May	Oct.	Dec.	Sept.
Chef-Boutonne (Deux-Sèvres)	1722–1792	June	May	April	Aug.	Oct.	Sept.
Avits (Tarn)	1692–1717	June	Jan.	Nov.	Feb.	Sept.	Oct.
Saint-Romain-d'Urfé (Loire)	1740–1749	June	May	July	Oct.	Sept.	Nov.
Crulai (Orne)	1700–1799	June	May	April	Sept.	Nov.	Oct.

Chapter 4

A Statistical

View of

European

Rural Life,

1600–1800

QUESTIONS TO CONSIDER

Each of the sources of evidence you considered in this chapter represents a piece of a puzzle that, when assembled, presents a picture of the life of the rural majority of seventeenth- and eighteenth-century Europe. Let us now begin to fit those pieces together.

Consider first what the various sources tell you about the health of seventeenth- and eighteenth-century Europeans in "average" times. How did the productivity of farming compare to that of today? What sort of diet did it provide Europeans of those centuries? Why would you not be surprised to learn that modern scientists have found evidence that nutritionally based ailments like rickets abounded among these people and that historians have discovered that they were of much shorter stature than twentieth-century Europeans? What would you conclude about this population's resistance to disease?

Next you should determine the frequency with which a physically vulnerable population faced the physical stress of nonaverage times. Note in Source 5 how disastrous an epidemic could be in early modern times. Then recall the sanitary conditions described by Pierre Goubert earlier in this chapter. How common do you think diseases other than the plague must have been, given such sanitary conditions and the physical condition of the population? To arrive at a partial answer to this question, count the demographic crises at Bresles-en-Beauvaisis (Source 7) in the 1655–

1745 period. How many times did burials exceed births in this period? How often, on the average, did crises combining disease and food shortage recur? To generalize from the French case, reflect how much more productive agriculture in the French zone of Europe was than in some other parts of the Continent. What groups in society, based on the evidence in Sources 8 through 10, were most vulnerable to disease and poor nutrition?

If demographic crises recurred with some frequency, especially in the seventeenth century, the effects were felt for years afterward. What effect did demographic crises have on later rates of marriages and births, according to the data in Source 6? Why do you think that population experienced little growth in the seventeenth and eighteenth centuries?

You should also consider the effect that climate and agricultural life had on those who survived the threats to life in seventeenth- and eighteenth-century Europe. How did the cycle of agriculture affect such basic events of human life as marriage and reproduction?

You also ought to consider the cultural ramifications of the material life we have examined in this chapter. How do you think an illiterate population, cut off by poor transportation from outside assistance in time of famine and also isolated from more sophisticated ideas originating in cities, explained the disasters that overtook it periodically? Why would you not be surprised to find in other historical sources a high level of superstition among Europe's peasant population and a persistence of beliefs in the existence of witches who were thought to bring evil upon their neighbors?

Finally, reconsider the full range of evidence to determine the possibilities for change in this lifestyle. What chance did scientific farming methods have to influence the agricultural methods of a widely illiterate European majority? Compare the overall literacy rate in northern Europe (higher than that in southern Europe) with eighteenth-century improvements in agricultural productivity. What correlation between increased literacy rates and farm output would you expect? If farm productivity could have been improved, what sort of effects do you think western Europe would have experienced?

As you formulate answers to these questions that transcend the lessons of the individual pieces of evidence and lead you to general conclusions, you should be on the way to putting together the puzzle. As you do so, you should be able to answer the main questions of this chapter. What were the natural forces that affected the majority of seventeenth- and eighteenth-century Europeans? How can we measure the effects of these forces on Europe's farming population? Can we discern any changes that might have allowed Europe's illiterate, rural majority to escape the grip of these natural forces?

EPILOGUE

The world we have sketched here was, until the late eighteenth century one of limited literacy, poverty, and precarious existence characterized by a stagnant or slowly growing population. Educational levels improved slowly in the late eighteenth century and more rapidly along with the spread of public education in the nineteenth century. But the biggest change was the transformation of the demographic system of western Europe.

After a century and a half of little growth, Europe's population rapidly expanded after about 1750. The population in England and Wales increased more than fivefold between 1750 and 1900 and that of France almost doubled in the same period. Other countries experienced similar dramatic population increases.

This population explosion was primarily the result of a reduced mortality rate. In particular, losses of life to famine and disease decreased. Famines declined in frequency and severity for several reasons. Some western European farmers applied more scientific techniques to improve their output, first in England and Holland but later elsewhere. New crops of American origin, like corn and the potato, were introduced to European agriculture. Yielding more food per acre than wheat and often cultivable on marginal lands unsuited for that grain, these crops also increased the food supply. All these developments were part of a phenomenon that many textbooks call the Agricultural Revolution, a process that greatly reduced the numbers

Chapter 4

A Statistical

View of

European

Rural Life,

1600–1800

of deaths from starvation or the effects of malnutrition.

Deaths from diseases also diminished in the eighteenth century, when physicians began inoculation for smallpox and more effective quarantining of infectious diseases. As a result of the more bountiful and reliable food supply and reduced mortality from disease, the population swelled.

A second transformation of society, the Industrial Revolution, also dramatically altered the lifestyle we examined in this chapter. Beginning in England in the late eighteenth century and later elsewhere in Europe, the Industrial Revolution drew increasingly numbers of people away from agriculture to employment in factories and residence in the cities that grew up around the new plants (see Chapters 6 and 8). The Agricultural Revolution aided this process by creating harvests so productive that a farming minority of the population could feed an urbanized majority employed in manufacturing and service industries. The result was an increasingly urbanized Europe.

The Industrial Revolution also helped to destroy the demographic system we explored in this chapter. Improved transportation, like the railroads made possible by the modern steel industry, permitted food products to be moved rapidly to areas in need of them and to eliminate the local famines we examined in Source 9. Some historians also argue that at least in England the Industrial Revolution may also have helped to increase the birth rate. Because marriage has always depended on the existence of the financial means to establish a new household, industrialization may have created the wealth necessary to allow more women than ever before to marry and to have children.

A variety of factors thus combined in the nineteenth and early twentieth centuries to alter beyond recognition the rural world we have explored. Its isolation bred of illiteracy, its poverty rooted in an unproductive agriculture, and its high mortality now represent a lifestyle foreign to modern Europe, a Western society preserved only in museums and history books.

CHAPTER FIVE

THE LIBERATOR-HERO

AND WESTERN REVOLUTIONS

During the late eighteenth century, successful revolts, failed uprisings, and both real and imagined revolutionary plots swept across much of Europe and the Americas. While visiting her native city of Liège in 1791, Théroinge de Méricourt, a woman who sympathized with and participated in the early stages of the French Revolution, was arrested and imprisoned by the Austrians. Believing she was a spy, the Austrians interrogated her, without success, and then sent for the prison doctor, who diagnosed her as suffering from "revolutionary fever."[1] In the eyes of many, Méricourt was not the only person struck down with "revolutionary fever." Indeed, according to historian R. R. Palmer, English conservative Edmund Burke "was so

afraid of invasion and revolution . . . that he gave orders for his remains to be secretly buried, lest triumphant democrats dig them up for desecration."[2]

Whatever their differences, the Western revolutionaries of the late eighteenth century were an extremely self-conscious lot. Convinced that they were altering history, for their own people as well as for all the world, these revolutionists wanted to justify their revolts as the fulfillment of a higher purpose (rather than a mere grab for power), as well as to pass on to future generations what they considered to be the true essence or meaning of their respective revolutions.

One way they were able to accomplish both objectives was through the creation of a *liberator-hero*, a person

---

1. Théroinge de Méricourt, real name Anne-Joseph Méricourt (1762–1817), was one of the many fascinating participants in the French Revolution. See Simon Schama, *Citizens: A Chronicle of the French Revolution* (New York: Alfred A. Knopf, 1989), pp. 462–463, 530, 605, 611, 873–875.

2. R. R. Palmer, *The Age of the Democratic Revolution: A Political History of Europe and America, 1760–1800*, 2 vols. (Princeton: Princeton University Press, 1959), vol. I, p. 5. According to Palmer, revolutions, threats of revolutions, or plots took place in what was to become the United States as well as in France, Ireland, the Netherlands, Switzerland, Milan, Rome, Naples, Poland, Hungary, Greece, Ecuador, Brazil, what would become Haiti, and in some of the German states.

who could be a *symbol* of the revolution both to contemporaries and to future generations. Through the use of speeches, eulogies, memorials, pageants, paintings, and statuary, the major essences, goals, and events of the Western revolutions were personified, and myths about these revolutions were created and imbued in their liberator-heroes.

In this chapter you will examine the creation of three liberator-heroes: George Washington of the American Revolution, Jean-Paul Marat of the French Revolution, and Toussaint Louverture of the Haitian Revolution. Using eulogies and contemporary portraits, you will be asked to analyze how the participants in each revolution attempted to fashion a liberator-hero who symbolized the character, goals, and nature of the revolution as the participants themselves understood it *and* as they wanted others to see it. How was George Washington used by his contemporaries as a symbol of the American Revolution? Jean-Paul Marat of the French Revolution? Toussaint Louverture of the Haitian Revolution? Although these revolutions had much in common and in many ways were intertwined, the American, French, and Haitian revolutions were profoundly different.

In Britain's North American colonies, a struggle for home rule evolved into a war for separation. In the 1760s and early 1770s an increasing number of people in Britain's North American colonies began to oppose taxation by the mother country, as well as what they feared was an erosion of their political rights. In 1775 these protests erupted into open warfare, and in the next year the colonies declared their independence from Great Britain and their intention to form a new nation. Independence and nationhood, however, were not actually achieved until the British gave up the armed struggle in 1781 and grudgingly recognized the former colonies' independence in 1783. For their part, the colonial elites who had led the fight for independence (New England and Middle Colonies merchants and lawyers and southern planters) did not want the war to be accompanied by democratic reforms, and were able to prevent such an upsurge by forming a new government that favored rule by the elite, property qualifications for voting, and other conservative measures.

After the opening battles of what would become the American Revolution (at Lexington and Concord on April 19, 1775, later referred to by Ralph Waldo Emerson as "the shot heard 'round the world"), revolutionary leaders in Britain's North American colonies[3] realized they needed a military leader who could organize the ragtag militia besieging the British forces in Boston into what would become the Continental Army. Reasoning that a man from the southern colonies would give the rebellion the unity it needed, Congress named

3. Canada was invited to join Britain's thirteen other North American colonies in the rebellion, but refused. See Justin H. Smith, *Our Struggle for the Fourteenth Colony: Canada and the American Revolution*, 2 vols. (New York: G. P. Putnam's Sons, 1907). See also George A. Rawlyk, *Revolution Rejected, 1775–1776* (Scarborough, Ont.: Prentice-Hall, 1968).

forty-three-year-old George Washington of Virginia. Washington was born on February 11, 1732,[4] into Virginia's minor gentry. Trained as a surveyor, as a young man his goal was a commission in the regular British army. The intercession of a friend secured Washington an officership in the Virginia militia and the potentially dangerous assignment (at the age of only twenty-one) of delivering to the French, poised along the western frontier, an ultimatum to leave what Virginians believed was British territory. The following year (1754), Washington, now a colonel in the militia, returned to the frontier to challenge the French, but he was forced to surrender a fort he had constructed (Fort Necessity, in present-day western Pennsylvania) and to return to eastern Virginia.

In 1755 Washington became an aide to General Edward Braddock, who led a force of 1,400 British regulars and 450 colonial militiamen on an expedition to capture Fort Duquesne (present-day Pittsburgh) in western Pennsylvania. About eight miles below the fort, the army was attacked and defeated by a combined force of Frenchmen and Native Americans. Braddock was mortally wounded, and Washington led the remnant of the force to safety, an accomplishment that earned him an international reputation. But in 1758, frustrated by his inability to secure a commission in the British army as well as by insufficient support for the Virginia militia's campaign in the West, he resigned his militia post and retired to his home, Mount Vernon.

Although not in the forefront of colonial leaders who urged resistance to the mother country, Washington was so well-known that he was elected to most of the major colonial congresses that met to protest British policies and, as noted above, was a popular choice to command the American army formed after the outbreak of hostilities at Lexington and Concord.

George Washington's principal accomplishments were organizing what became the United States Army (called the Continental Line and never numbering more than 18,000 troops); preventing desertions from decimating that force (he once wrote, "We shall have to detach half of the army to look for the other half"); and keeping that force in the field for six years of skirmishes and battles, many of which were lost. The British, however, faced with the defeat of General Cornwallis at Yorktown in 1781 and mounting opposition to the war at home, were forced to give up the struggle. After once again retiring to Mount Vernon, Washington was called back to service as the Constitutional government's first president (the article of the Constitution dealing with the executive branch was written with Washington in mind, hoping that he would accept the position). Having retired yet again in 1797, he died on December 14, 1799. By then, he was generally being referred to as the "father of his country," and was enshrined as the libera-

---

4. When the English changed from the Julian to the Gregorian calendar in 1752, eleven days were added to the calendar to realign it with the sun and stars. Therefore, Washington's birthday became February 22.

tor-hero of the United States, the symbol of the successful American Revolution.

The French Revolution was the result of the convergence of several problems that overtook the French monarchy in the 1780s. The most critical of these problems was the government's fiscal bankruptcy. As a consequence of the costly wars of the eighteenth century and a system of taxation that virtually exempted the nobility and the clergy from fiscal obligations, the French monarchy was deeply in debt by 1787.[5] Several finance ministers struggled with the crown's debts (which by 1788 had reached 4 billion livres and took 51 percent of the government's total revenues just to make the interest payments), but eventually all of them arrived at the same conclusion: bankruptcy could be avoided only through fundamental reforms that would tax the Church and nobility and not just the commoners.

In proposing such changes, however, the finance ministers encountered opposition from the noble judges of the great law courts (the *parlements*) who had to approve any new royal laws before they could be enforced. Such basic changes in taxation policy, they alleged, had to be approved by a nationwide representative body, and their objections forced the king to call for a meeting in 1789 of the Estates General, an elected assembly that had not met since 1614.

5. France's successful intervention in the American Revolution had cost the French government 2 billion livres, a figure that was four times the government's tax receipts in 1788.

The election of 1789 was held in a country suffering from enormous economic problems. Since 1705 France's population had increased by 24.5 percent, with no corresponding increase in the food supply. Poor harvests in 1788 and 1789 and a commercial depression in 1789 only made matters worse. Inflation of prices had increased the cost of living for the working person by 62 percent over the eighteenth century, while wages for construction workers had risen only 24 percent and agricultural workers' wages a meager 16 percent. Nearly 40 percent of France's population in 1789 was destitute, living by squatting on land they did not own, begging, charity, or crime.

The result of France's economic and political problems was the election of an Estates General that was prepared to seek far more than tax reform. When Louis XVI refused to approve voting rules for the Estates General that would have assured the representatives of the commoners (known as the Third Estate) a chance at enacting tax reform and of realizing some degree of political equality with the clergy and the nobility (the First and Second Estates), the king encountered the first act of revolution. Declaring themselves a National Assembly and the rightful representatives of all the French people, the representatives of the Third Estate pledged to draft a written constitution that would clearly limit royal authority—in essence making Louis XVI a constitutional monarch. When the king countered by ordering troops to disperse the National Assembly, the people of Paris took up arms and seized the strategically important fort and prison the Bastille on July 14, 1789. In the countryside, peasants attacked the castles and manor houses of their noble lords and broke into grain storage facilities.

Faced with mounting opposition and rising violence, Louis XVI ostensibly agreed to live within a new constitutional order. Taking the king at his word, the National Assembly began work on a constitution that would have made France a constitutional monarchy. But Louis never really accepted the new constitutional order, and in 1791 he attempted to flee to eastern France to assume leadership of counterrevolutionary forces. Captured and forcibly returned to Paris where he was virtually made a prisoner in his own country, Louis's situation was hopeless. In September 1792, the republic was proclaimed, Louis XVI was tried for treason and condemned in December 1792, and the monarch went to the guillotine on January 16, 1793. His wife Marie Antoinette (who probably never said, "Let them eat cake") followed soon thereafter and their son, next in line to the now nonexistent throne, died in prison in 1795.

Jean-Paul Marat was among the Jacobin radicals who were supported by the shopkeepers and craftsmen of Paris, known as *sans-culottes*,[6] in their

regicide[7] and their search for other enemies of the revolution. Marat was born on May 24, 1743, the oldest of six children in a lower-middle-class family (the family's original name had been Mara, but Jean-Paul changed his name to appear more French). Later admitting that his dominant passion was a love of glory (*amour de la gloire*), Marat became a prosperous physician who treated the wealthy and published his research on the medical properties of electricity. His friends called him a brilliant doctor-scientist-philosopher, while his detractors dubbed him a desperate charlatan. Drifting toward radicalism (driven, perhaps, by his rejection for admission to the Academy of Sciences), in February 1789 Marat published an attack on the government, calling for a constitutional monarchy with full political rights to the people. In September 1789, he began to publish his newspaper *L'Ami du Peuple* (*The Friend of the People*).

From the first, *L'Ami du Peuple* echoed Marat's fears of plots against the Revolution by its enemies, and his responses to such plots became increasingly radical. As early as October 1789 he called for a revolutionary dictatorship that would preserve the Revolution's gains. One month earlier, Marat declared that "five or six hundred heads cut off would have assured you peace, liberty and happiness." But by May 27, 1791, he had raised that number: "today fifty thousand would be necessary" to protect the Revolution. Seen by his opponents as a dangerous radical and blamed by the police for instigating

6. *sans-culottes* (**without breeches**): the shopkeepers and craftsmen of Paris so named because they wore clothing characteristic of their social group. Their garb included pants that extended to their shoe tops and not the elegant knee breeches of aristocrats. This group was unified by more than just a common mode of dress, however. It espoused a political ideology of direct democracy and an economic policy of government regulation of wages and prices to protect its economic security.

7. **Regicide**: the killing of a king.

an October 1789 march on the royal palace at Versailles, Marat was forced into hiding and fled briefly to England, but he soon returned to France. Continuing to publish his newspaper, Marat gained more power when he was elected to the National Convention in 1792.

Marat supported *sans-culottes* ideals of direct democracy, aid to the economically disadvantaged funded by a progressive income tax, state-sponsored vocational schools, and shorter terms of military service. These positions won him the support of the Parisian *sans-culottes* and the enmity of the more moderate Girondin faction in the Convention. Indeed, the Girondins secured Marat's indictment on charges of inciting insurrection, but he was acquitted of these capital charges and gained his revenge by playing a major role in the Parisian insurrection that purged the Convention of its Girondin members on June 2, 1793.

After June 2, 1793, Marat was much less active politically. He was dying from skin and lung diseases, and was forced to spend long hours in medicinal baths in his Paris apartment. It was there that he was visited by a young woman named Charlotte Corday on July 13, 1793. Corday was a Girondist sympathizer who had become convinced that radicals like Marat were destroying the Revolution. Gaining admission to Marat's bathroom by claiming to have information on counterrevolutionary plots, she stabbed the revolutionary leader to death. Apprehended immediately, the twenty-five-year-old Corday was guillotined on July 17. A magnificent funeral and numerous eulogies turned

Jean-Paul Marat into a revolutionary martyr and a liberator-hero. The ceremonies would have lasted longer but, in the hot Paris summer, Marat's body began to decompose. His embalmed heart was hung from the ceiling of the Cordeliers Club, but the remainder of Marat was quickly buried in the club's garden.

The search for enemies of the revolution led to the Reign of Terror of 1793–1794 in which perhaps as many as 40,000 citizens lost their lives. And their search for a secular state in which the Church would have no influence led the radicals to scrap the traditional calendar based on the Christian year in favor of a new revolutionary calendar that began counting years from 1791, when the new constitution came into force.

True stability, however, continued to elude France. Recurrent coups marked the rest of the decade until Napoleon Bonaparte's seizure of power in 1799 restored some measure of political stability.

Christopher Columbus had landed on the island he named Hispaniola (Little Spain) on December 6, 1492, and he claimed it for Spain.[8] French settlers began moving into the western part of the island in the late 1600s, and the Treaty of Ryswick (1697) officially divided the island between the two European nations, the French calling their portion Saint-Domingue and the Spanish calling theirs Santo Domingo. Gradually the French de-

---

8. The origin of the name Haiti is somewhat unclear. Many scholars believe that the Native American Arawaks who were living on the island when Columbus arrived called the island Haiti. But other scholars of the region disagree.

veloped a plantation system with approximately 3,000 plantations that raised sugar, coffee, cotton, and indigo. The Native American population, not immune to European diseases, was virtually wiped out. The French planters, therefore, relied on slave labor from Africa, importing over 800,000 Africans between 1680 and 1776. By 1787, the population of Saint-Domingue was composed of around 24,000 whites, 408,000 black slaves (approximately two-thirds of whom were African born, largely from the Congo and Angola), and 20,000 *gens de couleur* (mulattos and free blacks).

The death toll among the slave population was enormous; thus planters had to import Africans continuously to keep up the labor pool. Largely because a significant majority of the slave population had been born in freedom in Africa, slave resistance was a regular feature of life in the French colony. A large revolt took place in 1522 and four other armed conspiracies occurred between 1679 and 1704. Runaway slaves hid in the mountains, where, according to one European observer in 1705, "[t]hey gather together in the woods and live there exempt from service to their masters without any other leader but one elected among them." African culture among the slaves and runaways remained both vital and durable, including the practice of voodoo, an African form of worship that the French tried in vain to eradicate but that formed an important bond among the blacks—even those who had nominally been converted to the Catholic faith. In 1757 another widespread rebellion, the

Makandal conspiracy, broke out. Involving mostly African-born slaves, it sought to overthrow the white masters and win political independence. Crushed by the white planters, the conspirators were burned at the stake.

The French Revolution provided the opportunity for another revolt. Aware of revolutionary events in France, in 1791 mulattos sent a delegation to the National Assembly in Paris to secure the rights enumerated in France's Declaration of the Rights of Man and Citizen (1789). Being refused, mulattos rebelled against the white planters but were quickly overcome, as they had been in an earlier revolt in October 1790. Leaders of the uprising were executed and then decapitated, their heads placed on poles which were left standing for around three years as a warning to other would-be revolutionaries.

Once again, however, the French Revolution intruded on life in Saint-Domingue. Later in 1791, the National Assembly granted rights to all mulattos and all blacks born of free parents. When news of the National Assembly's actions reached the Caribbean colony (on June 30, 1791), whites were enraged. Civil war once again broke out between mulattos and whites.

In August 1791, the situation became even more complex—and bloody—by an uprising of the slaves. Many whites fled to U.S. seaports like Savannah, Charleston, and Baltimore, terrifying American plantation owners with reports of burning plantations, widespread killing, and atrocities. By 1793, slaves had built up an army of between 4,000 and 5,000 troops who were fierce, courageous, and tactically brilliant fighters. Led by Toussaint Louverture, this army beat back an attempted British invasion, a Spanish intrusion from Santo Domingo, and another uprising of mulattos in 1799.

François-Dominique Toussaint à Bréda was born on May 20, 1743, on the Bréda plantation in Saint-Domingue. The oldest of eight children, Toussaint's father had been born in Africa, captured in a war, and sold into slavery in the New World. Taught to read and write by a Roman Catholic priest, Toussaint was given more and more responsibility on the plantation until he was made coachman and livestock steward; the plantation's overseer (the owner lived in Paris) gave him forty acres and thirteen slaves to manage. Permitted to marry (a rarity for slaves in Saint-Domingue), Toussaint wed Suzanne Simone Baptiste, and the union produced two sons. Therefore, although Toussaint was technically a slave and no manumission papers ever were drawn up, essentially he was looked upon and treated as a free man (*affranchi*).

When the slave rebellion first broke out in August 1791, Toussaint played only a minor role and was believed to be conservative in his thinking (he had helped his plantation's white factor, or agent, escape from a mob of ex-slaves). Gradually his powerful and articulate speeches to the troops (Toussaint spoke both the Creole patois and his father's African tribal language, in addition to French) and his charisma, tactical genius, and emphasis on training and discipline lifted him to the position of commander of the rebellion.

Seeing an opportunity to drive the French from Saint-Domingue, Toussaint briefly sided with the Spanish. It was at this time that he wrote a letter to blacks and signed it Toussaint Louverture, which means *the opening*. "I thought it was a good name for bravery," Toussaint reflected. But when he learned that the National Convention in Paris had abolished slavery (in February 1794), he switched sides and led his army against the Spanish and the British invaders, both of whom gave up the fight. In 1796 Toussaint was named lieutenant governor of Saint-Domingue, put down an uprising of the mulattos in 1800, and in 1801 issued a constitution for the republic.

And yet Toussaint believed that Haiti's economic future was tied to that of France. In 1802, Napoleon Bonaparte revived French ambitions for an empire in the Western Hemisphere. Intending to reap enormous profits from the sugar and coffee trade and determined to restore slavery in order to do it, Napoleon sent a French invading army to the island in 1802. When the French army invaded the island in 1802, Toussaint, foolishly, was prepared to welcome it. His two sons were being educated in France (they were received by the Empress Josephine) and he had tried to convince the ex-slaves to adopt French ways (he criticized the low necklines of Haitian women's dresses).

Tricked into surrendering, Toussaint was hustled off to a prison in France (Fort de Joux), where he died on April 7, 1803. His entreaties to meet with Napoleon had gone unheeded. Yet the Haitians ultimately won their independence from the French, and Toussaint Louverture became the symbol of the revolution, the liberator-hero.

The French army, decimated by yellow fever, was forced to withdraw from Haiti, ending Napoleon's dreams of an American empire. It was at that point that he offered to sell the Louisiana Territory to the United States. The Republic of Haiti (so named in 1804) had secured its independence, but the instability and terror of the revolution did not cease for decades.

Thus each revolution—the American, the French, and the Haitian—chose a person who could stand as the symbol and the essence of its respective revolution. Your task in this chapter is to analyze how each liberator-hero was portrayed by his contemporaries, through eulogies and portraits, and how each portrayal informs us about the nature of each of the momentous revolutions of the eighteenth century.

SOURCES AND METHOD

In his provocative book *The Hero in History: A Study in Limitation and Possibility*, historian Sidney Hook observed that the "history of every nation is represented to its youth in terms of the exploits of great individuals—mythical or real. . . . The splendor, the power, the fame of the leader are shared imaginatively. New elements of meaning enter the lives of those who are emotionally impoverished."[9] When those nations are created by

revolutions (as were the United States, France, and Haiti), the leader is portrayed as the liberator-hero.

Revolutions have several means at their disposal to create and shape the image of the liberator-hero that they want to pass on to their contemporaries as well as to future generations. Special holidays, statuary, commemorative postage stamps, songs, and dramas are only a few of the ways that the image of the liberator-hero can be created and shaped. Two especially effective methods, however, are eulogies of the hero and paintings. How the liberator-hero is portrayed in eulogies and in comtemporary paintings can give us excellent clues as to how revolutionary leaders wanted others to see the essence or meaning of the revolution they had fomented.

Source 1, the eulogy to George Washington, is probably the most widely circulated of the more than four hundred that were delivered and published. It was commissioned by the Massachusetts legislature and delivered in Boston's Old South Meeting House by Fisher Ames on February 8, 1800.[10] Ames (1758–1808) was an attorney, a former congressman from Massachusetts, and a well-known conservative ally of Washington and Alexander Hamilton. How does Ames portray Washington? When he spoke of Washington conducting "a civil war with mildness, and a revolution with order," Ames

9. Sidney Hook, *The Hero in History: A Study in Limitation and Possibility* (New York: Humanities Press, 1943), pp. 8, 22.

10. The New York Public Library has collected 266 of the 440 Washington eulogies that still exist.

was telling his listeners (and, later, his readers) how *he* wanted them to think about the nature of the American Revolution. How did he want people to view that revolution? To Ames, what was the true glory of the American Revolution? As you read the eulogy carefully, think about how Ames was trying to portray Washington as the liberator-hero of the United States.

Jean-Paul Marat was murdered by Charlotte Corday when the French Revolution was in its most radical phase, the Terror of 1793–1794. Source 3 is the eulogy for Marat that was delivered to the National Convention by a Marat ally, F. E. Guiraut. Not much is known about Guiraut except that he was a member of the Paris Jacobin Club and a leader in the Social Contract Section of Paris. His eulogy of Marat seems to have been the most widely circulated tribute, appearing in pamphlet form and in the official bulletin of the Convention. How did Guiraut portray Marat as a liberator-hero? Using that portrayal, what did Guiraut (and, presumably, Marat) *want* the essence of the French Revolution to be? The name of the newspaper Marat published was *L'Ami du Peuple* (*The Friend of the People*). How do Guiraut's word plays on that title give you some important clues?

No formal eulogy of Toussaint Louverture is known to exist and, since he died in a French prison, it is possible that none ever was delivered. Source 5, however, is quite close to a eulogy, part of an 1814 manifesto written by Henri Christophe (1767–1820). A follower of Toussaint, Christophe was born in the British West Indies (either Grenada or St. Kitts),

taken to the French colony of Saint-Domingue, sold to a free black who owned a stable, was permitted to purchase his freedom, and became a waiter in a hotel. In 1811, eight years after Toussaint's death, Christophe proclaimed himself Henri I, King of Haiti. His 1814 manifesto was intended to rally Haitians to repulse a threatened French invasion of the island. What lessons did Christophe intend that his readers learn from the life of Toussaint? Toussaint attempted to create a Haiti in which whites, blacks, and mulattos could live in freedom and relative equality. What did Christophe think of Toussaint's goal? Finally, what does Christophe see as the true meaning of the Haitian Revolution?

With a bit of practice, portraits of liberator-heroes can be "read" by historians in order to understand how revolutionary leaders (through the artist) sought to create and shape the image of the liberator-hero and the image of the revolution as well. Examine each portrait carefully, noting how the subject is posed and dressed. Do other objects in the painting help to create and shape the image of the subject? Unlike photographs (especially those that appear in newspapers or magazines), nothing in a portrait is there by chance.

Source 2 is a painting of George Washington by Gilbert Stuart (1755–1828), one of the most noted portraitists of his time. Washington sat for the painting on April 12, 1796, and the work was finished the next year. Measuring almost eight feet by five feet, the painting is filled with clues. First of all, since Washington's role in the American Revolution was primarily a military one, why didn't Stuart choose to paint his subject in uniform and astride a horse (many portraitists of Washington did just that)? Also, examine closely Washington's facial expression. He had just purchased new dentures, which obviously did not fit well, but look beyond that. Look closely at his clothing, his pose, the books on the floor, the table leg, the chair in the background, the sheathed sword in Washington's hand. What clues do each of these provide? What is the overall image that Stuart sought to convey of Washington? Of the American Revolution?[11]

Source 4 is a painting of Marat by Jacques Louis David (1748–1825), undoubtedly France's best-known Neoclassical painter and an ardent supporter of the French Revolution. Given to oratorical outbursts almost as inflammatory as those of Marat himself, as an elected deputy to the National Convention he urged the statues of Louis XIV and Louis XV be destroyed and voted for the execution of Louis XVI. David arranged the pageant that accompanied Marat's funeral and presented his portrait of Marat to the National Convention on November 13, 1793. One knowledgeable critic has called it "one of the world's most skillfully executed propaganda pictures."[12]

David could have painted Marat addressing the National Convention, or writing articles for his newspaper, or addressing a crowd of Paris *sans-culottes*. And yet he chose to show his hero and political ally at the moment of his gruesome death, complete with bath water tinted with Marat's blood, the bloody wound, the knife on the floor, and the note Charlotte Corday had used to gain entrance to Marat's apartment in his hand. Why did he choose to do this? It is important to note that the macabre scene is historically inaccurate, since Marat's mistress and friends quickly carried him to his bed, where he expired. Why did David ignore the truth in his painting? What image of Marat did David seek to communicate? What image of the French Revolution did the thousands who viewed the painting receive? Thousands of cheap reproductions of this painting were distributed throughout France. Why was this done?

Unfortunately, no contemporary portrait of Toussaint Louverture by a Haitian artist is known to exist, and it is possible that one was never done. Source 6 is from the book *An Historical Account of the Black Empire of Hayti*, written in 1802 by Marcus Rainsford, a British officer, and published in London in 1805.[13] Rainsford had met and interviewed Toussaint and obviously admired him. The artist is identified

11. Washington sat for Stuart to paint the portrait's head only. Various models later posed for Stuart to paint the body. This particular portrait (Stuart actually did three portraits of Washington, plus numerous copies), known as the Lansdowne portrait, was sold to William Bingham to be hung at his country house (Lansdowne) outside Philadelphia. A copy was painted for a British friend of America. In 1800 the U.S. government purchased the painting for $800.

12. David Lloyd Dowd, *Pageant-Master of the Republic: Jacques-Louis David and the French Revolution* (Lincoln: University of Nebraska, 1948), p. 107.

13. Marcus Rainsford, *An Historical Account of the Black Empire of Hayti* (London: James Cunde, 1805). The portrait is opposite page 241.

only as J. Barlow, and about him we know nothing. There is no evidence that Barlow ever met Toussaint, and he may have been commissioned in London to illustrate Rainsford's book. But Rainsford almost certainly conferred with Barlow about how Toussaint should have been portrayed.

This presents the historian with a very difficult problem, for we cannot be sure that Barlow's portrait of Toussaint would have been similar to portraits by contemporary Haitian artists. How, then, can we use Barlow's portrait to analyze what Haitians thought of Toussaint as a liberator-hero? And

yet, since Rainsford knew Toussaint and admired him, we can suppose that Rainsford instructed Barlow to paint Toussaint Louverture *as Toussaint himself wanted to be portrayed*—as a liberator-hero.

Keeping that problem in mind, examine Barlow's illustration carefully, noting Toussaint's clothing, the fact that his right hand rests on his sword while his left hand holds a copy of Haiti's constitution, and the background matter. What image of Toussaint Louverture did Barlow seek to communicate? What image of the Haitian Revolution?

THE EVIDENCE

Source 1 from Fisher Ames, Works of Fisher Ames (*Boston: T. B. Wait and Co., 1809*), *pp. 115–133.*

1. Fisher Ames's Eulogy on Washington, Boston, February 8, 1800

Rome did not owe more to Fabius,[14] than America to Washington. Our nation shares with him the singular glory of having conducted a civil war with mildness, and a revolution with order.

The event of that war seemed to crown the felicity and glory both of America and its chief. Until that contest, a great part of the civilized world had been surprisingly ignorant of the force and character, and almost of the existence, of the British colonies. They had not retained what they knew, nor felt curiosity to know the state of thirteen wretched settlements, which vast woods enclosed, and still vaster woods divided from each other. They did not view the colonists so much a people, as a race of fugitives, whom want, and solitude, and intermixture with the savages, had made barbarians.

At this time, while Great Britain wielded a force truly formidable to the most powerful states, suddenly, astonished Europe beheld a feeble people, till

14. Fabius Maximus, hero of the Second Punic War, who adopted the military strategy whereby Rome was able to retain control of Italy in spite of the major successes of Hannibal.

[114]

then unknown, stand forth, and defy this giant to the combat. It was no un-equal, all expected it would be short. Our final success exalted their admiration to its highest point: they allowed to Washington all that is due to transcendent virtue, and to the Americans more than is due to human nature. They considered us a race of Washingtons, and admitted that nature in America was fruitful only in prodigies. . . .

Washington retired to Mount Vernon, and the eyes of the world followed him. He left his countrymen to their simplicity and their passions, and their glory soon departed. Europe began to be undeceived, and it seemed, for a time, as if, by the acquisition of independence, our citizens were disappointed. The confederation was then the only compact made "to form a perfect union of the states, to establish justice, to ensure the tranquillity, and provide for the security, of a nation;" and, accordingly, union was a name that still commanded reverence, though not obedience. The system called justice was, in some of the states, inequity reduced to elementary principles; and the publick tranquillity was such a portentous calm, as rings in deep caverns before the explosion of an earthquake. Most of the states then were in fact, though not in form, unbalanced democracies. Reason, it is true, spoke audibly in their constitutions; passion and prejudice louder in their laws. . . . It was scarcely possible that such governments should not be agitated by parties, and that prevailing parties should not be vindictive and unjust. Accordingly, in some of the states, creditors were treated as outlaws; bankrupts were armed with legal authority to be persecutors; and, by the shock of all confidence and faith, society was shaken to its foundations. Liberty we had, but we dreaded its abuse almost as much as its loss; and the wise, who deplored the one, clearly foresaw the other.

The peace of America hung by a thread, and factions were already sharpening their weapons to cut it. The project of three separate empires in America was beginning to be broached, and the progress of licentiousness[15] would have soon rendered her citizens unfit for liberty in either of them. An age of blood and misery would have punished our disunion: but these were not the considerations to deter ambition from its purpose, while there were so many circumstances in our political situation to favour it.

At this awful crisis, which all the wise so much dreaded at the time, yet which appears, on a retrospect, so much more dreadful than their fears; some man was wanting who possessed a commanding power over the popular passions, but over whom those passions had no power. That man was Washington.

His name, at the head of such a list of worthies as would reflect honour on any country, had its proper weight with all the enlightened, and with almost all the well disposed among the less informed citizens, and blessed be God! the constitution was adopted. Yes, to the eternal honour of America among the nations of the earth, it was adopted, in spite of the obstacles, which, in any other country, and, perhaps, in any other age of *this*, would have been

---

15. The lack of moral discipline or restraint.

insurmountable; in spite of the doubts and fears, which well-meaning prejudice creates for itself, and which party so artfully inflames into stubbornness; in spite of the vice, which it has subjected to restraint, and which is
therefore its immortal and implacable foe; in spite of the oligarchies in some
of the states, from whom it snatched dominion; it was adopted, and our
country enjoys one more invaluable chance for its union and happiness: invaluable!

No sooner did the new government begin its auspicious course, than order
seemed to arise out of confusion. Commerce and industry awoke, and were
cheerful at their labours; for credit and confidence awoke with them. Every
where was the appearance of prosperity; and the only fear was, that its
progress was too rapid to consist with the purity and simplicity of ancient
manners. The cares and labours of the president were incessant: his exhorta-
tions, example, and authority, were employed to excite zeal and activity for
the publick service: able officers were selected, only for their merits; and some
of them remarkably distinguished themselves by their successful management of the publick business. Government was administered with such integrity, without mystery, and in so prosperous a course, that it seemed to be
wholly employed in acts of beneficence. Though it has made many thousand
malcontents, it has never, by its rigour or injustice, made one man wretched.

Such was the state of publick affairs: and did it not seem perfectly to ensure
uninterrupted harmony to the citizens? Did they not, in respect to their government and its administration, possess their whole heart's desire? They had
seen and suffered long the want of an efficient constitution; they had freely
ratified it; they saw Washington, their tired friend, the father of his country,
invested with its powers: they knew that he could not exceed or betray them,
without forfeiting his own reputation. Consider, for a moment, what a reputation it was: such as no man ever before possessed by so clear a title, and in so
high a degree. His fame seemed in its purity to exceed even its brightness: office took honour from his acceptance, but conferred none. Ambition stood
awed and darkened by his shadow. For where, through the wide earth, was
the man so vain as to dispute precedence with him; or what were the honours
that could make the possessor Washington's superior? Refined and complex
as the ideas of virtue are, even the gross could discern in his life the infinite
superiority of her rewards. Mankind perceived some change in their ideas of
greatness: the splendor of power, and even of the name of conqueror, had
grown dim in their eyes. They did not know that Washington could augment
his fame; but they knew and felt, that the world's wealth, and its empire too,
would be a bribe far beneath his acceptance.

While the president was thus administering the government in so wise and
just a manner, as to engage the great majority of the enlightened and virtuous
citizens to co-operate with him for its support, and while he indulged the
hope that time and habit were confirming their attachment, the French revolution had reached that point in its progress, when its terrible principles
began to agitate all civilized nations. I will not, on this occasion, detain you to

express, though my thoughts teem with it, my deep abhorrence of that revolution; its despotism, by the mob or the military, from the first, and its hypocrisy of morals to the last. Scenes have passed there which exceed description, and which, for other reasons, I will not attempt to describe; for it would not be possible, even at this distance of time, and with the sea between us and France, to go through with the recital of them, without perceiving horrour gather, like a frost, about the heart, and almost stop its pulse. That revolution has been constant in nothing but its vicissitudes, and its promises; always delusive, but always renewed, to establish philosophy by crimes, and liberty by the sword. . . .

Who then, on careful reflection, will be surprised, that the French and their partisans instantly conceived the desire, and made the most powerful attempts, to revolutionize the American government? But it will hereafter seem strange that their excesses should be excused, as the effects of a struggle for liberty; and that so many of our citizens should be flattered, while they were insulted with the idea, that our example was copied, and our principles pursued. Nothing was ever more false, or more fascinating. Our liberty depends on our education, our laws, and habits, to which even prejudices yield; on the dispersion of our people on farms, and on the almost equal diffusion of property; it is founded on morals and religion, whose authority reigns in the heart; and on the influence all these produce on publick opinion, before *that* opinion governs rulers. *Here* liberty is restraint; *there* it is violence: *here* it is mild and cheering, like the morning sun of our summer, brightening the hills, and making the vallies green; *there* it is like the sun, when his rays dart pestilence on the sands of Africa. American liberty calms and restrains the licentious passions, like an angel that says to the winds and troubled seas, be still. . . .

It is not impossible, that some will affect to consider the honours paid to this great patriot by the nation, as excessive, idolatrous, and degrading to freemen, who are all equal. I answer, that refusing to virtue its legitimate honours would not prevent their being lavished, in future, on any worthless and ambitious favourite. If this day's example should have its natural effect, it will be salutary. Let such honours be so conferred only when, in future, they shall be so merited: then the publick sentiment will not be misled, nor the principles of a just equality corrupted. . . .

But such a chief magistrate as Washington appears like the pole star in a clear sky, to direct the skilful statesman. His presidency will form an epoch, and be distinguished as the age of Washington. Already it assumes its high place in the political region. Like the milky way, it whitens along its allotted portion of the hemisphere. The latest generations of men will survey, through the telescope of history, the space where so many virtues blend their rays, and delight to separate them into groups and distinct virtues. As the best illustration of them, the living monument, to which the first of patriots would have chosen to consign his fame, it is my earnest prayer to heaven, that our country may subsist, even to that late day, in the plenitude of its liberty and happiness, and mingle its mild glory with Washington's.

Source 2 from the White House Historical Association.

2. Gilbert Stuart, *George Washington* (The Lansdowne Portrait), 1797

Source 3 from J. Mavidal and E. Laurent, eds., Archives parlementaires de 1787 à 1860. Recueil complet des débats législatifs et politiques des chambres francaises, *1st series, volume 73 (Paris: Librairie administrative Paul Dupont, 1908), pp. 302–305. Translated by Julius R. Ruff.*

3. F. E. Guiraut, Funeral Oration for Marat, Paris, July 1793

Citizens:

A hideous night has just stretched its funeral crepe over us; the intrepid defender of liberty has become its martyr. Marat, Marat is no more.

People! It is true that you have lost your friend.[16] A monster vomitted up by tyranny has come to pierce his breast. You have seen his mortal wounds with your own eyes;[17] his body was cold and bloodied, sad remains which for you are the last witnesses of his fidelity.

His funeral, it is true, was one filled with our gratitude! You have carefully placed him in a tomb, you have covered him with garlands and flowers; and you have done more: you bathed him in your tears. Oh Marat, how glorious it is to die in the middle of your brothers! . . .

Marat was born, the son of a doctor, on May 24, 1743, in Boudry near Neuchâtel in a republican land, at the base of mountains that pierce the clouds and hold down Hell, near that city[18] where liberty has resided since its departure from Greece and Rome. . . .

He had a sickly childhood and a meticulous education. His mother enjoyed allowing him to taste the sweetness of philanthropy. From the age of eight, he could not bear any aspect of injustice or cruelty. Obedient, hardworking, he never knew the play of childhood, but made rapid progress in his studies. Reflective at fifteen, observant at eighteen, thinker at twenty-one, work was a basic need for him.

He spent twenty-five years in an intellectual retreat, engaged in the reading of the best books; he exhaustively studied morality, philosophy and politics. Like Plato he sometimes listened to his soul speak and at these moments, when filled with respect for the Creator and with admiration for all living beings, he weighed the vanity of human glory, searched the somber future, and looked for the man beyond the monument, . . . and like the famous Locke he, too, had a medical degree. He used his medical knowledge to enlighten, but practiced his profession little.

16. Note Guiraut's play on words here.

17. Marat's body was on view in the Church of the Cordeliers on July 16, along with the bathtub in which he was murdered and his bloody shirt.

18. The city here probably is Rousseau's hometown of Geneva.

Citizens! Follow Marat! Born for liberty, he early experienced acts of despotism caused by ignorance. He could not stand ignorance and, having identified it, would have abolished it in the twinkling of an eye if he could have. Instead, his imagination was kindled, and, impelled by his love of fame, he took his pen in a firm hand and set forth his metaphysical, anatomical and physiological works on man in eight volumes. . . .

Under the blissful influence of freedom, he extended his knowledge of human affairs to social relations. For Marat governments were a monstrosity, nothing but a mixture of extortions, crimes, and impudence. He knew governments' politics and he tried to overthrow their monstrous abuses. His stay in England furnished a good opportunity for such an attempt at the time of the Parliamentary election of 1774. Indeed Marat enjoyed this. Citizen of the world, he wrote of the state's attacks against liberty and the people, the ruses it employed, and the bloody scenes which accompany despotism. Finished and printed under the title *The Chains of Slavery*, his work could not be published. The English ministry had corrupted all, bought printers, publishers, and journalists, its gold infiltrating everywhere. The genius of Marat had shaken the operation of the throne. . . .

Then in 1789 the earthshaking reveille of liberty sounded. The people rose up, stamped its foot on the ground and the throne started to shake. Marat saw it already toppled. "Be watchful," he wrote to his fellow citizens, "the laurels are for you." Intrepid, courageous, he took responsibility for assuring the victory of the Revolution. He advised the people's representatives meeting at Versailles; in Paris he kept the people stirred up, and he was everywhere in the streets and roads fearing that liberty would escape his grasp. Marat was indignant at the deceptive scheme for double representation,[19] and he planned a constitution. He observed events. The people, he concluded, had been deceived, betrayed by its representatives, and he mounted a war to the death against the traitors.

Ignoring all other sentiments than the wish to see his homeland happy, Marat saw all the perils. He feared nothing. He resolved to fight all vices with a daily newspaper whose austere language would remind legislators of their principles, unmask scoundrels and corrupt officials, reveal their plots and sound the alarm bell in moments of danger.

Scarcely had he cast his glance on the Constituent Assembly, than innumerable plots were directed against him. He spoke the truth, his enemies wished

19. **double representation:** In late 1788 Louis XVI conceded a doubling of the number of Third Estate representatives in the Estates General to be elected in February–April 1789. This would have given the commoners a number of representatives roughly equal to those of the clergy and the nobility. What was not conceded was vote by head in place of vote by house. Because the Estates General was, in essence, a three-house legislature that required positive votes by all three estates or houses (the First Estate representing the clergy, the Second Estate the nobility, and the Third Estate the commoners), the maintenance of vote by house meant that the privileged groups could block reform legislation proposed by the commoners of the Third Estate.

to buy his silence. Necker[20] offered him a million in gold, but he refused it. They seized his presses, ordered his arrest, put a price on his head in vain efforts to silence him. His courage sustained him, his paper continued, his energy grew.

Lafayette beseiged his home with 12,000 men but Marat escaped, though his home was pillaged and he was reduced to misery.

In this dreadful situation, he was without domicile and soon without friends. Wandering from one neighborhood on the outskirts of Paris to another, pursued relentlessly, heaped with venom and pain, he was only the more formidable. Everywhere spied on, everywhere he escaped the fury of his enemies' knives. They could not silence him.

Lafayette spared no sacrifice in his search for Marat, stirring everyone out of their indifference. Marat found no refuge. He looked for an underground tunnel and took refuge in quarries of Montmartre. There, some good citizens were pleased to keep him; they brought him food which he received with gratitude. He clasped his bread, bathed it in his tears and gave to the state the life that had been sustained by hands of brotherhood.

When the constitution was proclaimed, Marat sensed that the new order of things could not last a long time. His eye discovered secret plots, and he told the people that the plotters wished to subjugate them and to restore Louis XVI to his former authority. He pursued the deputies of the Legislative Assembly, denouncing their treachery and venality, and found himself charged with a crime and the crowd at his heels. Passion dictated his actions. Didn't he write that "The defense of the people's rights is my supreme law"? Stronger than all the plotters together he defied them, scorned them, revealed conspiracies, and showed the need to exclude priests, nobles, financiers, creatures of the court, and tricksters from all public office.

The Revolution took some reactionary steps and public spirit seemed to weaken. Marat shook with indignation at the inactivity of patriots. He worried, he wished to electrify all souls and to achieve liberty. You should have seen him thus reduced, citizens, more unhappy than Diogenes[21] in his tub deprived of his light. Often in wet places, he had nothing to sleep on. Wasted by the most dreadful misery, he covered his body with a simple blue frock coat and his head with a handkerchief. With a handkerchief, alas, almost always soaked in vinegar in order to cool the ardor of his mind which could not allow the friends of liberty to sleep. He wrote with a writing case in his hand and his knees, supporting some sheets of paper, served

20. Jacques Necker was a Swiss banker who was made director of finances by Louis XVI in 1777, but who was dismissed when he attempted to reform France's tax structure. During the revolution he played a major role in trying to restructure the nation's finances.

21. Diogenes (412–323 B.C.) was a Greek philosopher who believed the only virtuous life was a simple one. He demonstrated this by discarding all his worldly possessions and living in a tub. Diogenes showed his contempt for his fellow Greeks by conducting daylight searches, complete with a lantern, for an honest man.

as his desk. His work was sold, people gave to him, and he lived on an *écu.* . . .[22]

Disgusted by bitterness, with France inundated by ministerial placards describing him as a ferocious beast, his latest efforts without effect, Marat recalled his reception in England. He left for that country, but was recognized at Amiens and an armed force was immediately assembled. He was surrounded but burst through the ranks of men and escaped. Heaven protected his life, the countryside aided his flight, and he arrived in Paris without shoes, his feet stained with his blood. Having barely survived, he sacrificed himself entirely for his cause and swore to conquer.

On August 10[23] the voice of the people made itself heard and toppled not enormous stones wet with the tears of the oppressed[24] but crowns, *fleurs de lis*[25] and gilded corridors. . . .

Marat was a lone mountain[26] and it was necessary to destroy him at any price. . . .

Respond, assassins of Marat! You who thrust the knife into his chest, have you, like him, any virtues to offer? Did you ever know this extraordinary mortal? He spent all his life in seclusion and thought but was persecuted by the envious and jealous, pursued by the forces of despotism, abandoned by the timid and weak, hated by those who are evil and corrupt, feared by the ambitious and conspirators, esteemed by the people, and slain by agents of fanaticism. Answer, assassins! Did you know him? . . .

Listen to the last words of this philosopher, citizens:

People! I was your representative. I defended your rights. I lived in misery, and I died in misery. People! Your confidence was too great and was always your misfortune. Cease to acclaim false idols. Your welfare depends on you. Know your dignity and your strength. Calculate your needs coldly. Faithful observer, no longer allow yourself to be enslaved. Crush intrigue, suppress ambition, scorn evil, esteem talent, honor virtue. . . .

People, do not let yourselves be led astray. Be on guard against those who would deceive you. Never again become the instrument of passion. Do not arm yourselves against your brothers but employ toward them all those means of reconciliation worthy of you. Everywhere arrest the most culpable enemies; they alone deserve to be punished.

People, cherish your liberty! All the social virtues should reign with it. Among you it is in an embryonic state. Be happy and enjoy the charms of philanthropy. Think sometimes of your friend; I make you the trustee of my heart.

22. **écu**: A coin of the Old Regime.

23. On August 10, 1792, Parisian crowds stormed the Tuileries Palace and effectively ended the monarchy founded by the Constitution of 1791.

24. Guiraut refers here to the crowd's capture of the Bastille prison in Paris on July 14, 1789.

25. **fleurs de lis**: A three-leaf lily that symbolized the Old Regime monarchy.

26. A clever reference on Marat's political faction, the Montagnard (mountain).

Oh Marat, the ever watchful and vigilant sentinel before our gate, we will never again hear: "Here is Marat, the friend of the people!"

Always present in our thought, we will never forget what you have done for us. . . .

Source 4 from Château de Versailles/Cliché des Musées Nationaux-Paris.

4. Jacques Louis David, *Portrait of Marat*, 1793

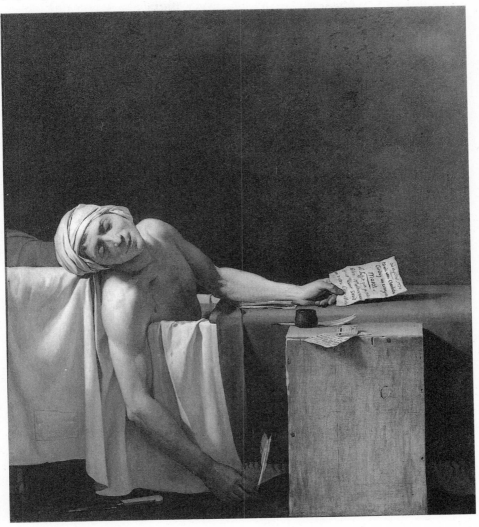

Source 5 from Toussaint L'Ouverture: Biography and Autobiography (*Boston: James Red-path, 1863*), *pp. 331–336.*

5. Henri Christophe, Manifesto, 1814

We have deserved the favors of liberty, by our indissoluble attachment to the mother country. We have proved to her our gratitude.

At the time when, reduced to our own private resources, cut off from all communication with France, we resisted every allurement; when, inflexible to menaces, deaf to proposals, inaccessible to artifice, we braved misery, famine, and privation of every kind, and finally triumphed over our enemies both within and without.

We were then far from perceiving that twelve years after, as the price of so much perseverance, sacrifice, and blood, France would deprive us in a most barbarous manner of the most precious of our possessions,—liberty.

Under the administration of Governor-General Toussaint L'Ouverture, Hayti arose from her ruins, and everything seemed to promise a happy future. The arrival of General Hédouville[27] completely changed the aspect of affairs, and struck a deadly blow to public tranquillity. We will not enter into the detail of his intrigues with the Haytian General, Rigaud,[28] whom he persuaded to revolt against the legitimate chief. We will only say, that before leaving the island, Hédouville had put everything into confusion, by casting among us the firebrands of discord, and lighting the torch of civil war.

Ever zealous for the reëstablishment of order and of peace, Toussaint L'Ouverture, by a paternal government, restored their original energy to law, morality, religion, education, and industry. Agriculture and commerce were flourishing; he was favorable to white colonists, especially to those who occupied new possessions; and the care and partiality which he felt for them went so far that he was severely censured as being more attached to them than to people of his own color. This negro wail was not without reason; for some months previous to the arrival of the French, he put to death his own nephew, General Moise, for having disregarded his orders relative to the protection of the colonists. This act of the Governor, and the great confidence which he had in the French Government, were the chief causes of the weak resistance which the French met with in Hayti. In reality, his confidence in that Government was

---

27. Hedouville was the commander of the French forces that Toussaint ultimately defeated in 1797–1798, forcing the French to abandon Haiti until the French invasion of 1802.

28. Rigaud had been second in command to Toussaint but broke with him and led the mulattos in a civil war against Toussaint in 1799–1800. Rigaud's revolt was brutally repressed and approximately 2,000 people were put to death.

so great, that the General had disbanded the greater part of the regular troops, and employed them in the cultivation of the ground.

Such was the state of affairs whilst the peace of Amiens[29] was being negotiated; it was scarcely concluded, when a powerful armament landed on our coasts a large army, which, attacking us by surprise, when we thought ourselves perfectly secure, plunged us suddenly into an abyss of evils.[30]

Posterity will find a difficulty in believing that, in so enlightened and philosophic an age, such an abominable enterprise could possibly have been conceived. In the midst of a civilized people, a horde of barbarians suddenly set out with the design of exterminating an innocent and peaceable nation, or at least of loading them anew with the chains of national slavery.

It was not enough that they employed violence; they also thought it necessary to use perfidy and villainy,—they were compelled to sow dissension among us. Every means was put in requisition to carry out this abominable scheme. The leaders of all political parties in France, even the sons of the Governor Toussaint, were invited to take part in the expedition. They, as well as ourselves, were deceived by that *chef-d'oeuvre*[31] of perfidy, the proclamation of the First Consul,[32] in which he said to us, 'You are all equal and free before God and the Republic;' such was his declaration, at the same time that his private instructions to General Leclerc[33] were to reëstablish slavery.

The greater part of the population, deceived by these fallacious promises, and for a long time accustomed to consider itself as French, submitted without resistance. The Governor so little expected the appearance of an enemy that he had not even ordered his generals to resist in case of an attack being made; and, when the armament arrived, he himself was on a journey toward the eastern coast. If some few generals did resist, it was owing only to the hostile and menacing manner in which they were summoned to surrender, which compelled them to respect their duty, their honor, and the present circumstances.

After a resistance of some months, the Governor-General yielded to the pressing entreaties and the solemn protestations of Leclerc, 'that he intended to protect the liberties of every one, and that France would never destroy so noble a work.' On this footing, peace was negotiated with France; and the Governor Toussaint, laying aside his power, peaceably retired to the retreat he had prepared for himself.

---

29. The Peace of Amiens (1802) brought a temporary end to the war between France and Great Britain, thus allowing Napoleon to plan an invasion of Haiti.

30. The French invasion of 1802.

31. *chef-d'oeuvre:* masterpiece.

32. Napoleon Bonaparte.

33. Leclerc was the commander of the 1802 French invasion force.

Scarcely had the French extended their dominion over the whole island and that more by roguery and deceit than by force of arms, than they began to put in execution their horrible system of slavery and destruction.

To hasten the accomplishment of their projects, mercenary and Machiavellian writers fabricated fictitious narratives, and attributed to Toussaint designs that he had never entertained. While he was remaining peaceably at home, on the faith of solemn treaties, he was seized, loaded with irons, dragged away with the whole of his family, and transported to France. The whole of Europe knows how he ended his unfortunate career in torture and in prayer, in the dungeon of the Château de Joux.

Such was the recompense reserved for his attachment to France, and for the eminent services he had rendered to the colony.

At the same time, notice was given to arrest all suspected persons throughout the island. All those who had shown brave and enlightened souls, when we claimed for ourselves the rights of men, were the first to be seized. Even the traitors who had most contributed to the success of the French army, by serving as guides to their advanced guard, and by exciting their compatriots to take vengeance, were not spared. At first they desired to sell them into strange colonies; but, as this plan did not succeed, they resolved to transport them to France, where overpowering labor, the galleys, chains, and prisons, were awaiting them.

Then the white colonists, whose numbers have continually increased, seeing their power sufficiently established, discarded the mask of dissimulation, openly declared the reëstablishment of slavery, and acted in accordance with their declaration. They had the impudence to claim as their slaves men who had made themselves eminent by the most brilliant services to their country, in both the civil and military departments. Virtuous and honorable magistrates, warriors covered with wounds, whose blood had been poured out for France and for liberty, were compelled to fall back into the bonds of slavery. These colonists, scarcely established in the possession of their land, whose power was liable to be overthrown by the slightest cause, already marked out and chose in the distance those whom they determined should be the first victims of their vengeance.

The proud and liberty-hating faction of the colonists, of those traffickers in human flesh, who, since the commencement of the revolution, had not ceased to impregnate the successive Governments in France with their plans, their projects, their atrocious and extravagant memorials, and everything tending to our ruin,—these factious men, tormented by the recollection of the despotism which they had formerly exercised at Hayti, a prey to their low and cruel passions, exerted all their efforts to repossess themselves of the prey which had escaped from their clutches. In favor of independence under the constitutional assembly, terrorists under the Jacobins, and finally, zealous Bonapartists, they knew how to assume the mask of any party, in order to obtain place and favor. It was thus, by their insidious counsels, they urged Bonaparte to undertake this iniquitous expedition to Hayti. It was this faction who, after having advised the expedition, furnished the pecuniary resources which were necessary, by means of subscriptions which were at this time commenced. In a word, it was this faction which caused the blood of our compatriots to flow in torrents,—which invented the exhausting tortures to which we were subjected; it is to these colonists that France owes the loss of a powerful army, which perished in the plains and marshes of Hayti; it is to them she owes the shame of an enterprise which has fixed an indelible stain on the French name. . . .

Source 6 from Marcus Rainsford, An Historical Account of the Black Empire of Hayti *(London: James Cundee, 1805), facing p. 241. Photo from Stock Montage, Inc.*

6. J. Barlow, *Portrait of Toussaint Louverture, c. 1805*

QUESTIONS TO CONSIDER

In this chapter, your task is *not* to find out what each revolutionary leader (Washington, Marat, and Toussaint) was *really* like. Instead, your task is to analyze how each leader's fellow revolutionists or contemporaries created and shaped an *image* of a liberator-hero, and through that image communicated to their contemporaries and to future generations the nature or essence of the revolution.

Fisher Ames's eulogy to George Washington is an excellent case in point. In spite of the fact that Washington's initial prominence came from his military leadership of the Continental Line, Ames spends almost no time on that aspect of Washington's life. Why do you think this is so? Instead, Ames concentrates on the years *after* the War for Independence, saying only that Washington and his fellow revolutionists (including Ames himself) "conducted a civil war with mildness, and a revolution with order." What did Ames mean by that statement?

Ames pictured a postwar decade of "awful crisis" and filled with "popular passions." To what was he referring? How did the Constitution solve those problems? Was the acceptance of the presidency by Washington a key factor in overcoming the crisis? How?

Washington was president when the French Revolution broke out in 1789. What opinions does Ames have of that revolution? What dangers does he see in it? On a related note, what does Ames consider the principal threat to the American Revolu-

tion? And, from that, what does Fisher Ames see as the true nature of the American Revolution? How can Washington be used to personify or symbolize that true nature?

Of Gilbert Stuart's 1797 portrait of Washington, William Kloss has remarked that no "other portrait conveys the unyielding resolve and severe dignity that made him the embodiment of the young Republic."[34] As you examine the painting, look first at the central figure. What is the expression on Washington's face? What is the significance of the body's pose? Why was he dressed in civilian clothes (the majority of paintings of Washington show him in military garb)? What is the significance of the sheathed sword in his left hand?

The table leg is formed to resemble a *fasces*, a band of rods that symbolized authority and justice in the Roman Republic. Does the chair behind Washington contain symbols equal to those of the table leg? What are the titles of the books in the painting and what is their importance? Is there anything else in the background that Stuart intended to be used as a symbol? Finally, by looking at Stuart's portrait what did he hope that viewers would see about George Washington? About the American Revolution?

The funeral oration for Jean-Paul Marat is a dramatically different eulogy from Fisher Ames's address. Guiraut begins by referring to Marat as a "martyr." A martyr to what? If Marat was a martyr to the French

34. William Kloss et al., *Art in the White House: A Nation's Pride* (Washington, D.C.: White House Historical Association, 1992), p. 66.

Revolution, what *particular aspect* of the revolution did he symbolize?

Guiraut intersperses his biographical sketch of his subject with numerous observations and judgments, as if Marat's early life was preparing him for the revolution. How does Guiraut accomplish this? What phases are particularly significant?

As the revolution began, what does Guiraut assert was Marat's warning? What did Marat fear? What message is Guiraut intending to communicate? Why were plots hatched against Marat? What lessons does Guiraut see in those conspiracies? What kind of French Revolution did Marat seek?

The "last words" attributed to Marat were actually those of Guiraut.[35] Through Marat, what does Guiraut see as true goals of the French Revolution? What are the dangers? Finally, how does Guiraut use the image of Marat to make him into a liberator-hero? What, in Guiraut's view, is the nature of the French Revolution?

As noted above, David's painting of Marat is a magnificent piece of political propaganda. In what ways is it so? Why did David choose to portray Marat in this way, in his grisly death? Why does David have Marat holding the note from Charlotte Corday? What does that say about David's view of the revolution?

At the bottom of the wooden box, David has painted the words *L'An Deux* (the Year Two). Since it was 1793, what is the significance of David's date? Finally, what reaction did David

hope viewers of the painting would have? How could Marat be used as a liberator-hero of the French Revolution?

Henri Christophe, like the preceding two eulogists, is using the career, the accomplishments, and the ideas of Toussaint Louverture to make a point. What is that point? In Christophe's view, what was Toussaint's fatal blunder? (It was *not* his being duped into surrendering.)

Toussaint Louverture tried to build a nation in which whites, blacks, and mulattos would live in peace and mutual trust. What does Henri Christophe think of that goal? How does Christophe use Toussaint as a *negative example* of the liberator-hero? What does that say about Christophe's notion of the true nature of the Haitian Revolution—or what that true nature *should* be?

Unlike Stuart and David, the artist who portrayed Toussaint Louverture probably never met his subject. Yet Marcus Rainsford may well have given Barlow enough details to make this a reasonably accurate portrait—at least according to Rainsford. Examine the artist's representation of Toussaint: his face, his physique, his clothing. What impressions was the artist seeking to convey? What is the significance of the sword and the document (Haiti's constitution, issued by Toussaint in 1801) in his hand? Of the Haitian Revolution?

Revolutionists face a dual challenge. The first challenge is to win their revolution. The second challenge is to preserve it and to pass it down to future generations. How do the three eulogists and the three artists attempt to do this?

35. Marat's actual last words were "Help, my dear, help!" Edward S. LeCompte, comp., *Dictionary of Last Words* (New York: Philosophical Library, 1955), p. 144.

EPILOGUE

As the "revolutionary fever" that "afflicted" Théroigne de Méricourt swept across the Western world in the late eighteenth century, revolutionists sought to justify, legitimate, and explain the true natures of their respective uprisings to their wary contemporaries as well as to generations yet unborn. To do this, they created the images of liberator-heroes, men and (occasionally) women who could be used as symbols of the revolution and through whose lives the true nature or essence of the revolution could be seen. Some, like Washington, became symbols of revolts that succeeded. Others, like Marat and Toussaint Louverture, became martyrs to a revolution not yet fulfilled. Nevertheless, each one became a liberator-hero, a construction through which the message of the revolution could be communicated.

George Washington became a symbol of a revolution that stopped (according to Fisher Ames) at precisely the right moment—not falling back into monarchy nor veering wildly into democracy. It was a revolution out of which reform and democratization would come gradually, wrenched by only one (albeit bloody) civil war. After his death in 1799, biographers made Washington into a symbol of that revolution. From the wildly creative biography by Mason Locke "Parson" Weems to the magisterial seven-volume work by Douglas Southall Freeman, George Washington continues to reign as the "Father of His Country."

Gilbert Stuart moved to Washington, D.C., soon after the nation's capital was relocated there. He continued to receive enormous fees for painting portraits of the new nation's political and commercial leaders, but died in debt in 1823. When British troops invaded Washington in 1814 (during the War of 1812 between the United States and Great Britain), Dolley Madison, wife of President James Madison, broke the Lansdowne portrait's frame and carried the canvas on its stretcher out of the city to save it from British mutilation. It was returned to the White House in 1817 and hangs there today, in the city that bears its subject's name.

Charlotte Corday went silently to the guillotine, refusing to disclose information on any plot against Jean-Paul Marat. The liberator-hero of the radicals at first was placed in a cave-like tomb on the grounds of the radical Cordeliers Club in Paris. Later Marat's body was moved to the Pantheon, the burial place of France's great figures. But in the conservative Thermidorian Reaction, it was once again moved to the Sainte-Genevieve Cemetery.

Jacques Louis David survived the French Revolution and became Napoleon Bonaparte's favorite painter (David did several famous paintings of Napoleon), in 1803 was made a knight of the French Legion of Honor, and in 1804 was named First Painter to the Emperor.[36] When Napoleon fell at Waterloo, David went into exile, continued to paint, and died in exile in Belgium in 1825.

36. David's 1808 portrait of Napoleon in his study has the well-known pose of the subject with his right hand inserted in his vest.

The popular revolution Marat, Guiraut, and David hoped for did not come. The French Revolution began to move into more conservative channels in 1795, capped by the coup d'etat of Napoleon Bonaparte in 1799. Napoleon's fall in 1815 restored the Bourbon monarchy to France, and the nation struggled gradually but perceptibly toward stability throughout the rest of the nineteenth and part of the twentieth centuries. Only after decades would Marat's goal of a democratic republic finally be achieved.

The French invasion of Haiti in 1802 was broken by a yellow fever epidemic which ravaged the French army. In 1804, Jean Jacques Dessalines, a black general, assumed the title of Emperor of Haiti, but was soon assassinated, to be followed by Henri Christophe. Henri I maintained power until 1820, when a paralytic stroke and yet another uprising led to his suicide (October 8, 1820). Since that time, the history of Haiti has been one of grinding poverty, political tyranny, and instability. In 1980 Haiti's illiteracy rate was 85 percent, its infant mortality rate 20 percent, and its per capita income a meager $219 per year. More recently, the United States has intervened in Haiti to install and prop up the government of President Jean Bertrand Aristide. A statue of Toussaint Louverture still stands in Port-au-Prince, a symbol to those who seek to continue the revolutionary struggle. In France, his grave was destroyed between 1876 and 1880 when alterations were made to the prison chapel.

CHAPTER SIX

LABOR OLD AND NEW:

THE IMPACT OF

THE INDUSTRIAL REVOLUTION

THE PROBLEM

The main difficulty did not ... lie so much in the invention of a proper self-acting mechanism for drawing and twisting cotton as in the distribution of the different members of the apparatus into one cooperative body, in impelling each organ with its appropriate delicacy and speed, and above all, in training human beings to renounce their desultory habits of work, to identify themselves with the unvarying regularity of work of the complex automation. It requires in fact a man of Napoleonic nerve and ambition to subdue refractory tempers of work people accustomed to irregular spasms of diligence, and to urge on his multifarious and intricate constructions in the face of prejudice, passion, and envy.

This is how Andrew Ure, an early and enthusiastic analyst of the Industrial Revolution, characterized the problems of industrial management in his book *The Philosophy of Manufacturers* (1835). In these few sentences

Ure identified the essence of the Industrial Revolution. As most Western Civilization courses correctly emphasize, the period of history this label describes did indeed represent an economic and technological revolution of the greatest magnitude. The manner in which the West produced its goods changed more in the century from 1750 to 1850 than in all the previous centuries of human history, making necessary, as Ure says, the solution of tremendous problems of technology and integration of industrial processes.

But the Industrial Revolution had another impact, one that Ure did not neglect, though he approached it from the managerial point of view in emphasizing the manager's need to train his employees. That Ure thought the disciplining of the work force was perhaps the manager's chief problem suggests the broad social impact of industrialization. The first generations of factory laborers encountered a world of work dramatically transformed from that of

Chapter 6

Labor Old

and New:

The Impact of

the Industrial

Revolution

their fathers and mothers, a laboring situation with which most were totally unfamiliar.

The work life of the preindustrial laborer certainly was not easy. Workdays were long, typically dawn to dusk, six days per week, and it was common for wives and children to labor alongside their husbands and fathers as part of a household economy. Indeed, for agricultural workers and craftsmen alike, labor took up so much of their time that little remained for other daily activities. The material rewards of labor often were meager, too; we saw the mass poverty of preindustrial Europe in Chapter 4. But preindustrial work, however long, hard, and unrewarding, had characteristics that distinguished it from early industrial labor.

Preindustrial work usually was conducted in and around the worker's residence. Such labor afforded the worker occasional variety and, in some instances, a measure of control over the pace of work. We may see this effect if we examine the various types of preindustrial workers. Agricultural workers certainly experienced periods of intensive labor, especially at spring plowing and at harvest time, but periods of less intensive labor, especially in the winter months, punctuated their work year and brought them a bit of respite from their duties.

Many of the skilled craftsmen who produced the consumer goods of preindustrial Europe were organized by trade into local, professional groups known as guilds. Guilds performed many functions for their members. By controlling the size of their member-

ship, guilds could limit the number of practitioners of a trade in their cities because practice of a trade often required guild membership. Such limitation of membership aimed at protecting the livelihoods of guild members by assuring that there would be sufficient work, and thus income, for each one. Guilds set prices for their products, as well, always at a level to assure an adequate income to guild members and to prevent ruinous price competition. Guilds assured the consumer a measure of protection, too. Guilds regulated the quality of their members' output and, by a system of training known as *apprenticeship,* guaranteed consumers that producers had sufficient skills in their trades to produce a fine product. Apprenticeship gave a craftsman the essential skills of his trade and most men followed apprenticeship with employment as *journeymen,* that is, as workers sufficiently skilled to command a daily wage in the shop of a guild master. Full guild membership, and the right to open one's own production unit in his trade, were reserved for those journeymen who completed a *masterpiece,* a fine example of their skills in their chosen profession, which won for them the title of guild master.

The production unit of a guild master afforded him some measure of freedom in plying his trade within guild regulations. The master supervised a production unit that often included members of his family, apprentices, and sometimes journeymen. The master set the pace for himself and his workers, who, particularly in Catholic countries, might look forward to a number of religious holidays, civic festivals, and fairs to interrupt their year's labor.

In the later centuries of the preindustrial age, another kind of labor began to emerge. Called the *putting-out system,* this form of employment became common in textile production. A merchant would purchase the raw material, often wool, and deliver it to various rural workers who would spin, weave, dye, and finish the cloth using traditional methods. Often workers were farm families who took in textile work to supplement their incomes. Merchants sought such rural workers because they worked cheaply and because they were beyond the jurisdiction of urban authorities, who limited textile production to guild members. The putting-out system allowed merchants to gather large numbers of workers under their control and thus organize production more efficiently. Even workers in this more disciplined mode of production enjoyed some freedom in organizing their work, however, despite the low wages that often kept them in poverty. For example, consider a weaver employed as part of the putting-out system. The weaver might enjoy "holy Monday," that is, a prolongation of the Sabbath, by taking the first day of the week off. The weaver might also take a few hours off on Tuesday and Wednesday as well, completing the week's required production only by working all night Thursday and Friday. No matter how he or she scheduled his or her work time, however, the choice was the weaver's. The worker had some control over the labor.

Indeed, all these factors that somewhat lessened the intensity of preindustrial labor have led some historians to idealize preindustrial work. It is important that we do not follow their example. By perhaps the most important measure of a laborer's work life—the standard of living it supports—it is by no means certain that early industrial employment represented an overall worsening of workers' living conditions. Historians continue to debate the issue of standard of living, examining diverse data on wages, diet, and housing; the problem clearly is a complex one. Whereas the preindustrial skilled craftsman was generally well rewarded for his work, the agricultural laborer and putting-out worker usually were not, and peasant families on the Continent sometimes lived a subsistence existence. For some rural workers, early industrial labor may actually have improved their standard of living.

Industrial labor, however, definitely brought all those employed in the new mills, factories, and mines a new style of work. Hours in the new establishments remained long, but the work year was interrupted by fewer holidays because factory owners could maximize returns on their massive investments in plants and machines only by using them to their fullest. Labor by whole families often continued, too, but the factory system separated them from their homes, and the tasks and workplaces of family members were very

Chapter 6

Labor Old

and New:

The Impact of

the Industrial

Revolution

different. Husbands endured the heaviest labor in textile mills or mines. Their wives, research has shown, most often remained at home, keeping house, caring for young children and often laboring many hours in low-paying tasks that could be done at home—"slop work," that is, needle trades, bookbinding, millinery, or other such occupations. Only a minority of married women worked in early mills and mines. Children and unmarried women, however, went out to work in mills, where their hands were better suited to intricate machinery than men's, or in mines, where their small statures allowed them to move more easily than men through low mine tunnels. Their wages always were very low.

Most significantly, perhaps, the worker lost control over the pace of his or her work. Modern factory production dictated that workers serve these new machines that had taken over the productive role. Barring breakdowns, the machine's pace never varied; the new work was monotonous. Workers found themselves endlessly repeating the same tasks in the production process with little autonomy. In addition, industrial work imposed a new punctuality on workers. For the factory system to function smoothly, all had to be at their work stations on time and remain there except during scheduled breaks. "Holy Monday" and unscheduled leisure time threatened the smooth operation of an industrial establishment. Early mines and factories posed significant safety problems, too, as we will see.

How did the first generations of industrial workers respond to such fundamental changes? Some adapted. Others proved incapable of adjusting to the new working conditions, and absenteeism (especially on Mondays), chronic tardiness, and workers' inability to keep pace with machines plagued many early mills. Many other workers experienced a growing inner alienation, identified by such observers of industrialism as Karl Marx, that manifested itself in various forms of asocial behavior. When economic conditions were good and jobs were plentiful, early mills had problems with frequent employee resignations. Some mills experienced as much as 100 percent annual employee turnover.

Other new social problems also accompanied industrialization. Urban expansion accompanied the factory system (see Chapter 8), reflecting the movement of many rural families to growing cities in search of factory employment. Such moves separated the new arrivals from friends and from the social controls of village life. In the city they often found not only the poverty of early industrial work but also the anonymity of urban life and the wealth of modern society displayed by the privileged classes. The result was a rapid rise of crimes against property accompanying urban growth. Older social problems persisted, too. Preindustrial workers frequently consumed alcohol in excess as an escape from their tedious work lives. Indeed, "holy Monday" often reflected the effects of a worker's weekend of alcohol abuse. The early industrial age was little different. One English clergyman described to a committee of Parliament the sight of twelve-year-old coal miners staggering with drink.

The human response to this fundamental change in work thus assumed many forms, but these did not include organized resistance to the machine age by industrial workers. Those employed in early mills and mines often were illiterate and consequently difficult to mobilize for collective actions such as strikes. Moreover, laws like the English Combination Acts (1799, 1800) and the French Le Chapelier Law (1791) actually forbade worker organizations; the few early unions were illegal and secretive. The only overt resistance to industrialization, therefore, came not from industrial workers but from one group of preindustrial laborers, namely, the artisans. This class had a high rate of literacy and thus were aware that the new machines ultimately threatened both their livelihoods and their work autonomy. They lashed out with acts of machine smashing. English machine smashers were called *Luddites* after one Ned Ludd, who supposedly originated their movement.

Machine smashing, of course, could not stop industrialization, and workers in early mines and mills became the objects of an increasingly stringent discipline aimed at forcing their acceptance of the new labor. Overseers beat child laborers. Managers fined or dismissed adults and sometimes blacklisted particularly difficult workers to deny them any employment.

In this chapter you will be asked to contrast the working conditions of the preindustrial and industrial ages. How did industrial labor differ from preindustrial work? How did such labor evolve? What effects did the new labor have on the first generations of men, women, and children in Europe's mills and mines?

SOURCES AND METHOD

The central questions of this chapter require your analysis of both preindustrial and industrial labor. As an aid to this analysis, the evidence for this chapter is accordingly divided into two groups, one relating to the preindustrial age (the "old labor") and the other to the industrial era (the "new labor").

Let us begin our consideration of the old labor with its most traditional form, agricultural labor. Source 1 is the work of Sébastien Le Prestre de Vauban (1633–1707). Vauban was a brilliant military engineer whose skill in designing fortifications and conducting sieges for the army of Louis XIV of France propelled him to the highest rank in the army, Marshal of France. But Vauban's interests were not narrowly military in scope. This highly intelligent and observant man wrote extensively on a variety of problems, authoring treatises on agriculture, construction, and the need for religious toleration in an age of widespread persecution of religious minorities. The selection from Vauban's writings presented in Source 1 is

Chapter 6

Labor Old

and New:

The Impact of

the Industrial

Revolution

drawn from one of his last works, a proposal for reforming the tax system of early-eighteenth-century France with the goals of both greater equity in assessing the tax burden and increased revenues to balance the royal budget. To adequately present his ideas, Vauban undertook a description of the economic situations of his fellow Frenchmen in this work that gives the student of the eighteenth century a number of insights into the lot of common people who left little other record of their activities. In reading this source pay particular attention to the agricultural workers Vauban describes. This group owned little property, but instead worked the lands of others. Lacking land of their own, this group of workers possessed a certain mobility that would lead many of their number to factory employment a century after Vauban's analysis of their situation. How long was the agricultural work year of this group? Why were the earnings of such people from agriculture insufficient? What sort of nonagricultural employment did members of the family unit undertake?

In Source 2, you encounter further evidence on agricultural labor that presents working conditions of farm workers in England almost a century and a half after Vauban wrote. Source 2 offers you for the first time a type of evidence you will analyze several times in this chapter, the record of hearings on early industrial working conditions conducted by legislative committees. From such records committee members drew up recommendations that often resulted in legislation to improve working conditions

in early mills, factories, and mines. These records have a great advantage for the historian because they also offer a glimpse into the world of the illiterate laboring poor of an earlier age. Secretaries to the investigating committees often took down the testimony of witnesses verbatim, providing an enduring record of all the difficulties of labor in the early industrial era. Mrs. Britton labored in the old style as an agricultural worker, but she brought a unique perspective to her testimony to a committee of the British Parliament because she once had worked in a factory also. What were the work conditions and the standard of living of agricultural workers like Mrs. Britton and her husband? How did agricultural labor compare with factory labor for Mrs. Britton?

With Source 3 we turn to the labor of the preindustrial craftsman. The evidence on craftsmen's labor opens with a summary of holidays in a textile-producing city, Lille, France, in the seventeenth century. How would you characterize the pace of labor in Lille, a city whose work calendar was not unusual in Catholic Europe?

Source 4 presents excerpts from guild regulations in the Prussian woolen industry. The Industrial Revolution began in England in the mid-eighteenth century but affected the Continent much later, only in the first decades of the nineteenth century. Thus these guild regulations dating from 1797 describe the traditional labor of many Europeans. In reading them, ask yourself what sort of labor conditions these regulations sustained. A worker's demonstration of his mastery of all the processes of producing wool cloth won him the "freedom of the guild" and its privileges. The latter involved the right to establish his own production unit and market his goods, as well as guild assistance when old age or illness prevented work. What sort of limits on the activities of guild members accompanied these freedoms? What do you think were the reasons for these restrictions? What efforts to protect both the consumer and the guild members' market can you discern in these restrictions? Why was the putting-out system explicitly forbidden to guild members? What specifically in all these restrictions seems intended to create a protected monopoly for producers?

Source 5 describes another facet of the old style of labor in textile production, namely, the putting-out system. It is the work of François-Alexandre Frédéric, Duke of La Rochefoucauld-Liancourt (1747–1827), an astute observer of the social and economic problems of his day who applied his energy and wealth in various reform schemes, including experimental farms and an early cotton mill. La Rochefoucauld wrote persuasively on the need for improved poor relief and better education for all Frenchmen. Here, to support his call for social change, La Rochefoucauld provides a good description of the putting-out system in his travel account of 1781 to 1783. Who was employed in textiles in Rouen? What does the duke tell you about the quantity of production in Rouen, despite the continued use of hand looms? How did the organization of this work, the quantity of production,

and the destinations of its products foreshadow certain features of the industrial age?

Source 6, "The Clothier's Delight," is a popular song, a type of source you have not yet studied in Volume II. Historians examine songs as evidence of popular culture to understand the attitudes and lives of men and women who were often illiterate. We must understand that such songs may exaggerate their message a bit to achieve their desired effect among unsophisticated audiences. Nevertheless we do have in this song some evidence of broad trends in the putting-out system and the concerns of those employed in it by English clothiers. Who controlled the material in this production process? Were the weavers and other textile workers the independent producers described in the guild regulations? Why did the workers view the clothiers as adversaries? How did the clothiers control the workers?

Next, consider the evidence on the new labor, that is, the work of the industrial age. Sources 7 and 8 in this section are regulations governing the conditions of work in early industrial enterprises. In using such material, the historian must remember that it describes the behavior prescribed by persons in authority; such regulations may not describe the actual comportment of those whose behavior the statutes aimed to control. Indeed, we can assume frequent conflict between the prescribed rules and the actual behavior of working people as workers adapted to the new conditions of industrial work.

Examine the work code for the foundry and engineering works in

Chapter 6
Labor Old
and New:
The Impact of
the Industrial
Revolution

Moabit, an industrial suburb of Berlin, Germany, in 1844 (Source 7). What sort of habits did these regulations seek to inculcate in the foundry workers? Notice also the pay practices described in paragraph 18. Why would management have adopted these? What disadvantages did they represent for the worker?

The apprenticeship agreement for girls as silk workers in rural Tarare, France (Source 8), retains the terminology of the old labor in designating new workers as apprentices, but it lays down industrial-age work rules for governing young women. Examine the agreement carefully, noting its disciplinary features. How long was the apprenticeship? When were wages paid? What happened if a girl left before the completion of her apprenticeship? What were the work hours? In what ways did management seek to increase production? Such mills as this were established in rural areas, away from cities like Lyons, where male preindustrial silk weavers had a centuries-long history of guild organization (and of unrest). Given that information, can you discern why the mill's location was chosen and why a female work force was sought? What attractions did the mill, with its long workday, offer unmarried rural women who otherwise would have been reluctant to seek industrial employment away from home?

The testimony of William Cooper to the Sadler Committee of the British Parliament (Source 9) provides dramatic evidence about the conditions of industrial labor in early textile mills. What effect did mill labor have on Cooper? What were the hours of work? How did overseers enforce punctuality and a faster work pace on young workers? Were conditions within the mills conducive to good health? Compare his height to that of his father. What could have accounted for Cooper's shorter stature? When he had health problems and was unable to work, what recourse did Cooper have?

Source 10 also describes the condition of labor in the textile industry, but it records the lot of women fifty or more years after William Cooper's experiences in the mills. Had working conditions improved very much since Cooper's day? How long was the workday? Did the work demand exceptional energy or skill from the workers? How did management impose discipline in such matters as punctuality?

With the selections brought together as Source 11, you will once more analyze the records of English parliamentary inquiries, but this time the committees examined coal mine labor in the 1840s. Read first the testimony of Joseph Staley. Note his position in the mine. How might this have affected his conclusion about his miners' health? How many boys did he employ and what ages were they? What sort of labor did the boys do? What were their hours? Analyze the testimony of William Jagger. What age was he? How long had he worked in the mine? What were his hours? What do his testimony and the comment by the investigator following that testimony tell you about work conditions and mine safety?

With the testimony of Patience Kershaw we have a record of women's labor in the mines. What sort of labor did Kershaw do? What weight of coal did she move daily? What health effects did such labor have on women like Kershaw and her sisters? What impression did she make on the parliamentary investigator, as indicated in his comment following her testimony?

Industrialization transformed the Western world in many ways, and we will examine aspects of its consequences in other chapters of this book as well (see especially Chapters 8 and 14). Your analysis of the evidence presented here should aid you in understanding one aspect of that transformation: the emergence of a new world of industrial labor and how it affected men and women of the eighteenth and nineteenth centuries.

THE EVIDENCE

THE OLD LABOR

Source 1 from Sebastien Le Prestre de Vauban, Project d'une Dixme royale, *ed. by E. Coornaert (Paris: Alcan, 1933) reprinted in Pierre Goubert,* The Ancien Régime: French Society, 1600–1750, *trans. by Steve Cox (New York: Harper and Row, 1974), pp. 116–118.*

1. Agricultural Labor Described by Vauban, about 1700

. . . It only remains to take stock of two million men[1] all of whom I suppose to be day-laborers or simple artisans scattered throughout the towns, *bourgs*[2] and villages of the realm.

What I have to say about all these workers . . . deserves serious attention, for although this sector may consist of what are unfairly called the dregs of the people, they are nonetheless worthy of high consideration in view of the services which they render to the State. For it is they who undertake all the great tasks in town and country without which neither themselves nor others could live. It is they who provide all the soldiers and sailors and all the serving women; in a word, without them the State could not survive. It is for this reason that they ought to be spared in the matter of taxes, in order not to burden them beyond their strength. . . .

1. Vauban wrote in an age that had no modern census data to accurately assess the size of a population. His figures here, at best, are an estimate. Indeed, modern demographic historians generally find Vauban's population data highly inaccurate.

2. **bourgs:** market towns.

Chapter 6

Labor Old

and New:

The Impact of

the Industrial

Revolution

Among the smaller fry, particularly in the countryside, there are any number of people who, while they lay no claim to any special craft, are continually plying several which are most necessary and indispensable. Of such a kind are those we call *manoeuvriers*, who, owning for the most part nothing but their strong arms or very little more, do day- or piece-work for whoever wants to employ them. It is they who do all the major jobs such as mowing, harvesting, threshing, woodcutting, working the soil and the vineyards, clearing land, ditching, carrying soil to vineyards or elsewhere, labouring for builders and several other tasks which are all hard and laborious. These men may well find this kind of employment for part of the year, and it is true that they can usually earn a fair day's wage at haymaking, harvesting and grape-picking time, but the rest of the year is a different story. . . .

It will not be inappropriate [to give] some particulars about what the country day-laborer can earn.

I shall assume that of the three-hundred and sixty-five days in the year, he may be gainfully employed for one hundred and eighty, and earn nine *sols*[3] a day. This is a high figure, and it is certain that except at harvest and grape-picking time most earn not more than eight *sols* a day on average, but supposing we allow the nine *sols*, that would amount to eighty-five *livres* and ten *sols*, call it ninety *livres*, from which we have to deduct his liabilities (taxes plus salt[4] for a family of four, say 14l. 16s.) . . . leaving seventy-five *livres* four *sols*.

Since I am assuming that his family . . . consists of four people, it requires not less than ten *septiers*[5] of grain, Paris measure, to feed them. This grain, half wheat, half rye . . . commonly selling at six *livres* per *septier* . . . will come to sixty *livres*, which leaves fifteen *livres* 4 *sols* out of seventy-five *livres* four *sols*, out of which the labourer has to find the price of rent and upkeep for his house, a few chattels, if only some earthenware bowls, clothing and linen, and the needs of his entire family for one year.

But these fifteen *livres* four *sols* will not take him very far unless his industry[6] or some particular business supervenes and his wife contributes to their income by means of her distaff,[7] sewing, knitting hose or making small quan-

3. **sol:** sou.

4. Salt was subject to a form of tax in France before 1789. Tax farmers purchased the exclusive right to sell this dietary necessity to the public. The public was required by law to buy a certain amount of salt per year from these monopolists; in paying the price of the salt, buyers also paid a salt tax, the *gabelle*, to the tax farmers, who turned the proceeds of this over to the government. This form of taxation kept salt prices artificially high in much of France and was deeply resented by many taxpayers.

5. **septier:** a unit of measure in use in France prior to the Revolution of 1789. Its precise size varied from one district to another; hence here Vauban must specify that he is using the Parisian *septier*. Ten Parisian *septiers* would have equaled about 15.5 hectoliters or 43 bushels.

6. Many rural workers would have been employed in some phase of textile production, like weaving.

7. **distaff:** a staff that holds unspun flax or wool during the process of spinning such material into thread. The word can also refer to women's work or interests, because spinning was women's work.

tities of lace . . . also by keeping a small garden or rearing poultry and perhaps a calf, a pig or a goat for the better-off . . . ; by which means he might buy a piece of larding bacon and a little butter or oil for making soup. And if he does not additionally cultivate some small allotment, he will be hard pressed to subsist, or at least he will be reduced, together with his family, to the most wretched fare. And if instead of two children he has four, that will be worse still until they are old enough to earn their own living. Thus however we come at the matter, it is certain that he will always have the greatest difficulty in seeing the year out. . . .

Source 2 from British Parliamentary Papers: Reports of Special Assistant Poor Law Commissioner on the Employment of Women and Children in Agriculture *(London: William Clowes and Sons for Her Majesty's Stationery Office, 1843), pp. 66–67.*

2. Testimony of an Agricultural Worker's Wife and Former Factory Worker, 1842[8]

Mrs. *Britton*, Wife of _____ *Britton*, of *Calne, Wiltshire*, Farm-labourer, examined.

I am 41 years old; I have lived at Calne all my life. I went to school till I was eight years old, when I went out to look after children. At ten years old I went to work at a factory in Calne, where I was till I was 26. I have been married 15 years. My husband is an agricultural labourer. I have seven children, all boys. The oldest is fourteen, the youngest three-quarters of a year old. My husband is a good workman, and does most of his work by the lump, and earns from 9s. to 10s. a-week pretty constantly, but finds his own tools,—his wheelbarrow, which cost 1l., pickaxe, which cost 3s., and scoop, which cost 3s.[9]

I have worked in the fields, and when I went out I left the children in the care of the eldest boy, and frequently carried the baby with me, as I could not

---

8. This testimony was delivered before a Parliamentary Committee studying the employment of women and children in British agriculture.

9. **by the lump:** Mr. Britton was paid by the job rather than by the hour or day. English coinage mentioned in this and following selections (with the abbreviations for each denomination where appropriate) includes:
   £ or l.: pound sterling.
   s.: shilling; 20 shillings to 1 pound sterling.
   d.: pence (from Latin *denari*); 12 pence to 1 shilling.
   crown: a coin worth 5 shillings.
   groat: a coin worth 4 pence.

Chapter 6

Labor Old

and New:

The Impact of

the Industrial

Revolution

go home to nurse it. I have worked at hay-making and at harvest, and at other times in weeding and keeping the ground clean. I generally work from half-past seven till five, or half-past. When at work in the spring I have received 10*d*. a-day, but that is higher than the wages of women in general; 8*d*. or 9*d*. is more common. My master always paid 10*d*. When working I never had any beer, and I never felt the want of it. I never felt that my health was hurt by the work. Hay-making is hard work, very fatiguing, but it never hurt me. Working in the fields is not such hard work as working in the factory. I am always better when I can get out to work in the fields. I intend to do so next year if I can. Last year I could not go out, owing to the birth of the baby. My eldest boy gets a little to do; he don't earn more than 9*d*. a-week; he has not enough to do. My husband has 40 lugs[10] of land, for which he pays 10*s*. a-year. We grow potatoes and a few cabbages, but not enough for our family; for that we should like to have forty lugs more. We have to buy potatoes. One of the children is a cripple, and the guardians[11] allow us two gallons of bread a-week for him.[12] We buy two gallons more, according as the money is. Nine people can't do with less than four gallons of bread a-week. We could eat much more bread if we could get it; sometimes we can afford only one gallon a-week. We very rarely buy butcher's fresh meat, certainly not oftener than once a-week, and not more than sixpenny worth. I like my husband to have a bit of meat, now he has left off drinking. I buy $\frac{1}{2}$ lb. butter a-week, 1 oz. tea, $\frac{1}{2}$ lb. sugar. The rest of our food is potatoes, with a little fat. The rent of our cottage is 1*s*. 6*d*. a-week; there are two rooms in it. We all sleep in one room, under the tiles. Sometimes we receive private assistance, especially in clothing. Formerly my husband was in the habit of drinking, and everything went bad. He used to beat me. I have often gone to bed, I and my children, without supper, and I have had no breakfast the next morning, and frequently no firing.[13] My husband attended a lecture on teetotalism one evening about two years ago, and I have reason to bless that evening. My husband has never touched a drop of drink since. He has been better in health, getting stouter, and has behaved like a good husband to me ever since. I have been much more comfortable, and the children happier. He works better than he did. He can mow better, and

10. **lug:** an old English measure of area equal to 49 square yards. The Brittons' 40 lugs would, therefore, have equaled 1,960 square yards, less than half of a full acre, which is 4,840 square yards.

11. **guardian:** Poor Law official.

12. **two gallons of bread:** the gallon as a gauge of wheat and other dry material is an archaic English measure, the weight of which was far from standard in the British Isles. Sources refer to gallons of wheat weighing anywhere from 8 to almost 10 pounds. If we assume a gallon to have been 9 pounds in the case of the Brittons, we find that the family claims to have required a minimum of 36 pounds of bread per week. For this time, in which bread was the basic dietary element of the poor, demographic historians assume an adult to have consumed 2 pounds per day. Even if the family comprised only two adults and the rest children, these were extremely short rations.

13. **firing:** that is, no morning hearth fire for want of the cost of fuel.

that is hard work, and he does not mind being laughed at by the other men for not drinking. I send my eldest boy to Sunday school; them that are younger go to the day school. My eldest boy never complains of work hurting him. My husband now goes regularly to church: formerly he could hardly be got there.

Source 3 from Alain Lottin, Chavatte, ouvrier lillois. Un contemporain de Louis XIV *(Paris: Flammarion, 1979), pp. 323–324.*

3. The Work Year in 17th-century Lille, France

Holidays in Seventeenth-Century Lille

January	Monday following Epiphany (January 6)
22 January	Feast of St. Vincent
25 January	Feast of St. Paul's Conversion
February	Ash Wednesday
22 February	Feast of the Chair of St. Peter
March or April	Tuesday of Holy Week until the Thursday after Easter (eight working days)
3 May	Feast of the Finding of the True Cross
9 May	Feast of St. Nicholas
May or June	Feast of Pentecost (seventh Sunday after Easter): Pentecost eve through the following Thursday (five days)
5 June	Corpus Christi
9 June or second Sunday in June	Municipal procession accompanied by banquets
11 June	Feast of St. Barnabas
June	Thursday after municipal procession is a holiday
2 July	Feast of the visitation of the Virgin
1 August	Feast of St. Peter in Chains
3 August	Feast of St. Stephen
29 August	Feast of the Beheading of St. John the Baptist, followed by five days off
1 October	Feast of St. Remy
18 October	Feast of St. Luke
1 November	All Saints Day
24–31 December	Christmas (eight days)

This represents a total of forty-four days off, in addition to Sundays.

Chapter 6

Labor Old

and New:

The Impact of

the Industrial

Revolution

Sources 4 and 5 from Sidney Pollard and Colin Holmes, editors, Documents in European Economic History, *vol. 1,* The Process of Industrialization, 1750–1870 *(New York: St. Martin's, 1968), pp. 45–48, pp. 91–92.*

4. Guild Regulations in the Prussian Woolen Industry, 1797

§ 760

Although it is laid down in the General Privilege (8 Nov. 1734) that it shall not be necessary to produce a masterpiece in order to gain the master's freedom; yet it was ruled afterwards: that anyone aspiring to the freedom of the gild, shall (22 November 1772) apart from being examined by the Inspector of Manufactures and the Gild Master whether he be properly experienced in sorting and fulling, wool shearing and preparing and threading the looms, also weave a piece of cloth of mixed colour from wool dyed by himself.

§ 765–§ 771

The woollen weavers may sell by retail and cutting-up home produced cloths and baizes[14] on condition that they and their fellow gild members may not only sell in their own town the goods made locally, but may also offer them for sale at fairs and annual markets. The latter, however, is limited to this extent (1772 and 1791): that a gild member may not take part in any market or fair unless he has at least 12 pieces of cloth for sale, though it is permissible (18 December 1791) for two of them to enter a fair and to offer cloth for sale if they have at least 12 pieces of cloth between them; at the same time, this privilege is extended also to weavers (1772) who are no longer practising their trade themselves.

The woollen weavers of Salzwedel, however, may not sell the cloths produced by themselves, by retail and cutting-up, even in their own town, because the local cloth cutters' and tailors' gild enjoys, according to its old privilege (1233, 1323 and last confirmed on 26 January 1715) the sole right of cutting up woollen and similar cloth for sale, so that neither the local merchants, nor the mercers, nor the woollen weavers of the town, whose rights were recently confirmed, have the right to cut up woollen cloth for sale.

Woollen weavers may not trade in woollen cloths made outside their own town, unless they have been specially granted this right, because this would infringe the privileges granted to the merchants. . . .

14. **baize:** a soft woolen fabric.

Neither finishers nor croppers,[15] dyers or other craftsmen (1772) are permitted to trade in woollen cloths or undertake putting-out agencies on pain of losing their craft privileges.

In the countryside (28 August 1723, 14 November 1793) neither linen (?) weavers, nor vergers[16] or schoolmasters, nor husbandmen themselves, are permitted to manufacture woollen or worsted cloth not even for their own use. Neither are town linen weavers permitted to make goods wholly of wool.

Woollen weavers are permitted to dye their own cloths, but neither they nor the merchants are permitted to have the cloths made in the Electoral Mark finished or dyed in foreign towns, on pain of confiscation of the goods. While the export of unfinished and undyed cloths is permissible (1772), merchants and woollen weavers should be persuaded (26 October and 10 November 1791) to export only dyed and finished cloths.

Woollen weavers may not (1772) keep their own tenting frame and stretch their own cloths, but must leave this finishing process to the cloth finishers. They have however the concession (28 October and 11 November 1773) that they may keep 10–12 frames, but on these they may only stretch $\frac{3}{4}$ widths, and twill flannels. . . .

§ 798

On pain of requisition and, for repeated offences, on pain of loss of the freedom of the gild, better yarn may not be used for the ends of pieces of cloth than is used for the middle. No weaver is permitted to keep frames of his own, on pain of loss of his gild freedom, and he is obliged to take his cloths to the master shearmen; tanned wool and wool-fells may not be woven into pieces, but must be made only into rough goods and horse blankets. Finally it is laid down in detail how each type of woollen and worsted cloth shall be manufactured; and weavers have been advised several times to observe closely the detailed rules and regulations of the woollen and worsted order (20 September 1784, 9 September and 8 October 1787). . . .

§ 800

It is further laid down as a general rule, that all cloths shall be viewed by sworn aulnagers,[17] of whom eight shall be elected in large companies, six in medium sized ones, and two to four among small ones, and they shall be viewed three times, and sealed accordingly after each time. The first viewing shall determine that the piece is woven with sufficient and satisfactory yarn, woven sufficiently closely and without flaws, and of the correct length and

15. **cropper:** the craftsmen who sheared the nap from woolen cloth.
16. **verger:** a parish official generally charged with care of the interior of a church.
17. **aulnager:** an official charged with measuring and inspecting woolen cloth.

Chapter 6

Labor Old

and New:

The Impact of

the Industrial

Revolution

width. The second, held on the frame, shall determine whether the cloth is overstretched, and has wholly pure wool, is fulled cleanly and free of errors in fulling, and the third, held on the frame after dyeing, whether it has suffered by the dyeing.

5. La Rochefoucauld Describes the Putting-Out System in Rouen, France, 1781–1783

I then saw the material called cotton check (*cotonnades*). There are all sorts of cotton manufacture made up at Rouen and in the area 15 leagues[18] around it. The peasant who returns to the plough to work his fields, sits at his cotton frame and makes either *siamoises*[19] or ticking or even white, very fine, cotton cloth. One must admire the activity of the Normans. This activity does not interfere at all with their daily work. Land is very dear and consequently very well cultivated. The farmer works on the land during the day and it is in the evening by the light of the lamp that he starts his other task. His workers and his family have to help. When they have worked all week they come into the town with horses or carts piled up with material. Goods are sold in the Hall, which is all that remains of the palace of the former Dukes of Normandy, on Thursdays. It is a truly wonderful sight. It takes place at a surprising speed. Almost 800,000 francs worth of business is transacted between 6.00 and 9.00 in the morning. Among those who do the buying there are many agents who buy for merchants and then the goods pass to America, Italy and Spain. The majority goes to America. I have seen many pieces destined to become shirts for negroes; but their skin will be seen through the material, since the cloth is thin and almost sufficiently coarse to make ticking. It costs 17, 20 and even 25 francs per aune[20] in the Hall.

18. **league:** a league equals 2.764 miles.
19. **siamoises:** common cotton goods.
20. **aune:** an old French measurement unit for textiles; equal to 45 inches.

Source 6 from James Burnley, The History of Wool and Wool Combing *(London: Sampson Low, Marston, Searle and Rivington, Ltd., 1889), pp. 160–163.*

6. "The Clothier's Delight; or, the Rich Men's Joy, and the Poor Men's Sorrow, Wherein Is Exprest the Craftiness and Subtility of Many Clothiers in England by Beatting Down their Workmen's Wages," Song, 18th century

Of all sorts of callings that in England be,
There is none that liveth so gallant as we;
Our trading maintains us as brave as a knight,
We live at our pleasure, and take our delight;
We heapeth up riches and treasure great store,
Which we get by griping and grinding the poor.
    And this is a way for to fill up our purse,
    Although we do get it with many a curse.

Throughout the whole kingdom, in country and town,
There is no danger of our trade going down,
So long as the Comber[21] can work with his comb,
And also the Weaver weave with his lomb;[22]
The Tucker[23] and Spinner[24] that spins all the year,
We will make them to earn their wages full dear.
    And this is the way, &c.

In former ages we us'd to give,
So that our work-folks like farmers did live;
But the times are altered, we will make them know
All we can for to bring them all under our bow;

21. **comber:** person who performed one of the processes in finishing raw wool, the combing out of the wool.
22. **lomb:** archaic spelling of *loom.*
23. **tucker:** in the processing of wool, person who performs the task of *fulling* the wool, that is, cleaning, shrinking, and thickening the fabric with moisture, heat, and pressure.
24. **spinner:** person who spun the raw wool into thread on a spinning wheel or other device.

Chapter 6

Labor Old

and New:

The Impact of

the Industrial

Revolution

We will make to work hard for sixpence a day,[25]
Though a shilling they deserve if they had their just pay.
    And this is the way, &c.

And first for the Combers, we will bring them down
From eight groats a score unto half a crown.
If at all they murmur, and say 'tis too small,
We bid them choose whether they will work at all:
We'll make them believe that trading is bad;
We care not a pin, though they are ne'er so sad.
    And this is the way, &c.

We'll make the poor Weavers work at a low rate;
We'll find fault where there's no fault, and so we will bate;[26]
If trading grows dead, we will presently show it;
But if it grows good, they shall never know it;
We'll tell them that cloth beyond sea will not go,
We care not whether we keep clothing or no.
    And this is the way, &c.

Then next for the Spinners we shall ensue,
We'll make them spin three pound instead of two;
When they bring home their work unto us, they complain,
And say that their wages will not them maintain;
But if that an ounce of weight they do lack,
Then for to bate threepence we will not be slack.
    And this is the way, &c.

But if it holds weight, then their wages they crave,
We have got no money, and what's that you'd have?
We have bread and bacon and butter that's good,
With oatmeal and salt that is wholesome for food;
We have soap and candles whereby to give light,[27]
That you may work by them so long as you have light.
    And this is the way, &c.

25. There were 12 pence to a shilling; hence sixpence represented a 50 percent pay cut. In the next verse the value of 8 groats was 32 pence; half a crown was worth 30 pence. Thus the song portrays the clothiers as seeking to reduce wages a small and perhaps unnoticed amount, 2 pence.

26. **bate:** to beat back or reduce a worker's wages.

27. This whole verse refers to a practice, theoretically illegal in England after 1701, of paying putting-out workers in textiles with goods, not cash. This practice kept workers dependent on their employers because they lacked hard currency when they were paid in such commodities as bread, bacon, butter, oatmeal, salt, soap, and candles. That the practice endured despite the law is indicated by additional laws directed against it as late as 1779.

We will make the Tucker and Shereman understand
That they with their wages shall never buy land;
Though heretofore they have been lofty and high
Yet now we will make them submit humbly;
We will lighten their wages as low as may be,
We will keep them under in every degree.
    And this is the way, &c.

And thus we do gain all our wealth and estate,
By many poor men that work early and late;
If it were not for those that do labour full hard,
We might go and hang ourselves without regard;
The Combers, the Weavers, the Tuckers also,
With the Spinners that work for wages full low.
    By these people's labour we will up our purse, &c.

Then hey for the Clothing Trade, it goes on brave;
We scorn for to toyl and moyl,[28] nor yet to slave.
Our workmen do work hard, but we live at ease;
We go when we will, and come when we please;
We hoard up our bags of silver and gold;
But conscience and charity with us are cold.
    By poor people's labour, &c.

THE NEW LABOR

Source 7 from Sidney Pollard and Colin Holmes, editors, Documents in European Economic History, *vol. 1,* The Process of Industrialization, 1750–1870 *(New York: St. Martin's, 1968), pp. 534–536.*

7. Rules for Workers in the Foundry and Engineering Works of the Royal Overseas Trading Company, Berlin, 1844

In every large works, and in the co-ordination of any large number of workmen, good order and harmony must be looked upon as the fundamentals of success, and therefore the following rules shall be strictly observed.

    Every man employed in the concern named below shall receive a copy of these rules, so that no one can plead ignorance. Its acceptance shall be deemed to mean consent to submit to its regulations.

28. **toyl and moyl:** archaic spellings of *toil* and *moil*—that is, work and drudgery.

Chapter 6

Labor Old

and New:

The Impact of

the Industrial

Revolution

(1) The normal working day begins at all seasons at 6 a.m. precisely and ends, after the usual break of half an hour for breakfast, an hour for dinner and half an hour for tea, at 7 p.m., and it shall be strictly observed.

Five minutes before the beginning of the stated hours of work until their actual commencement, a bell shall ring and indicate that every worker employed in the concern has to proceed to his place of work, in order to start as soon as the bell stops.

The doorkeeper shall lock the door punctually at 6 a.m., 8.30 a.m., 1 p.m. and 4.30 p.m.

Workers arriving 2 minutes late shall lose half an hour's wages; whoever is more than 2 minutes late may not start work until after the next break, or at least shall lose his wages until then. Any disputes about the correct time shall be settled by the clock mounted above the gatekeeper's lodge.

These rules are valid both for time- and for piece-workers, and in cases of breaches of these rules, workmen shall be fined in proportion to their earnings. The deductions from the wage shall be entered in the wage-book of the gatekeeper whose duty they are: they shall be unconditionally accepted as it will not be possible to enter into any discussions about them.

(2) When the bell is rung to denote the end of the working day, every workman, both on piece- and on day-wage, shall leave his workshop and the yard, but is not allowed to make preparations for his departure before the bell rings. Every breach of this rule shall lead to a fine of five silver groschen to the sick fund. Only those who have obtained special permission by the overseer may stay on in the workshop in order to work.—If a workman has worked beyond the closing bell, he must give his name to the gatekeeper on leaving, on pain of losing his payment for the overtime.

(3) No workman, whether employed by time or piece, may leave before the end of the working day, without having first received permission from the overseer and having given his name to the gatekeeper. Omission of these two actions shall lead to a fine of ten silver groschen payable to the sick fund.

(4) Repeated irregular arrival at work shall lead to dismissal. This shall also apply to those who are found idling by an official or overseer, and refuse to obey their order to resume work.

(5) Entry to the firm's property by any but the designated gateway, and exit by any prohibited route, e.g., by climbing fences or walls, or by crossing the Spree, shall be punished by a fine of fifteen silver groschen to the sick fund for the first offences, and dismissal for the second.

(6) No worker may leave his place of work otherwise than for reasons connected with his work.

(7) All conversation with fellow-workers is prohibited; if any worker requires information about his work, he must turn to the overseer, or to the particular fellow-worker designated for the purpose.

(8) Smoking in the workshops or in the yard is prohibited during working hours; anyone caught smoking shall be fined five silver groschen for the sick fund for every such offence.

(9) Every worker is responsible for cleaning up his space in the workshop, and if in doubt, he is to turn to his overseer.—All tools must always be kept in good condition, and must be cleaned after use. This applies particularly to the turner, regarding his lathe.

(10) Natural functions must be performed at the appropriate places, and whoever is found soiling walls, fences, squares, etc., and similarly, whoever is found washing his face and hands in the workshop and not in the places assigned for the purpose, shall be fined five silver groschen for the sick fund.

(11) On completion of his piece of work, every workman must hand it over at once to his foreman or superior, in order to receive a fresh piece of work. Pattern makers must on no account hand over their patterns to the foundry without express order of their supervisors. No workman may take over work from his fellow-workman without instruction to that effect by the foreman.

(12) It goes without saying that all overseers and officials of the firm shall be obeyed without question, and shall be treated with due deference. Disobedience will be punished by dismissal.

(13) Immediate dismissal shall also be the fate of anyone found drunk in any of the workshops.

(14) Untrue allegations against superiors or officials of the concern shall lead to stern reprimand, and may lead to dismissal. The same punishment shall be meted out to those who knowingly allow errors to slip through when supervising or stocktaking.

(15) Every workman is obliged to report to his superiors any acts of dishonesty or embezzlement on the part of his fellow workmen. If he omits to do so, and it is shown after subsequent discovery of a misdemeanour that he knew about it at the time, he shall be liable to be taken to court as an accessory after the fact and the wage due to him shall be retained as punishment. Conversely, anyone denouncing a theft in such a way as to allow conviction of the thief shall receive a reward of two Thaler, and, if necessary, his name shall be kept confidential.—Further, the gatekeeper and the watchman, as well as every official, are entitled to search the baskets, parcels, aprons etc. of the women and children who are taking the dinners into the works, on their departure, as well as search any worker suspected of stealing any article whatever. . . .

(18) Advances shall be granted only to the older workers, and even to them only in exceptional circumstances. As long as he is working by the piece, the workman is entitled merely to his fixed weekly wage as subsistence pay; the extra earnings shall be paid out only on completion of the whole piece contract. If a workman leaves before his piece contract is completed, either of his own free will, or on being dismissed as punishment, or because of illness, the partly completed work shall be valued by the general manager with the help

Chapter 6

Labor Old

and New:

The Impact of

the Industrial

Revolution

of two overseers, and he will be paid accordingly. There is no appeal against the decision of these experts.

(19) A free copy of these rules is handed to every workman, but whoever loses it and requires a new one, or cannot produce it on leaving, shall be fined $2\frac{1}{2}$ silver groschen, payable to the sick fund.

Moabit, August, 1844.

Source 8 from Erna Olafson Hellerstein, L. P. Hume, and K. M. Offen, editors, Victorian Women: A Documentary Account of Women's Lives in Nineteenth-Century England, France, and the United States *(Stanford, California: Stanford University Press, 1981), pp. 394–396.*

8. Apprenticeship Contract for Young Women Employed in the Silk Mills of Tarare, France, 1850s

MILLING, REELING, AND WARP-PREPARATION OF SILKS

Conditions of Apprenticeship

Art. 1. To be admitted, young women must be between the ages of thirteen and fifteen, of good character and in good health, intelligent and industrious, and must have been vaccinated. They must present their birth certificate, a certificate of vaccination, and a trousseau.

Art. 2. Girls who are accepted by the establishment will be placed in milling, reeling, or warp[29] preparation by the director, according to the needs of the establishment and their intelligence.

Art. 3. During the apprenticeship period, the pupil will be paid wages, fed, lodged, given heat and light, and laundry *for her body linen only*; she will also be furnished with aprons.

Art. 4. The pupil promises to be obedient and submissive to the mistresses charged with her conduct and instruction, as well as to conform to the rules of the establishment.

Art. 5. In case of illness the director will notify the father or guardian of the sick apprentice, and if her state necessitates a leave, it will be granted until her recovery.

Art. 6. If the sick pupil remains in the establishment, every care necessitated by her condition will be given to her.

---

29. **warp:** in the weaving process, threads placed lengthwise in the loom. They were woven with threads called the *weft* or *woof* placed perpendicularly to them.

Art. 7. In case of illness or any other serious cause that warrants her leaving, the apprentice who must absent herself from the establishment will be obligated to prolong her apprenticeship during a time equal to that of her absence.

Art. 8. The director alone has the right to authorize or refuse leaves. They will be granted only on the request of the father or guardian of the pupil.

Art. 9. Apprenticeship is for three consecutive years, *not including an obligatory trial month.* In order to encourage the pupil, she will be paid:

1st year:	a wage of 40 to 50 francs
2nd year:	" " " 60 to 75 "
3rd year:	" " " 80 to 100 "

After the apprenticeship the wage will be established according to merit.

At the end of the apprenticeship, a gratuity of 20 francs will be given to the apprentice to reward her for her exactitude in fulfilling her engagements.

Art. 10. The effective work time is twelve hours. Summer and winter, the day begins at 5 o'clock and ends at 7:15.

Breakfast is from 7:30 to 8:15; lunch is from 12:00 to 1:00; snack is from 5:00 to 5:30; supper is at 7:15.

After the second year, pupils will receive lessons in reading, writing, and arithmetic. They will be taught to sew and do a little cooking.

Art. 11. As a measure of encouragement and with no obligation, it is established that at the end of each month the young people will be graded as follows:

1st class, gift for the month 1 fr. 50 c.	
2nd class	1 " —
3rd class	50 c.
4th class	—[30]

Each month a new classification will take place, and the young person will rise or fall according to her merit. This classification will be based on an overall evaluation of conduct, quantity and quality of work, docility and diligence, etc.

Art. 12. Wages are not due until the end of the year. They will be paid during the month following their due date. Gifts, incentive pay, and compensation for extra work will be paid each month.

Art. 13. Any apprentice who leaves the establishment before the end of her term, or who has been dismissed for bad conduct, conspiracy, rebellion, laziness, or a serious breach of the rules loses her rights to wages for the current

---

30. Abbreviations for French currency.
    fr.: franc.
    c.: centime, 100 centimes to 1 franc.

Chapter 6

Labor Old

and New:

The Impact of

the Industrial

Revolution

year; beyond this, in such a case, the father or guardian of the pupil agrees to pay the director of the establishment the sum of one hundred francs to indemnify him for the non-fulfillment of the present agreement: half of this sum will be given to the *bureau de bienfaisance*[31] in the pupil's parish.

Art. 14. If, during the first year, apprentice is recognized as unfit, despite the agreement and in the interest of both parties the director reserves the right to send her away without indemnity.

Art. 15. The apprentice who leaves the establishment at the end of the first month under the pretext that she cannot get used to the place, will pay 50 centimes per day toward the costs she has occasioned, as well as her travel expenses.

Art. 16. On her arrival, the apprentice will submit to inspection by the house doctor. Any girl who has a skin disease or who is found to be sickly will not be accepted and will be sent away immediately at her own expense.

Contract

The undersigned _____ the manufacturer, and have made the following contract:

M. _____ , having read and understood the conditions of apprenticeship stipulated above in sixteen articles, declares that he accepts them for _____ aged _____ , present and consenting, and pledges to execute them and have them executed in all their contents by _____ . M. _____ , manufacturer, pledges likewise to execute the above conditions insofar as they concern him.

The present agreement is consented to for *Three years* beginning on _____ .

Made and signed in duplicate _____

_____   _____

Father or Guardian   Director

P.S. Girls will not be admitted on Sundays or holidays.[32]

---

31. **Bureau de bienfaissance:** Catholic social welfare organization.

32. That is, girls were not admitted to employment in the mill on Sundays or holidays.

Source 9 from British Parliamentary Papers: Reports from Committees, *vol. 15*, Labour of Children in Factories *(London: House of Commons, 1832), pp. 6–13.*

9. Report of the Sadler Committee, 1832[33]

William Cooper, called in; and Examined.

What is your business?—I follow the cloth-dressing at present.

2. What is your age?—I was eight-and-twenty last February.

3. When did you first begin to work in mills or factories?—When I was about 10 years of age.

4. With whom did you first work?—At Mr. Benyon's flax[34] mills, in Meadowland, Leeds.

5. What were your usual hours of working?—We began at five, and gave over at nine; at five o'clock in the morning.

6. And you gave over at nine o'clock?—At nine at night.

7. At what distance might you have lived from the mill?—About a mile and a half.

8. At what time had you to get up in the morning to attend to your labour?—I had to be up soon after four o'clock.

9. Every morning?—Every morning.

10. What intermissions had you for meals?—When we began at five in the morning, we went on until noon, and then we had 40 minutes for dinner.

11. Had you no time for breakfast?—No, we got it as we could, while we were working.

12. Had you any time for an afternoon refreshment, or what is called in Yorkshire your "drinking?"—No; when we began at noon, we went on till night; there was only one stoppage, the 40 minutes for dinner.

13. Then as you had to get your breakfast, and what is called "drinking" in that manner, you had to put it on one side?—Yes, we had to put it on one side; and when we got our frames doffed, we ate two or three mouthfuls, and then put it by again.[35]

14. Is there not considerable dust in a flax mill?—A flax mill is very dusty indeed.

33. **Sadler Committee:** the Committee on the Bill to Regulate the Labour of Children in the Mills and Factories of the United Kingdom.

34. **flax:** a plant whose fiber is manufactured into linen for thread or weaving into fabrics.

35. Vocabulary of the textile mill:
    frame: the water frame, an early spinning machine.
    doff: the task, in the industrial spinning process, of removing spindles filled with yarn from the spinning machine.
    bobbin: a reel, cylinder, or spoollike apparatus on which thread is wound.

Chapter 6
Labor Old
and New:
The Impact of
the Industrial
Revolution

15. Was not your food therefore frequently spoiled?—Yes, at times with the dust; sometimes we could not eat it, when it had got a lot of dust on.

16. What were you when you were ten years old?—What is called a bobbin-doffer; when the frames are quite full, we have to doff them.

17. Then as you lived so far from home, you took your dinner to the mill?—We took all our meals with us, living so far off.

18. During the 40 minutes which you were allowed for dinner, had you ever to employ that time in your turn in cleaning the machinery?—At times we had to stop to clean the machinery, and then we got our dinner as well as we could; they paid us for that.

19. At these times you had no resting at all?—No.

20. How much had you for cleaning the machinery?—I cannot exactly say what they gave us, as I never took any notice of it.

21. Did you ever work even later than the time you have mentioned?—I cannot say that I worked later there: I had a sister who worked up stairs, and she worked till 11 at night, in what they call the card-room.

22. At what time in the morning did she begin to work?—At the same time as myself.

23. And they kept her there till 11 at night?—Till 11 at night.

24. You say that your sister was in the card-room?—Yes.

25. Is not that a very dusty department?—Yes, very dusty indeed.

26. She had to be at the mill at five, and was kept at work till eleven at night?—Yes.

27. During the whole time she was there?—During the whole time; there was only 40 minutes allowed at dinner out of that.

28. To keep you at your work for such a length of time, and especially towards the termination of such a day's labour as that, what means were taken to keep you awake and attentive?—They strapped us at times, when we were not quite ready to be doffing the frame when it was full.

29. Were you frequently strapped?—At times we were frequently strapped.

30. What sort of strap was it?—About this length [*describing it*].

31. What was it made of?—Of leather.

32. Were you occasionally very considerably hurt with the strap?—Sometimes it hurt us very much, and sometimes they did not lay on so hard as they did at others.

33. Were the girls strapped in that sort of way?—They did not strap what they called the grown-up women.

card: a tool used to comb out textile fibers (wool, flax, etc.) in preparation for spinning them into thread.

gigger: person who worked in the gigging process, a step in dressing wool cloth in which loose fibers were drawn off of the fabric and in which the fabric's nap is raised. The process used **teasles,** thistlelike plants that hooked the fabric and raised it.

boiler: part of the processing of wool involved boiling and scrubbing to remove oils.

primmer, brusher: workers involved in the final preparation of woolen cloth.

34. Were any of the female children strapped?—Yes; they were strapped in the same way as the lesser boys. . . .

44. Were your punishments the same in that mill as in the other?—Yes, they used the strap the same there.

45. How long did you work in that mill?—Five years.

46. And how did it agree with your health?—I was sometimes well, and sometimes not very well.

47. Did it affect your breathing at all?—Yes; sometimes we were stuffed.

48. When your hours were so long, you had not any time to attend to a day-school?—We had no time to go to a day-school, only to a Sunday-school,[36] and then with working such long hours we wanted to have a bit of rest, so that I slept till the afternoon, sometimes till dinner, and sometimes after.

49. Did you attend a place of worship?—I should have gone to a place of worship many times, but I was in the habit of falling asleep, and that kept me away; I did not like to go for fear of being asleep.

50. Do you mean that you could not prevent yourself from falling asleep, in consequence of the fatigue of the preceding week?—Yes. . . .

85. After working at a mill to this excess, how did you find your health at last?—I found it very bad indeed; I found illness coming on me a long time before I fell down.

86. Did you at length become so ill as to be unable to pursue your work?—I was obliged to give it up entirely.

87. How long were you ill?—For six months.

88. Who attended?—Mr. Metcalf and Mr. Freeman.

89. What were you told by your medical attendants was the reason of your illness?—Nothing but hard labour, and working long hours; and they gave me up, and said no good could be done for me, that I must go into the country.

90. Did this excessive labour not only weaken you, but destroy your appetite?—It destroyed the appetite, and I became so feeble, that I could not cross the floor unless I had a stick to go with; I was in great pain, and could find ease in no posture.

91. You could drink in the meantime, if you could not eat?—Yes, I could drink.

92. But you found that did not improve your health?—No.

93. Has it been remarked that your excessive labour from early life has greatly diminished your growth?—A number of persons have said that such was the case, and that I was the same as if I had been made of iron or stone.

94. What height are you?—About five feet. It is that that has hindered me of my growth.

95. When you were somewhat recovered, did you apply for labour?—I applied for my work again, but the overlooker said I was not fit to work; he was

---

36. **Sunday school:** churches often ran schools for mill children on their day off (Sunday) to teach the rudiments of reading and writing along with religious instruction.

Chapter 6

Labor Old

and New:

The Impact of

the Industrial

Revolution

sure of that, and he would not let me have it. I was then obliged to throw myself on the parish.[37]

96. Have you subsisted on the parish ever since?—Yes.

97. Have you been always willing and anxious to work?—I was always willing and anxious to work from my infancy.

98. Have you been on the parish since your severe illness?—Yes.

99. How long is that ago?—Six months. When I was ill I got something from the Society; they relieved me then, but when I became better I received no benefit from it.

100. Yours is not what is called a Friendly Society?—No, it is what we call Odd Fellows.[38]

101. And they do not extend relief after a certain period?—Not after you get better. . . .

124. You say that you had no time to go to school during the week, but that you went on Sunday?—I went on Sunday; I had no time to go to a day-school.

125. Can you read or write?—I can read, but I cannot write. . . .

142. If you had refused to work over-hours, would they have turned you off altogether?—Yes, they would have turned us off. If one will not do it, another will.

143. At this particular period, when you were thus over-worked, were there not a great number of able-bodied individuals in Leeds totally out of employment?—A great number. A few individuals have it all, and the rest, of course, are obliged to apply to the parish.

144. If you had refused to work the over-work, there were plenty of others willing to undertake it?—That is very true.

145. And they were people able to perform the sort of work you were engaged in?—They were.

146. You of course know your trade?—Yes.

147. Were those people out of work persons who could have undertaken your situation?—They were out of work.

148. At the time that you were working these over-hours were there a great many out of work in Leeds?—Yes.

149. And were they capable of doing your work?—Yes, capable of doing the same work.

150. Do you work anywhere now?—I have not worked anywhere for rather more than a year. I have been constantly out to seek for employment since I have been better.

37. **on the parish:** under existing English laws, poor relief was the responsibility of the local parish.

38. **Friendly Society, Odd Fellows Society:** organizations founded to benefit workers through "self-help." They took up small weekly sums from their members and used the funds thus collected to aid sick or injured members unable to work, or to assist the widows and orphans of members.

151. How are you supported?—By the town.

152. Do you mean by the parish?—Yes.

153. Of what place?—Leeds. . . .

184. How did you contrive to be awake so early in the morning?—My father used to call me up.

185. Did he get up so early as that for his own business?—He got up on purpose to call me.

186. How many hours did he work in a day at his own business?—Sometimes from five in the morning till eight at night.

187. You say he was a shoemaker?—Yes.

188. Then, according to this, he worked more hours than you did?—I think not so long.

189. Did your father take his regular intervals for his meals?—I should think so.

190. And walked about to market for his family; had he not many pauses in his labour?—He worked at home, and therefore could do as he pleased. . . .

198. Has your health improved since you left off working long hours?—I am a deal better than I was; but I believe that if I could have got work, and have had something to support me, I should have recruited my health better. I have been very poorly kept for these last six months, having been out of work. I have only half a crown a week allowed from the parish for my wife and myself.

199. When you were working the long hours, were there any people in the same employment, when you were a gigger, for instance, who were working the short hours?—Yes; some mills were working short hours in the same line; there were none in the same room that worked less hours than I did.

200. That did not depend on your choice, did it?—They would not let us have it of our own choice; we might either do it or leave it.

201. Suppose it was left to you, would you prefer a moderate degree of labour with lower wages, to high wages with this excessive labour?—I would rather have short hours and moderate wages, than great wages and long hours. I should be a great deal better.

202. Of course you do not mean to say that these long hours have continued in mills and factories when trade has slackened; has not the excessive labour somewhat abated when there is not such a brisk trade?—It has abated when there was not a brisk trade; when there was, it was again increased for those that were working, who were not willing to lose their employment, and so they submitted, or they must have gone travelling about the streets, and applied to the parish. But if the hours of work had not been then so much increased, more hands would have got employment. There would have been not so many over-worked, and not so many without any thing to do; it would have been share and share alike. . . .

206. When you were working these very long hours in a mill as a gigger and boiler, had you the liberty, if you wished to be away for a day or part of a

Chapter 6

Labor Old

and New:

The Impact of

the Industrial

Revolution

day, to send another person to do your work?—Yes; if we were poorly, we had liberty to send another person in our place.

207. If you wished to rest for half a day, you could send another man in your place?—I was once poorly, and I sent another workman, and they let me have the job again; now that I have been ill six months, they will not let me have the job again. . . .

217. Do you think you would be able to stand your work?—I should like to try; I cannot bear to go wandering about the streets. . . .

220. Is being a gigger harder than the others?—Yes, gigging is very hard work; the fleeces are so heavy and full of water, and you have to stand in this position [*describing it*] to support them and turn the fleece over; if you are not over strong it makes you rather deformed in your legs.

221. At what age do people generally begin gigging?—Some begin about 15, 16 or 17, and some lads begin when about 14.

222. At what age did your father die?—He was 60 when he died.

223. Have you seen the man lately who is doing your work at Mr. Brown's?—Yes.

224. Is he in good health?—I do not know; I must not say a thing that I do not know; it is a good while since I saw him.

225. Was your father a tall or a short man?—He stood about five feet seven.

226. And you are five feet?—Yes.

227. Have you any brothers or sisters?—Two brothers and a sister.

228. Do they work in the same trade?—I have a brother working now at the same trade; he was seventeen the 14th of last February.

229. Has he good health?—He had not over good health when I came from Leeds.

Source 10 from Sidney Pollard and Colin Holmes, editors, Documents in European Economic History, *vol. 2,* Industrial Power and National Rivalry *(New York: St. Martin's, 1972), pp. 322–323.*

10. Working Conditions of a Female Textile Worker in Germany, 1880s and 1890s

In the weaving sheds the girls work in an atmosphere which, on the third day of my work there, gave me bad lung catarrh; tiny flakes of the twisted wool fill the air, settle on dress and hair, and float into nose and mouth; the machines have to be swept clean every two hours; the dust is breathed in by the girls, since they are not allowed to open the windows. To this has to be added the terrible nerve-racking noise of the rattling machines so that no one can hear himself speak. No communication with one's neighbour is possible except by shouting on the top of one's voice. In consequence, all the girls have screeching, irritating voices: even when the shop has gone quiet, at the end of the working day, on the street, at home, they never converse quietly like other people, their conversation is a constant yelling, which produces the impression among outsiders that they are quarrelling.

It is truly a miracle that so many girls still look fresh and blooming, and that they still feel like singing at work, usually sentimental folk songs. . . .

Many girls work happily, particularly those weaving small carpets or curtains woven as one piece who can observe the building up of the pattern. They love their machines like loving a faithful dog; they polish them, and tie coloured ribbons, little pictures of saints and all sorts of gaudy tinsel given to them by their sweethearts at the summer fairs, to the crossbars.

The girls work hard, very hard, and quite a few told me how they collapsed with the exertion of the first four weeks of work, and how most of them suffer for months with irritations of the lung and throat until they get used to the dust. To this has to be added the poor, miserable food, the short periods of rest in rooms which don't deserve the name of "dwelling"—and yet the girls remain cheerful, healthy, lively and enterprising.

I have always watched this with admiration; I could not have stood this for long. I could not take anything in the morning beside coffee; only in the evening I hurried, totally exhausted, to my hotel, to swallow some nourishing food with great difficulty. . . .

No one would dream of stopping work and taking a rest even when suffering from violent headache or toothache, not even a quarter of an hour of being late was tolerated without a substantial fine at the end of the week. . . .

The work of the carpet weavers should not be underrated, it is anything but monotonous or repetitive. When working the complex Turkish patterns, the weaver has to catch the exact moment for changing the different coloured reels. She has to think and coordinate, calculate and pay attention and concentrate all her thoughts. This work requires far more mental activity and sense of responsibility than the crochet work and needlework done by hundreds of girls of society, year after year, in expectation of the shining knight who would one day come and rescue them.

Most factories start work at half past six, pause for breakfast from 8 to 8.30, dinner 12–1; at 4 there are 20–30 minutes for tea, and work goes on until 7. On Saturdays work ends at 5.30, in order to give time to the workers to clean the machines thoroughly and to oil them by 6; Mondays, work starts half an hour later probably because all the girls have a hangover from Sunday.

Chapter 6

Labor Old

and New:

The Impact of

the Industrial

Revolution

Source 11 from British Parliamentary Papers: Reports from Commissioners: Children's Employment (Mines), *vol. 17*, Appendix to the First Report of the Commissioners (Mines) *(London: William Clowes for Her Majesty's Stationery Office, 1842), pp. 39, 103, 107–108.*

11. Report on the Employment of Children in British Mines, 1841–1842

May 14, 1841.

No. 49. Mr. *Joseph Staley*, Managing Partner in Coal-works at Yate Common, in the parish of Yate (Two Pits), carried on under the firm of *Staley* and *Parkers*:

Employ from 30 to 35 hands; not more than five or six boys under 13; the two youngest are from eight to nine years old, who work with their father; perhaps three boys not more than 10 years of age; they assist in cutting and carting out the coal from a one-foot seam; no doorboys employed, because there is sufficient ventilation without being particular about closing them; the carters generally manage the doors as they pass; the boys earn from 6s. to 9s. per week when they get handy at cutting; have not more than three or four under 18; all over 15 are earning nearly men's wages—say 15s. per week; the men earn from 18s. to 20s.; considers two tons a fair day's work; wages paid in money every Saturday; the older boys receive their own; the boys, in carting out the coals from the *googs* [narrow inclined planes up which the coal is pulled by a chain and windlass], when short distances, draw by the *girdle* or *lugger, i.e.* a rope round the waist, with an iron hook depending in front, to which a chain, passing between the legs, is attached; if for longer distances, they use wheeled-carriages on a railway; no horses are employed under ground at present; the smaller boys do not tug more than 1 cwt.[39] at a time; the carts generally hold about 2 cwt. each; the thickest vein is two feet six inches, and is worked by the young men; the boys cart through a two feet six inches passageway; the young men have four feet, there being a bed of soft stuff above the coal, to cut away before they come to the roof; the shaft is 45 fathoms,[40] worked by a steam-engine, and strong-plaited rope; thinks rope decidedly safer than chain, as it gives more timely notice of any defect, by a strand or two giving way, whereas a link of iron is sometimes near breaking, a good while before it is discovered, and then separates on a sudden. Has had many years' experience in Staffordshire and Derbyshire, having been brought up a collier; say for 40 years; has been engaged 23 years in this coal-field; the work-

39. **cwt.:** hundredweight, i.e., 100 pounds.

40. **fathom:** a fathom equals 6 feet; the shaft of 45 fathoms thus extended 270 feet below the earth's surface.

ings are quiet dry; a pumping-engine of 60-horse power, is constantly at work when there is water; three or four days a-week is sufficient in summer; hours of work average eight to nine hours a-day; no night-work at present; always employ two sets when it occurs.

Some of the boys and young persons attend the Church Sunday-school, and others the Dissenting Sunday-school; most of them can read a little; look clean and tidy on Sundays; thinks there are no healthier boys in the country.

MESSRS. WILLSON, HOLMES, AND STOCKS, QUARRY-HOUSE PIT.

No.6. *William Jagger*, aged 11.   May 6:

I am a hurrier[41] for my father, Benjamin Jagger; have been in here four years and upwards; I come to work at seven o'clock, and go home at four, five, and six; I get breakfast afore I come down; I get my dinner down here, I get it about one o'clock; I don't know how long I am taking it; I get it as I can; I go to work directly after; I get currant-cake and buttered cake sometimes, never any meat; I get a bit of meat for supper when I go up. I went to day-school often; I comed to work about half a year; I go to Sunday-school now at church; I cannot read or write. I have got to hurry a corve 400 yards; I don't know what weight it is [$2\frac{1}{2}$ cwt.]; it runs upon rails; I push the corves; some of the boys push when there is no rail. I do not oft hurt my feet; I never met with an accident. The men serve me out sometimes—they wallop me; I don't know what for, except 'tis when I don't hurry fast enough; I like my work very well; I would rather hurry than set cards.

The mainway of this pit is 3 feet 6 inches high and 400 yards in length; seams 17 inches thick; gear in good order; shaft not walled up. At the moment of stepping out of the corve at the pit's bottom, a stone weighing from five to seven pounds fell in the water close by my feet from the unlined shaft near the top, or from the bank, a circumstance at once illustrative of the importance of protecting persons in their descent, by walling up the sides of the shaft, and thereby preventing loose measures from falling.

41. Mining vocabulary:
   hurrier: person who drew a wagon loaded with coal through mine tunnels to the shaft up which the load would be raised to the earth's surface.
   corve: small wagon for carrying coal or ore in a mine.
   getter: person who cut the coal from the seam. Young male hurriers, who often suffered stunted growth because of their excessive labor in moving coal as children, often graduated to the occupation of getter. Short stature was an asset in the restricted spaces of mine tunnels. The mining commission report from which this testimony is drawn notes that getters described themselves as "mashed up."

Chapter 6

Labor Old

and New:

The Impact of

the Industrial

Revolution

MR. JOSEPH STOCKS, BOOTH TOWN PIT, HALIFAX.

No. 26. *Patience Kershaw, aged 17.*   May 15:

My father has been dead about a year; my mother is living and has ten children, five lads and five lasses; the oldest is about thirty, the youngest is four; three lasses go to mill; all the lads are colliers, two getters and three hurriers; one lives at home and does nothing; mother does nought but look after home.

All my sisters have been hurriers, but three went to the mill, Alice went because her legs swelled from hurrying in cold water when she was hot. I never went to day-school; I go to Sunday-school, but I cannot read or write; I go to pit at five o'clock in the morning and come out at five in the evening; I get my breakfast of porridge and milk first; I take my dinner with me, a cake, and eat it as I go; I do not stop or rest any time for the purpose; I get nothing else until I get home, and then have potatoes and meat, not every day meat. I hurry in the clothes I have now got on, trousers and ragged jacket; the bald place upon my head is made by thrusting the corves; my legs have never swelled, but sisters' did when they went to mill; I hurry the corves a mile and more under ground and back; they weigh 3 cwt.; I hurry 11 a-day; I wear a belt and chain at the workings to get the corves out; the getters that I work for are *naked* except their caps; they pull off all their clothes; I see them at work when I go up; sometimes they beat me, if I am not quick enough, with their hands; they strike me upon my back; the boys take liberties with me sometimes, they pull me about; I am the only girl in the pit; there are about 20 boys and 15 men; all the men are naked; I would rather work in mill than in coal-pit.

This girl is an ignorant, filthy, ragged, and deplorable-looking object, and such a one as the uncivilized natives of the prairies would be shocked to look upon.[42]

QUESTIONS TO CONSIDER

Let us bring together your findings on the old and new labor of European working men and women. Your goal is to understand the changes affecting them in the late eighteenth and nineteenth centuries and how these changes came about. You may want to review the questions in Sources and Method before continuing your study of the evidence.

First, consider the length of time workers devoted to labor. Was the preindustrial workday much different in length from the early industrial age workday? Note especially the

---

42. This comment by the mine commissioners is amplified elsewhere in their report, where they note that Kershaw worked in a mine whose tunnels contained 3 or 4 inches of water at all times and that she moved her corve 1,800 to 2,000 yards on each trip.

findings of the Sadler Committee on the workdays of William Cooper, employed in industrial labor, and his father, a craftsman of the old school. Next, consider the number of workdays per year. Both old and new labor generally required a six-day workweek. But reexamine the holidays at Lille, remembering to punctuate the work year with a liberal number of "holy Mondays." On how many days per year did Vauban estimate his workers were employed in agriculture? Compare this quantity of work with that demanded of William Cooper. Like many nineteenth-century miners, this textile worker could probably have looked forward to holidays only on Christmas, Easter Monday, and the Monday after Pentecost. What other time off from work could he have expected? What effect did the Industrial Revolution have on the annual quantity of work for many laborers?

Those employed in both old and new styles of labor certainly worked hard. But the quality, pace, and discipline of their respective work situations certainly vary. Let us first consider the quality or nature of the old labor. What sort of variety characterized the work of agricultural workers like those described by Vauban and Mrs. Britton? Where was much of their work carried on? Where did most industrial-age labor take place? Why do you think Mrs. Britton testified that she preferred physically taxing agricultural work to factory labor? Why do you think William Cooper would have preferred the craftsman's work of his father to industrial labor? How do you think the necessity of

working with machinery would have shaped Cooper's opinion? What basic qualitative differences distinguished the old from the new labor?

Consider the pace of work. Who set the pace for guild members? Who set the pace in the putting-out system, the factory, and the mine? Notice the discipline of the industrial-era workplace, too. What sort of punishments and incentives prodded employees to work quickly? Considering conditions of preindustrial labor, why do you think the specific regulations in Source 8 were necessary? Recall the statement by Andrew Ure that opened this chapter. What were management's goals in imposing this kind of discipline?

Other changes in labor also accompanied the Industrial Revolution. What do the testimonies from the coal miners and the records of French and German textile workers tell us about the labor of women in the industrial age? Reexamine Mrs. Britton's testimony. In what setting did she labor after her marriage? What effect might female and child industrial labor have had on the family? What educational opportunities existed for boys and girls in industrial labor?

Finally, let us consider the health and safety of workers under both the old and the new systems. Which style of labor do you think Mrs. Britton and William Cooper would have considered more healthful? What hazards awaited textile workers like Cooper and miners like William Jagger and Patience Kershaw?

In other ways, old and new labor were not quite so different. Ideally,

Chapter 6
Labor Old
and New:
The Impact of
the Industrial
Revolution

any job should provide some security of continuing employment. How did the Prussian guild regulations seek to protect the markets and incomes of the textile workers? Did any other workers, old or new, benefit from such efforts to protect job security? Consider the problems of Mr. Britton and Vauban's workers, the effect of cycles of economic prosperity and depression on William Cooper and his fellow textile workers, and the experiences of putting-out workers described in the song. Did any of them have hopes of continuing employment opportunity?

Consider, too, the problems all these workers confronted when illness, injury, or economic conditions denied them employment. What recourse did Mrs. Britton and her family have in the face of poverty? Did William Cooper have any additional resources to draw on when illness struck? Were they sufficient for his needs?

Your comparative analysis of this chapter's sources provides one more insight into the industrialization of Western Europe. Economic historians speak of *proto-industrialization,* a process that paved the way for industrialization by organizing production into larger units employing traditional technologies. Industrial capitalists later combined experience in such organization with new machines to produce the Industrial Revolution. To understand this process, consider what the factory system meant: large units of production, controlled by capitalists prepared to organize labor and resources for a profit, and competition among producers who sought worldwide markets. What evidence of mod-

ern industrial organization do you find in the putting-out system? In what ways did it occupy a transitional role? Were its methods of production old or new? Was its organization of production old or new? How were its labor-management relations similar to those of the industrial age? Compare the discipline Andrew Ure advocated for industrial managers with the alleged goal of the clothiers in the popular song. What significance do you attach to the putting-out workers' complaint that they could no longer buy land? Would you say they were slipping into a work status like that of later industrial workers?

Now you are ready to provide detailed answers to the main questions of this chapter: What was the nature of the new labor? How did it evolve? How did it differ from the old labor? Be sure to base your responses on the evidence you have assessed.

EPILOGUE

A combination of developments served to improve conditions for later generations of workers. Early industrial workers won such improvements in their lot only slowly and with considerable struggle, however. The right to take part in government by voting was one common demand of nineteenth-century workers in a Europe that accorded a political voice, if at all, only to the wealthy and privileged. Workers in England began to win the vote only in 1867 after considerable agitation; a revolution in France in 1848 established the right of universal suffrage for men. Elsewhere the vote came more slowly, and Russian workers lacked voting rights until 1906.

In the more democratic Western European nations, a widened right to vote in the nineteenth century made political institutions more responsive to workers' needs. During that century legislation passed by several European parliaments sought to regulate working conditions for women and children, to establish minimum safety standards, and to begin to provide the accident, health, and old age insurance plans that protect modern workers. Real improvements, however, often lagged behind such legislation. Early wage, hour, and safety regulations ran counter to an important political philosophy of the nineteenth century, liberalism (see Chapter 7), which viewed such legislation as interference in freedom of management. Early regulations thus frequently lacked enough officials to enforce them by comprehensive factory inspections. If you refer to William Cooper's testimony, you will find him completely unaware of a parliamentary act to regulate work hours, eloquent proof of this early lack of enforcement. Governments were slow to create the machinery necessary to enforce these rules.

The nineteenth century also witnessed an often bitter struggle by workers to form their own organizations promoting their common welfare. Because unions and strikes, as we have seen, were illegal in many countries, the first worker organizations of the early nineteenth century often were self-help groups such as the one that aided William Cooper. Only after much struggle did governments in countries like England and France legalize labor unions and the right to strike.

The legalization of unions, however, allowed industrial workers to take collective action in strikes to win better wages and conditions. Early strikes often produced bloody conflict between labor on one side and management, sometimes backed by police or the army in the name of keeping order, on the other. The first major victory for a noncraft union, however, occurred in the London dockworkers' strike of 1889. Twentieth-century developments have improved the lot of workers in other ways, especially through increased leisure time realized in the forty-hour workweek and paid vacations.

Improvements in wages and working conditions, however, did not change the basic nature of modern factory labor. In the industrial workplace, the pace of work continued to be set by machines, granting little independence to the individual worker, who remained a human cog in the greater modern industrial machine. Though most workers adjusted to this kind of labor, manifestations of their discontent have not disappeared entirely. In 1968, as you will see in Chapter 14, millions of French workers went on strike and occupied their factories. One of their chief demands was for a concept they called *autogestion*, that is, some voice in the workplace decisions that governed their lives on the job.

Chapter 6
Labor Old
and New:
The Impact of
the Industrial
Revolution

Such demands by employees have not gone entirely unheeded by management. There have been efforts to reintroduce some worker input in the production process through such practices as quality circles, in which workers engaged in the same phases of production meet periodically to discuss their jobs and to make suggestions for improving the production process. Other experiments in such industries as automobile assembly have sought to involve individual workers in several phases of the production process as a way of mitigating the monotony of assembly-line work. Nevertheless, for the majority of Western workers today the basic nature of industrial employment, as symbolized by the production line, remains unchanged.

CHAPTER SEVEN

TWO PROGRAMS FOR
SOCIAL AND POLITICAL
CHANGE: LIBERALISM
AND SOCIALISM

THE PROBLEM

"Workingmen of all countries unite!" proclaimed Karl Marx and Friedrich Engels in *The Communist Manifesto* of 1848, urging working people to overthrow the capitalist system and end the working conditions of the early Industrial Revolution, which we explored in Chapter 6. Marx and Engels were partisans in a nineteenth-century ideological clash in which they and other proponents of socialism opposed liberalism, the dominant doctrine among the rising class of factory owners and managers. Nineteenth-century liberals and socialists differed greatly in their views on such issues as the definition of freedom and democracy, the role of government, and their visions of the future.

We must be careful in this chapter to understand liberalism in its nineteenth- and not its twentieth-century sense. For most twentieth-century Americans, *liberalism* describes an ideology that represents an activist role for government in assuring the basic needs of its citizens in a variety of areas, including civil rights, material wants, and health and safety protection. In the nineteenth century liberals sought to maximize the freedom of the individual from government control. Drawing on traditions restricting royal authority that dated back to medieval times, liberals saw in the French Revolution the essential victory they sought to win all over Europe. In destroying the Old Regime with its absolute monarchy and privilege for the aristocratic few, the Revolution had created a new political order based on individual freedom. Everywhere, liberals sought to draft constitutions that would limit royal authority and ensure basic individual rights. The citizen was to be safe from arbitrary arrest and was to enjoy freedom of speech, assembly, religion, and the press.

Chapter 7

Two Programs

for Social

and Political

Change:

Liberalism

and Socialism

For the early or classical liberals, individual freedom did not, however, mean political democracy, a voice for all in government. The constitutional arrangements created by liberals usually included some sort of property qualification to vote. Most liberals were members of the middle classes and believed that, to exercise the right to vote, a citizen had to have some stake in the existing social and economic order in the form of property. The majority lacked sufficient wealth to vote in all early-nineteenth-century countries under liberal rule. But one liberal French minister, François Guizot, noted that the poor possessed full freedom to increase their wealth so that they could acquire property and participate in political life! Extreme as this view may seem to us, it does express the liberal faith that peaceful political change was possible. The key for the success of such a system of government was the establishment of a society of laws protecting individual freedoms.

Liberal economic thought was also a doctrine of absolute freedom. Liberals opposed the guild and aristocratic privileges that had limited career opportunities in Old Regime Europe. Thus individual economic opportunity, embodied in the opening of all careers to citizens on the basis of their talents, not their titles, became the central liberal economic tenet. But liberals' faith in economic freedom had far greater implications.

Liberals believed that immutable natural laws, like supply and demand, regulated economic life. Government interference in economic life, they believed, not only violated these laws but individual freedom as well. Based in large part on the writings of such classical liberal economists as the Englishmen Adam Smith (1723–1790), Thomas Malthus (1766–1834), and David Ricardo (1772–1823), liberal economic thought defended the right of early industrial employers to be free of government regulation. Their doctrine was summed up in the French phrase *laissez faire* (literally, "leave it alone").

Socialists differed from liberals in seeing the French Revolution of 1789 as simply the first step in revamping Europe's old order. The Revolution had established individual freedom but not political democracy. More important for socialists, the Revolution had not brought social democracy. To achieve this goal, they advocated a more equitable distribution of society's wealth. Their message, as you might imagine, had considerable appeal to those workers employed in the mills, factories, and mines of the early Industrial Revolution whose lot we explored in Chapter 6.

Some early socialist thinkers expressed the view that economic equality could be realized by peaceful evolutionary change. Karl Marx applied the label "utopian" to those thinkers because of the impracticality, in his view, of their schemes. Charles Fourier (1771–1837) advocated a restructuring of society around essentially agricultural communities that represented an attempt to turn the clock back to a preindustrial economy. Louis Blanc (1811–1882) advocated state assistance in the creation of worker-owned units of production that was difficult to imagine in a Europe dominated by the liberal ideology of government noninterference in economic life. But some utopian socialists, notably Robert Owen (1771–1858), who created a model industrial town around his textile mills in New Lanark, Scotland, achieved real improvements for working people.

Utopian socialism did not transform society. Some of its ideas, however, did influence other socialist thinkers, including Karl Marx, who advocated a revolutionary transformation of society. Indeed, revolutionary socialism gained large numbers of working-class followers and by the middle and late nineteenth century threatened Western Europe's liberal political leaders with the possibility of a complete overhaul of society in the name of political and social democracy.

Nineteenth-century liberalism and socialism both produced important thinkers who analyzed the ills of their society and advanced not only plans for change but critiques of the opposing ideology. What visions of the future did liberals and socialists propose? How did they hope to realize their ideals? How did their ideologies differ? Your task in this chapter is to answer these questions by examining the ideas of two nineteenth-century political and social theorists.

SOURCES AND METHOD

Liberalism and socialism each had large numbers of eloquent proponents in the nineteenth century. This chapter presents you with samples of liberal and socialist thought in the nineteenth century drawn from the writings of but one advocate of each cause. Your sources in this chapter are the works of the liberal Alexis de Tocqueville and the revolutionary socialist Karl Marx. These two thinkers have been selected because they expressed strikingly different views on similar subjects; the historical development of the West, the nature of democracy, and the role of revolution. Tocqueville and Marx also analyzed the French Revolution of 1848, a topic you may wish to review in your textbook. Their contrasting views on the same issues will provide the basis for your answers to the general questions on liberalism and socialism.

In analyzing the works of Tocqueville and Marx, you must understand that these works were polemic in character—that is, they were all written to advocate the causes espoused by their authors. All such works may be expected to emphasize their authors' viewpoints and summarily to dismiss opposing points of view that may have considerable validity. Because each theorist was an eloquent advocate of his cause, some examination of their separate backgrounds and viewpoints is necessary to permit you to analyze their ideas fruitfully.

Alexis Charles Henri Clerel de Tocqueville was born in 1805, the son of an aristocratic father who hoped for the restoration of the French monarchy destroyed by the Revolution of 1789. When Napoleon's fall from power finally brought a restored monarchy, the Tocquevilles rose to positions of importance in govern-

Chapter 7

Two Programs

for Social

and Political

Change:

Liberalism

and Socialism

ment. Alexis de Tocqueville's talents gained early recognition with his appointment as a judge at the youthful age of twenty-one. It was not as a jurist, however, that Tocqueville gained fame but rather as a liberal political theorist and as an early student of what we would call today sociology and political science.

In 1831 Tocqueville and his longtime friend, Gustave de Beaumont, undertook a fact-finding tour in the United States to study that country's pioneering penitentiary system. For nine months Tocqueville and Beaumont traveled through the United States, observing prisons and much more. The fruit of their trip was a study of prisons written largely by Beaumont and Tocqueville's observations on American society and government, published as *Democracy in America* (1835–1840). Tocqueville's keen analysis of American society in the latter work gained him immediate international recognition, and he received an honor unusual for a person of his age: election to the French Academy in 1841.[1]

In 1839 Tocqueville had already won election to the French Chamber of Deputies, which permitted him an active role in French politics. He joined the opposition to the government of King Louis Philippe and rejected es-

pecially the monarchy's restriction of the right to vote to wealthy Frenchmen. As a deputy, Tocqueville wrote a report on slavery that contributed to its abolition in France's colonies. Further, in a speech to the Chamber of Deputies in January 1848 during a period of apparent political calm, his analysis of social conditions led him to predict the imminence of revolution. Indeed, it broke out less than four weeks later.

Despite his opposition to Louis Philippe, Tocqueville long had criticized revolution, perceiving a danger that individual liberty could be lost in revolutionary enthusiasm. Nevertheless, he gained election to the legislature of the new Second Republic created by the Revolution of 1848 and took part in the drafting of its constitution, arguing unsuccessfully against a directly elected president. He correctly foresaw the possibility that an ambitious demagogue could sway the people to gain election and threaten democracy. In December 1848, the victor in the presidential elections was Louis-Napoleon Bonaparte. This nephew of Emperor Napoleon I destroyed the republic in favor of an authoritarian empire, naming himself Emperor Napoleon III.[2] Tocqueville retired permanently from public life after Bonaparte's seizure of power,

1. **French Academy:** an association of scholars, writers, and intellectual leaders founded in 1635 to maintain the purity of the French language and establish standards of correct usage. The Academy has only forty members, called the "immortals," who vote to fill vacancies in their ranks caused by deaths of members. The dignity of such election is usually confined to persons of advanced years and long-proven merit.

2. **Emperor Napoleon III:** Bonapartists recognize the son of Emperor Napoleon I (ruled 1804–1814, 1815) as Napoleon II. But Napoleon II never actually ruled France. Aged three years when his father abdicated, he was taken to Vienna by his maternal grandfather, the Emperor of Austria, and spent his brief life there until his death in 1832.

unable to support the new, undemocratic regime.

Returning to writing, Tocqueville produced two more important works before his death from tuberculosis in 1859. The first was his *Recollections* of the Revolution of 1848 and the Second Republic, based on his experiences in Paris in 1848 and 1849; the second was a study of the French Revolution of 1789, *The Old Regime and the Revolution.* Both works demonstrate again Tocqueville's liberal ideology and political astuteness.

In reading the selections by Tocqueville, you should ascertain the nature of his liberal thought. In Source 1, what does Tocqueville identify as the main trend in historical development? What implications did this trend, which he found strong in America, have for Europe's existing class structure? What problems does Tocqueville in Source 2 find accompanying American democracy? What threatened the individual? What danger did centralized authority pose? In Source 3 Tocqueville treats revolution. Why does he see the danger of revolution diminishing with the advance of political democracy? Does he find revolution justified at times?

Sources 3 and 4 provide you with summations of Tocqueville's political thought and his view of the future. Under what sort of government had he spent his youth? What did it contribute to his political thought?

Born in Germany in 1818, thirteen years after Tocqueville, Karl Marx was the advocate of a very different political order, one of socialist revolution. The son of a successful attorney, Marx enjoyed an excellent education. He studied law first and then philosophy, a field in which he completed the doctoral degree that normally would have led to an academic career. Young Marx, however, was an advocate of political and economic democracy whose growing radicalism and atheism precluded such a career. When he turned instead to journalism, his ideas quickly offended the Prussian censors, who suppressed his newspaper.

Marx left Germany in 1843 for Paris, a city in which there was considerable discussion of utopian socialist ideas. Perhaps the greatest single event in Marx's two-year stay in Paris was his meeting with the young businessman, Friedrich Engels, with whom he was to enjoy a lifelong friendship. Engels shared Marx's socialist ideas, gave him intellectual support, and provided financial aid that allowed Marx to devote his life to writing.

French authorities expelled Marx for his radical political ideas in 1845. He moved to Brussels, Belgium, where he and Engels wrote *The Communist Manifesto,* an abstract declaration of war between the working class and their capitalist exploiters. Belgian authorities ultimately also expelled Marx. Back in Paris by March 1848, Marx, like Tocqueville, based his writings on some firsthand experience of the French Revolution of 1848. He also returned to Germany during 1848 before settling in England in 1849, where he spent the rest of his life.

Marx's poor command of spoken English and his illegible handwriting precluded his employment in

Chapter 7

Two Programs

for Social

and Political

Change:

Liberalism

and Socialism

white-collar jobs, and he and his family often lived in poverty when there were delays in Engels's generosity. In England Marx drew on his own excellent education, his knowledge of French socialist thought from his Paris days, and his daily research in the British Museum Library to refine his views on socialist revolution. He wrote studies of contemporary events, including *Class Struggles in France* and *The Eighteenth Brumaire of Louis Bonaparte,* which dealt with the French Revolution of 1848 and its aftermath. The final product of his labors was the first volume of *Capital* (1867), a work Engels completed after Marx's death in 1883.

Marx was not to witness the implementation of his ideals during his life. His chief attempt at revolutionary organization, the International Workingmen's Association or First International, founded in 1864, broke up as a result of ideological disputes in 1876. In those disputes the always irascible Marx found his viewpoints challenged by another revolutionary activist, Mikhail Bakunin (1814–1876). Marx, who prided himself on what he believed was the scientific certainty of his ideas, found Bakunin insufficiently "scientific" and ruptured socialist unity in securing the latter's expulsion from the association. Bakunin went on to become one of the founders of modern anarchism, a movement advocating the destruction of all institutions of modern society. Marx spent the few years remaining before his death in 1883 drained

and embittered by his struggle in the International and by family problems. He died believing that his ideas would have little impact. Nevertheless, his writings became the basis for the international socialist movement.

As you read the selections by Marx, you should answer a number of questions to aid you in formulating your responses to the central problems of this chapter. Marx, like Tocqueville, had a definite view of history. Examine Source 5, a selection from *The Communist Manifesto.* What basic event, according to Marx, has characterized and shaped all historical development? Why does Marx find the latest phase of history, modern middle-class ("bourgeois") capitalism, particularly oppressive? What is Marx's view of the free economy advocated by nineteenth-century liberals?

In Source 6 Marx deals with the French Revolution of 1848. That revolution, of course, failed to bring the working classes to power. Whom did it bring to power in France? In Source 7 we have Marx's statement of his ideals in government. Marx proclaims that he advocates democracy. How does that democracy differ from the kind of democracy acceptable to liberals like Tocqueville?

Now you are ready to read the selections with an eye to answering the main questions of this chapter: What were Tocqueville's and Marx's separate political visions? How did they hope to see their visions realized? How did these two thinkers and their liberal and socialist ideologies differ?

THE EVIDENCE

ALEXIS DE TOCQUEVILLE

Sources 1 and 2 from Alexis de Tocqueville, Democracy in America, *edited by J. P. Mayer and Max Lerner, translated by George Lawrence (New York: Harper & Row, 1965), pp. 3–5, 610–611, 613, 618; pp. 231–233, 665, 667–669.*

1. Tocqueville's View of History

No novelty in the United States struck me more vividly during my stay there than the equality of conditions. It was easy to see the immense influence of this basic fact on the whole course of society. It gives a particular turn to public opinion and a particular twist to the laws, new maxims to those who govern and particular habits to the governed.

I soon realized that the influence of this fact extends far beyond political mores and laws, exercising dominion over civil society as much as over the government; it creates opinions, gives birth to feelings, suggests customs, and modifies whatever it does not create.

So the more I studied American society, the more clearly I saw equality of conditions as the creative element from which each particular fact derived, and all my observations constantly returned to this nodal point.

Later, when I came to consider our own side of the Atlantic, I thought I could detect something analogous to what I had noticed in the New World. I saw an equality of conditions which, though it had not reached the extreme limits found in the United States, was daily drawing closer thereto; and that same democracy which prevailed over the societies of America seemed to me to be advancing rapidly toward power in Europe. . . .

A great democratic revolution is taking place in our midst; everybody sees it, but by no means everybody judges it in the same way. Some think it a new thing and, supposing it an accident, hope that they can still check it; others think it irresistible, because it seems to them the most continuous, ancient, and permanent tendency known to history. . . .

Running through the pages of our history, there is hardly an important event in the last seven hundred years which has not turned out to be advantageous for equality.

The Crusades and the English wars decimated the nobles and divided up their lands. Municipal institutions introduced democratic liberty into the heart of the feudal monarchy; the invention of firearms made villein and noble equal on the field of battle; printing offered equal resources to their minds; the post brought enlightenment to hovel and palace alike; Protestantism maintained that all men are equally able to find the path to heaven.

Chapter 7

Two Programs

for Social

and Political

Change:

Liberalism

and Socialism

America, once discovered, opened a thousand new roads to fortune and gave any obscure adventurer the chance of wealth and power.

If, beginning at the eleventh century, one takes stock of what was happening in France at fifty-year intervals, one finds each time that a double revolution has taken place in the state of society. The noble has gone down in the social scale, and the commoner gone up; as the one falls, the other rises. Each half century brings them closer, and soon they will touch.

And that is not something peculiar to France. Wherever one looks one finds the same revolution taking place throughout the Christian world.

WHY GREAT REVOLUTIONS
WILL BECOME RARE

When a people has lived for centuries under a system of castes and classes, it can only reach a democratic state of society through a long series of more or less painful transformations. These must involve violent efforts and many vicissitudes, in the course of which property, opinions, and power are all subject to swift changes.

Even when this great revolution has come to an end, the revolutionary habits created thereby and by the profound disturbances thereon ensuing will long endure.

As all this takes place just at the time when social conditions are being leveled, the conclusion has been drawn that there must be a hidden connection and secret link between equality itself and revolutions, so that neither can occur without the other.

On this point reason and experience seem agreed.

Among a people where ranks are more or less equal, there is no apparent connection between men to hold them firmly in place. None of them has any permanent right or power to give commands, and none is bound by his social condition to obey. Each man, having some education and some resources, can choose his own road and go along separately from all the rest.

The same causes which make the citizens independent of each other daily prompt new and restless longings and constantly goad them on.

It therefore seems natural to suppose that in a democratic society ideas, things, and men must eternally be changing shape and position and that ages of democracy must be times of swift and constant transformation.

But is this in fact so? Does equality of social conditions habitually and permanently drive men toward revolutions? Does it contain some disturbing principle which prevents society from settling down and inclines the citizens constantly to change their laws, principles, and mores? I do not think so. The subject is important, and I ask the reader to follow my argument closely.

Almost every revolution which has changed the shape of nations has been made to consolidate or destroy inequality. Disregarding the secondary causes which have had some effect on the great convulsions in the world, you will

[178]

almost always find that equality was at the heart of the matter. Either the poor were bent on snatching the property of the rich, or the rich were trying to hold the poor down. So, then, if you could establish a state of society in which each man had something to keep and little to snatch, you would have done much for the peace of the world. . . .

Such men are the natural enemies of violent commotion; their immobility keeps all above and below them quiet, and assures the stability of the body social.

I am not suggesting that they are themselves satisfied with their actual position or that they would feel any natural abhorrence toward a revolution if they could share the plunder without suffering the calamities; on the contrary, their eagerness to get rich is unparalleled, but their trouble is to know whom to despoil. The same social condition which prompts their longings restrain them within necessary limits. It gives men both greater freedom to change and less interest in doing so.

Not only do men in democracies feel no natural inclination for revolutions, but they are afraid of them.

Any revolution is more or less a threat to property. Most inhabitants of a democracy have property. And not only have they got property, but they live in the conditions in which men attach most value to property. . . .

Therefore the more widely personal property is distributed and increased and the greater the number of those enjoying it, the less is a nation inclined to revolution.

Moreover, whatever a man's calling and whatever type of property he owns, one characteristic is common to all.

No one is fully satisfied with his present fortune, and all are constantly trying a thousand various ways to improve it. Consider any individual at any period of his life, and you will always find him preoccupied with fresh plans to increase his comfort. Do not talk to him about the interests and rights of the human race; that little private business of his for the moment absorbs all his thoughts, and he hopes that public disturbances can be put off to some other time.

This not only prevents them from causing revolutions but also deters them from wanting them. Violent political passions have little hold on men whose whole thoughts are bent on the pursuit of well-being. Their excitement about small matters makes them calm about great ones. . . .

There are also other, and even stronger, reasons which prevent any great change in the doctrines of a democratic people coming about easily. I have already indicated them at the beginning of this book.

Whereas, in such a nation, the influence of individuals is weak and almost nonexistent, the power of the mass over each individual mind is very great. . . .

Whenever conditions are equal, public opinion brings immense weight to bear on every individual. It surrounds, directs, and oppresses him. The basic constitution of society has more to do with this than any political laws. The

Chapter 7
Two Programs
for Social
and Political
Change:
Liberalism
and Socialism

more alike men are, the weaker each feels in the face of all. Finding nothing that raises him above their level and distinguishes him, he loses his self-confidence when he comes into collision with them. Not only does he mistrust his own strength, but even comes to doubt his own judgment, and he is brought very near to recognizing that he must be wrong when the majority hold the opposite view. There is no need for the majority to compel him; it convinces him.

Therefore, however powers within a democracy are organized and weighted, it will always be very difficult for a man to believe what the mass rejects and to profess what it condemns.

This circumstance is wonderfully favorable to the stability of beliefs.

2. Tocqueville on the Problems of Democracy

TYRANNY OF THE MAJORITY

I regard it as an impious and detestable maxim that in matters of government the majority of a people has the right to do everything, and nevertheless I place the origin of all powers in the will of the majority. Am I in contradiction with myself?

There is one law which has been made, or at least adopted, not by the majority of this or that people, but by the majority of all men. That law is justice.

Justice therefore forms the boundary to each people's right.

A nation is like a jury entrusted to represent universal society and to apply the justice which is its law. Should the jury representing society have greater power than that very society whose laws it applies?

Consequently, when I refuse to obey an unjust law, I by no means deny the majority's right to give orders; I only appeal from the sovereignty of the people to the sovereignty of the human race. . . .

Omnipotence in itself seems a bad and dangerous thing. I think that its exercise is beyond man's strength, whoever he be, and that only God can be omnipotent without danger because His wisdom and justice are always equal to His power. So there is no power on earth in itself so worthy of respect or vested with such a sacred right that I would wish to let it act without control and dominate without obstacles. So when I see the right and capacity to do all given to any authority whatsoever, whether it be called people or king, democracy or aristocracy, and whether the scene of action is a monarchy or a republic, I say: the germ of tyranny is there, and I will go look for other laws under which to live.

My greatest complaint against democratic government as organized in the United States is not, as many Europeans make out, its weakness, but rather its irresistible strength. What I find most repulsive in America is not the extreme freedom reigning there but the shortage of guarantees against tyranny.

When a man or a party suffers an injustice in the United States, to whom can he turn? To public opinion? That is what forms the majority. To the legislative body? It represents the majority and obeys it blindly. To the executive power? It is appointed by the majority and serves as its passive instrument. To the police? They are nothing but the majority under arms. A jury? The jury is the majority vested with the right to pronounce judgment; even the judges in certain states are elected by the majority. So, however iniquitous or unreasonable the measure which hurts you, you must submit.[3]

But suppose you were to have a legislative body so composed that it represented the majority without being necessarily the slave of its passions, an executive power having a strength of its own, and a judicial power independent of the other two authorities; then you would still have a democratic government, but there would be hardly any remaining risk of tyranny.

WHAT SORT OF DESPOTISM DEMOCRATIC NATIONS HAVE TO FEAR

I noticed during my stay in the United States that a democratic state of society similar to that found there could lay itself peculiarly open to the establishment of a despotism. And on my return to Europe I saw how far most of our princes had made use of the ideas, feelings, and needs engendered by such a state of society to enlarge the sphere of their power. . . .

---

3. [Tocqueville's note:] At Baltimore during the War of 1812 there was a striking example of the excesses to which despotism of the majority may lead. At that time the war was very popular at Baltimore. A newspaper which came out in strong opposition to it aroused the indignation of the inhabitants. The people assembled, broke the presses, and attacked the house of the editors. An attempt was made to summon the militia, but it did not answer the appeal. Finally, to save the lives of these wretched men threatened by the fury of the public, they were taken to prison like criminals. This precaution was useless. During the night the people assembled again; the magistrates having failed to bring up the militia, the prison was broken open; one of the journalists was killed on the spot and the others left for dead; the guilty were brought before a jury and acquitted.

I once said to a Pennsylvanian: "Please explain to me why in a state founded by Quakers and renowned for its tolerance, freed Negroes are not allowed to use their rights as citizens? They pay taxes; is it not right that they should vote?"

"Do not insult us," he replied, "by supposing that our legislators would commit an act of such gross injustice and intolerance."

"So, with you, Negroes do have the right to vote?"

"Certainly."

"Then how was it that at the electoral college this morning I did not see a single one of them in the meeting?"

"That is not the fault of the law," said the American. "It is true that Negroes have the right to be present at elections, but they voluntarily abstain from appearing."

"That is extraordinarily modest of them."

"Oh! It is not that they are reluctant to go there, but they are afraid they may be maltreated. With us it sometimes happens that the law lacks force when the majority does not support it. Now, the majority is filled with the strongest prejudices against Negroes, and the magistrates do not feel strong enough to guarantee the rights granted to them by the lawmakers."

"What! The majority, privileged to make the law, wishes also to have the privilege of disobeying the law?"

Chapter 7

Two Programs

for Social

and Political

Change:

Liberalism

and Socialism

Our contemporaries are ever a prey to two conflicting passions: they feel the need of guidance, and they long to stay free. Unable to wipe out these two contradictory instincts, they try to satisfy them both together. Their imagination conceives a government which is unitary, protective, and all-powerful, but elected by the people. Centralization is combined with the sovereignty of the people. That gives them a chance to relax. They console themselves for being under schoolmasters by thinking that they have chosen them themselves. Each individual lets them put the collar on, for he sees that it is not a person, or a class of persons, but society itself which holds the end of the chain.

Under this system the citizens quit their state of dependence just long enough to choose their masters and then fall back into it.

A great many people nowadays very easily fall in with this brand of compromise between administrative despotism and the sovereignty of the people. They think they have done enough to guarantee personal freedom when it is to the government of the state that they have handed it over. That is not good enough for me. I am much less interested in the question who my master is than in the fact of obedience. . . .

Subjection in petty affairs is manifest daily and touches all citizens indiscriminately. It never drives men to despair, but continually thwarts them and leads them to give up using their free will. It slowly stifles their spirits and enervates their souls, whereas obedience demanded only occasionally in matters of great moment brings servitude into play only from time to time, and its weight falls only on certain people. It does little good to summon those very citizens who have been made so dependent on the central power to choose the representatives of that power from time to time. However important, this brief and occasional exercise of free will will not prevent them from gradually losing the faculty of thinking, feeling, and acting for themselves, so that they will slowly fall below the level of humanity.

I must add that they will soon become incapable of using the one great privilege left to them. Those democratic peoples which have introduced freedom into the sphere of politics, while allowing despotism to grow in the administrative sphere, have been led into the strangest paradoxes. For the conduct of small affairs, where plain common sense is enough, they hold that the citizens are not up to the job. But they give these citizens immense prerogatives where the government of the whole state is concerned. They are turned alternatively into the playthings of the sovereign and into his masters, being either greater than kings or less than men. When they have tried all the different systems of election without finding one to suit them, they look surprised and go on seeking for another, as if the ills they see did not belong much more to the constitution of the country itself than to that of the electoral body.

It really is difficult to imagine how people who have entirely given up managing their own affairs could make a wise choice of those who are to do that for them. One should never expect a liberal, energetic, and wise government to originate in the votes of a people of servants.

Source 3 from Alexis de Tocqueville, Democracy in America, *edited by J. P. Mayer and Max Lerner, translated by George Lawrence (New York: Harper & Row, 1965), pp. 674–675 (first part); and J. P. Mayer, editor, Alexander Teixeira De Mattos, translator,* The Recollections of Alexis de Tocqueville *(New York: Meridian, 1959), pp. 63, 68–71 (second part).*

3. Tocqueville on Revolution

[The general danger of revolution]

There are some habits, some ideas, and some vices which are peculiar to a state of revolution and which any prolonged revolution cannot fail to engender and spread, whatever may be in other respects its character, object, and field of action.

When in a brief space of time any nation has repeatedly changed its leaders, opinions, and laws, the men of that nation will in the end acquire a taste for change and grow accustomed to see all changes quickly brought about by the use of force. Then they will naturally conceive a scorn for those formalities of whose impotence they have been daily witnesses, and they will be impatient to tolerate the sway of rules which they have so often seen infringed.

As ordinary ideas of equity and morality are no longer enough to explain and justify all the innovations daily introduced by revolution, men fall back on the principle of social utility, political necessity is turned into a dogma, and men lose all scruples about freely sacrificing particular interests and trampling private rights beneath their feet in order more quickly to attain the public aim envisaged.

Such habits and ideas, which I call revolutionary since all revolutions give rise to them, are seen as much in aristocracies as among democratic peoples. But in the former case they are often less powerful and always less permanent, because there they come up against habits, ideas, faults, and eccentricities which are opposed to them. They therefore vanish of their own accord when the revolution is at an end and the nation recovers its former political ways. However, that is not always the case in democratic countries, for in them there is always a danger that revolutionary instincts will mellow and assume more regular shape without entirely disappearing, but will gradually be transformed into mores of government and administrative habits.

Hence, I know of no country in which revolutions are more dangerous than in a democracy, because apart from the accidental and ephemeral ills which they are ever bound to entail, there is always a danger of their becoming permanent, and one may almost say, eternal.

I think that resistance is sometimes justified and that rebellion can be legitimate. I cannot therefore lay it down as an absolute rule that men living in times of democracy should never make a revolution. But I think that they, more than others, have reason to hesitate before they embark on such an enterprise and that it is far better to put up with many inconveniences in their present state than to turn to so dangerous a remedy.

Chapter 7

Two Programs

for Social

and Political

Change:

Liberalism

and Socialism

[*Tocqueville on the Revolution of 1848
in France*]

*My Explanation of the 24th of February and My Thoughts as to Its
Effects upon the Future*[4]

And so the Monarchy of July[5] was fallen, fallen without a struggle, and before rather than beneath the blows of the victors, who were as astonished at their triumph as were the vanquished at their defeat. . . .

I had spent the best days of my youth amid a society which seemed to increase in greatness and prosperity as it increased in liberty; I had conceived the idea of a balanced, regulated liberty, held in check by religion, custom and law; the attractions of this liberty had touched me; it had become the passion of my life; I felt that I could never be consoled for its loss, and that I must renounce all hope of its recovery.

I had gained too much experience of men to be able to content myself with empty words; I knew that, if one great revolution is able to establish liberty in a country, a number of succeeding revolutions make all regular liberty impossible for very many years.

I could not yet know what would issue from this last revolution, but I was already convinced that it could give birth to nothing that would satisfy me; and I foresaw that, whatever might be the lot reserved for our posterity, our own fate was to drag on our lives miserably amid alternate reactions of licence and oppression. . . .

I spent the rest of the day with Ampère, who was my colleague at the Institute,[6] and one of my best friends. He came to discover what had become of me in the affray, and to ask himself to dinner. I wished at first to relieve myself by making him share my vexation. . . .

I saw that he not only did not enter into my view, but that he was disposed to take quite an opposite one. Seeing this, I was suddenly impelled to turn against Ampère all the feelings of indignation, grief and anger that had been accumulating in my heart since the morning; and I spoke to him with a violence of language which I have often since recalled with a certain shame, and which none but a friendship so sincere as his could have excused. I remember saying to him, *inter alia.*[7]

---

4. On Thursday, February 24, 1848, King Louis Philippe abdicated the throne in the face of the Paris revolution and fled the capital for England.

5. **Monarchy of July:** the term often used for the regime of King Louis Philippe because that government came to power in July 1830.

6. **Institute:** Institut de France, the cultural institution including the French Academy, of which Tocqueville was a member. **Jean-Jacques Ampère:** (1800–1864), a philologist and professor of French literature.

7. **inter alia:** Latin, among other things.

"You understand nothing of what is happening; you are judging like a poet or a Paris cockney.[8] You call this the triumph of liberty, when it is its final defeat. I tell you that the people which you so artlessly admire has just succeeded in proving that it is unfit and unworthy to live a life of freedom. Show me what experience has taught it! Where are the new virtues it has gained, the old vices it has laid aside? No, I tell you, it is always the same, as impatient, as thoughtless, as contemptuous of law and order, as easily led and as cowardly in the presence of danger as its fathers were before it. Time has altered it in no way, and has left it as frivolous in serious matters as it used to be in trifles."

After much vociferation we both ended by appealing to the future, that enlightened and upright judge who always, alas! arrives too late.

Source 4 from Roger Boesche, editor, James Toupin and Roger Boesche, translators, Alexis de Tocqueville: Selected Letters on Politics and Society *(Berkeley: University of California Press, 1985), pp. 112–113.*

4. Tocqueville's Ideals of Government (letter to Eugène Stoffels)[9]

I do not think that in France there is a man who is less revolutionary than I, nor one who has a more profound hatred for what is called the revolutionary spirit (a spirit which, parenthetically, is very easily combined with the love of an absolute government). What am I then? And what do I want? Let us distinguish, in order to understand each other better, between the end and the means. What is the end? What I want is not a republic, but a hereditary monarchy. I would even prefer it to be legitimate rather than elected like the one we have, because it would be stronger, especially externally. What I want is a central government energetic in its own sphere of action. Energy from the central government is even more necessary among a democratic people in whom the social force is more diffused than in an aristocracy. Besides our situation in Europe lays down as imperative law for us in what should be a thing of choice. But I wish that this central power had a clearly delineated sphere, that it were involved with what is a necessary part of its functions and not with everything in general, and that it were forever subordinated, in its tendency, to public opinion and to the legislative power that represents this public opinion. I believe that the central power can be invested with very great

8. **Cockney:** generally a person of the lower classes born in London's East End. In this context it refers to someone from that same class in Paris.
9. **Eugène Stoffels (1805–1852):** an official in Metz, France and a friend of Tocqueville from their days together in secondary school.

Chapter 7
Two Programs
for Social
and Political
Change:
Liberalism
and Socialism

prerogatives, can be energetic and powerful in its sphere, and that at the same time provincial liberties can be well developed. I think that a government of this kind can exist, and that at the same time the majority of the nation itself can be involved with its own affairs, that political life can be spread almost everywhere, the direct or indirect exercise of political rights can be quite extensive. I wish that the general principles of government were liberal, that the largest possible part were left to the action of individuals, to personal initiative. I believe that all these things are compatible; even more, I am profoundly convinced that there will never be order and tranquility except when they are successfully combined.

As for the means: with all those who admit that we must make our way gradually toward this goal, I am very much in accord. I am the first to admit that it is necessary to proceed slowly, with precaution, with legality. My conviction is that our current institutions are sufficient for reaching the result I have in view. Far, then, from wanting people to violate the laws, I profess an almost superstitious respect for the laws. But I wish that the laws would tend little and gradually toward the goal I have just indicated, instead of making powerless and dangerous efforts to turn back. I wish that the government would itself prepare mores and practices so that people would do without it in many cases in which its intervention is still necessary or invoked without necessity. I wish that citizens were introduced into public life to the extent that they are believed capable of being useful in it, instead of seeking to keep them away from it at all costs. I wish finally that people knew where they wanted to go, and that they advanced toward it prudently instead of proceeding aimlessly as they have been doing almost constantly for twenty years.

KARL MARX

Source 5 from Karl Marx and Friedrich Engels, The Communist Manifesto, *translated by Samuel Moore (New York: Penguin, 1977), pp. 79–83, 85–92, 95–96.*

5. Marx's View of History

1
BOURGEOIS AND PROLETARIANS[10]

The history of all hitherto existing society is the history of class struggles.

Freeman and slave, patrician and plebeian, lord and serf, guild-master[11] and journeyman, in a word, oppressor and oppressed, stood in constant op-

---

10. **bourgeois, proletarian:** "By bourgeoisie is meant the class of modern Capitalist, owners of the means of social production and employers of wage labour. By proletariat, the class of modern wage-labourers who, having no means of production of their own, are reduced to selling their labour power in order to live" (note by Engels to the English edition, 1888).

11. **guild-master:** "that is, a full member of a guild, a master within, not a head of a guild" (note by Engels to the English edition, 1888).

position to one another, carried on an uninterrupted, now hidden, now open fight, a fight that each time ended, either in a revolutionary reconstitution of society at large, or in the common ruin of the contending classes.

In the earlier epochs of history, we find almost everywhere a complicated arrangement of society into various orders, a manifold gradation of social rank. In ancient Rome we have patricians, knights, plebeians, slaves; in the Middle Ages, feudal lords, vassals, guild-masters, journeymen, apprentices, serfs; in almost all of these classes, again, subordinate gradations.

The modern bourgeois society that has sprouted from the ruins of feudal society has not done away with class antagonisms. It has but established new classes, new conditions of oppression, new forms of struggle in place of the old ones.

Our epoch, the epoch of the bourgeoisie, possesses, however, this distinctive feature: it has simplified the class antagonisms. Society as a whole is more and more splitting up into two great hostile camps, into two great classes directly facing each other: Bourgeoisie and Proletariat.

From the serfs of the Middle Ages sprang the chartered burghers of the earliest towns. From these burgesses the first elements of the bourgeoisie were developed.

The discovery of America, the rounding of the Cape, opened up fresh ground for the rising bourgeoisie. The East-Indian and Chinese markets, the colonization of America, trade with the colonies, the increase in the means of exchange and in commodities generally, gave to commerce, to navigation, to industry, an impulse never before known, and thereby, to the revolutionary element in the tottering feudal society, a rapid development.

The feudal system of industry, under which industrial production was monopolized by closed guilds, now no longer sufficed for the growing wants of the new markets. The manufacturing system took its place. The guild-masters were pushed on one side by the manufacturing middle class; division of labour between the different corporate guilds vanished in the face of division of labour in each single workshop.

Meantime the markets kept ever growing, the demand ever rising. Even manufacture no longer sufficed. Thereupon, steam and machinery revolutionized industrial production. The place of manufacture was taken by the giant, Modern Industry, the place of the industrial middle class, by industrial millionaires, the leaders of whole industrial armies, the modern bourgeois.

Modern industry has established the world market, for which the discovery of America paved the way. This market has given an immense development to commerce, to navigation, to communication by land. This development has, in its turn, reacted on the extension of industry; and in proportion as industry, commerce, navigation, railways extended, in the same proportion the bourgeoisie developed, increased its capital, and pushed into the background every class handed down from the Middle Ages.

Chapter 7

Two Programs
for Social
and Political
Change:
Liberalism
and Socialism

We see, therefore, how the modern bourgeoisie is itself the product of a long course of development, of a series of revolutions in the modes of production and of exchange.

Each step in the development of the bourgeoisie was accompanied by a corresponding political advance of that class. An oppressed class under the sway of the feudal nobility, an armed and self-governing association in the medieval commune;[12] here independent urban republic (as in Italy and Germany), there taxable "third estate" of the monarchy (as in France), afterwards, in the period of manufacture proper, serving either the semi-feudal or the absolute monarchy as a counterpoise against the nobility, and, in fact, corner-stone of the great monarchies in general, the bourgeoisie has at last, since the establishment of Modern Industry and of the world market, conquered for itself, in the modern representative State, exclusive political sway. The executive of the modern State is but a committee for managing the common affairs of the whole bourgeoisie.

The bourgeoisie, historically, has played a most revolutionary part.

The bourgeoisie, wherever it has got the upper hand, has put an end to all feudal, patriarchal, idyllic relations. It has pitilessly torn asunder the motley feudal ties that bound man to his "natural superiors," and has left remaining no other nexus between man and man than naked self-interest, than callous "cash payment." It has drowned the most heavenly ecstasies of religious fervour, of chivalrous enthusiasm, of philistine sentimentalism, in the icy water of egotistical calculation. It has resolved personal worth into exchange value, and in place of the numberless indefeasible chartered freedoms, has set up that single, unconscionable freedom—Free Trade. In one word, for exploitation, veiled by religious and political illusions, it has substituted naked, shameless, direct, brutal exploitation.

The bourgeoisie has stripped of its halo every occupation hitherto honoured and looked up to with reverent awe. It has converted the physician, the lawyer, the priest, the poet, the man of science, into its paid wage-labourers.

The bourgeoisie has torn away from the family its sentimental veil, and has reduced the family relation to a mere money relation. . . .

The bourgeoisie cannot exist without constantly revolutionizing the instruments of production, and thereby the relations of production, and with them the whole relations of society. Conservation of the old modes of production in unaltered form, was, on the contrary, the first condition of existence for all earlier industrial classes. Constant revolutionizing of production, uninterrupted disturbance of all social conditions, everlasting uncertainty and agita-

12. **commune:** "the name taken, in France, by the nascent towns even before they had conquered from their feudal lords and masters local self-government and political rights as the 'Third Estate.' Generally speaking, for the economical development of the bourgeoisie, England is here taken as the typical country; for its political development, France" (note by Engels to the English edition, 1888). "This was the name given their urban communities by the townsmen of Italy and France, after they had purchased or wrested their initial rights of self-government from their feudal lords" (note by Engels to the German edition, 1890).

tion distinguish the bourgeois epoch from all earlier ones. All fixed, fast-frozen relations, with their train of ancient and venerable prejudices and opinions are swept away, all new-formed ones become antiquated before they can ossify. All that is solid melts into air, all that is holy is profaned, and man is at last compelled to face with sober senses, his real conditions of life, and his relations with his kind.

The need of a constantly expanding market for its products chases the bourgeoisie over the whole surface of the globe. It must nestle everywhere, settle everywhere, establish connexions everywhere. . . .

Modern bourgeois society with its relations of production, of exchange and of property, a society that has conjured up such gigantic means of production and of exchange, is like the sorcerer, who is no longer able to control the powers of the nether world whom he has called up by his spells. For many a decade past the history of industry and commerce is but the history of the revolt of modern productive forces against modern conditions of production, against the property relations that are the conditions for the existence of the bourgeoisie and of its rule. It is enough to mention the commercial crises that by their periodical return put on its trial, each time more threateningly, the existence of the entire bourgeois society. In these crises a great part not only of the existing products, but also of the previously created productive forces, are periodically destroyed. In these crises there breaks out an epidemic that, in all earlier epochs, would have seemed an absurdity—the epidemic of over-production. . . .

And how does the bourgeoisie get over these crises? On the one hand by enforced destruction of a mass of productive forces; on the other, by the conquest of new markets, and by the more thorough exploitation of the old ones. That is to say, by paving the way for more extensive and more destructive crises, and by diminishing the means whereby crises are prevented.

The weapons with which the bourgeoisie felled feudalism to the ground are now turned against the bourgeoisie itself.

But not only has the bourgeoisie forged the weapons that bring death to itself; it has also called into existence the men who are to wield those weapons—the modern working class—the proletarians.

In proportion as the bourgeoisie, i.e., capital, is developed, in the same proportion is the proletariat, the modern working class, developed—a class of labourers, who live only so long as they find work, and who find work only so long as their labour increases capital. These labourers, who must sell themselves piecemeal, are a commodity, like every other article of commerce, and are consequently exposed to all the vicissitudes of competition, to all the fluctuations of the market.

Owing to the extensive use of machinery and to division of labour, the work of the proletarians has lost all individual character, and, consequently, all charm for the workman. He becomes an appendage of the machine, and it is only the most simple, most monotonous, and most easily acquired knack, that

Chapter 7

Two Programs

for Social

and Political

Change:

Liberalism

and Socialism

is required of him. Hence, the cost of production of a workman is restricted, almost entirely, to the means of subsistence that he requires for his maintenance, and for the propagation of his race. . . .

Modern industry has converted the little workshop of the patriarchal master into the great factory of the industrial capitalist. Masses of labourers, crowded into the factory, are organized like soldiers. As privates of the industrial army they are placed under the command of a perfect hierarchy of officers and sergeants. Not only are they slaves of the bourgeois class, and of the bourgeois State; they are daily and hourly enslaved by the machine, by the overlooker, and, above all, by the individual bourgeois manufacturer himself. The more openly this despotism proclaims gain be its end and aim, the more petty, the more hateful and the more embittering it is. . . .

The proletariat goes through various stages of development. With its birth begins its struggle with the bourgeoisie. At first the contest is carried on by individual labourers, then by the work-people of a factory, then by the operatives of one trade, in one locality, against the individual bourgeois who directly exploits them. They direct their attacks not against the bourgeois conditions of production, but against the instruments of production themselves; they destroy imported wares that compete with their labour, they smash to pieces machinery, they set factories ablaze, they seek to restore by force the vanished status of the workman of the Middle Ages.

At this stage the labourers still form an incoherent mass scattered over the whole country, and broken up by their mutual competition. If anywhere they unite to form more compact bodies, this is not yet the consequence of their own active union, but of the union of the bourgeoisie, which class, in order to attain its own political ends, is compelled to set the whole proletariat in motion, and is moreover yet, for a time, able to do so. At this stage, therefore, the proletarians do not fight their enemies, but the enemies of their enemies, the remnants of absolute monarchy, the landowners, the non-industrial bourgeois, the petty bourgeoisie. Thus the whole historical movement is concentrated in the hands of the bourgeoisie; every victory so obtained is a victory for the bourgeoisie.

But with the development of industry the proletariat not only increases in number; it becomes concentrated in greater masses, its strength grows, and it feels that strength more. The various interests and conditions of life within the ranks of the proletariat are more and more equalized, in proportion as machinery obliterates all distinctions of labour, and nearly everywhere reduces wages to the same low level. The growing competition among the bourgeois, and the resulting commercial crises, make the wages of the workers ever more fluctuating. The unceasing improvement of machinery, ever more rapidly developing, makes their livelihood more and more precarious; the collisions between individual workmen and individual bourgeois take more and more the character of collisions between two classes. Thereupon the workers begin to form combinations (Trades Unions) against the bourgeois; they club together in order to keep up the rate of wages; they found permanent associations in order to make provision beforehand for these occasional revolts. Here and there the contest breaks out into riots.

Now and then the workers are victorious, but only for a time. The real fruit of their battles lies, not in the immediate result, but in the ever-expanding union of the workers. This union is helped on by the improved means of communication that are created by modern industry and that place the workers of different localities in contact with one another. It was just this contact that was needed to centralize the numerous local struggles, all of the same character, into one national struggle between classes. But every class struggle is a political struggle. And that union, to attain which the burghers of the Middle Ages, with their miserable highways, required centuries, the modern proletarians, thanks to railways, achieve in a few years. . . .

Of all the classes that stand face to face with the bourgeoisie today, the proletariat alone is a really revolutionary class. The other classes decay and finally disappear in the face of modern industry; the proletariat is its special and essential product.

The lower middle class, the small manufacturer, the shopkeeper, the artisan, the peasant, all these fight against the bourgeoisie, to save from extinction their existence as fractions of the middle class. They are therefore not revolutionary, but conservative. Nay more, they are reactionary, for they try to roll back the wheel of history. . . .

In the conditions of the proletariat, those of old society at large are already virtually swamped. The proletarian is without property; his relation to his wife and children has no longer anything in common with the bourgeois family relations; modern industrial labour, modern subjection to capital, the same in England as in France, in America as in Germany, has stripped him of every trace of national character. Law, morality, religion, are to him so many bourgeois prejudices, behind which lurk in ambush just as many bourgeois interests.

All the preceding classes that got the upper hand sought to fortify their already acquired status by subjecting society at large to their conditions of appropriation. The proletarians cannot become masters of the productive forces of society, except by abolishing their own previous mode of appropriation, and thereby also every other previous mode of appropriation. They have nothing of their own to secure and to fortify; their mission is to destroy all previous securities for, and insurances of, individual property.

All previous historical movements were movements of minorities, or in the interest of minorities. The proletarian movement is the self-conscious, independent movement of the immense majority, in the interest of the immense majority. The proletariat, the lowest stratum of our present society, cannot stir, cannot raise itself up, without the whole superincumbent strata of official society being sprung into the air.

Chapter 7

Two Programs

for Social

and Political

Change:

Liberalism

and Socialism

2
PROLETARIANS AND COMMUNISTS

In what relation do the Communists stand to the proletarians as a whole?

The Communists do not form a separate party opposed to other working-class parties.

They have no interests separate and apart from those of the proletariat as a whole.

They do not set up any sectarian principles of their own, by which to shape and mould the proletarian movement.

The Communists are distinguished from the other working-class parties by this only: 1. In the national struggles of the proletarians of the different countries, they point out and bring to the front the common interests of the entire proletariat, independently of all nationality. 2. In the various stages of development which the struggle of the working class against the bourgeoisie has to pass through, they always and everywhere represent the interests of the movement as a whole.

The Communists, therefore, are on the one hand, practically, the most advanced and resolute section of the working-class parties of every country, that section which pushes forward all others; on the other hand, theoretically, they have over the great mass of the proletariat the advantage of clearly understanding the line of march, the conditions, and the ultimate general results of the proletarian movement.

The immediate aim of the Communists is the same as that of all the other proletarian parties: formation of the proletariat into a class, overthrow of the bourgeois supremacy, conquest of political power by the proletariat.

The theoretical conclusions of the Communists are in no way based on ideas or principles that have been invented, or discovered, by this or that would-be universal reformer.

They merely express, in general terms, actual relations springing from an existing class struggle, from a historical movement going on under our very eyes. The abolition of existing property relations is not at all a distinctive feature of Communism.

All property relations in the past have continually been subject to historical change consequent upon the change in historical conditions.

The French Revolution, for example, abolished feudal property in favour of bourgeois property.

The distinguishing feature of Communism is not the abolition of property generally, but the abolition of bourgeois property. But modern bourgeois private property is the final and most complete expression of the system of producing and appropriating products, that is based on class antagonisms, on the exploitation of the many by the few.

In this sense, the theory of the Communists may be summed up in the single sentence: Abolition of private property.

Source 6 from Karl Marx, The Class Struggles in France (1848–1850), *edited by C. P. Dutt (New York: International Publishers, 1964), pp. 33–34, 39–40, 50–52, 55, 56, 58–59.*

6. Marx on the Revolution of 1848 in Paris

1
FROM FEBRUARY TO JUNE 1848

With the exception of a few short chapters, every important part of the annals of the revolution from 1848 to 1849 carries the heading: Defeat of the revolution!

But what succumbed in these defeats was not the revolution. It was the pre-revolutionary traditional appendages, results of social relationships, which had not yet come to the point of sharp class antagonisms—persons, illusions, conceptions, projects, from which the revolutionary party before the February Revolution was not free, from which it could be freed, not by the victory of February, but only by a series of defeats.

In a word: revolutionary advance made headway not by its immediate tragi-comic achievements, but on the contrary by the creation of a powerful, united counter-revolution, by the creation of an opponent, by fighting whom the party of revolt first ripened into a real revolutionary party.

To prove this is the task of the following pages.

I. THE DEFEAT OF JUNE 1848

After the July Revolution, when the Liberal banker, Laffitte, led his godfather, the Duke of Orleans, in triumph to the Hôtel de Ville,[13] he let fall the words: "From now on the bankers will rule." Laffitte had betrayed the secret of the revolution. . . .

It was not the French bourgeoisie that ruled under Louis Philippe, but a fraction of it, bankers, Stock Exchange kings, railway kings, owners of coal and iron works and forests, a section of landed proprietors that rallied around them—the so-called finance aristocracy. It sat on the throne, it dictated laws in the Chambers, it conferred political posts from cabinet portfolios to the tobacco bureau.

The real industrial bourgeoisie formed part of the official opposition, *i.e.*, it was represented only as a minority in the Chambers. . . .

The petty bourgeoisie of all degrees, and the peasantry also, were completely excluded from political power. Finally, in the official opposition or

---

13. **Hôtel de Ville:** City Hall. The Duke of Orleans emerged from the July Revolution as King Louis Philippe.

Chapter 7
Two Programs
for Social
and Political
Change:
Liberalism
and Socialism

entirely outside the *pays légal*,[14] there were the ideological representatives and spokesmen of the above classes, their savants, lawyers, doctors, etc., in a word: their so-called talents. . . .

The Provisional Government which emerged from the February barricades, necessarily mirrored in its composition the different parties which shared in the victory.[15] It could not be anything but a compromise between the different classes which together had overturned the July throne, but whose interests were mutually antagonistic. A large majority of its members consisted of representatives of the bourgeoisie. . . . The working class had only two representatives, Louis Blanc and Albert. . . .

Up to noon on February 25, the republic had not yet been proclaimed; on the other hand, the whole of the Ministries had already been divided among the bourgeois elements of the Provisional Government and among the generals, bankers and lawyers of the *National*. But the workers were this time determined not to put up with any swindling like that of July 1830. They were ready to take up the fight anew and to enforce the republic by force of arms. With this message, Raspail betook himself to the Hôtel de Ville. In the name of the Parisian proletariat he commanded the Provisional Government to proclaim the republic; if this order of the people were not fulfilled within two hours, he would return at the head of 200,000 men. The bodies of the fallen were scarcely cold, the barricades were not yet cleared away, the workers not yet disarmed, and the only force which could be opposed to them was the National Guard. Under these circumstances the prudent state doubts and juristic scruples of conscience of the Provisional Government suddenly vanished. The interval of two hours had not expired before all the walls of Paris were resplendent with the tremendous historical words:

> *République française! Liberté, Egalité, Fraternité!*[16] . . .

The proletariat, by dictating the republic to the Provisional Government and through the Provisional Government to the whole of France, stepped into the foreground forthwith as an independent party, but at the same time challenged the whole of bourgeois France to enter the lists against it. What it won

14. **pays légal:** literally, "legal country." Here Marx refers to the fact that the monarchy established by the July Revolution created a very limited right to vote. One had to possess a substantial amount of property to qualify for the right to vote, with the result that only 170,000 men, out of a population of about 30,000,000, qualified to vote for the Chamber of Deputies in the 1830s.

15. In his work, *The Eighteenth of Brumaire of Louis Bonaparte* (New York: International Publishers, 1935), p. 101, Marx referred to the participation of a broad spectrum of social groups in the February Revolution as the "Universal brotherhood swindle." This means that, in his view, the lower classes were seduced into revolutionary action by bourgeois promises of democracy unfilled in the postrevolutionary government.

16. **Republique française: Liberté, Egalité, Fraternité:** "The French Republic: Liberty, Equality, Fraternity," the motto of the Revolution of 1789.

was the terrain for the fight for its revolutionary emancipation, but in no way this emancipation itself! . . .

A hundred thousand workers thrown on the streets through the crisis and the revolution were enrolled by the Minister Marie in so-called National *Ateliers*![17] Under this grand name was hidden nothing but the employment of the workers on tedious, monotonous, unproductive earthworks at a wage of 23 sous.[18] English *workhouses* in the open—that is what these National *Ateliers* were. . . .

All the discontent, all the ill humour of the petty bourgeois was simultaneously directed against these National *Ateliers*, the common target. With real fury they reckoned up the sums that the proletarian loafers swallowed, while their own situation became daily more unbearable. A state pension for sham labour, that is socialism! they growled to themselves. They sought the basis of their misery in the National *Ateliers*, the declarations of the Luxembourg,[19] the marches of the workers through Paris. And no one was more fantastic about the alleged machinations of the Communists than the petty bourgeoisie who hovered hopelessly on the brink of bankruptcy.[20] . . .

In the National Assembly all France sat in judgment on the Paris proletariat. It broke immediately with the social illusions of the February Revolution; it roundly proclaimed the bourgeois republic, nothing but the bourgeois republic. It at once excluded the representatives of the proletariat, Louis Blanc and Albert, from the Executive Commission appointed by it; it threw out the proposal of a special Labour Ministry,[21] and received with stormy applause the statement of the Minister Trélat: "The question is merely one of bringing labour back to its old conditions."

17. **Atelier:** workshop. The National Ateliers were government-funded projects to provide work to the unemployed.

18. **23 sous:** The sou was a French coin worth 5 centimes (100 centimes to 1 franc). Thus Marx cites a wage of a little over 1 **franc** per day for the labor. Initially, wages in the workshops were 2 francs per day for laborers and 1 franc per day for those unemployed for whom labor could not be found. Even 2 francs per day was less than the usual wage for skilled artisans like tailors and shoemakers.

19. **The Luxembourg:** the revolutionary government established a commission to study labor problems; chaired by the socialist Louis Blanc and composed of representatives of various trades, it was headquartered in the Luxembourg Palace. The commission secured the government's enactment of a ten-hour workday in Paris and a twelve-hour workday in the provinces. This reform would have reduced most workers' hours of labor had it been enforced by government supervision.

20. One of the causes of the Revolution of 1848 was a general European economic crisis in 1846–1848 that had its origins in agricultural problems. Potato harvests were disastrously deficient in Ireland and other countries in 1845–1848 because of a blight. Weather factors conspired to reduce wheat harvests in these same years, creating rising food prices and general distress in the economies of most European countries.

21. The National Assembly, elected by universal manhood suffrage in April 1848, had a moderate to conservative majority: of the 900 members, about 500 were moderate republicans and 300 were monarchists. In such a chamber, proposals for a Ministry of Labor and for a guaranteed right to work proposed by Louis Blanc gained little support.

Chapter 7

Two Programs

for Social

and Political

Change:

Liberalism

and Socialism

But all this was not enough. The February republic was won by the workers with the passive support of the bourgeoisie. The proletarians regarded themselves, and rightly, as the victors of February, and they made the proud claims of victors. They had to be vanquished on the streets, they had to be shown that they were worsted as soon as they fought, not with the bourgeoisie, but against the bourgeoisie. Just as the February republic, with its socialist concessions, required a battle of the proletariat, united with the bourgeoisie, against monarchy, so a second battle was necessary in order to sever the republic from the socialist concessions, in order to officially work out the bourgeois republic as dominant. The bourgeoisie had to refute the demands of the proletariat with arms in its hands. And the real birthplace of the bourgeois republic is not the February victory; it is the June defeat. . . .

The Executive Commission began by making entry into the National *Ateliers* more difficult, by turning the day wage into a piece wage, by banishing workers not born in Paris to Sologne, ostensibly for the construction of earthworks. These earthworks were only a rhetorical formula with which to gloss over their expulsion, as the workers, returning disillusioned, announced to their comrades. Finally, on June 21, a decree appeared in the *Moniteur*,[22] which ordered the forcible expulsion of all unmarried workers from the National *Ateliers,* or their enrolment in the army.

The workers were left no choice: they had to starve or start to fight. They answered on June 22 with the tremendous insurrection in which the first great battle was joined between the two classes that split modern society. It was a fight for the preservation or annihilation of the bourgeois order. The veil that shrouded the republic was torn to pieces.

It is well known how the workers, with unexampled bravery and talent, without chiefs, without a common plan, without means and, for the most part, lacking weapons, held in check for five days the army, the Mobile Guard, the Parisian National Guard, and the National Guard that streamed in from the provinces. It is well known how the bourgeoisie compensated itself for the mortal anguish it underwent by unheard of brutality, and massacred over 3,000 prisoners.[23] . . .

By making its burial place the birth place of the bourgeois republic, the proletariat compelled the latter to come out forthwith in its pure form as the state whose admitted object is to perpetuate the rule of capital, the slavery of labour. With constant regard to the scarred, irreconcilable, unconquerable enemy—unconquerable because its existence is the condition of its own life—bourgeois rule, freed from all fetters, was bound to turn immediately into

22. **Moniteur:** a journal that published parliamentary debate and government decrees.

23. Marx does not wildly exaggerate the losses here. Casualties in the actual fighting and in the retribution following it were high.

bourgeois terrorism. With the proletariat removed for the time being from the stage and bourgeois dictatorship recognised officially, the middle sections, in the mass, had more and more to side with the proletariat as their position became more unbearable and their antagonism to the bourgeoisie became more acute. Just as earlier in its upsurge, so now they had to find in its defeat the cause of their misery. . . .

Only through the defeat of June, therefore, were all conditions created under which France can seize the initiative of the European revolution. Only after baptism in the blood of the June insurgents did the tricolour[24] become the flag of the European revolution—the red flag.

And we cry: *The revolution is dead!—Long live the revolution!*

Source 7 from Karl Marx and Friedrich Engels, The Communist Manifesto, *translated by Samuel Moore (New York: Penguin, 1977), pp. 104–105.*

7. Marx's Ideals of Government and Economy

We have seen above, that the first step in the revolution by the working class, is to raise the proletariat to the position of ruling class, to win the battle of democracy.

The proletariat will use its political supremacy to wrest, by degrees, all capital from the bourgeoisie, to centralize all instruments of production in the hands of the State, i.e., of the proletariat organized as the ruling class; and to increase the total of productive forces as rapidly as possible.

Of course, in the beginning, this cannot be effected except by means of despotic inroads on the rights of property, and on the conditions of bourgeois production; by means of measures, therefore, which appear economically insufficient and untenable, but which, in the course of the movement, outstrip themselves, necessitate further inroads upon the old social order, and are unavoidable as a means of entirely revolutionizing the mode of production.

These measures will of course be different in different countries.

Nevertheless, in the most advanced countries, the following will be pretty generally applicable:

1. Abolition of property in land and application of all rents of land to public purposes.

2. A heavy progressive or graduated income tax.

3. Abolition of all right of inheritance.

4. Confiscation of the property of all emigrants and rebels.

24. **tricolor:** the three-colored flag, composed of vertical stripes of blue, white, and red, adopted in the 1789 Revolution and today the flag of France.

Chapter 7

Two Programs

for Social

and Political

Change:

Liberalism

and Socialism

5. Centralization of credit in the hands of the State, by means of a national bank with State capital and an exclusive monopoly.

6. Centralization of the means of communication and transport in the hands of the State.

7. Extension of factories and instruments of production owned by the State; the bringing into cultivation of wastelands, and the improvement of the soil generally in accordance with a common plan.

8. Equal liability of all to labour. Establishment of industrial armies, especially for agriculture.

9. Combination of agriculture with manufacturing industries; gradual abolition of the distinction between town and country, by a more equable distribution of the population over the country.

10. Free education for all children in public schools. Abolition of children's factory labour in its present form. Combination of education with industrial production, &c., &c.

When, in the course of development, class distinctions have disappeared, and all production has been concentrated in the whole nation, the public power will lose its political character. Political power, properly so called, is merely the organized power of one class for oppressing another. If the proletariat during its contest with the bourgeoisie is compelled, by the force of circumstances, to organize itself as a class, if, by means of a revolution, it makes itself the ruling class, and, as such, sweeps away by force the old conditions of production, then it will, along with these conditions, have swept away the conditions for the existence of class antagonisms and of classes generally, and will thereby have abolished its own supremacy as a class.

In place of the old bourgeois society, with its classes and class antagonisms, we shall have an association, in which the free development of each is the condition for the free development of all.

QUESTIONS TO CONSIDER

Tocqueville and Marx pose different responses to many of the same issues in the selections presented in this chapter. Your basic task in answering the main questions of this chapter is to compare their ideas.

Central to the thought of both men is a certain vision of historical evolution. Indeed, Marx called himself a "scientific socialist" because, in his view, he had discovered the im-

mutable course of historical development. What was this historical process for Marx? What patterns of history did Tocqueville identify? As you continue your study of modern Western history in this course, consider which of these thinkers' ideas seem most adequately to have predicted the political and economic development of the West.

Both Marx and Tocqueville address the problem of revolution in the selections that you have read. First consider Tocqueville. What threats to democracy did he see emerging in the West? Why did he believe that revolution was not likely to be a threat to democracy? What dangers, according to Tocqueville, did revolution pose when it did erupt? Do Tocqueville's liberal principles admit any circumstances under which society should resort to revolution as a means of change? Recall Tocqueville's attitude toward the government of King Louis Philippe in Source 3. Why did Tocqueville oppose the Revolution of 1848 despite this view?

Let us now analyze Marx's ideas on revolution. Examine the historical role for revolution that Marx believed he has found. Why does Marx see the middle class, those who owned the factories and embraced liberal ideas, as revolutionary? In what ways, according to Marx, was capitalism sowing the seeds of its destruction? What class would challenge the factory owners in revolution? What vision of the future did that class have, according to Marx? Did they want the political democracy Tocqueville was prepared to accept or a broader reorganization of society? How did Marx and Tocqueville differ in their views of the desirability of revolution?

Both authors also wrote on the same revolution, the French uprising of 1848, providing us a further opportunity to contrast their views. As your study of the 1848 revolutions no doubt has demonstrated, it is impossible to consider the uprising of that year a success. Whether revolutionaries' goals were nationalist or liberal, the revolutions ended everywhere in defeat. This was certainly the case in France, where the conflict of June 1848 between the government of the Second Republic and the Parisian unemployed created the political climate for the election of Louis-Napoleon Bonaparte.

How did each author view the revolution of 1848? What guiding emotion do you detect in Tocqueville's *Recollections* of February 24, 1848? What was its source? In formulating your answer, consult the selection in which Tocqueville discusses general aspects of revolution and expresses his ideals in government. What is Marx's view of the failure of the June 1848 revolt? Why was the victory that emerged in 1848 an essential step for Marx toward the final revolution?

Finally, let us compare the political and economic ideals advocated by the liberal Tocqueville and the socialist Marx. Your task here is made more challenging by the assertion of both these political thinkers that they advocated democracy. To understand the differences between them, review their writings to determine how each defined "democracy." Is Tocqueville's conception of democracy expressed primarily in terms of political participation? Is there any room in his thought for social democracy, that is, a more egalitarian distribution of society's wealth? How does Tocqueville characterize his political thought in Source 4? Recall France's history of recurring revolution. Why might he accept a monarch in Europe and an elected head of government in America?

Sources 5 through 7 express especially clearly Marx's democratic philosophy. Did Marx believe in political democracy? How is he concerned

Chapter 7

Two Programs

for Social

and Political

Change:

Liberalism

and Socialism

with social democracy? Who would control property, credit, and the means of production in his ideal society? What answers does Marx have to such abuses of industrialization as child labor? What impact would his system have on the lives of its citizens?

Finally, consider the two thinkers' views on the role of government. What role does Tocqueville assign to the government in the lives of its citizens? How does that view mark him as a nineteenth-century liberal? What sort of postrevolutionary government does Marx envision? How does it differ from Tocqueville's ideal? Are there areas where Marx and Tocqueville might agree?

With answers to these fairly specific questions in mind, you are now ready to answer the general questions presented earlier in this chapter: What visions of the future did liberals and socialists propose? How did they hope to realize their ideals? How did their ideologies differ?

EPILOGUE

The selections in this chapter present two contrasting nineteenth-century visions of Western society. Most of what you have read appeared around the middle of the nineteenth century, much of it in the midst of the West's last general outbreak of revolution in 1848. Because both authors wrote about that event and had a definite view of revolution, perhaps it is appropriate to examine briefly how their predictions fared after 1848.

The events of 1848 shook Tocqueville's faith in the growth of democracy founded on limited government and increasing equality of property as well as in political stability and evolutionary change based on respect for the rule of law. Indeed, he wrote to his friend Eugène Stoffels of events in France with considerable despair in 1850:

> What is clear to me is that for sixty years we have fooled ourselves by believing that we could see the end of revolution. The revolution was thought to have finished at 18 *brumaire,* the same was thought in 1814; I thought myself in 1830 that it could well be at an end . . . I was wrong. It is clear today . . . not only that we have not seen the end of the immense revolution which started before our time, but that today's child will probably not see it.[25]

Tocqueville died in 1859 questioning his vision of the future, and Marx lived on until 1883, also disillusioned, as we have noted, by his own apparent failure decisively to affect the socialist movement. Events after their deaths would have surprised both men. Political change in much of Europe proved to be far more evolution-

25. Tocqueville to Eugène Stoffels, quoted in Jack Lively, *The Social and Political Thought of Alexis de Tocqueville* (Oxford: Clarendon Press, 1962), p. 211. The radical leaders of the French Revolution of 1789–1799 had sought to break with the traditional Western calendar and its Christian observances. Thus they created a new calendar devoid of Christian holidays and with renamed months. The date 18 *brumaire* was the day in 1799 that marked Napoleon's seizure of power in France; 1814 was the year of the restoration of the French monarchy after Napoleon's fall; 1830, of course, was the year King Louis Philippe came to power.

ary than revolutionary in the years after 1848, thanks to several developments predicted neither by Tocqueville nor by Marx.

The liberal ideology represented by Tocqueville became less and less a narrow doctrine of individual freedom. Later liberals, like the Englishman John Stuart Mill (1806–1873), emphasized that economic liberty reached its limits when it allowed employers to abuse their employees with the low wages and poor working conditions we examined in Chapter 6. Consequently they supported legislation to rectify many of the worst abuses of industrial employment. Such liberals also believed in political democracy and won extended franchises in countries like England and Italy.

Communist revolution occasionally did break out as Marx had predicted. But he utterly misjudged the historical developments that produced such revolutions. Writing from the vantage point of the early Industrial Revolution, Marx assumed that working-class misery would only intensify and produce communist revolution in the most industrialized nations. Instead, Marx's revolution broke out in places where he never would have expected it. Peasant populations in countries either on the threshold of industrialization, like Russia in 1917, or not yet industrialized, like China and Vietnam in the 1940s and 1950s, have been the chief adherents of communist revolution. Marx had believed peasants incapable of such ideological mobilization, counting them a politically inert "sack of

potatoes." And, contrary to Marx's prediction that communism would constitute the final stage of human development, such regimes, like that in the former Soviet Union, were breaking down by the early 1990s.

In much of the industrialized West the widened right to vote, in fact, engendered a new kind of evolutionary socialism quite distinct from Marx's revolutionary socialism. The German Eduard Bernstein (1850–1932) was among the first to recognize that working-class voting rights eliminated the need for Marx's class warfare and revolution. Armed with the vote, Bernstein emphasized, workers could elect parliaments favoring their needs and peacefully win a better life through legislation. The need for revolution was at an end.

In the twentieth century, socialist parties committed to political democracy, and sometimes allied with liberals, have been instrumental in bringing greater social equality for working people in much of Western Europe. In modern England, France, Italy, Germany, and other nations, legislation improving working conditions and wages as well as establishing the protection of health and unemployment insurance and old age pensions stands as monument to the widened vote created by liberals and the use of that vote by democratic socialists. The consequent improvement in working-class conditions ultimately resulted in the decline in broad popular appeal experienced by Marxian revolutionary socialists in much of the West.

CHAPTER EIGHT

VIENNA AND PARIS,

1850–1930:

THE DEVELOPMENT OF

THE MODERN CITY

The nineteenth century was a period of great change in Europe. Just as the Industrial Revolution transformed the Continent's mode of production and, as we have seen in Chapter 6, its patterns of work, it also greatly accelerated the urbanization of the West. Individual cities grew rapidly as they drew large numbers of immigrants from rural areas searching for industrial jobs, and society was transformed as urban rather than rural life became the lifestyle of the majority. By the second half of the nineteenth century, over half of the population of England and Wales, the original centers of the Industrial Revolution, dwelt in cities, and Germany and other countries reached that level of urban concentration of population within several decades.

Unfortunately for the residents of Europe's growing nineteenth-century cities, living conditions in these centers often were very difficult. This is how one French author described Paris in 1848:

If you contemplate from the summit of Montmartre or any other hill in the neighborhood, the congestion of houses piled up at every point of a vast horizon, what do you observe? Above, a sky that is always overcast, even on the finest day. Clouds of smoke, like a vast floating curtain, hide it from view. A forest of chimneys with black or yellowish chimneypots renders the sight singularly monotonous. . . . Looking at it, one is tempted to wonder whether this is Paris; and, seized with sudden fear, one is reluctant to venture into this vast maze, in which a million beings jostle each other, where the air, vitiated by unhealthy effluvia, rising in a poisonous cloud, almost obscures the sun. Most of the streets in this wonderful Paris are nothing but filthy alleys forever damp from a reeking flood. Hemmed in between two rows of tall houses, they never get the sun; it reaches only the tops of the chimneys dominating them. To catch a glimpse of the sky you have to look straight up above your head. A haggard and sickly crowd perpetually throngs these streets, their feet in the gutter, their noses in infection, their eyes outraged by the most repulsive garbage at every street corner. The best-paid workmen live in these streets. There are alleys, too, in which two cannot walk abreast, sewers of ordure and mud, in which the stunted dwellers daily inhale death. These are the streets of old Paris, still intact.[1]

Rapid population growth overwhelmed the capacity of early-nineteenth-century municipal governments to provide for the needs of their new citizens. The problems described in the quotation were almost universal. Many cities in Continental Europe remained hemmed in by medieval or early modern fortifications designed to protect much smaller populations from military attack. Even without this obstacle to expansion, however, urban spread was limited by the almost complete absence of cheap, public transportation. People had to live close to their jobs because they walked to them, and essentially medieval residential patterns persisted in which craftsmen and merchants dwelled behind or above their places of business and poorer persons occupied the upper floors of the same buildings.

1. H. Lecouturier, *Paris incompatible avec la République, plan d'un nouveau Paris où les révolutions seront impossibles* (Paris: 1848), quoted in Louis Chevalier, *Laboring Classes and Dangerous Classes in Paris during the First Half of the Nineteenth Century,* trans. by Frank Jellinek (Princeton: Princeton University Press, 1981), p. 155. Montmartre is the highest point in Paris.

The growing urban population within the old walls led to an increasingly dense pattern of residence. Landlords added additional floors to existing buildings, cut up once spacious apartments into many smaller living units, erected inferior dwellings in courtyards and other open spaces, and rented basement and attic rooms. Sunlight and fresh air disappeared as building heights increased along narrow, medieval streets. Basements formed particularly unhealthy dwellings; they often leaked and seldom received sunlight or ventilation. With little but musty, stale air available to them, it was a custom of basement residents to get an occasional "airing" out of doors.

Simple movement of people was a problem in the streets of such cities. Lacking sidewalks, pedestrians competed with horse-drawn vehicles for the opportunity to move through cramped streets wet with household waste water and soiled by horse droppings. A trip across a major city, which today would require a matter of minutes by subway, consumed considerably more time in the early nineteenth century. Many cities were almost strangled by such transportation difficulties within their old walls.

Rapid population growth in the limited spaces of many cities produced serious health and social problems. Extremely primitive methods for disposal of human wastes often polluted water supplies, and in the first decades of the nineteenth century, sewers in Paris and other cities emptied into the very rivers that were the main sources of municipal water. Under such conditions, disease spread

Chapter 8

Vienna

and Paris,

1850–1930:

The Development

of the Modern

City

rapidly, and life could be short. Epidemics of cholera, a disease often transmitted by polluted drinking water, struck many cities in the nineteenth century, and 20,000 persons died in one outbreak of the disease in Paris in 1832. Indeed, well into the nineteenth century, most cities retained an age-old urban demographic pattern in which death rates among their citizens exceeded birth rates. The limited urban population growth that occurred prior to about 1850 was almost entirely the result of immigration to the cities from rural areas.

A rapidly rising crime rate was probably the most vexing of the social consequences of urban growth. Urban life often plunged unskilled immigrants of rural origin into deep poverty. Though crime sometimes stemmed from poverty, certain features of urban life encouraged it. The social controls of rural village life largely were absent in the cities, where the anonymity of the individual in the urban mass facilitated lawbreaking. Police resources for controlling such behavior were limited or nonexistent during the first half of the nineteenth century, too. The pioneering effort at urban crime control, the London Metropolitan Police Force, was created only in 1829, and was imitated widely only after 1850.

In fact, only after about 1850 can we find Western society systematically attempting to solve the real problems of urban life. Collectively these responses transformed city life and produced our modern pattern of urban life. Several nineteenth-century developments made possible this important transformation of city

life. We should note first that the power of central governments grew everywhere. The state's ability to command resources in the form of taxes financed many improvements. Its growing bureaucracy also provided the personnel to undertake the first modern urban planning. And its need to maintain order in growing cities demanded improved police services and better street lighting to inhibit crime, wider streets to allow for troop movements in case of urban rebellion, and better sanitation to protect the health of its citizens and taxpayers.

The Industrial Revolution played a major role in the urban transformation, too. It created new technologies whose application to city life would improve conditions, and it produced wealth, increasingly shared by more and more persons, which would finance private projects of urban building and improvement. Industrialization also sustained a new consumer-oriented economy characterized by the mass distribution of the products of the new factories to large urban markets. Modern science played a part in urban improvements, too. The work of Louis Pasteur (1822–1895) and other scientists made possible purer water and food to protect public health.

The combination of these nineteenth-century developments would transform the Western city by 1930. Your problem in this chapter is to examine the physical expressions and social consequences of this transformation in two major cities: Paris, France, and Vienna, Austria. How were these cities physically reshaped in response to early-nineteenth-century problems? How did this physical transformation affect the lifestyle of urban dwellers?

SOURCES AND METHOD

In order to analyze this chapter's sources, you will require some specific information on nineteenth-century Paris and Vienna. In the 1870s Paris and Vienna respectively were Europe's second and third largest cities; only the population of Greater London was larger. As the political capitals of their nations and as major cultural, commercial, and industrial centers, they experienced rapid growth in much of our period from 1850 to 1930. The population of Paris grew from 547,000 persons in 1800 to 2,714,000 persons a century later, a growth rate of 496 percent. For the same period, Vienna's population grew even more rapidly: from 247,000 persons to 1,675,000 persons, for a growth rate of 678 percent.[2] With such rapid growth, Paris and Vienna experienced the full range of urban problems we examined earlier in this chapter. The two cities' responses to these problems typify those of most Continental European cities in our period. But to analyze our evidence on these changes, some background on Paris and Vienna is necessary.

Unlike English cities, which early abandoned their defensive walls because of the protection from attack afforded all of England by its surrounding seas, most Continental European cities retained their walls into the nineteenth century because of the probability of military assault. Thus Paris traditionally had been confined by fortifications against attackers and by barriers erected to enforce the collection of taxes on goods entering the city. Within those confines the city described at the beginning of this chapter developed. Only in the 1850s did major improvements of the central city begin. But these improvements in Paris were centrally planned because the national government administered the French capital through its Prefect of the Seine Department.[3] Change in Paris could come about rapidly as a result, since the financial resources of the national government could be brought to the process, and the prestige of that government aided private investment schemes for civic improvements like new housing.

From 1852 to 1870 Emperor Napoleon III governed France. He personally drafted detailed plans for the improvement of Paris and entrusted these to his energetic prefect of the Seine, Baron Georges Eugène Haussmann (1809–1891). Haussmann's projects combined government initiative

2. B. R. Mitchell, *European Historical Statistics 1750–1970*, abridged edition (New York: Columbia University Press, 1978), pp. 12–15. This is the source for all population statistics through 1970 in this chapter.

3. In 1791 the Legislative Assembly divided France into eighty-three departments for administrative purposes. Paris was the Department of the Seine until twentieth-century reforms subdivided the metropolitan area into a number of new departments in the interest of efficiency. Napoleon I instituted the office of the prefect as the central government's administrator in each department.

Chapter 8
Vienna
and Paris,
1850–1930:
The Development
of the Modern
City

and money with private capital, and his results were sweeping and rapid. He cut new boulevards through the warren of narrow, medieval streets in the city's center and began the construction of peripheral boulevards along the line of the tax wall of 1784 that once enclosed the city. The new boulevards were wide. Indeed, some of them were almost 400 feet in width. Such street-building efforts eased movement of goods and persons through the city and improved health standards by opening the center of Paris to more light and fresh air. At the same time the city's physical appearance changed dramatically as private investors erected new apartment buildings along Haussmann's broad boulevards.

Matters of public health also occupied Haussmann. The government greatly expanded the Paris sewer system and built aqueducts to bring clean drinking water into the city. Haussmann's work also added parks to the cityscape of Paris where residents could enjoy recreational opportunities and unrestricted sunlight and fresh air. Former royal hunting preserves at the western and eastern borders of the city, the Bois de Boulogne (the Boulogne Wood) and the Bois de Vincennes (the Vincennes Wood), became great new public parks, and Haussmann added major new inner-city parks with the Buttes-Chaumont, Monceau, and Montsouris parks.

Urban improvements continued in Paris after Haussmann. More major new thoroughfares opened, including the Avenue de l'Opéra in 1877, and public transportation soon flowed on the new boulevards. Paris had had slow-moving and rather expensive horse-drawn buses called omnibuses since 1828. But the new boulevards permitted the city to lead Europe in the introduction of horse-drawn tramcars running much more quickly on steel tracks. By the end of the nineteenth century electrification of trams provided increasingly efficient and inexpensive public transportation. And in 1900 the city opened a subway system, the Métropolitain, which many urban transportation specialists regard as the world's most comprehensive public transportation system.

The twentieth century also witnessed greater attention to solving the housing problems of working people in Paris. The apartment buildings constructed along Haussmann's boulevards, built at private expense, were intended for a market that would provide real estate investors a good return on their capital. These new buildings housed the middle- and upper-class Parisians who, like their counterparts throughout Continental Europe, preferred the city to the suburbs, which already drew affluent English and Americans out of their cities. These new buildings and Haussmann's boulevards, however, destroyed much old working-class housing, and Paris's near suburbs, like those of many European cities, became zones of cheap worker housing as well as home to industries too large for the city itself.

Much of this housing for workers was of poor quality, however, because building expenses had to be kept low to keep rents affordable. Also to keep prices low, such housing was densely built; in Paris, working-class suburbs often had greater densities of population than the central city. Worse still, there was an increasing shortage of low-cost housing in the early twentieth century in Paris. Rent controls made necessary by World War I (1914–1918) continued until after World War II (1939–1945) and made private construction of low-cost housing unprofitable. As a result, French national and city governments cooperated to construct low-cost housing called HBM (Habitation de Bon Marché, that is, inexpensive housing). Built as multistoried apartment buildings, some of this new housing arose in the zone occupied by Paris's most recent city wall, which was built in 1841–1845 and which the government razed after World War I.

Vienna, like Paris, sustained a rapid and planned transformation from a congested, walled city to a modern metropolis in the nineteenth century. As in Paris, the initiative came from the central government. In December 1857, Emperor Francis Joseph ordered the destruction of Vienna's fortifications and the implementation of a plan for his capital's expansion into the area of the old walls and the open spaces, called the *glacis*, surrounding them.[4] Just as Haussmann had promoted the construction of peripheral boulevards along the old tax wall of Paris, Viennese planners mapped out a broad system of boulevards, collectively called the *Ringstrasse*, along the old defense lines. As in Paris this new boulevard system was grand: the Ringstrasse's builders made it 2.5 miles long and 185 feet wide. Along it rose new public buildings and privately financed apartment buildings.

Just as in Paris, such construction affected the human geography of Vienna. The old city within the walls had been densely populated before 1857, but never squalid. The Imperial Court resided within the walls and many of Austria's great nobles maintained residences nearby. Most of Vienna's suburbs, on the other hand, had long contained the residences of the economically disadvantaged, living in densely built tenements of two- and three-room apartments, structures Viennese called "rent barracks" and "bed bug castles." The construction of the Ringstrasse reinforced this segregation, as its new apartment buildings became the residences of affluent families whose wealth derived from new industries or service in the expanding governmental institutions of nineteenth-century Austria-Hungary. Even though the city of Vienna annexed numerous suburbs in 1867 and again in 1890, many neighborhoods just beyond the Ringstrasse retained their working-class character.

A new street system encouraged public transportation development in Vienna as it did in Paris. Horse-drawn trams began to run in 1868, and these were electrified at the turn of the century. Also at the century's end, in 1894, the city began construction of a peripheral railroad, the Stadtbahn (or S-Bahn), that ran in

4. Early modern fortifications customarily were surrounded by a *glacis,* an unbuilt area intended to provide free fire zones for the fortifications' defenders. By the nineteenth century, as artillery ranges increased, these zones often had become quite broad indeed. In Vienna's case, the glacis was 1,485 feet wide. Destruction of constraining fortifications was a common feature of urban development in the nineteenth and early twentieth centuries. The following cities tore their defensive walls down in the years indicated: Brussels (1830s), Geneva (1851), Barcelona (1854), Basel (1860–67), Madrid (1868), and Bologna (1902).

Chapter 8

Vienna

and Paris,

1850–1930:

The Development

of the Modern

City

tunnels for about a quarter of its 16.5-mile route. A true subway system was planned, too, but World War I prevented its construction, and Vienna opened its subway system only in 1980.

Late-nineteenth-century Viennese planners effected many other improvements in their city. They initiated a system providing pure water to the city in 1860 and rechanneled the Danube in 1870–1875 to prevent dangerous flooding. Most importantly, they, like Haussmann, opened parks to provide healthful recreation opportunities for citizens. The Ringstrasse itself included a great deal of green space, but the most important park opened to citizens in the 1880s when Emperor Francis Joseph turned a former hunting preserve on the Danube River over to the city. This new park, the Prater, had some 3,200 acres that by the end of the nineteenth century offered something for almost everyone. It had paths for walking, riding, or bicycling, lakes for boating, soccer fields, an amusement park with a large Ferris wheel, and Europe's largest outdoor theater.

Such development made Vienna a much more attractive city by the outbreak of World War I in 1914. But that war drastically changed the city. Austria-Hungary broke up at the war's end, and Vienna found itself not the political and cultural center of a cosmopolitan empire of 54 million, but the capital of a republic of 6 million, and one-third of those residents lived in Vienna. The capital of the small Republic of Austria faced great problems. Population growth outstripped the construction of new, privately owned housing even before World War I, and wartime rent controls, as in Paris, ended most private construction during and after the war. Thus the city found itself with a major housing shortage at the war's end, when soldiers returned from the army to marry and establish families and as refugees from the former empire's territories crowded the city.

In Vienna, as in Paris and many other cities, government action sought to address this and other problems. The postwar constitution of Austria gave Vienna the status of a province with authority to raise and spend substantial revenues. The government of this city was in the hands of the Socialist party until 1934, and that party used public funds for the construction of 63,924 low-cost housing units to meet the housing shortage and to provide better residences for those dwelling in Vienna's tenements. Other projects improved recreational opportunities and included public swimming pools and a 60,000-seat stadium in the Prater.

Now let us use this background material on Paris and Vienna to consider the evidence. Your sources for answering the questions posed in this chapter are of two chief types. You first encounter pictorial evidence, a type of historical source that you have analyzed in earlier chapters. In the present chapter you will wish to examine this evidence carefully, to discern the solutions to the urban problems that the pictures present. The pictures also present various architectural answers to the problems of living in the city. You should consider carefully the solutions posed by architects and builders to society's needs, because architecture is an important source for the historian. Architects do not design for themselves, but at the commission of their customers. As a result, their designs generally reflect the needs and values of their employers.

This chapter presents a second kind of evidence, one which so far you have not analyzed extensively, in the form of maps and city plans. Maps are important records of human activity that often are underused by historians. Many historians simply employ maps to illustrate their narratives, as a military historian frequently does when he or she presents a map to describe a battle. Other social scientists, like sociologists and human geographers, make more extensive use of maps. Their study of maps as primary sources allows them to discover basic elements of human activity such as residential patterns. It is in this fashion that you should view the maps.

Let us now apply these general guidelines to analysis of specific pieces of evidence. Sources 1 through 3 provide pictorial evidence on the pre-industrial city. Observe the pictures carefully, recalling our description of such cities in The Problem section of this chapter. Source 1 is a picture of Vienna in 1850, before the Ringstrasse development, showing the city walls and the glacis. What is your impression of the city within those walls? In which direction have buildings grown because of the city's confinement within these walls? What sort of opportunities did the glacis offer urban planners?

Sources 2 and 3 take us within early-nineteenth-century Paris. Consider Source 2, a photograph of the rue Bernard de Palissy. What kind of housing did such a street seem to offer? What do you think the population density in such a neighborhood would have been? Consider health conditions. How much sunlight probably reached the residences on this street? Given the city's lack of sewers in the early nineteenth century, what function do you think the central gutter performed? Why do you think such a street would offend your senses and prove unhealthful? Source 3 is a photograph of leather workshops along the Bièvre River. This district was in a densely populated area of the city on a river flowing into the Seine River from which Parisians drew much of their drinking water in the early nineteenth century. Leather processing produces strong chemical odors and much toxic waste. Why do you think the workshops were built along the Bièvre? What sort of health impact do you suppose these workshops had?

Sources 4 and 5 present you a map and photograph of Vienna's Ringstrasse. Study the map in Source 4. It shows central Vienna with the Danube Canal curving across the lower right of the map near building Number 13. What evidence of deliberate planning efforts do you see in the development? Does the Ringstrasse, which intermingled new apartment buildings with both public and commercial buildings, seem to have certain functional zones? Why might you conclude that commerce occupied one zone? Moving along the Ringstrasse,

Chapter 8

Vienna

and Paris,

1850–1930:

The Development

of the Modern

City

what sort of functional change do you observe at the area's first building, the Votivkirche, a church built in the 1850s in thanks for the emperor's escape from an assassination attempt? What sort of institutions surround the Hofburg or imperial palace?

Source 5 offers you a photograph of key Ringstrasse buildings. Do you find any harmony of architectural styles in the public buildings? Why do you think architects adopted classical Greek architecture for the houses of Parliament? Why might they have adopted Gothic architecture for the city hall? Do you think such tactics heightened the sense of different functional zones within the Ringstrasse? Consider the scale of the boulevard. How might its great width have improved communications and public health?

In Sources 6 through 9, you must analyze evidence on Paris. The map in Source 6 is particularly rich in detail on the city improvements wrought by Baron Haussmann during the Second French Empire. How has Haussmann improved Paris streets? What other transportation improvements do you find on the map? Consider, too, the impact Haussmann's work had on the quality of life for Parisians. How many new parks were opened during Haussmann's tenure in office? What problems dictated the aqueducts in the lower center of the map and in its upper right? What do you notice about the city's growth? What suburbs did it annex to provide for growth?

Sources 7 through 9 illustrate a major project in Paris's nineteenth-century improvements, the Avenue de l'Opéra, and Source 7 is a map showing the creation of the avenue. Haussmann began this broad avenue in the 1850s to provide better communication in western Paris, but it was completed only in 1878 after he left office. The complexities of property acquisition for the new street played a major role in its delayed completion. What was the street pattern in this area of the city before the avenue's construction? What effects do you think the avenue had on its district? Refer to Source 8 as well now. How does this photograph affect your opinion of the complexity of this project? How would your assessment of the project's difficulty change knowing that street builders had to level a large hill, the Butte Saint-Roch, to provide a level path for the avenue? What sort of housing, judging by Source 8, was removed to make way for the avenue? Refer to Source 9 at this juncture, a photograph of the completed avenue looking toward the new opera house that opened in 1875. How did the avenue improve communications in the city? What health benefits probably resulted from its construction? What sort of housing seems to surround the avenue?

Sources 10 through 12 provide you with detailed examples of the housing built along the Ringstrasse and Haussmann's new streets. Examine Source 10, paying particular attention to the ornamentation around the windows and their size in this building constructed in the late nineteenth century, before elevators came into widespread use. What about the building's façade suggests to you that the building's upper floors might contain less prestigious, cheaper, and smaller apartments than the lower floors? Why might you conclude that, in the absence of elevators, some former patterns of social segregation by floor persisted?

Source 11 is an engraving of a building typical of those that arose along Haussmann's new boulevards in Paris. Such structures usually had shops facing the street on the ground floor with apartments on upper floors. Access to the buildings' residential sections often was through a large double door (at lower left in the picture) leading past the lodging of a *concièrge*, who controlled access to the building and who kept it clean, to an inner courtyard.

Source 12 illustrates an architect's plan for another such apartment building. Such plans, showing the building literally as it would look if you removed its roof and looked down into it, are easy to read, when you know a few rules. On this plan doorways are shown as openings in the dark outline of the building and windows are shown as the white, narrower areas in the building's outline. The rest of the features of the building may be analyzed through the keys.

Remember that architects design buildings with a definite clientele in mind. Examine the apartment on the ground floor, as well as the two apartments found on each of the first, second, and third floors (floors above the third contained smaller apartments and servants' quarters). How many rooms do these apartments contain? Consider, too, other features like service staircases, stables, and coach houses. What do these features

of the building floor plan suggest to you about the types of residents expected for these apartments? Compare your conclusions with those you derived from analyzing the exterior decoration of the Vienna apartment building in Source 10. Why might you conclude that the same class of resident lived in both the Vienna and Paris buildings?

Sources 13 and 14 present examples of the recreational areas added to nineteenth-century cities. Source 13 is a photograph of the Prater in the late nineteenth century. What sort of diversions did this part of the great park offer? What developments in nineteenth-century urban life would have made such a place more accessible to citizens of all classes? Source 14 illustrates Haussmann's Buttes-Chaumont Park, constructed in 1864–1867 near Belleville, one of the nineteenth-century worker suburbs annexed by Paris. On an area formerly occupied by quarries and dumps, Haussmann's engineers created a lake surrounded by a dramatically landscaped park with a view of the entire Paris area. What sort of economic activities surround the park? What do the presence of these activities suggest to you about the suburbs of cities like Paris and Vienna?

Sources 15 through 17 focus on the near suburbs of both cities. Source 15 is a photograph of the working-class neighborhood of Belleville. What sort of concentration of people might you imagine inhabited a narrow street such as this one? Having examined the landscape around Buttes-Chaumont Park in Source 14, examine

Chapter 8

Vienna

and Paris,

1850–1930:

The Development

of the Modern

City

Source 16, a picture of a suburban factory that opened in 1873 at Ivry. Why might you conclude that such suburbs would have been rather unhealthy places of residence? Turn to Source 17, which illustrates Viennese worker housing. Why do you find late-nineteenth-century conditions in Vienna little different from those in Paris?

Sources 18 through 21 illustrate the impact of the Industrial Revolution on urban life. Sources 18 and 19 in particular show new modes of transportation made possible by industrialization. The Stadtbahn, or S-Bahn, encircled Vienna and buses and electric trolleys, like those of Paris, appeared on the streets of all European cities. The fares on such vehicles were low at all times and often were discounted for workers at rush hours. What impact might the availability of such transportation have had on worker living patterns? Since public transportation ran seven days per week, why do you think recreational opportunities for workers increased?

The vast array of products from Industrial Age factories required mass markets, and urban marketing techniques developed accordingly. Sources 20 and 21 illustrate two aspects of urban merchandising. Source 20 is a photograph of the Passage de l'Opéra in Paris, one of 137 enclosed shopping promenades flourishing in the city by 1828. Notice the display windows designed to foster consumer interest in the shops' merchandise. What aspects of early-nineteenth-century Parisian streets probably made window-shopping the stores lining such streets difficult or unpleasant and made passages such as this one at-

tractive? By the mid-nineteenth century such shopping passages grew, in some cities, to multilevel structures of many shops called bazaars or galleries. By the 1860s consolidation of the small shops in such structures under one management created that urban institution we call the department store. Source 21 illustrates the interior of one of Paris's major department stores. Why might such an institution only have developed in an urban area? Why do you think the decoration and displays of such a store would have encouraged purchases of the products of new factories? Since early department stores sold only for cash, what social group do you think patronized these establishments in the late nineteenth and early twentieth centuries?

Our final sources illustrate post–World War I answers to the problems of city life whose growing complexity dictated state rather than private action. Almost all major European cities built public, low-cost housing for workers after World War I. Source 22 illustrates the largest such Viennese housing project, the Karl Marx Hof, which provided homes for 5,000 persons in 1,382 apartments. Such projects really were small cities, equipped with common laundries, child-care facilities, and parklike courtyards. Contrast this block of apartments with the tenements in Source 17. Why would you think that such large complexes would have been more healthful for workers than the old tenements?

Source 23 is a floor plan of a Parisian low-cost housing project with two apartments sharing a common stair. The Parisian solution to the housing shortage differed in detail, but not substance, from the Viennese apartments of the Karl Marx Hof. Observe the floor plans carefully. What common late-twentieth-century amenities are missing? Floor plans always show placement of radiators. Do you find any? Indeed do you find any other heat source for multiroom apartments than fireplaces? While each apartment has a toilet, does each have a shower? Notice the sizes of the rooms. How do they compare with those to which you are accustomed? For what class of residents do you think such apartments were designed?

Source 24 is a photo of Vienna's Kongressbad swimming pool. It was one of the largest pools in Europe, measuring 66' × 330'. Built at public expense, such a pool represented the culmination of many trends. Why would such projects as this pool, which attracted 450,000 bathers in 1930, have been virtually impossible without developments in public transportation during our period? How do the pool and public housing developments reflect a changed government attitude toward the solution of urban problems from that of the earlier nineteenth century?

As you examine the evidence that follows, you should be able to formulate answers to this chapter's central questions. How were these cities physically reshaped in response to the problems of the early nineteenth century? How did this physical transformation affect the lifestyles of urban dwellers?

Chapter 8
Vienna
and Paris,
1850–1930:
The Development
of the Modern
City

Source 1 from Donald J. Olsen, The City as a Work of Art (New Haven: Yale University Press, 1986), p. 61. Photograph: Historisches Museum der Stadt Wien.

1. **Vienna in 1850**

Source 2 from Donald J. Olsen, The City as a Work of Art *(New Haven: Yale University Press, 1986), p. 222. Photograph: © Photothèque des Musées de la Ville de Paris/Cliché Lauros-Giraudon by SPADEM.*

2. A Paris Street in the 1850s: The Rue Bernard de Palissy

Chapter 8
Vienna
and Paris,
1850–1930:
The Development
of the Modern
City

Source 3 from Mark Girouard, Cities and People: A Social and Architectural History *(New Haven: Yale University Press, 1985), p. 298. Photograph: © Photothèque des Musées de la Ville de Paris/by SPADEM.*

3. Leather Workshops on the Bièvre River in Paris in the Mid-19th Century

Source 4 from Wolfgang Braunfels, translated by Kenneth J. Northcott, Urban Design in Western Europe: Regime and Architecture, 900–1900 *(Chicago: University of Chicago Press, 1988), p. 304.*

4. Schematic Drawing of the Viennese Ringstrasse and Its Major Buildings

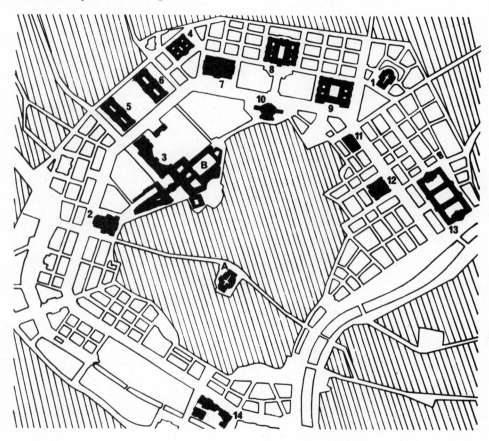

Key

Pre-1857 Buildings
A St. Stephen's Cathedral
B *Hofburg* (Imperial Palace)

Post-1857 Buildings
1 Votivkirche (the Votive Church or
  Church of the Divine Savior)
2 Opera House
3 New Hofburg
4 Courthouse
5 Art History Museum
6 Natural History Museum
7 Parliament

8 City Hall
9 University
10 Burgtheater
11 Banking Union
12 Stock Exchange
13 Army Barracks
14 School of arts and crafts

Chapter 8

Vienna

and Paris,

1850–1930:

The Development

of the Modern

City

Source 5 from William M. Johnston, Vienna, Vienna: The Golden Age, 1815–1914 *(New York: Clarkson N. Potter, 1981), p. 128. Photograph courtesy of Mondadori Press.*

5. Vienna Ringstrasse in the Late 19th Century

The Parliament building is in the foreground; city hall is the spired building in the upper left; the university is the domed building right of center; and the Burgtheater appears in the upper right.

Source 6 from Thomas F. X. Noble et al., Western Civilization: The Continuing Experiment (Boston: Houghton Mifflin, 1994), p. 953.

6. Paris, 1850–1870

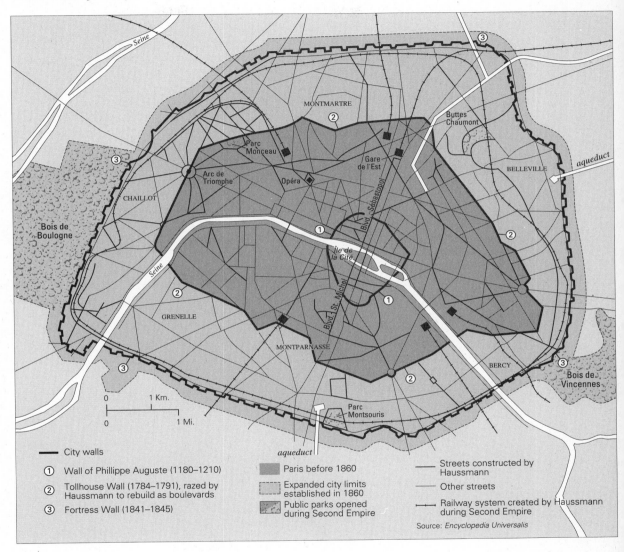

City walls

① Wall of Phillippe Auguste (1180–1210)

② Tollhouse Wall (1784–1791), razed by Haussmann to rebuild as boulevards

③ Fortress Wall (1841–1845)

aqueduct

▨ Paris before 1860

⬚ Expanded city limits established in 1860

▨ Public parks opened during Second Empire

— Streets constructed by Haussmann

— Other streets

⊢⊣ Railway system created by Haussmann during Second Empire

Source: *Encyclopedia Universalis*

Chapter 8
Vienna
and Paris,
1850–1930:
The Development
of the Modern
City

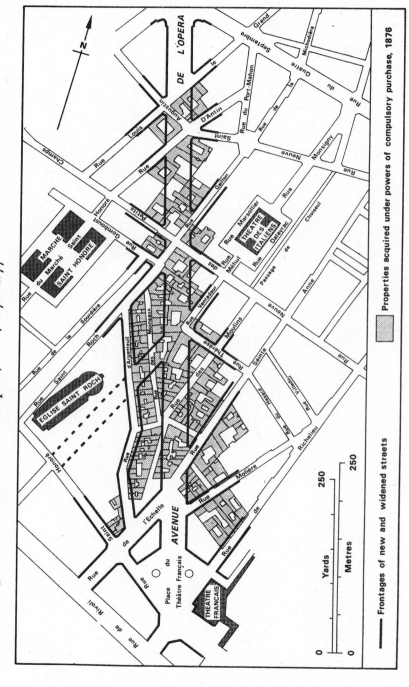

Source 7 from Anthony Sutcliffe, The Autumn of Central Paris: The Defeat of Town Planning, 1850–1870 (Montreal: McGill-Queens University Press, 1971), p. 48.

7. The Completion of the Avenue de l'Opéra, Paris, 1876–1877

Source 8 from Photothèque des Musées de la Ville de Paris/Cliché Dubuisson by SPADEM.

8. Clearing Old Neighborhoods for the Avenue de l'Opéra, Paris, 1876

Chapter 8

Vienna

and Paris,

1850–1930:

The Development

of the Modern

City

Source 9 from F. Roy Willis, Western Civilization, *Vol. IV,* From the Seventeenth Century to the Contemporary Age *(Lexington, Mass.: D. C. Heath, 1985), 4th ed., p. 269. Photograph by H. Roger-Viollet.*

9. Avenue de l'Opéra, Paris, Late 19th Century

Source 10 from Donald J. Olsen, The City as a Work of Art *(New Haven: Yale University Press, 1986), p. 156. Original source: fur Kunstgeschichte Institut Universität Wien. Photograph by Johanna Fiegl.*

10. Ringstrasse Apartment Building, Schottenring 25

Chapter 8

Vienna

and Paris,

1850–1930:

The Development

of the Modern

City

Source 11 from David H. Pinkney, Napoleon III and the Rebuilding of Paris *(Princeton: Princeton University Press, 1958), Plate 16. Original Source:* The Builder *(London), XVI (March 6, 1858).*

11. A Paris Apartment Building, Late 19th Century

Source 12 from Donald J. Olsen, The City as a Work of Art *(New Haven: Yale University Press, 1986), p. 118. Original source:* Revue générale d'architecture, *XVIII (1860), p. 41.*

12. Floor Plan of Apartment Building at 39, Rue Neuve des Mathurins, Paris

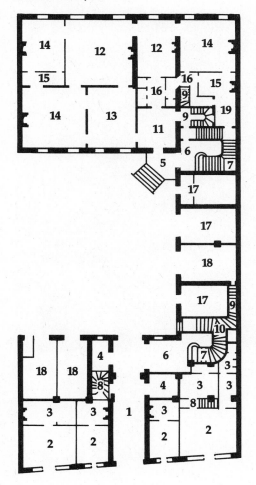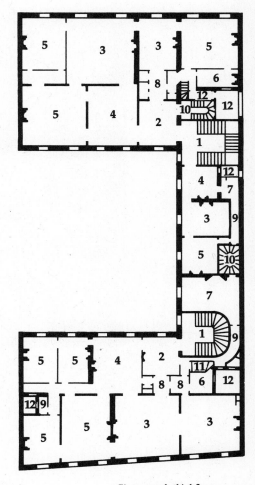

Ground floor

1 Passage from carriage entrance to courtyard
2 Shops
3 Shop backrooms
4 Concierge residence and kitchen
5 Entry steps
6 Grand staircase vestibule
7 Grand staircase

8,9,10 Service staircases
11 Antechamber
12 Parlors
13 Dining rooms
14 Bedrooms
15 Bathrooms
16 Cloakroom
17 Stables
18 Coach house
19 Light/air shafts

First, second, third floors

1 Grand staircase
2 Antechambers
3 Parlors
4 Dining rooms
5 Bedrooms
6 Bathrooms
7 Kitchens
8 Cloakrooms
9 Corridors
10,11 Service stairs
12 Light/air shafts

Chapter 8
Vienna
and Paris,
1850–1930:
The Development
of the Modern
City

Source 13 from William M. Johnston, Vienna, Vienna: The Golden Age, 1815–1914 *(New York: Clarkson N. Potter, 1981), p. 228. Photograph courtesy of Raccolta delle Stampe Bertarelli, Milan, Italy.*

13. The Prater, Vienna

Source 14 from Maurice Agulhon et al., Histoire de la France urbaine, *vol. IV:* La ville de l'âge industriel: Le cycle haussmannien *(Paris: Éditions du Seuil, 1983), p. 48. Photograph from Bibliothèque Historique de la Ville de Paris/Seuil.*

14. The Buttes-Chaumont Park, Paris

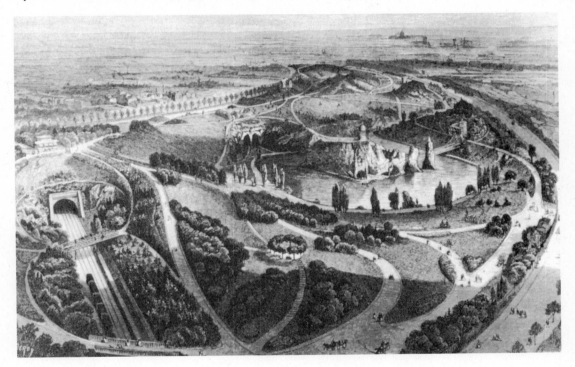

Chapter 8
Vienna
and Paris,
1850–1930:
The Development
of the Modern
City

Source 15 from Lapi-Viollet.

15. A 19th-Century Parisian Working-Class Suburb in Belleville

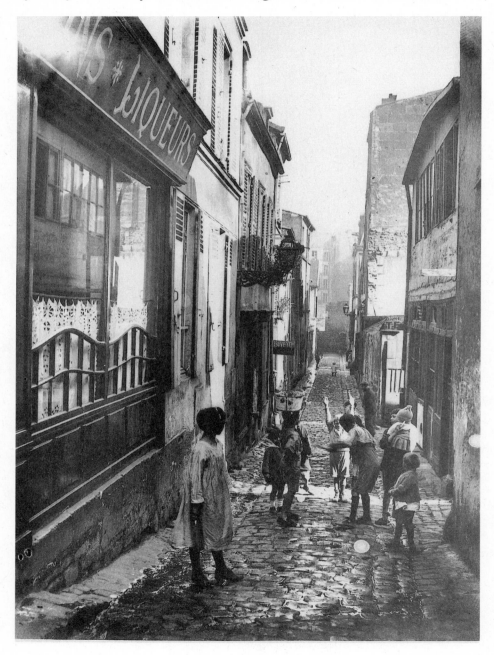

Source 16 from Maurice Agulhon et al., Histoire de la France urbaine, *vol. IV:* La ville de l'age industriel: Le cycle haussmanien *(Paris: Editions du Seuil, 1983), p.202. Photograph courtesy of Archives Seuil, Paris.*

16. The Lemoine Forges at Ivry, 1881

Chapter 8
Vienna
and Paris,
1850–1930:
The Development
of the Modern
City

Source 17 from Helmut Gruber, Red Vienna: Experiment in Working-Class Culture, 1919–1934 *(New York: Oxford University Press, 1991), p. 47. Original source: Verein für Geschichte der Arbeiterbewegung, Vienna.*

17. Vienna Workers' Tenement, Early 20th Century

Source 18 from William M. Johnston, Vienna, Vienna: The Golden Age, 1815–1914 *(New York: Clarkson N. Potter, 1981), p. 240. Photograph courtesy of Mondadori Press.*

18. The Vienna S-Bahn and Its Schönbrunn Station, Built Between 1894 and 1897

Source 19 from Maurice Agulhon, et al., Histoire de la France urbaine, *Vol. IV:* La ville de l'âge industriel: Le cycle haussmannien *(Paris: Éditions du Seuil, 1983), p. 350. Photograph by Harlingue/Viollet.*

19. The Gare de l'Est Bus and Tramway Stop in 1936

Source 20 from Donald J. Olsen, The City as a Work of Art *(New Haven: Yale University Press, 1986), p. 226. Photograph: © Photothèque des Musées de la Ville de Paris/Cliché Lauros-Giraudin by SPADEM.*

20. The Passage de l'Opéra, Paris, Between 1856 and 1865

Chapter 8
Vienna
and Paris,
1850–1930:
The Development
of the Modern
City

Source 21 from Maurice Agulhon, et al., Histoire de la France urbaine, *Vol. IV:* La ville de l'âge industriel: Le cycle haussmannien *(Paris: Éditions du Seuil, 1983), p. 227. Photograph by Roger-Viollet.*

21. The Galeries Lafayette Department Store, Paris, Early 20th Century

Source 22 from Paul Hoffmann, Viennese: Splendor, Twilight, and Exile *(New York: Doubleday, 1988). Photograph from Austrian Press and Information Service.*

22. The Karl Marx Hof, Erected 1927–1929

Chapter 8

Vienna

and Paris,

1850–1930:

The Development

of the Modern

City

Source 23 from Norma Evenson, Paris: A Century of Change, 1878–1978 *(New Haven: Yale University Press, 1979), p. 219. Original source:* La vie urbaine *(Published by the Institut d'Urbanisme de Paris), No. 18, Nov. 15, 1933.*

23. Floor Plan of Parisian HBM (Low-Cost Housing) Apartments, 1933

Key

Chambre = room
Salle à manger = dining room
Cuisine = kitchen
Douche = shower
W.C. = toilet
= fireplace

Room Measurements

2.70 × 4.60 m = 8.9 × 15.2 feet
3.00 × 5.00 m = 9.9 × 16.5 feet
2.80 × 4.60 m = 9.25 × 15.2 feet
2.60 × 4.60 m = 8.6 × 15.2 feet
19 sq. meters = 205 sq. ft.
7 sq. meters = 75.6 sq. ft.

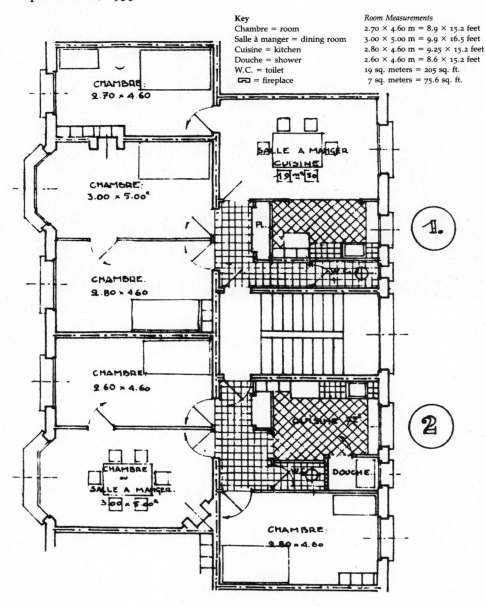

Source 24 from Helmut Gruber, Red Vienna: Experiment in Working-Class Culture, 1919–1934 *(New York: Oxford University Press, 1991), p. 122. Original source: Verein für Geschichte der Arbeiterbewegung, Vienna.*

24. Kongressbad, Vienna, One of Europe's Largest Pools, About 1930

Chapter 8

Vienna

and Paris,

1850–1930:

The Development

of the Modern

City

QUESTIONS TO CONSIDER

In the previous sections of this chapter, we have considered each city individually. To answer the chapter's central questions we now need to study the cities jointly, drawing general trends from their individual experiences in urban development.

Consider first the core of the cities. Notice the street patterns and recall the problems that faced early-nineteenth-century cities. What common approaches to street building do you find in Paris and Vienna? Notice how the ring boulevards of Vienna connect every area of the city with the riverfront. Notice how Haussmann's boulevards facilitate direct north-south and east-west movement in Paris. Why did city and national governments lay out such streets? What facilities for recreation do you find incorporated into many of the cities? Consult especially the maps of Paris and Vienna. Why do you think a Parisian or Viennese of 1800 would have had difficulty recognizing his or her city in 1900?

Improvements in the urban cores of cities benefited all to some extent. Let us look more deeply into these physical improvements, however, to discern if one class, at least initially, benefited more than others from private and government initiatives for municipal improvements. Consult the sources to determine the kinds of buildings arising in the central cities in the late nineteenth century. Paris and Vienna continued to employ a large part of their central cores for residential use. What classes seem to

have occupied the new buildings constructed along Haussmann's boulevards and the Ringstrasse boulevards in Vienna? Where do the sources for Paris and Vienna suggest that persons of lower income were forced to live when the wealthy appropriated much of the central city for residential purposes? Why do you find an economically segregated housing pattern evolving? How might transportation developments have supported residential segregation?

Reflect also on the buildings erected at public expense in the second half of the nineteenth century, remembering all the while that universal, free public education became a reality only in the late nineteenth or early twentieth centuries in most countries. The opera in Paris, completed in 1875, typifies such buildings, as do the museums and theaters built in Vienna in the same period. What social groups do you think initially benefited most from such institutions? What does this tell you about the groups most influencing late-nineteenth-century politics? Why would you perhaps agree with those historians who call the nineteenth century the century of the middle class?

The right to vote became increasingly universal among European males in the late nineteenth and early twentieth centuries. Indeed, in many countries all women also gained the vote after World War I. At the same time, political parties addressing working-class needs arose in many countries. What evidence do you see of such new political empowerment in Parisian and Viennese urban development in early twentieth century?

Why do you think improved, low-cost public transport would have allowed lower income groups an improved lifestyle by the early twentieth century?

Finally, consider whether the developments reflected in your sources, including the construction projects, the railroads, the sewers, and water supply systems, would have been possible without the advances of industrialization. Why can you say with some justice that the Industrial Revolution helped to solve in the second half of the nineteenth century some of the problems it created in the first half?

After considering the sources as a unit, you should be ready to formulate answers to the chapter's main questions. How were the cities physically reshaped in response to the problems of the first decades of the early nineteenth century? How did this physical transformation affect the lifestyle of urban dwellers?

EPILOGUE

The development of Paris and Vienna after our period typifies one major trend in twentieth-century urban affairs: the end of urban growth in much of the West. Northern Europe led the way as its rapid nineteenth-century population growth ended by the first decades of the twentieth century. The dramatic growth of urban populations characteristic of the nineteenth century ended as overall population growth rates diminished. Indeed, many cities had an actual decline in population in the twentieth century, and this was the case with Paris and Vienna.

The chief cause of Vienna's population decline was Austria-Hungary's defeat in World War I. The peace treaties ending that war left Vienna the capital of a truncated Austria, a city with the buildings for imperial glory, but without the old imperial territory and population. Vienna's population growth ended with the empire and the city's population ac-tually shrank. The 1910–11 population was 2,031,000 people; the city's population in 1981 was 1,504,200.

Paris better illustrates trends in modern urban life because twentieth-century warfare less seriously affected that city. Paris continues to be a major cultural hub and twentieth-century improvements have made it a bit more livable, although modern ecological problems like air pollution from large concentrations of motor vehicles are posing new problems for solution. Nevertheless Paris reached its population peak in 1920–21 at 2,907,000 persons and is now inhabited by 2,188,918.[5]

Urban growth ceased in Paris and many other cities in the twentieth century in large part due to suburbanization that is much more extensive than that of the nineteenth century. In the nineteenth century, as we've seen, suburban growth fol-

5. Other major cities reached their population peaks as follows: Amsterdam, 1960–61; Birmingham, 1950–51; Glasgow, 1940–41; London, 1940–41; Manchester, 1930–31; Rotterdam, 1960–61; Stockholm, 1960–61.

Chapter 8

Vienna

and Paris,

1850–1930:

The Development

of the Modern

City

lowed the roads, railroads, and later subways. In the twentieth century, limited access highways also have abetted suburban sprawl, but the social divisions of the nineteenth century persist. Paris continues to have a greater portion of its population ranked among economically and professionally higher status groups than the rest of France, but its suburbs still have a marked working-class complexion. Improved transportation has carried the working classes to communities more distant from the capital. The often drab working-class outer districts of Paris and its near suburban communities until recently have reflected their social composition at election time, voting so heavily for socialist or communist candidates committed to workers' causes that they have been nicknamed "the Red Belt."

In fact, suburbanization has become so extensive that modern planners in Western Europe are being forced to direct its course the way nineteenth-century planners tried to shape urban development. In the late twentieth century French planners, for examples, have begun to lay out large population centers on the distant periphery of Paris. Such centers, like Cergy-Pontoise, northeast of Paris, are suburban in their location and connected to the city by train and highway, but are almost urban in their population density. The modern city thus continues as the locus of Western civilization, but it is now a smaller city influencing a much broader area.

CHAPTER NINE

EXPANSION AND PUBLIC

OPINION: ADVOCATES OF

THE "NEW IMPERIALISM"

THE PROBLEM

From the 1870s until around 1905, Western nations engaged in a brief but extremely intense period of imperial expansion. In one sense, of course, this was not entirely a new phenomenon. From the sixteenth through the eighteenth centuries, the emerging nations of Western Europe had struggled over possession of the New World. Between roughly 1815 and 1871, the West, beset with internal problems, had engaged in only limited attempts at colonialism, but some nations, principally England, nevertheless had sought to expand their economic spheres of influence. In some ways, then, the "new imperialism" of the late nineteenth century was not dramatically different from the old.

Yet to many living at the time (as well as to a number of later historians), the imperialism of the late nineteenth and early twentieth centuries seemed markedly different from earlier forms of territorial expansion. For one thing,

the number of contestants for empire had increased with the addition of the newly formed nations of Germany and Italy. Indeed, even the United States, itself a nation composed of former European colonies, joined in the headlong scramble for new territories. The increased number of empire-seeking nations probably contributed to the speed with which unclaimed areas were brought under Western control.

Another factor that made the colonial expansion of the late nineteenth and early twentieth centuries appear "new" was that many people believed this was their nation's last opportunity to build or enlarge an empire. Only Africa and parts of Asia remained vulnerable to imperialistic ventures. Awareness of this fact filled the nations of the West with a sense of urgency: if a nation did not acquire colonies quickly, other nations would do so. This feeling of urgency doubtless contributed to the speed of empire building as well as to the heightened sense of national competition

Chapter 9
Expansion
and Public
Opinion:
Advocates of
the "New
Imperialism"

for greatness. So powerful was this sentiment that by the turn of the century almost all of Africa and parts of Asia had fallen under Western control and the West, accurately or not, could boast of itself as the master of much of the world.

A third factor that made the "new imperialism" seem different from the old was that advocates and opponents of colonial expansion felt the need to sway public opinion. Before the late eighteenth century, public opinion was not considered a crucial factor when monarchs or bodies representing a limited electorate decided what policies their respective governments should pursue. To be sure, certain powerful interest groups had to be consulted or appealed to, but the opinion of the general public was rarely heeded. The expansion of the electorate,[1] however, together with increased educational opportunities and literacy, the corresponding mass circulation of newspapers, and the evolution of modern political campaign techniques, served to make the general public more aware of their governments' policies and even to have a limited voice in the shaping of those policies. Hence, supporters or opponents of particular policies were obliged to appeal to—and, in some cases, manipulate—public opinion. Thus, the new imperialism also appeared different in that it was warmly debated not only in palaces and parliaments but also in the streets, the press, the workingmen's halls, and

the public houses ("pubs") of the Western nations.

No historical trend such as the new imperialism takes place in a vacuum, unaffected by other trends and events that precede and parallel it and, in some cases, help to cause it. In the West, several important developments in the second half of the nineteenth century not only acted to create the new imperialism but also helped impart to that movement its particular shape and character.

One of the most important occurrences in the West preceding and paralleling the new imperialism was that of rapid population growth. Between 1850 and 1900, the population of Europe (including Russia) increased 54 percent, from approximately 274 million to 423 million. Germany's population jumped over 62 percent, Great Britain's 41 percent, Italy's around 41 percent, and Belgium's 48 percent. This population boom was primarily the result of falling death rates, in turn caused by the controlling of epidemic diseases, increased food production, and improvements in transportation that allowed food supplies to reach cities and regions of local famines. In the United States, where massive immigration from Europe supplemented large natural increase, the population increased an astounding 227 percent.[2]

This dramatic jump in population, especially in the cities of Europe, created a serious need for jobs, particularly in the nonagricultural sector. The pressure for greater employment in turn increased Europe's demand

---

1. The expansion of the electorate took place in the United Kingdom in 1867–1884, in Germany in 1871, in France in 1875, and in Italy in 1913.

2. Between 1846 and 1900, the number of emigrants from Europe to the United States and Latin American probably exceeded 30 million.

for raw materials for industrial production and markets for those manufactured goods. Moreover, in some areas of Europe (notably Italy), the rise in rural population put a heavy strain on land and agricultural resources, which resulted in increased emigration. It is easy to imagine how these problems, caused by population pressures, might be linked to calls for expansionism.

A second important trend during this time was the spread and apparent peaking of the Industrial Revolution. By the latter part of the nineteenth century, much of the West had joined in the Industrial Revolution and thus (as noted earlier) needed raw materials and, equally important, markets for manufactured goods. A severe depression, which struck Europe and the United States in 1873 and lasted into the 1890s, made it impossible for the West to consume all the manufactured goods it could produce. Unless industries were to shut down, bringing on massive unemployment, new markets would have to be found. With most of the Western countries erecting protective tariff barriers to keep out each other's manufactured goods, these new markets would have to be found outside the West, in areas that could be exploited almost at will.

The Industrial Revolution not only provided an incentive for a new upsurge of imperialism, it also gave the West the means to accomplish this expansion. Technological improvements, especially in transportation and communications, allowed Western mercantile and financial houses gradually to draw much of the world into

an integrated global market dominated by Western merchants and financiers. As English economist Stanley Jevons boasted in 1866:

> The several quarters of the globe are our willing tributaries. The plains of North America and Russia are our cornfields; Chicago and Odessa our granaries; Canada and the Baltic our forests; Australia contains our sheep farms, and in South America are our herds of oxen . . . the Chinese grow tea for us; and coffee, sugar and spice arrive from East Indian plantations. Spain and France are our vineyards, and the Mediterranean our fruit garden.[3]

Advances in medicine and in weapons technology made it further possible for Westerners to subdue non-Western peoples and live for extended periods in non-Western climates. Great Britain, for example, acquired the Upper Nile River area in 1898, but only after slaughtering 20,000 tribesmen at Omdurman, thanks to the newly invented machine gun. As Hilaire Belloc's "Modern Traveler" would sing,

Whatever happens, we have got
The Maxim gun; and they have not.[4]

A third important trend that contributed to late-nineteenth-century imperialism was that of intensified

3. Quoted in R. R. Palmer and Joel Colton, *A History of the Modern World* (New York: Alfred A. Knopf, 1965), pp. 574–575.

4. Quoted in Roland Oliver and G. N. Sanderson, *The Cambridge History of Africa* (Cambridge: Cambridge University Press, 1985), vol. 6, p. 98. The Maxim gun was the brainchild of British engineer Sir Hiram Maxim, who in 1889 perfected the machine gun.

Chapter 9

*Expansion
and Public
Opinion:
Advocates of
the "New
Imperialism"*

competition among Western nations. It was obvious at the time to many people that Western nations did not have to seize non-Western territories in order to dominate them economically. Moreover, some of the territories that Western nations colonized could offer no immediate profits to their conquerors. Yet in this era of intensified rivalry, colonies were widely regarded as assets that could be exploited in the increased competition among Western nations and also as potential military bases to protect the extraction of raw materials and the maintenance of trade lanes. Safe harbors and coaling stations for a modern steam-powered navy were seen as critically important to each Western nation's power and survival. At the same time, no single country could be allowed to gain an advantage over others in the rush for colonies and the establishment of national "greatness." Thus U.S. President William McKinley justified taking the Philippine Islands partly to keep them out of the hands of any other national competitor seeking to exploit Asia and the Pacific. Truly, heightened national competition, along with other trends, helped renew the spirit of imperialism in the West. With the new nations of Germany and Italy and the newly imperialistic United States added to the race, the scramble for colonies at times seemed almost frantic.

Paralleling the rise in imperialistic sentiment were two important and, in some ways, contradictory intellectual trends. The first of these was Social Darwinism, a system of ideas that spread rapidly throughout the West in the second half of the nineteenth century. An application of the theories of biological evolution to human affairs, Social Darwinism taught that peoples, like species, were engaged in a life-or-death struggle to determine the "survival of the fittest." Those classes or nations that emerged triumphant in this struggle were considered the most fit, hence best suited to carry on the evolution of the human race. Therefore the subjugation of weak peoples by strong ones was not only in accordance with the laws of nature, it was bound to result in a more highly civilized world as well. Most celebrated among the Social Darwinists was the Englishman Herbert Spencer, a diminutive and eccentric writer who became a worldwide celebrity through his writings. (A letter was once addressed to him, "Herbert Spencer. England. And if the postman doesn't know the address, he ought to." It was delivered.)

Although Spencer himself disapproved of imperialism, it is easy to see how his writings could be used as a justification for empire building. At the conclusion of the Spanish-American War in 1898, whereby the United States acquired its empire from Spain, Senator Henry Cabot Lodge justified the transfer of colonies by asserting that "Spain . . . has proved herself unfit to govern, and for the unfit among nations there is no pity in the relentless world-forces which shape the destinies of mankind."[5]

At the same time that many in the West embraced this notion of a strug-

5. Henry Cabot Lodge, *The War With Spain* (New York: Harper and Brothers, 1899), p. 2.

gle for survival between the "fittest" and the "unfit" (a doctrine with strong racist overtones), they also adopted the concept of the "White Man's Burden." This concept held that it was the duty of the "fittest" not so much to destroy the "unfit" as to "civilize" them; white people, according to this view, had a responsibility to educate the rest of the world to the norms of Western society. As racist as Social Darwinism, the belief in the White Man's Burden downplayed the idea of a struggle for survival between peoples and emphasized the "humanitarian" notion of bringing the benefits of "civilization" to the "uncivilized." Using this argument, many in the West justified imperialism as an obligation, a sacrifice that God had charged the "fittest" to make. In his 1876 speech to the International Conference of Geographers, King Leopold II of Belgium declared:

> The matter which brings us together today is one most deserving the attention of the friends of humanity. For bringing civilization to the only part of the earth [Africa] which it has not yet reached and lightening the darkness in which whole peoples are plunged is, I venture to say, a crusade worthy of this century of progress. . . .[6]

Although the doctrine of the White Man's Burden differed in tone from that of Social Darwinism, one can see that its practical results might well be the same.

6. From Henri Brunschwig, *French Colonialism 1871–1914: Myths and Realities* (New York: Praeger, 1966), p. 35.

Thus, a number of important trends preceded and paralleled the rising imperialist tide in the West in the late nineteenth and early twentieth centuries. As we shall see, not only did these demographic, economic, technological, diplomatic, and intellectual trends profoundly alter the lives and attitudes of most Westerners, but they also gave power to the expansionist surges of the new imperialism.

Your task in this chapter is to analyze the writings of important advocates of imperialism from four of the most active expansionist nations: Germany, Great Britain, France, and Italy. What were the main arguments used by each spokesman in favor of colonial expansion? How did each attempt to appeal to public opinion? Finally, how can their speeches and writings help us identify the principal motives and justifications for the new imperialism?

SOURCES AND METHOD

One of the most significant currents in the West during the last half of the nineteenth century was the popular identification of the common people with the symbols and traditions of their respective nations. Although roots of this modern sense of nationalism can be found in Napoleonic France, this tendency gained enormous strength and momentum in the latter part of the nineteenth century, fueled by national holidays and celebrations (Bastille Day in France, begun in 1880; Queen Victoria's jubilees in Great Britain in 1887 and 1897; the

Chapter 9

Expansion
and Public
Opinion:
Advocates of
the "New
Imperialism"

massive funerals of King Victor Emmanuel II of Italy in 1878 and of Tsar Alexander III of Russia in 1894), the erection of enormous monuments to the nation (the Eiffel Tower in France; the Washington Monument in the United States; the national monument to William I of Germany), the renovation of capital cities on magnificent scales (London, Paris, Berlin, Vienna, Rome, and Washington, D.C.), the commemoration of national heroes and historical events on postage stamps, and the creation or re-creation of international athletic competitions (the Davis Cup in tennis in 1900; the Olympic Games, revived in 1896). This new sense of popular nationalism in which people of different classes, religions, and ethnic groups identified with the nation itself rather than with its monarch or government or with their own particular groups was a crucial step in the creation of the modern nation-state. Against the powerful force of modern nationalism, competing ideas such as Marxism had little initial effect.[7]

And yet, if the people were expected to identify with their nation, it seemed logical that their opinions about that nation and the policies of its government ought to be heard. And although few advocated actual rule by "the people," the prevailing sentiment was that their opinions should at least be heeded. Indeed, the few remaining autocrats, like the stubborn Nicholas II of Russia, would ignore

7. For an excellent discussion of this trend, see Eric Hobsbawm and Terence Ranger, eds., *The Invention of Tradition* (Cambridge: Cambridge University Press, 1983), especially pp. 263–307.

this impulse at their peril—and to their ultimate destruction. Therefore, when some political leaders in the West began to embrace imperialist ideas and ventures, they had to appeal to the populace for their support.

The evidence in this chapter, selections from five writings and one speech, is arranged in chronological order. Source 1 is from the extremely popular short book *Bedarf Deutschland der Kolonien?* (*Does Germany Need Colonies?*) by Friedrich Fabri (1824–1891), a long-time inspector of the Barmen Rhine Mission in German Southwest Africa. Originally published in 1879, the book was so popular that it ran through numerous editions in the late nineteenth and early twentieth centuries (the edition you will be reading was the original one, published in 1879).

Source 2 is from an 1883 letter written by John Gibson Paton (1824–1907) to James Service, governor-general of Australia. Paton was a Scotsman who in 1857 was ordained by the Reformed Presbyterian Church of Scotland and sent to be a missionary in the New Hebrides Islands (east of Australia). Missionaries such as Paton at first glance may not appear to be very important or influential. Yet their writings and occasional lectures during visits home had an enormous impact on churchgoers, and most of the men in the congregation were voters. For example, in 1889 fear of Scottish Presbyterian voters prompted Lord Salisbury to alter Great Britain's policy toward Nyasaland in southeast Africa. In 1889, Paton's autobiography (actually written by his brother from Paton's notes and letters) was published and was an extremely popular volume (a children's edition appeared in 1892).

Source 3 is a selection from an 1890 work by Jules Ferry (1832–1893). Born into a solidly bourgeois and well-to-do family (his father was a lawyer), Ferry had enough money to travel, study, take up painting, and write. He was a Republican who approved of the overthrow of Napoleon III (although he winced at the fact that the Emperor's downfall had been brought on by Prussia) and served as the premier of France's Third Republic twice between 1880 and 1885. Although Ferry came late to his advocacy of imperialism, his popularity made him an important figure in appealing to the people of France to support the building of the second colonial empire. He was responsible for the French annexation of Tunisia.

Source 4 is from a speech made by Joseph Chamberlain (1836–1914), a wealthy manufacturer and member of the British Parliament since 1876, to a city relief association on January 22, 1894. Chamberlain, a former mayor of Birmingham (1873–1875) who was an advocate of social reforms to aid the working classes, was invited to speak at the meeting, which was called to discuss widespread unemployment and hard times in Birmingham.

The fifth piece of evidence is taken from a book that gained wide circulation in Italy, *Cose affricane* (*Concerning Africa*) (Milan, 1897), by Ferdinando Martini. Martini (1841–1928) was a well-known author, playwright, theater producer, and government offi-

cial (he was governor of the Italian colony Eritrea from 1897 to 1900). *Cose affricane* was written in the wake of the Italian defeat by Ethiopia when Italy attempted to seize that African nation. This was a major humiliation for Italy.

The final piece of evidence (Source 6) is a selection from the enormously popular book *With Kitchener to Khartum* (1898) by British journalist and war correspondent George Warrington Steevens (1869–1900). In 1884, General Charles Gordon was sent by the British government to suppress a rebellion in the Sudan that threatened the stability of Egypt. Surrounded at Khartoum, Gordon and his force were wiped out on January 25, 1885, before relief could reach them (the reaction in Great Britain was about the same as the shock Americans felt zwhen they learned of the "last stand" of General George Armstrong Custer in 1876). When Major General Horatio Herbert Kitchener was ordered to smash the rebellion and avenge Gordon, Steevens went along as a war correspondent for the London *Daily Mail*. His vivid dispatches were read avidly throughout Great Britain and later collected into the book *With Kitchener to Khartum*. Steevens died of typhoid fever during the siege of Ladysmith (in Natal) during the Boer War.

All the pieces of evidence presented here were designed to influence or sway public opinion on imperialistic ventures. To help you answer the central questions in this chapter, you will want to examine each piece of evidence for the following points:

Chapter 9

Expansion

and Public

Opinion:

Advocates of

the "New

Imperialism"

(1) Does the author identify a problem or problems which he thinks imperialism can solve? What are they? If more than one, which is the most important? How will imperialism solve it? (2) How (if at all) does the author regard the "host populations" in the regions to be colonized? What adjectives, if any, are used to describe them? Does the author mention what effect Western imperialism will have on the "host populations"? (3) How does the author deal (if at all) with opponents of imperialism? How are they characterized? (4) How (if at all) does the author connect imperialism with one or more of the parallel trends and events? (5) In what other ways does the author attempt to influence public opinion?

Remember that each piece of evidence may include more than one reason to undertake imperialistic ventures. It would be helpful to take notes as you examine the evidence.

Keep the central questions in mind: What were the main arguments used by the six advocates of imperialism in favor of colonial expansion? How did each spokesman attempt to appeal to public opinion? How can these selections aid in identifying the principal motives and justifications for the new imperialism?

THE EVIDENCE

Source 1 from Friedrich Fabri, Bedarf Deutschland der Kolonien? *(Gotha: Friedrich Andreas Berthes, 1879), pp. 106–108. Translated by Christiane M. Hunley.*

1. Friedrich Fabri's *Bedarf Deutschland der Kolonien?*, 1879

But should not the German nation who is fundamentally so very capable, so seaworthy, so industrially and commercially minded, more than others suited for agricultural colonization, equipped with an abundant number of available labourers, like no other of the modern culture-people, should not precisely this nation successfully pave the way on this new course? The more we are convinced, all the less we doubt that the colonial question has already become today a vital question for the development of Germany. This question well-considered, but also vigorously handled will be of the most beneficial effects on our economic situation as well as on our entire national development. Alone the fact that there is a new question which has a polymorphic importance for the German people is truly an untouched, virginal ground that can prove to be salutary in many directions. Many things in the new nation are already made bitter through unproductive political quarreling, soured and poisoned, so that the notification of a new promising course of national development will produce a liberating effect, as the national spirit is stimulated in many ways. This would be delightful as well as a profit. By all means, more important is the consideration that one nation which is led to the height of political power can only maintain its historical position as long as it understands and proves itself as a bearer of a cultural mission. This is at the same time the only way which guarantees the existence and growth of the national well-being, the necessary foundation for a lasting development of power. The times, in which Germany contributed almost exclusively intellectual and literary activity to the tasks of our century, are over. We have become politically minded and powerful. But the political power when experiencing the absence of ulterior motive pushes itself in the foreground of the national goals, leads to harshness, yes, even to barbarism, should it not be ready and willing to serve for the ideal, moral, and economic culture-tasks of its time. The French national economist, Leroy Beaulieu, closes his work on colonization with the following words: "That nation is the greatest in the world which colonizes the most; if it is not today, it will be tomorrow." No one can deny that in this direction all other countries are by far surpassed by England. One has, of course, especially in Germany during the last decade, often heard about the declining power of England. Who only understands to appreciate political power of one nation—as it has in our iron era become almost customary—by the number of combat-ready troops, may prove easily such an opinion. Who, on the other hand, looks at the globe and notes the constantly increasing colonial possessions of Great Britain, how it extracts the strength from them, the skill with which it governs them, and above all, the dominant position which the Anglo-Saxon strain occupies in the overseas territories; such a discourse will appear to him as the reasoning of a bourgeois. The fact that England maintains its world-wide possessions, its politically dominant position over all seas with a number of troops which is scarcely one-fourth of the troops of one of our continental military nations, is not only a great economic advantage, but also at the same time a striking proof of the solid power and cultural strength that England has. Great Britain, of course, will today keep away as far as possible from mass warfare on the continent, or will only go into action with dependable allies which does not harm in any way the political power of this isolated state. In any case, it would be wise, if we Germans would learn about colonial skills from our Anglo-Saxon cousins and would begin—in a friendly competition—to strive after them. When the German Reich centuries ago was at the peak of the states in Europe, it was the Number One trade and seapower. Should the New German Reich wish to prove and maintain its newly won position of power for a long time, it will have to take up the same culture-mission and delay no longer to acknowledge its colonial task anew.

Chapter 9

Expansion

and Public

Opinion:

Advocates of

the "New

Imperialism"

Source 2 from John G. Paton (Senior Missionary, New Hebrides Mission) to the Hon. James Service (Governor-General of Australia), August 1883, quoted in Louis L. Snyder, editor, The Imperialism Reader *(Princeton, N.J.: D. Van Nostrand, 1962), pp. 295–297.*

2. Letter from John G. Paton to James Service Urging British Possession of the New Hebrides, 1883

The Hon. James Service,
Premier

Sir:

For the following reasons we think the British government ought now to take possession of the New Hebrides group of the South Sea islands, of the Solomon group, and of all the intervening chain of islands from Fiji to New Guinea.

1. Because she has already taken possession of Fiji in the east, and we hope it will soon be known authoritatively that she has taken possession of New Guinea at the northwest, adjoining her Australian possessions, and the islands between complete this chain of islands lying along the Australian coast. Taking possession of the New Hebrides would not add much to her expenses, as her governments on Fiji and New Guinea with the visits of her men-of-war passing through the group of the New Hebrides and intervening islands on their way to New Guinea, would almost be sufficient for all her requirements on the islands between.

2. The sympathy of the New Hebrides natives are all with Great Britain, hence they long for British protection, while they fear and hate the French, who appear eager to annex the group, because they have seen the way the French have treated the native races in New Caledonia, the Loyalty Islands, and other South Sea islands.

3. Till within the past few months almost all the Europeans on the New Hebrides were British subjects, who long for British protection.

4. All the men and all the money (over £140,000) used in civilizing and Christianizing the New Hebrides have been British. Now fourteen missionaries and the Dayspring mission ship, and about 150 native evangelists and teachers are employed in the above work on this group, in which over £6000 yearly of British and British-colonial money is expended; and certainly it would be unwise to let any other power now take possession and reap the fruits of all this British outlay.

5. Because the New Hebrides are already a British dependency in this sense—all its imports are from Sydney and Melbourne and British colonies, and all its exports are also to British colonies.

6. The islands of this group are generally very rich in soil and in tropical products so that if a possession of Great Britain, and [if] the labour traffic stopped so as to retain what remains of the native populations on them, they would soon, and for ages to come, become rich sources of tropical wealth to these colonies, as sugar cane is extensively cultivated on them by every native of the group, even in his heathen state. For natives they are an industrious, hard-working race, living in villages and towns, and, like farmers, depending on the cultivation and products of the ground for their support by their plantations. The islands also grow maize, cotton, coffee, arrowroot, and spices, etc., and all tropical products could be largely produced on them.

7. Because if any other nation takes possession of them, their excellent and spacious harbors, as on Efate, so well-supplied with the best fresh water, and their near proximity to Great Britain's Australasian colonies, would in time of war make them dangerous to British interests and commerce in the South Seas and her colonies.

8. The thirteen islands of this group on which life and property are now comparatively safe, the 8,000 professed Christians on the group, and all the churches formed among them, are by God's blessing the fruits of the labours of British missionaries, who, at great toil, expense, and loss of life, have translated, got printed, and taught the natives to read the Bible in part or in whole in nine different languages of this group, while 70,000 at least are longing and ready for the gospel. On this group twenty-one members of the mission families died or were murdered by the savages in beginning God's work among them, not including good Bishop Peterson, of the Melanesian mission, and we fear all this good work would be lost if the New Hebrides fall into other than British hands.

9. Because we see no other way of suppressing the labour traffic in Polynesia, with all its many evils, as it rapidly depopulates the islands, being attended by much bloodshed, misery, and loss of life.[8] It is an unmitigated evil to the natives, and ruinous to all engaged in it, and to the work of civilizing and Christianizing the islanders, while all experience proves that all labour laws and regulations, with government agents and gunboats, cannot prevent such evils, which have always been the said accompaniments of all such traffic in men and women in every land, and because this traffic and its evils are a sad stain on our British glory and Australasian honor, seeing Britain has done so much to free the slave and suppress slavery in other lands.

For the above reasons, and others that might be given, we sincerely hope and pray that you will do all possible to get Victoria and the other colonial

---

8. For decades the South Sea Islands had been plagued by unscrupulous men known as "blackbirders" who abducted laborers and sold them as slaves to work in the cotton fields of Fiji and Queensland, the sugar fields of New Caledonia, and the sheep stations of Australia. See Cyril S. Belshaw, *Changing Melanesia: Social Economics and Cultural Contact* (London: Oxford University Press, 1954), pp. 17–19.

Chapter 9
Expansion
and Public
Opinion:
Advocates of
the "New
Imperialism"

governments to help and unite in urging Great Britain at once to take possession of the New Hebrides group. Whether looked at in the interests of humanity, or of Christianity, or commercially, or politically, surely it is most desirable
that they should be at once British possessions; hence we plead for your judi-
cious and able help, and remain, your humble servant,

JOHN G. PATON
Senior Missionary
New Hebrides Mission

Source 3 from Jules Ferry, Tonkin et la Mère-Patrie *(1890), translated by and quoted in Har-
vey Goldberg, editor,* French Colonialism *(New York: Rinehart & Co., 1959), pp. 3–4.*

3. Jules Ferry's Appeal to the French to Build the 2nd Colonial Empire, 1890

Colonial policy is the child of the industrial revolution. For wealthy countries
where capital abounds and accumulates fast, where industry is expanding
steadily, where even agriculture must become mechanized in order to survive, exports are essential for public prosperity. Both demand for labor and
scope for capital investment depend on the foreign market. Had it been possible to establish, among the leading industrial countries, some kind of rational
division of production, based on special aptitudes and natural resources, so
that certain of them engaged in, say, cotton and metallurgical manufacture,
while others concentrated on the alcohol and sugar-refining industries, Europe might not have had to seek markets for its products in other parts of the
world. . . . But today every country wants to do its own spinning and weaving, forging and distilling. So Europe produces, for example, a surplus of
sugar and must try to export it. With the arrival of the latest industrial giants,
the United States and Germany; of Italy, newly resurrected; of Spain, enriched
by the investment of French capital; of enterprising little Switzerland, not to
mention Russia waiting in the wings, Europe has embarked on a competitive
course from which she will be unable to turn back.

All over the world, beyond the Vosges and across the Atlantic, the raising of
high tariffs has resulted in an increasing volume of manufactured goods, the
disappearance of traditional markets, and the appearance of fierce competition. Countries react by raising their own tariff barriers, but that is not
enough. . . . The protectionist system, unless accompanied by a serious colonial policy, is like a steam engine without a safety valve. An excess of capital
invested in industry not only reduces profits on capital but also arrests the
rise of wages. This phenomenon cuts to the very core of society, engendering

passions and countermoves. Social stability in this industrial age clearly depends on outlets for industrial goods. The beginning of the economic crisis, with its prolonged, frequent strikes—a crisis which has weighed so heavily on Europe since 1877—coincided in France, Germany, and England with a marked and persistent drop in exports. Europe is like a commercial firm whose business turnover has been shrinking for a number of years. The European consumer-goods market is saturated; unless we declare modern society bankrupt and prepare, at the dawn of the twentieth century, for its liquidation by revolution (the consequences of which we can scarcely foresee), new consumer markets will have to be created in other parts of the world. . . . Colonial policy is an international manifestation of the eternal laws of competition.

Without either compromising the security of the country or sacrificing any of its past traditions and future aspirations, the Republicans have, in less than ten years, given France four kingdoms in Asia and Africa. Three of them are linked to us by tradition and treaty. The fourth represents our contribution to peaceful conquest, the bringing of civilization into the heart of equatorial Africa. Suppose the Republic had declared, with the doctrinaires of the Radical school, that the French nation ends at Marseilles. To whom would Tunisia, Indochina, Madagascar, and the Congo belong today?

Source 4 from Joseph Chamberlain, M. P., Foreign & Colonial Speeches *(London: George Routledge & Sons, 1897), pp. 131–139.*

4. Joseph Chamberlain, Speech to the West Birmingham Relief Association, January 22, 1894

We must look this matter in the face, and must recognise that in order that we may have more employment to give we must create more demand. (Hear, hear.) Give me the demand for more goods and then I will undertake to give plenty of employment in making the goods; and the only thing, in my opinion, that the Government can do in order to meet this great difficulty that we are considering, is so to arrange its policy that every inducement shall be given to the demand; that new markets shall be created, and that old markets shall be effectually developed. (Cheers.) You are aware that some of my opponents please themselves occasionally by finding names for me—(laughter)—and among other names lately they have been calling me a Jingo.[9] (Laughter.) I am no more a Jingo than you are. (Hear, hear.) But for the reasons and arguments I have put before you tonight I am convinced that it is a necessity as

9. **Jingo:** a belligerent patriot; a chauvinist.

Chapter 9

Expansion

and Public

Opinion:

Advocates of

the "New

Imperialism"

well as a duty for us to uphold the dominion and empire which we now possess. (Loud cheers.) For these reasons, among others, I would never lose the hold which we now have over our great Indian dependency—(hear, hear)—by far the greatest and most valuable of all the customers we have or ever shall have in this country. For the same reasons I approve of the continued occupation of Egypt; and for the same reasons I have urged upon this Government, and upon previous Governments, the necessity for using every legitimate opportunity to extend our influence and control in that great African continent which is now being opened up to civilisation and to commerce; and, lastly, it is for the same reasons that I hold that our navy should be strengthened—(loud cheers)—until its supremacy is so assured that we cannot be shaken in any of the possessions which we hold or may hold hereafter.

Believe me, if in any one of the places to which I have referred any change took place which deprived us of that control and influence of which I have been speaking, the first to suffer would be the working-men of this country. Then, indeed, we should see a distress which would not be temporary, but which would be chronic, and we should find that England was entirely unable to support the enormous population which is now maintained by the aid of her foreign trade. If the working-men of this country understand, as I believe they do—I am one of those who have had good reason through my life to rely upon their intelligence and shrewdness—if they understand their own interests, they will never lend any countenance to the doctrines of those politicians who never lose an opportunity of pouring contempt and abuse upon the brave Englishmen, who, even at this moment, in all parts of the world are carving out new dominions for Britain, and are opening up fresh markets for British commerce, and laying out fresh fields for British labour. (Applause.) If the Little Englanders[10] had their way, not only would they refrain from taking the legitimate opportunities which offer for extending the empire and for securing for us new markets, but I doubt whether they would even take the pains which are necessary to preserve the great heritage which has come down to us from our ancestors. (Applause.)

When you are told that the British pioneers of civilisation in Africa are filibusters,[11] and when you are asked to call them back, and to leave this great continent to the barbarism and superstition in which it has been steeped for centuries, or to hand over to foreign countries the duty which you are unwilling to undertake, I ask you to consider what would have happened if 100 or 150 years ago your ancestors had taken similar views of their responsibility? Where would be the empire on which now your livelihood depends? We should have been the United Kingdom of Great Britain and Ireland; but those vast dependencies, those hundreds of millions with whom we keep up a mu-

10. **Little Englanders:** Britain's anti-imperialists.

11. **filibuster:** a person engaged in a private military action against a foreign government.

tually beneficial relationship and commerce would have been the subjects of other nations, who would not have been slow to profit by our neglect of our opportunities and obligations. (Applause.)

Let me give you one practical illustration, in order to show what ought to be done, and may be done, in order to secure employment for our people. I will take the case of a country called Uganda, of which, perhaps, you have recently heard a good deal. A few years ago Uganda was only known to us by the reports of certain enterprising and most venturesome travellers, or by the accounts which were given by those self-denying missionaries who have gone through all these wild and savage lands, endeavouring to carry to the people inhabiting them the blessings of Christianity and civilisation. (Applause.) But within very recent times English authority has been established in Uganda, and an English sphere of influence has been declared. Uganda is a most fertile country. It contains every variety of climate; in a large portion of it European colonisation is perfectly feasible; the products are of the utmost richness; there is hardly anything which is of value or use to us in our commerce which cannot be grown there; but in spite of these natural advantages, during the past generation the country has been desolated by civil strife and by the barbarities of its rulers, barbarities so great that they would be almost incredible if they did not come to us on the authority of thoroughly trustworthy eye-witnesses.

All that is wanted to restore this country to a state of prosperity, to a commercial position which it has never attained before, is settled peace and order. (Hear, hear.) That peace and order which we have maintained for so long in India we could secure by a comparatively slight exertion in Uganda, and, when this is proposed to us, the politicians to whom I have referred would repudiate responsibility and throw back the country into the state of anarchy from which it has only just emerged; or they would allow it to become an appendage or dependency of some other European nation, which would at once step in if we were to leave the ground free to them. I am opposed to such a craven policy as this. (Applause.) I do not believe it is right. I do not believe it is worthy of Great Britain; and, on the contrary, I hold it to be our duty to the people for whom at all events we have for the time accepted responsibility, as well as to our own people, even at some cost of life, some cost of treasure, to maintain our rule and to establish settled order, which is the only foundation for permanent prosperity. When I talk of the cost of life, bear in mind that any cost of life which might result from undertaking this duty would be a mere drop in the ocean to the bloodshed which has gone on for generations in that country before we ever took any interest in it.

But I will go further than that. This rich country should be developed. It is at the present time 800 miles from the sea, and unless we can reach a country by the sea we cannot obtain its products in a form or at a cost which would be likely to be of any use to us, nor can we get our products to them. Therefore

Chapter 9

Expansion

and Public

Opinion:

Advocates of

the "New

Imperialism"

what is wanted for Uganda is what Birmingham has got—an improvement scheme. (Laughter.) What we want is to give to this country the means of communication by a railway from the coast which would bring to that population—which is more intelligent than the ordinary populations in the heart of Africa—our iron, and our cloths, and our cotton, and even our jewelry, because I believe that savages are not at all insensible to the delights of personal adornment. (Laughter.) It would bring to these people the goods which they want and which they cannot manufacture, and it would bring to us the raw materials, of which we should be able to make further use.

Now, it is said that this is the business of private individuals. Private individuals will not make that railway for fifty years to come, and for the good reason that private individuals who go into investments like railways want to see an immediate prospect of a return. They cannot afford to go for ten or twenty years without interest on their money, and accordingly you will find that in undeveloped countries no railway has ever been made by private exertion, but has always been made by the prudence and foresight and wisdom of a government. . . .

Source 5 from Ferdinando Martini, Cose affricane: da Saati ad Abba Carmina: discoursi e scritti *(Milan: Fratelli Treves, 1897), pp. 122, 136, 140. Translated by Gina Pashko.*

5. Ferdinando Martini, from *Cose affricane*, 1897

Italy has 108 inhabitants per square kilometer; France has only 73. In proportion to its territory, only three countries in Europe surpass Italy in population density: Belgium, Holland, and Great Britain. If we continue at this rate, Italy will soon take the lead: in the decade of 1871–1881, the birth rate exceeded the death rate by seven percent, and in the following years, by eleven percent. Every year 100,000 farmers and agricultural laborers emigrate from Italy. In spite of this immense exodus, the country witnesses its place in the family of civilized people growing smaller and smaller as it looks on with fear for its political and economic future. In fact, during the last eighty years, the English-speaking population throughout the world has risen from 22 to 90 million; the Russian-speaking population from 50 to 70; and so forth, down to the Spanish-speaking population, who were 18 million and are now 39. On the other hand, the Italian-speaking population has only increased from 20 to 31 million, and most of this growth has taken place within Italy's own geographical borders. This is not very surprising. At first, our emigrants were spreading Italy's name, language, and prestige in foreign countries, but since all, or nearly all, of them went to highly developed areas, their sons and grandsons were surrounded and attracted to the life of the vigorous people of the nations giving them hospitality, and ended up by forgetting the language of their fathers and forefathers. Now they merely increase the population of other nations, like branches that are grafted on a plant of a different species. . . .

Realizing that our stubbornness and our mistakes have cost us so much in the past and continue to cost us today, I believe that, even leaving aside all other considerations and taking into account only expenditures and the chances of success, it is less secure and more expensive to endeavor to cultivate three million hectares of barren land in Italy than to insure the prosperity of a large agricultural colony in Eritrea. . . .

Source 6 from G. W. Steevens, With Kitchener to Khartum, *first published* 1898 *(London: Greenhill Books photocopy of 1898 original, 1990), pp. 317–322.*

6. G. W. Steevens on the Sudan, 1898

The curtain comes down; the tragedy of the Sudan is played out. Sixteen years of toilsome failure, of toilsome, slow success, and at the end we have fought our way triumphantly to the point where we began.

It has cost us much, and it has profited us—how little? It would be hard to count the money, impossible to measure the blood. Blood goes by quality as well as quantity; who can tell what future deeds we lost when we lost Gordon . . .? By shot and steel, by sunstroke and pestilence, by sheer wear of work, the Sudan has eaten up our best by hundreds. Of the men who escaped with their lives, hundreds more will bear the mark of its fangs till they die; hardly one of them but will die the sooner for the Sudan. And what have we to show in return?

At first you think we have nothing; then you think again, and see we have very much. We have gained precious national self-respect. We wished to keep our hands clear of the Sudan; we were drawn unwillingly to meddle with it; we blundered when we suffered Gordon to go out; we fiddled and failed when we tried to bring him back. We were humiliated and we were out of pocket; we had embarked in a foolish venture, and it had turned out even worse than anybody had foreseen. Now this was surely the very point where a nation of shopkeepers should have cut its losses and turned to better business elsewhere. If we were the sordid counter-jumpers that Frenchmen try to think us, we should have ruled a red line, and thought no more of a worthless land, bottomless for our gold, thirsty for our blood. We did nothing such. We tried to; but our dogged fighting dander would not let us. We could not sit down till the defeat was redeemed. We gave more money; we gave the lives of men we loved—and we conquered the Sudan again. Now we can permit ourselves to think of it in peace.

Chapter 9

Expansion

and Public

Opinion:

Advocates of

the "New

Imperialism"

The vindication of our self-respect was the great treasure we won at Khartum, and it was worth the price we paid for it. Most people will hardly persuade themselves there is not something else thrown in. The trade of the Sudan? For now and for many years you may leave that out of the account. The Sudan is a desert, and a depopulated desert. Northward of Khartum it is a wilderness; southward it is a devastation. It was always a poor country, and it always must be. Slaves and ivory were its wealth in the old time, but now ivory is all but exterminated, and slaves must be sold no more. Gum-arabic and ostrich feathers and Dongola dates will hardly buy cotton stuffs enough for Lancashire to feel the difference. . . .

It will recover—with time, no doubt, but it will recover. Only, meanwhile, it will want some tending. There is not likely to be much trouble in the way of fighting: in the present weariness of slaughter the people will be but too glad to sit down under any decent Government. There is no reason—unless it be complications with outside Powers, like France or Abyssinia—why the old Egyptian empire should not be reoccupied up to the Albert Nyanza and Western Darfur. But if this is done—and done it surely should be—two things must be remembered. First, it must be militarily administered for many years to come, and that by British men. Take the native Egyptian official even today. No words can express his ineptitude, his laziness, his helplessness, his dread of responsibility, his maddening red-tape formalism. His panacea in every unexpected case is the same. "It must be put in writing; I must ask for instructions." He is no longer corrupt—at least, no longer so corrupt as he was—but he would be if he dared. The native officer is better than the civilian official; but even with him it is the exception to find a man both capable and incorruptible. To put Egyptians, corrupt, lazy, timid, often rank cowards, to rule the Sudan, would be to invite another Mahdi as soon as the country had grown up enough to make him formidable.

The Sudan must be ruled by military law strong enough to be feared, administered by British officers just enough to be respected. For the second point, it must not be expected that it will pay until many years have passed. The cost of a military administration would not be very great, but it must be considered money out of pocket. . . .

Well, then, if Egypt is not to get good places for her people, and is to be out of pocket for administration—how much does Egypt profit by the fall of Abdullahi and the reconquest of the Sudan? Much. Inestimably. For as the master-gain of England is the vindication of her self-respect, so the master-gain of Egypt is the assurance of her security. As long as dervish raiders loomed on the horizon of her frontier, Egypt was only half a State. She lived on a perpetual war-footing. . . . Without us there would have been no Egypt to-day; what we made we shall keep.

That is our double gain—the vindication of our own honour and the vindication of our right to go on making Egypt a country fit to live in. Egypt's gain is her existence to-day. The world's gain is the downfall of the worst tyranny in the world, and the acquisition of a limited opportunity for open trade. The Sudan's gain is immunity from rape and torture and every extreme of misery.

The poor Sudan! The wretched, dry Sudan! Count up all the gains you will, yet what a hideous irony it remains, this fight of half a generation for such an emptiness. People talk of the Sudan as the East; it is not the East. The East has age and colour; the Sudan has no colour and no age—just a monotone of squalid barbarism. It is not a country; it has nothing that makes a country. Some brutish institutions it has, and some bloodthirsty chivalry. But it is not a country: it has neither nationality, nor history, nor arts, nor even natural features. Just the Nile—the niggard Nile refusing himself to the desert—and for the rest there is absolutely nothing to look at in the Sudan. Nothing grows green. . . .

QUESTIONS TO CONSIDER

Begin by examining each piece of evidence separately. Your task is to identify the principal arguments each speaker used to support imperialist ventures by his nation. To help you complete that task, recall the questions in Sources and Method: (1) What problem or problems does the speaker identify that he claims imperialism will solve? (2) How does the speaker regard the "host populations" of the regions to be colonized? (3) How does the speaker treat (if at all) the opponents of imperialism? How does he characterize them? (4) Does the speaker connect imperialism with other important and simultaneous trends and events? If so, how?

Friedrich Fabri offered many reasons for Germany getting into the imperialist "scramble." And yet, in essence he put forth three principal reasons. What does he mean when he refers to the "unproductive political quarreling" that is going on within the new German state? How does he

propose that colonialism can solve that problem? Second, recall that Germany was a very new nation in 1879 (when Fabri's work first appeared). What material gains might this new nation realize through imperialism? What nonmaterial gains might be made? Finally, Fabri spends a good deal of time analyzing the British. What does he want his readers to conclude? Was his work likely to produce some sort of rivalry between Germany and Great Britain? In your view, what is Fabri's strongest argument?

In his letter to the governor-general of Australia, missionary John G. Paton listed nine reasons why the British government should "take possession of the New Hebrides group of the South Sea islands." In your opinion, which of Paton's nine reasons were intended to impress the governor-general? Of the nine reasons, which ones do you think Paton cared about the most? How does Paton characterize the "host population" in the New Hebrides? What does that characterization reveal about Paton's thinking?

Chapter 9

Expansion

and Public

Opinion:

Advocates of

the "New

Imperialism"

Many Westerners would have agreed with Jules Ferry when he wrote that "Colonial policy is the child of the industrial revolution." And yet Ferry went on to explain precisely how, in his view, this "child" was born. In his opinion, what might the industrialized nations of the West have done in order to avoid colonization? What, therefore, made that colonization inevitable? What role was played by high tariffs? According to Ferry, what would have happened to Tunisia, Indochina (Vietnam), Madagascar, and the Congo had the French not enveloped them? Why would that have been undesirable?

Historian Henri Brunschwig claims that Britain's was the most commercially motivated imperialism of all European nations. Does Joseph Chamberlain's speech support Brunschwig's hypothesis? How does Chamberlain attempt to convince the British working classes that imperialism will help them? Is the argument convincing?

Chamberlain barely referred to the "host populations." When he did, however, how did he portray them? On another note, how did Chamberlain characterize British anti-imperialists?

Chamberlain struck a responsive chord (as evidenced by the applause he received) when he referred to "those self-denying missionaries who have gone through all these wild and savage lands." What is the nature of that appeal to the working people of Birmingham? Finally, what principal trends and events does Chamberlain link to imperialism? In what way does he make those connections?

In contrast, in what ways did Ferdinando Martini see Italy's situation as unique among European nations? How does he see the power and prestige of Italy changing? What accounts for that change? More important, how might building an empire help to solve Italy's problems?

War correspondent Steevens admitted that Britain's conquest of the Sudan would reap no economic gains for many years. How, then, did he justify what he admitted was the enormous expenditure of blood and treasure? How would Great Britain benefit? How can Steevens's view of Britain's benefits be contrasted with those of Chamberlain? How would Egypt benefit? How does Steevens view the "host population"? Do you think he believed it capable of being "civilized"?

After reading all the selections and answering these questions, look at the six pieces of evidence collectively. What were the most important arguments imperialists used in trying to influence public opinion? How did they view the "host populations"? The anti-imperialists? Did the arguments in favor of imperialism differ significantly from nation to nation? If so, can you explain these differences?

EPILOGUE

The brief imperialistic surge of the late nineteenth and early twentieth centuries profoundly altered the history of the world. Because of it, most of the earth's lands fell under Western political and economic influence.

In 1880 only about 10 percent of Africa was controlled by European nations; by 1900, however, only Ethiopia and Liberia had been able to resist the imperialist onslaught. In Asia, Western nations acquired some territory and effectively dominated the trade of most of the rest of the continent. And when Europe greedily eyed the vulnerable nations of Latin America, the United States—by 1900 itself a colonial power—announced that, in effect, that area fell within its national "sphere of influence." Indeed, by 1905 the nations of the West had come to believe that they were the center of the universe and that the rest of the earth existed to work for, produce profits for, and please the peoples of Europe and the United States. In their arrogance as the self-proclaimed "fittest" peoples in the world, most Westerners believed this dominance was only right and just.

This is not to say, however, that all Westerners approved of empire building. Though a minority, these critics of imperialism were extremely vocal and their criticisms could not be entirely ignored. In England, economist J. A. Hobson attacked colonialism as economically unprofitable to all but a few and morally bankrupting to the West. He characterized his foes, the advocates of imperialism as "parasites upon patriotism." For his part, Vladimir Ilyich Lenin, soon to be leader of the Bolshevik Revolution, saw imperialism as the last stage of capitalism, which ultimately would lead to war and revolution. Building upon the work of Hobson, Lenin argued that investors were actually exporting investment capital from Europe to the developing colonies, to the detriment of the workers in the West. Instead of helping workers, therefore, it was Lenin's contention that colonial expansion actually hurt them.

In France, the critics of imperialism were equally vocal. Writer Anatole France in 1904 warned that French imperialism was for the adventures of the French military, and that its ultimate result was a kind of civic barbarism. For his part, socialist Jean Jaurès argued that the "host populations" would not remain a subjugated people for long, and that France was opening a Pandora's box that it would be unable to close.

In the United States, anti-imperialists counted among their number industrialist Andrew Carnegie, author Mark Twain, philosopher William James, reformer Jane Addams, and political leader William Jennings Bryan. Yet these and other voices, though loud and articulate, for the most part went unheeded amid the almost frantic scramble for colonial possessions.

Armed with hindsight, we can see that these critics of colonialism had much stronger arguments than their contemporaries either realized or appreciated. For one thing, few of these colonies could provide the markets for European manufactured goods that Ferry and Chamberlain claimed. For example, between 1909 and 1913, tropical Africa represented only about 2 percent of Great Britain's total non-European trade.

Moreover, acquiring and administering an empire was an enormously expensive process, draining off funds

Chapter 9

Expansion

and Public

Opinion:

Advocates of

the "New

Imperialism"

that might have been used for economic and social reforms. Snuffing out resistance to colonial rule required the maintenance of a strong military presence that often responded to anti-Western upsurges with extreme brutality. In China, resistance to imperialism was countered with naval bombardments of cities and wholesale executions of resisters. In the Philippines, the United States used approximately 74,000 troops to crush the movement for independence, resorting to torture, repression, and other atrocities in order to "civilize" the Filipinos. In the Congo Free State, agents of Leopold II resorted to forced labor and incredibly brutal treatment, including mutilations of protestors, in order to extract ivory and rubber.[12] In truth, colonialism could be both an exceedingly expensive and a morally reprehensible activity.

Finally, the scramble for empire heightened the rivalry and conflict among Western nations and was one factor leading to World War I in 1914. In 1898 England and France very nearly came to blows at Fashoda (on the upper Nile River) until the French backed down. In 1905 Germany's attempts to intrude into Morocco almost brought it to war with France

until the Algeciras Conference of 1906 awarded control of Morocco to the French. In 1904–1905, Russian imperialism in East Asia brought Russia into a war with Japan in which it suffered a humiliating defeat. As Western nations looked for power vacuums to exploit in Africa, China, and the Balkans, the threat of armed hostilities increased. Indeed, it was Russia's efforts to penetrate the Balkan tinderbox that led directly to war in 1914.

At the same time, the West's control of its newly acquired territories was never strong. Movements for national independence constantly had to be put down. Efforts to "westernize" Africans and Asians were never very successful, except among some of the elites of those regions. Though an increasing number of non-Westerners gradually came to embrace Western technology and political ideas in the twentieth century, they nevertheless insisted that the West should withdraw so they could govern themselves. Thus, later movements for independence often tended to be "anti-Western" as well, to purge those societies of westernized elites, if not of Western technology. Within a half-century, all the empires built by the West in the late nineteenth century would be in shambles. For a time, the West lived in an imperialistic sunshine. Yet—to paraphrase Herman Melville—the brighter the sunshine, the greater the resulting shadows.

---

12. The situation in the Congo Free State, Leopold's personal possession, became so scandalous that the king was forced to turn over control to the Belgian government in 1908.

CHAPTER TEN

TO THE AGE ITS ART,[1]

1870–1920

During World War I, a small group of writers and artists came together in Zurich, Switzerland, to form the core of a movement they called Dada.[2] They chose the name intentionally, precisely because it is a meaningless, nonsensical word conveying their reaction to a West capable of the carnage of the Great War. Dadaists saw everything in Western civilization as absurd and futile, the products of a world become increasingly mechanistic, and they gave form to their vision in startling literary and artistic innovations designed to mock conventional modes of expression. A dadaist poet cut words randomly from newspapers, dropped them into a bag and shook them up, then drew them out and assembled them in the order they emerged as a nonsensical poem.[3] A dadaist artist displayed his version of Leonardo da Vinci's *Mona Lisa*, faithful to the original save for a mustache added, an act that at the time appeared shockingly disrespectful of artistic conventions.[4] In such ways did dadaists call into question all traditional values and modes of expression.

Although the Dada movement had spent itself by 1924, it was nonetheless a highly significant cultural phenomenon, marking the culmination of a number of developments in Western thought that, taken together,

1. "To the age its art": Part of the inscription on the façade of the House of the Secession in Vienna, Austria, built in 1898 as a gallery home for the work of the group of artists calling themselves the Secession because of their break with artistic conventions of the late nineteenth century. The full inscription is: "To the age its art. To the art its freedom."

2. **Dada:** the precise origin of this term has been explained in various ways. It means "hobbyhorse" in French, and one version of its origin holds that it was selected by a random opening of a French dictionary at the word *dada*. Others explain "Dada" as the "Da, Da," that is "Yes, Yes," of the Romanian conversation of one of its founders. Whatever its actual origins, the term was nonsensical to most Europeans in 1918. The original Dada *Manifesto* issued in Berlin in 1918 is reprinted in Hans Richter, *Dada: Art and Anti-Art,* trans. David Britt (New York: Oxford University Press, 1978), pp. 104–07.

3. Tristan Tzara (1896–1963).

4. Marcel Duchamp (1887–1968).

represented for many an intellectual crisis, a real challenge to traditional values and beliefs during the period from about 1870 to 1920.

The traditional values and beliefs of most nineteenth-century Westerners were founded on the tenets of Judeo-Christian religion and the legacy of the eighteenth-century Enlightenment. From the Bible, most Westerners derived their faith in a Creator. From the Enlightenment, they drew a belief in the rational nature of humans and their ability to use their intellectual gifts to understand and master the physical world (see Chapter 3). In the last years of the nineteenth century and the first years of the twentieth century, however, the findings of physical and social scientists called traditional values and beliefs into question while failing to advance an alternative faith. At the same time, as we will see, the art of the age reflected an increasing knowledge of the physical world and the diminished authority of old standards of thought and behavior. We will note here only the more important late-nineteenth-century developments in Western knowledge that contradicted traditional thought, some aspects of which continue to stir controversy a century later.

Western religious beliefs met challenges on several fronts after 1870. The pioneering English biologist Charles Darwin (1809–1882) had presented his theory of evolution as it applied to animals in his 1859 classic, *On the Origin of Species*. In 1871 Darwin published what was for many a more disturbing work, *Descent of Man*, in which he applied his evolu-

tionary theories to mankind.[5] Educated Westerners suddenly found that their religious beliefs, grounded on the story of the Creation in the Bible's book of Genesis, conflicted with the rational framework of the natural science in which they also put great stock. The result was a crisis of belief that still manifests itself in parts of the West in struggles over the content of public school biology courses.

At the same time that Darwin's work challenged one basic article of the Judeo-Christian faith, archaeological and biblical studies diminished the uniqueness of the Judeo-Christian heritage. Increasing Western knowledge of ancient Middle Eastern civilization, for example, revealed a great cultural kinship between the Hebrews of the Old Testament and the Babylonians and other ancient peoples. Similarly, scholars of the New Testament period found remarkable parallels to the story of the life of Christ in non-Christian cultures. Was the Judeo-Christian heritage, based on a belief in the Jews as God's chosen people and in a Savior of humankind, as unique as it had previously seemed? The debate still continues between religious fundamentalists and those who accept an increasing body of knowledge founded on scholarship and not faith.

As modern scholarship challenged traditional religious thought, it also raised doubts about the intellectual legacy of the eighteenth century. A central tenet of the Enlightenment held

5. The full titles of these works were *On the Origin of Species by Means of Natural Selection or the Preservation of Favored Races in the Struggle for Life* and *The Descent of Man in Relation to Sex.*

that reason was the supreme and exclusive achievement of humankind. The work by psychological and biological researchers in the late nineteenth and early twentieth centuries, however, cast increasing doubt on the validity of that belief. Wilhelm Wundt (1832–1920) opened the first experimental psychology laboratory at the University of Leipzig in 1870. His purpose was to conduct experiments on animal subjects to demonstrate that the animal mind and the human mind were fundamentally similar. The Russian physiologist Ivan Pavlov (1849–1936), conducting similar laboratory experiments with dogs in the 1890s, determined that certain responses in his subjects could be conditioned—that is, learned and unlearned. The emerging behaviorist school of psychology to which Pavlov's experiments contributed held that most human actions and emotions, like those of the laboratory dogs, could be similarly conditioned. The human mind suddenly seemed quite similar to that of the animal. Such a concept did not accord with the Enlightenment belief in human rationality. Even more destructive of reason as the cornerstone of human behavior was the work of the Austrian physician Sigmund Freud (1856–1939).

Freud began his pioneering work in mental disorders in the 1880s, achieving success with a therapeutic process in which he allowed his patients to talk freely about their childhood memories, their emotions, and their fantasies. The result of his work was the modern school of psychoanalysis and a very unsettling view of the human mind. Freud and other psychological researchers posited the existence of the human unconscious, an irrational and inaccessible portion of the psyche that exerted tremendous influence, through feelings and impulses repressed from consciousness, on human behavior. Indeed, for Freud, the unconscious was a virtual battleground of conflicting inner forces. The *id* embodied base and instinctual drives, such as sex and violence, which demanded immediate, hedonistic gratification. The *superego*, on the other hand, embraced the conventions of society and the strictures of religion that aimed at repressing such impulses. Between these two extremes was the *ego*, the mediating point of consciousness in which some sort of balance between the hedonistic drives of the id and the repressive tendencies of the superego had to be achieved for the well-balanced mind. The goal of Freud's psychoanalysis was to defuse potentially dangerous unconscious impulses by making them conscious, that is, drawing them into the patient's field of awareness, where they could then be examined and treated.

After Freud, reason could no longer be upheld as the motivating principle of human behavior. The optimistic view of progress—that is, that history and human development moved toward better and better forms—also declined as a result of the work of two pioneering sociologists, the Frenchman Emile Durkheim (1858–1917) and the German Max Weber (1864–1920). In examining his society, Durkheim found that modern times in the West were not necessarily an improvement over the past. In medieval and early modern Europe, social station was determined at birth and traditional social values and religious strictures dictated the individual's comportment within his or her station. In the modern Western world, however, the individual enjoyed greater freedom at the same time that the force of traditional religious and social controls waned. Anarchy threatened society, and *anomie*, a loss of personal direction resulting from the collapse of moral guidelines, afflicted the individual and contributed, Durkheim said, to the West's high rate of suicide. Consequently, he believed, the modern world required a new, secular moral order.

Max Weber examined the results of the Enlightenment effort to explain the physical world scientifically and to organize governments rationally around constitutions and bureaucratic procedures. The results had been high scientific accomplishment and stable government won at the cost of human creativity and personal freedom. The modern institutions of the state and corporations aim at domination of the individual. Thus Weber pessimistically concluded his essay "Politics as a Vocation" with the words: "Not summer's bloom lies ahead of us, but rather a polar night of icy darkness and hardness. . . ."[6] Progress, for Weber and others, was a mixed blessing.

Other social theorists advanced a different but equally disturbing view

6. Quoted in H. H. Gerth and C. Wright Mills, editors and translators, *From Max Weber: Essays in Sociology* (New York: Oxford University Press, 1946), p. 128.

of the world, one marked by strife, violence, and conflict. Marxists, as we saw in Chapter 7, found human existence to be dominated by class conflict; other thinkers advanced equally unsettling visions of human conflict. An important tenet of Enlightenment thought was the basic equality of all humans. Yet some nineteenth-century thinkers, in their enthusiasm for the new scientific discoveries of the age, applied Darwin's biological theory of evolution to society as a whole. Emphasizing the struggle for existence that they found in Darwin's work, they claimed that a process of "survival of the fittest" characterized modern human society. All people were not created equal; rather, the stronger or more intelligent had a right to triumph and survive in life's struggle, whereas others did not. Such an application of Darwin's ideas, known as Social Darwinism, could be used, for example, to justify imperialism on the grounds that a "superior" people had a right to rule an "inferior" people (see Chapter 9). According to this view, despite the progressive improvement predicated by Enlightenment thinkers, human beings still were engaged in a primal struggle for existence.

Philosophers, too, joined in the criticism of the Christian tradition, the Enlightenment, and the modern world. Indeed, the German philosopher Friedrich Nietzsche (1844–1900) offered the most thoroughgoing rebuttal of Enlightenment thought and everything associated with it. Nietzsche saw the modern world in decay because its elevation of reason had undermined the capacity to feel pas-

ity of social labour cease to be a source of poverty and oppression for the hitherto exploited classes and become a source of supreme welfare and all-round, harmonious improvement. This social transformation means the emancipation not only of the proletariat but of the whole human race as suffering under present circumstances. It can only be achieved by the working class, however, because all other classes, despite conflicts of interest between them, take their stand on the private ownership of the means of production and have as their common goal the preservation of the foundations of present-day society.

The struggle of the working class against capitalist exploitation is of necessity a political struggle. The working class cannot wage its economic struggles and develop its economic organisation without political rights. It cannot effect the switch of the means of production to common ownership without first acquiring political power.

The task of the Social Democratic Party is to mould that struggle of the working class into a conscious, uniform process and direct it towards its immutable goal.

The interests of the working class in all countries with a capitalist mode of production are the same. With the growth of world trade and production for the world market the position of workers in one country is becoming increasingly dependent on the position of workers in all other countries. The emancipation of the working class is thus a task in which the workers of all civilised countries are equally involved. Recognising this, the Social Democratic Party of Germany feels and declares itself to be one with the class-conscious workers of all other countries.

The Social Democratic Party of Germany is thus fighting not for new class privileges and prerogatives but for the abolition of class rule and of classes themselves and for equal rights and equal obligations for all without distinction of sex and birth. Armed with these opinions it campaigns in present-day society not only against the exploitation and oppression of wage workers but against every kind of exploitation and oppression, be it directed against a class, a party, a sex, or a race.

On the basis of these principles the Social Democratic Party of Germany demands firstly:

1. Universal, equal, direct suffrage with secret balloting for all German citizens of twenty and over without distinction of sex for all elections and votes. A proportional-representation system, and until that is introduced the statutory re-drawing of constituency boundaries after every census. Two-year legislative periods. Elections and votes to be held on a statutory public holiday. Remuneration of elected representatives. The abolition of any restriction of political rights except in the event of legal incapacitation.

2. Direct legislation by the people through the medium of rights of proposal and rejection. Self-determination and self-government of the people at

amounts of energy. Einstein's work brought the world to the threshold of the atomic age while discrediting the long-held tenets of absolute time and space.

The greatest challenge to the world view of nineteenth-century Westerners, however, came not as abstract theory but devastating reality: World War I (see Chapter 11). Many intellectuals and artists initially joined their fellow citizens in welcoming a war that they believed would revitalize the West. In that conflagration, however, every belligerent government harnessed modern science and industry to its war effort. The result was bloodletting on an unprecedented scale that caused intellectuals and artists to despair of traditional values—the mood represented by the Dada movement. As the Dada *Manifesto* declared: "After the carnage, we keep only the hope of a purified humanity."

By the early decades of the twentieth century, then, the patterns of nineteenth-century Western thought seemed under assault on every front. As old ways of thinking fell to the new discoveries in the physical and social sciences, Western artistic expression cast off old norms as well, often with provocative results. To take the example of music, a number of composers of the early twentieth century abandoned traditional harmonies in their compositions, producing a new dissonant sound. The first performance in 1913 of a ballet, *The Rite of Spring,* by one of these composers, Igor Stravinsky (1882–1971), almost provoked a Paris audience to riot. To composers like Stravinsky, harmony no longer seemed appropriate in a world of discord.

Reflecting the trends of the period 1870 to 1920, another art form, painting, also abandoned traditional conventions during this time of intellectual crisis. Your goal in this chapter is to examine the magnitude of the transformations in Western thought of this period by analyzing the works of a group of major painters. How do the paintings reflect a break with traditional artistic standards? What trends can be traced from each artist's work? How did artists reveal the intellectual currents of the period in their works?

SOURCES AND METHOD

This chapter introduces you to a primary source historians traditionally have used in studying a past era—its art. Analysis of a period's works of art can provide the historian with an excellent entry into the intellectual life of that epoch because art often reflects the thought of its age. But we must be clear about what is and is not part of the analytical process you must carry out with this chapter's evidence.

The evidence should not be the object of your aesthetic analysis, that is, your attempt to determine which paintings express your individual concept of beauty. We all have opinions and preferences regarding art, especially the modern art this chapter presents. Consequently, you might be inclined simply to dismiss some of the paintings reproduced here as "strange looking" because they do not accord with your individual taste.

You should, however, analyze the paintings in the context of their times. To help focus your analysis, the paintings selected all have a common subject, the human form, to enable you to appreciate the different visions artists brought to the problem of portraying their fellow humans. They also are arranged roughly chronologically to show you both traditional nineteenth-century art before 1870 and some of its main trends over the half-century from 1870 to 1920. You should attempt to assess the impact that these works would have had on their contemporary viewers. Try to imagine yourself as an educated Western European born about 1850 and living until 1920. You would have reached maturity about 1870 and, in the course of your lifetime, would have experienced tremendous change. Materially, you would have been born in an age in which most people traveled by foot or horse and carriage and would have lived to see people traveling by train, automobile, and airplane. Your messages in later life would be carried by telephone and telegraph, and the diseases that threatened your parents would be only a memory by your middle years. In the course of your lifespan of seventy years, then, your material world would have been totally transformed. So, too, would have been your culture's art. Would you have found this transformation unsettling? To supplement your analysis, a brief introduction to the artists whose work this chapter presents is necessary.

Sources 1 and 2, representing two conventional styles of nineteenth-century art, are works whose style would have seemed familiar to their viewers. They are the starting point for your analysis of artistic trends. The French painter Jean-Auguste Dominique Ingres (1780–1867) was an exponent of the neoclassical style of painting. Art historians apply the label "neoclassical" to Ingres and other artists of his period who found much of their inspiration in classical subjects. In the execution of their works these artists sought to duplicate the harmony, balance, and realism they found in Greek and Roman art. They also often presented classical themes in their works. Source 1, *The Apotheosis of Homer*, is an example of such a work and of the techniques of many early-nineteenth-century artists. In Source 1 Ingres presents his vision of the reception of the Greek poet Homer into the ranks of the gods, symbolized in the painting by his coronation. What do you notice about Ingres's conception of this scene that illustrates classical values of harmony and balance? What in the artist's technical execution of this mythical scene would lead you to characterize his efforts as almost photographic in detail?

Source 2, *Greece Expiring on the Ruins of Missolonghi,* by Eugène Delacroix (1798–1863), is an example of nineteenth-century romanticism. Romanticism arose in large part as a reaction to the Enlightenment with its emphasis on a rational interpretation of the human experience. In literature

[269]

and art, exponents of the romantic impulse sought to recover the emotion and drama of life. In thus approaching art, many romantic artists were in conscious revolt against the formalism of neoclassical artists like Ingres. The Greek rebellion of the 1820s against Turkey excited European romantics because it was the war for independence of the land of Homer and Plato; and one English romantic poet, Lord Byron, died in Greece seeking to join the rebel cause. Delacroix's painting shows a Greek fighter crushed in the ruins of the city of Missolonghi, where the Greek defenders succumbed in 1826 to a long siege by the Turks. (Missolonghi, not inconsequentially, was the site of Byron's death.) The woman's gesture of defenseless resignation reflects Greek martyrdom. What view of the world and the role of human beings in it did Delacroix convey? What view of the individual does the image of "Greece" convey to you? Compare the paintings of Delacroix and Ingres. Certainly the artists reflected two very different philosophies. Nevertheless, what similarities do you find in their portrayal of the human form?

As your analysis moves beyond Source 2, you must be careful to assess the paintings in light of the intellectual breakthroughs we have just examined. Remember, too, that by 1850 the invention of the camera, with its ability to produce accurate images, obliged artists to make a serious reevaluation of the function of their art. What was the purpose of the labor involved in re-creating the details in Sources 1 and 2 in portraits when a photograph would capture an even more accurate image?

In Source 3 we encounter the work of an artistic movement that reflected the late nineteenth century's interest in science and the reassessment of the artistic function prompted by the camera. With the impressionist artists who flourished especially in France in the 1870s and 1880s, we see a reconsideration of the whole function of painting that relegated portraiture to the photographer. We also find a systematic attempt, much in the vein of modern science, to portray the artist's subjects with an accuracy that would convey to the viewer the subtle effects of light and shadow as they actually appeared to the human eye.

Some impressionists executed their works with large splashes of color. Georges Seurat (1859–1891) moved beyond this technique to a postimpressionism that he called pointilism in which he created pictures with intricate arrangements of tiny dots of color, the result of his study of scientific theories of color perception. *A Sunday Afternoon on the Island of La Grande Jatte* shows excursioners on an island in the river Seine near Paris. What was the artist's purpose in this painting? Why did he pay so little apparent attention to developing the individual characteristics of the persons in his painting? How would you characterize the figures in *La Grande Jatte*?

In the 1870s many viewed impressionism and the work of Seurat as a dramatic revolt against artistic conventions, but far more was to come.

The Dutchman Vincent van Gogh (1853–1890) studied the impressionists and moved beyond them. He gloried in the use of broad brush strokes to express his excitement and emotions in a picture, distorting images in that quest. His work thus makes him an early exponent of another style of art, expressionism. A deeply religious man, van Gogh sought to express his personal vision of his subjects while also seeking in them what he called "that something of the eternal which the halo used to symbolize."[7] Source 4, his portrait *La Berceuse* (The Cradle Rocker), employs startling colors: the woman's hair is orange, her dress green, the wallpaper background green and pink flowers, and the floor red. What feelings did the artist seek to express here? Compare *La Berceuse* with the work of Ingres. Why did van Gogh engage in such obvious distortions of the human shape?

Paul Gauguin (1848–1903) also emerged from the impressionists to create a style called symbolism. Gauguin had two careers, first as a successful Parisian stockbroker, then as an impoverished artist. Indeed, he left his family and business for his art in 1883. In rejecting his middle-class past, he also rejected much of modern industrial society. Gauguin found that Westerners had lost much of life's emotions and mystery in their progress toward the industrial age with its concern for material gain. Western art, he believed, reflected this loss, and he sought to reinfuse the missing

emotion into his paintings by studying the art of non-Western peoples. Gauguin spent most of his last years in the South Pacific trying to capture the spirit of non-Western art. A number of artists followed Gauguin's lead in exploring non-Western art, especially after World War I, which convinced them of the bankruptcy of Western culture and values. Indeed, later artists sought non-Western inspiration more widely than Gauguin; many, for example, incorporated African art forms in their work. In Source 5, Gauguin's painting *Manao Tupapau—The Spirit of the Dead Watches*, how has he added non-Western elements in achieving his artistic goal? How did he inject a fantastic element into Western art?

Source 6, *The Dream,* is the work of Frenchman Henri Rousseau (1844–1910). A self-taught artist, Rousseau spent the first half of his adulthood as a government customs inspector, and his paintings reflect his lack of traditional training. *The Dream* is a fantastic, impossible, and highly detailed scene that conveys Rousseau's view of life. What does the choice of a dream as his subject tell you about the artist's outlook? Does the artist present a realistic group of figures in the nude, the lions, and the snake charmer? Why might you think that Rousseau sought to paint the same natural and non-Western settings that Gauguin did?

The work of the Norwegian artist Edvard Munch (1863–1948) reflected the influence of van Gogh, Gauguin, and the philosophical thought of his day. His *The Scream,* Source 7, is an expressionist work. Even more than

---

7. Quoted in H. W. Janson, *History of Art: A Survey of the Major Visual Arts from the Dawn of History to the Present Day* (New York: Harry N. Abrams and Prentice-Hall, 1962), p. 507.

van Gogh, however, Munch subordinated detail and character study to a strong message. What sentiments does the central figure convey in *The Scream*? How does the artist's treatment of the background magnify the feelings of the central character? What might the artist be saying about the central figure's relationships with other people?

The work of van Gogh and Gauguin influenced other artists as well. Exhibits of their works in Paris during the first years of the twentieth century inspired a group of young artists to break so much with artistic conventions that their contemporaries called them *les Fauves*, or "The Wild Beasts." And in Vienna, a group of artists, calling themselves "The Secession" to reflect their abandonment of traditional modes of artistic expression, flourished in the last decades of the nineteenth century and in the twentieth century prior to World War I. The leading artist in this group was Gustav Klimt (1862–1918), a contemporary of Freud, in whom we can plainly see the intellectual and artistic turmoil of this period. Like other artists Klimt challenged stylistic convention. But what really made his work especially controversial was his apparent rejection of the norms of morality and good taste embraced by late-nineteenth- and early-twentieth-century, middle- and upper-class Europeans and his negation of that group's faith in the eventual triumph of liberal ideas and scientific progress (see Chapter 7).

Controversy engulfed Klimt when he was commissioned by the government to provide paintings for the ceremonial hall ceilings of the new University of Vienna building (see Chapter 8). Klimt's commission was to portray "Philosophy," "Medicine," and "Jurisprudence," and his work was expected to have reflected the nineteenth century's scientific and intellectual triumphs and the growth of political liberalism with its concern for justice for all. Instead Klimt provided paintings, controversial in the extreme because they were to have been paid for with public funds, that offered primitive sexuality and death, the expression of all of the dark forces that questioned the very idea of progress. The government rejected the paintings, for not only did they question the progress of the age, they also caused many in the public to charge Klimt with creating pornography.

Source 8 presents one of Klimt's best-known paintings, *The Kiss*, a work completed in 1907–1908 after the university controversy. This painting reflects Klimt's rebellion in several ways. Its background color is gold, demonstrating Klimt's interest in pre-twentieth-century media, especially Byzantine gold mosaics. What else do you notice about it? Why would its divorce from reality lead you to consider this abstract art? The painting contains a great deal of symbolism, too. How do you think many in early-twentieth-century audiences responded to the rectangles on the cloak of the male figure and the ovals on that of the female when you understand that these forms were generally taken to symbolize the genital organs of each figure? Why do you think Klimt's art might have been the most controversial of all?

A young Spanish artist, Pablo Picasso (1881–1973), moved to Paris in 1900 and immediately reflected in his work the influence of many of the artists we have discussed. Yet Picasso went beyond them in the extent of his break with artistic tradition. Source 9, *Les Demoiselles d'Avignon,* shocked Picasso's audiences in several ways in 1907. First, its subject is a group of prostitutes on Avignon Street in Barcelona. Second, it is an early expression of the cubist style in art, in which the artist used a variety of wedges and angles to create his picture.

In *Les Demoiselles d'Avignon,* Picasso abandoned traditional rules of perspective as well as any effort to portray the human form accurately. Some found his cubism almost an attempt to portray his subjects geometrically; others remarked that Picasso's women looked like arrangements of broken pieces of glass. Certainly, too, this work represents Picasso's exploration of forms of artistic expression from Africa and parts of the non-Western world. Why do you think Picasso abandoned artistic conventions? Can you discern any parallels between Picasso's art and the physical science of Einstein and others? What trend in modern art is reflected in the two faces on the picture's right?

Picasso was one of a number of abstract artists at work early in the twentieth century. Abstract art puts primary emphasis on the structure, not the subject, of the picture. Another abstract artist was the German George Grosz (1893–1959), who joined the Dada movement after World War I. Grosz's works show cubist influ-

ences in a type of collage technique; they also frequently have a social message, as in Source 10, *Germany, A Winter's Tale.* Completed amid the famine and defeat that overtook Germany in the last days of World War I, this painting presents Grosz's views on the war and the society that produced it. The central figure is an "average" German surrounded by a kaleidoscope of Berlin scenes. What do you notice about the plate in front of him? What comment does this make on the Germany of 1918? What social groups do the three figures at the bottom represent? What roles did they play in pre-1918 German society, according to the artist? What vision of German society in 1918 does the background convey?

The final artist whose work appears in our evidence is the Frenchman Marcel Duchamp (1887–1968). Duchamp joined the Dada movement in despair after World War I, and it was he who created the *"Mona Lisa"* with the mustache that we described earlier in this chapter. Even before the war, however, his work challenged all artistic conventions. Source 11, *Nude Descending a Staircase, Number 1,* challenged traditionalists who found little here resembling a human being. It also challenged the artistic rebels of the day; cubists, accustomed to presenting static forms, rejected the obvious motion of Duchamp's figure. Cubists forced the picture's removal from the major modern art exhibit in Paris in 1912, and traditionalists were scandalized when the picture appeared at the Armory Show of modern art in New York in 1913. Why do you think the artist rejected any attempt to portray the human form accurately? What manner of comment on the machine age might this work be making? How and why were artists like Duchamp striving for a new and more subjective reality?

Using this background on the painters, turn now to the evidence. As you look at the paintings, seek to assess the magnitude of the changes in Western thought in the period 1870–1920. How do the paintings reflect a break with traditional artistic standards? What trends can be traced from each artist's work? How did the artists reveal the intellectual currents of the period in their works?

Source 1 from Musée du Louvre, Paris.

1. Jean-Auguste Dominique Ingres, *The Apotheosis of Homer*, 1827

Source 2 from the Musée des Beaux Arts, Bordeaux/Cliché des Musées Nationaux-Paris.

2. Eugène Delacroix, *Greece Expiring on the Ruins of Missolonghi*, 1827

3. Georges Seurat, A Sunday Afternoon on the Island of La Grande Jatte, 1884–1886

Source 4 from the Stichting Kröller-Müller, Otterlo.

4. Vincent van Gogh, *La Berceuse*, 1889

Source 5 from the Albright-Knox Art Gallery, Buffalo, New York (A. Conger Goodyear Collection). Oil on burlap mounted on canvas, 28½″ × 38 ⅜″.

5. Paul Gauguin, *Manao Tupapau—The Spirit of the Dead Watches*, 1892

Source 6 from Collection, The Museum of Modern Art, New York (Gift of Nelson A. Rockefeller). 6'8½" × 9'9½".

6. Henri Rousseau, *The Dream*, 1910

Source 7 from the Nasjonalgalleriet, Oslo. Photograph by J. Lathion.

7. Edvard Munch, *The Scream*, 1893

Source 8 from Galerie Welz, Salzburg, reprinted in Carl E. Schorske, Fin-de-Siècle Vienna: Politics and Culture *(New York: Vintage Books, 1981), Plate viii. Photograph: Erich Lessing/Art Resource, NY.*

8. Gustav Klimt, *The Kiss*, 1907–1908

9. Pablo Picasso, *Les Demoiselles d'Avignon*, 1907

Source 10 formerly from the Collection Garvens, Hanover, Germany (painting has been lost).

10. George Grosz, *Germany, A Winter's Tale*, 1918

11. Marcel Duchamp, *Nude Descending a Staircase, Number 1, 1911*

QUESTIONS TO CONSIDER

As we saw in Chapter 8, free public education was becoming more widely available in Western Europe by the late nineteenth century. The number of people with sufficient education to understand intellectual trends grew rapidly in the years before 1920. Consequently, the shifts in thinking we are examining in this chapter were evident to a considerably larger audience than that of the Enlightenment (Chapter 3). Many in this growing educated class must have found the upheavals in the natural sciences, philosophy, and art of their day unpredictable and disturbing.

At the most basic level, consider the changes in art in the period 1870 to 1920. Contrast Sources 1 and 2 with the art that follows. How do you think nineteenth-century audiences would have received the impressionists' offerings after a steady diet of works like Sources 1 and 2? How would you account for the following reaction in 1876 by one French journalist to an early impressionist exhibit?

The Rue le Peletier is a road of disasters. After the fire at the Opera, there is now yet another disaster there. An exhibition has just been mounted at Durand-Ruel [gallery] which allegedly contains paintings. I enter and my horrified eyes behold something terrible. Five or six lunatics, among them a woman, have joined together and exhibited their works. I have seen people rock with laughter in front of these pictures, but my heart bled when I saw them. These would-be artists call themselves revolutionaries, "Impressionists." They take a piece of canvas, colour and brush, daub a few patches of colour on them at random, and sign the whole thing with their name. It is a delusion of the same kind as if the inmates of Bedlam picked up stones from the wayside and imagined they had found diamonds.[8]

But the art of the period was the result of an aesthetic impulse far more significant than change for the sake of change, and perhaps all the more significant for that reason. Art reflected a new view of the world and the place of the individual in it. You must now examine the paintings reproduced here in light of the emerging intellectual outlook we examined at the outset of this chapter. How did the impressionists respond to the great faith in science that characterized their age? Why do you find in the work of the postimpressionist Seurat far less emphasis on the individual than in the work of Ingres and Delacroix? What vision of life does Seurat express? What philosophical changes (and responses by educated persons to those changes) might this diminished importance have represented? How does Seurat's view of the individual contrast with that of later artists like Picasso?

Van Gogh's portrait *La Berceuse* offered its viewers an expression of the artist's sentiments. Why was van Gogh expressing his own feelings

8. Quoted in E. H. Gombrich, *The Story of Art* (New York: Phaidon, 1971), pp. 392–393. **Bedlam:** the early English institution for the insane.

through the medium of another individual rather than creating a photolike replica of that person? What developments in nineteenth-century thought did he reflect in this study of his subject?

In the works of Gauguin we find a search for an art with more meaning than that produced by Western civilization, which the artist found sterile. How would those familiar with the work of Nietzsche, Durkheim, Weber, and perhaps Marx have interpreted Gauguin's work? Remember, too, that Gauguin painted during the age of imperialism (see Chapter 9). How does his art stand in relation to his age's avowed belief in the superiority of Western civilization, the rallying point of the Social Darwinists?

Munch's *The Scream* brings together in one work of art many tendencies in late-nineteenth- and early-twentieth-century thought. Recall the ideas of Durkheim and Weber. Why did Munch portray his subject as a solitary individual? What do you think provoked the agonized scream? Although Munch's work predated most of Freud's great writings, why might you think that Munch and Freud shared a common view of the human psyche?

Consider next Klimt's *The Kiss*. Why do you think Freud's work on the human mind might have influenced Klimt? Many viewers of Klimt's work would have seen it as an attack. What was the artist attacking? George Grosz satirized the world in which he lived. Recall particularly the ideas of the pioneering German sociologist Max Weber and the steril-

ity he found in an increasingly bureaucratized world. What elements of Weber's thought do you find embodied in Grosz's response to German society?

You may find that Picasso's *Les Demoiselles d'Avignon* reflects several trends in Western thought. What is the significance of mathematical and geometric relationships in the cubist approach to the human form? What contrasting message is given by the masklike faces on the right of the picture? How do they reflect some of the same influences Gauguin experienced? What was the effect of the age's ideas on Picasso?

Consider Rousseau's *The Dream*. In one of his most significant works, *The Interpretation of Dreams* (1900), Freud sought to understand the irrational side of the human psyche, the unconscious, by explaining the psychological meaning of dreams. How does Rousseau's vision of reality coincide with Freud's? What significance might you ascribe to the nude and the powerful lions in the context of Freud's work?

The final painting is Duchamp's nude. Review our findings on the paintings that precede his chronologically. Why are you probably not surprised to find in his work a painting totally devoid of anything resembling the human form? What trends in art culminate in Duchamp's work? Remember that he eventually became a dadaist. Can you detect in the nude a message about the machine age and its impact on the individual?

As you answer these questions, you should gain a better understanding of the sweeping intellectual changes that overtook the late-nineteenth- and early-twentieth-century Western world. The dadaist outlook on Western civilization, described in the introduction to this chapter, embodied one extreme reaction to those changes, and the art we have studied presents other responses. You should now be able to answer the central questions of this chapter: How did the paintings reflect a break from traditional artistic standards? What trends can be identified in each artist's work? Finally, how did the artists collectively reveal the intellectual currents of the period?

EPILOGUE

In a sense, this chapter presents a turning point in the history of Western civilization. The West after 1920 was in many ways a far less secure place than the West of the eighteenth and nineteenth centuries, when Europe had been equally secure in its world power and its world view. The nineteenth century in particular had produced a standard of living in the West higher than ever before enjoyed by people anywhere. Westerners were convinced of their primacy.

As the nineteenth century drew to a close, however, many Europeans looked to a disturbing future. Certainly the trends in art we have observed here continued. Dadaism gave way to surrealism, which drew on the artist's unconscious. Later, abstract expressionism and other styles would also develop to present viewers with even greater challenges to their interpretive skills. Other undercurrents were even more distressing, however. Intellectually, the authority of the old faiths and tenets that long had guided Westerners eroded for many persons, and the consequent questioning of traditional values and practices invaded every area of human endeavor. Internationally, the strength of the European powers was challenged by the rise of non-European nations like the United States and Japan. Politically, the nineteenth-century faith in democracy would be challenged by twentieth-century totalitarian movements that reminded many of the threat Max Weber saw in an irrational but charismatic leader (see Chapter 13). Technologically, humankind's progress meant that it had developed unprecedented ability to destroy life (see Chapter 11). Economically, nineteenth-century bourgeois capitalism faced the challenge of communist revolution. The art of the period 1870–1920 reflected all these disturbing developments.

Indeed, the art produced after 1920 by surrealist, abstract expressionist, and other modern artists mirrored the changes in the West that came with accelerating speed after the period we have examined in this chapter. Einstein's work unlocked the destructive possibilities of the atom, and Western science was to create technologies of war far in excess of those employed in World War I. In the giant corporations that came to dominate the Western economy, the individual's significance diminished still further. Using the analytical technique you have mastered in this chapter, you may wish to continue exploring the ideological messages of modern art beyond the period 1870–1920.

CHAPTER ELEVEN

WORLD WAR I:

TOTAL WAR

In the first days of August 1914, every major capital city in Europe was the scene of enthusiastic patriotic demonstrations in favor of the declarations of war that began World War I. All confidently predicted victory for their own nation, and all expected a short war. Emperor William II (Kaiser Wilhelm II) told German troops departing for the front, "You will be home before the leaves have fallen from the trees." The war indeed ended in autumn, but it was the autumn of 1918, not 1914. Previous military history did not prepare Europeans in any way for the war they were to undertake in 1914.

Europe's last general war had ended in 1815 with Napoleon's defeat at Waterloo. Subsequent nineteenth-century conflicts never involved all the great powers, and they were invariably short wars. The Prussians, for example, had defeated Austria in six weeks during the Austro-Prussian War of 1866. In the last nineteenth-century conflict involving

major powers, the Franco-Prussian War of 1870–1871, France and Prussia had signed an armistice after a little over twenty-seven weeks of combat.

These nineteenth-century wars after Waterloo were also highly limited conflicts, involving relatively small professional armies whose weapons and tactics differed little from those of the Napoleonic era. Civilian populations seldom felt much impact from such conflicts, although Paris endured a siege of eighteen weeks in the Franco-Prussian War.

The war on which Europeans so enthusiastically embarked in 1914 proved a far different one than the 1870–1871 conflict. The prewar alliance system meant that, for the first time in a century, all the great powers were at war, making the scope of the hostilities greater than in any recent fighting. Moreover, the conflict quickly became a world war as the belligerents fought one another outside Europe and as non-European powers such as Japan and the United States joined the ranks of warring nations.

Even more significant than the number of nations engaged in the conflict, however, was the nature of the war they fought. The Industrial Revolution of the nineteenth century had brought technical changes to warfare that were to transform the 1914 conflict into the Western world's first modern, total war. This would be a war of tremendous cost to both soldiers and civilians, a struggle requiring effort and sacrifice by every citizen of the warring countries.

Modern railroads and motorized transport permitted belligerent nations to bring the full weight of their new industrial strengths to the battlefields of World War I. Both sides for the first time made extensive use of the machine gun as well as new, longer-range heavy artillery. Whole new weapons systems included flame throwers, poison gas, the tank, the airplane, the lighter-than-air dirigible, and the submarine.

Generals trained in an earlier era of warfare failed at first to understand the increased destructive capacity of these new weapons and practiced military tactics of 1870 in fighting the war's first battles. As before, they attacked the enemy with massed infantrymen armed with bayonets fixed, flags flying, drums sounding, and led by officers in dress uniforms complete with white gloves. This was the kind of war Europeans had enthusiastically anticipated in 1914, but because of modern firepower, casualties in such attacks were extremely heavy—indeed, completely unprecedented.

Especially in Western Europe, such losses resulted in increased reliance on what has been called the "infantryman's best friend," the shovel. To avoid the firepower of the new modern weaponry, opposing armies dug into the earth, and by Christmas 1914 they opposed each other in 466 miles of trenches stretching through France from the English Channel to the border of Switzerland. These trenches represented stalemate. They were separated by "No Man's Land," the open space an attacker had to cross to reach the enemy. Swept with machine gun and artillery fire and blocked by barbed wire and other obstacles, "No Man's Land" was an area that an attacking force could cross only with great losses. In such circumstances, neither side could achieve the traditional decisive breakthrough into the enemy's lines. Field Marshal Horatio Kitchener, an experienced commander of the old school of warfare and British Secretary for War until 1916, expressed the frustration of many about such combat: "I don't know what is to be done—this isn't war."

In their efforts to achieve victory, generals and statesmen sought to break the stalemate in a number of ways that extended the impact of World War I. The warring nations mobilized unprecedented numbers of men; over 70 million were called to military service. Never before had so large a part of Europe's population been put in uniform: England mobilized 53 percent of its male population of military age in 1914–1918, and France and Germany called on the service of some 80 percent of their males of draft age.

Each government involved took unprecedented steps to meet its forces' needs for food, material, and ammunition. Governments rationed consumer goods to provide for their armies. England and Germany asserted extraordinary government control over raw materials, privately owned production facilities, and civilian labor in the name of war production.

Civilians felt the war in other ways, too. The stalemate meant a long war, and governments soon recognized they could not maintain their war efforts during a long conflict if civilian morale broke. Each warring government therefore attempted to exert total control over news and public opinion, often at the expense of its citizens' rights. They censored the press, used propaganda to maintain civilian morale, and placed critics under surveillance or arrest.

Each warring nation also recognized the equal importance of the home front to their enemies in achieving victory. As a result, civilians experienced the war in unprecedented ways. Blockades by surface fleets and submarine attacks on shipping aimed at slowing war production and destroying civilian morale by cutting off vital shipments of raw materials and food to enemy countries. New weapons systems also placed civilians in actual physical danger. Warring nations dropped bombs on their enemies' cities from dirigibles and primitive bomber aircraft, and long-range artillery rained shells on population centers miles from battlefronts.

This was the world's first total war; until the outbreak of another such war in 1939, participants remembered it as the "Great War." Your task in this chapter is to assess the all-encompassing nature of modern warfare through several different kinds of sources. Why was World War I different from previous wars? What impact did it have on the soldiers at the front? How did it affect civilians at home?

SOURCES AND METHOD

As we have seen in Chapter 10, artists and intellectuals at first joined other Europeans in welcoming World War I. They believed that the conflict would sweep away a decadent cultural life and replace it with one more vital. Many talented and well-educated men sought to hasten this cultural transformation by volunteering for military service. Front-line combat, however, soon showed these young men that they were caught up in a war unlike any previous struggle. Conscious of the uniqueness of their battlefield experience and aware that their front-line service would leave them forever changed, many made an effort to record their experiences. Letters, diaries, autobiographical works, paintings, and sketches by individual soldiers all supplement the dry official records kept by war ministries of the participating countries and give the historian an excellent sense of battlefield realities and their impact. Your main sources in this chapter comprise creative works, in the form of poetry and fiction, in which a number of talented soldiers sought to convey the experience of modern war and its effect on them.

Literature can be a valuable source for the student of history in understanding the past. We must, however, stay fully aware of its limits as well as its value. The utility of literature as a historical source is somewhat limited by its very nature: as the product of an individual, it reflects personal and social perspectives that must be identified. Most of the authors represented here, for example, came from the middle or upper classes because such individuals, not the sons of the working classes, had the education to write works of enduring significance. With such a social background many served as officers, and the conditions they endured were in some ways better than those of the enlisted men: the war was often significantly worse for a private than for a captain.

Individuals have opinions, too, and opinions often invade war literature. The soldier often portrayed himself as a victim of forces beyond his control: a powerful government, modern technology, or the military authorities. As historians, we must note these opinions because they convey to us the individual's reaction to the war, but we must look beyond them as well to discern the objective wartime conditions the author was recording.

Not all chroniclers of the war were equally well placed to understand the war. We must ask if each work was based on actual front-line experience. If not, we should discount it as historical evidence. We must also ask if an author's work was written in the midst of war, in which case it may reflect the passions of the moment. If the work was written after the war, the author's selective memory for certain facts may have influenced his or her work. The evidence in this chapter presents works by front-line authors written both at the time of their experiences as well as after the war. Indeed, the great majority of literary works on the war appeared, like the literature on Vietnam, about a decade after the cessation of hostilities. Perhaps a gestation period is necessary for the minds of many to analyze the combat experience. If that is the case, we must recognize the frailty of the human memory and measure the message of postwar literature against those writings composed in the heat of battle.

Once the various viewpoints and perspectives are identified, however, a student of history can obtain an excellent sense of World War I through works of poetry and fiction. These works present the war in human terms far more vividly than do government reports and statistics. To assist your reading, some information on each of the writers presented here is in order.

Rupert Brooke (1887–1915), the author of Source 1, was a graduate of Cambridge University and one of England's most promising young poets when he enlisted in September 1914 as a sublieutenant in the Royal Naval Division, a land force attached to the British Navy. After brief service in Belgium in 1914, his unit was dispatched to the Middle East in 1915 as part of the British and French attack on the Turks at Gallipoli—a strategy designed to open the straits to the Black Sea so that Western supplies could reach Russia. (The attack itself, in which many Australian and New Zealand troops perished, was generally deemed a disaster.) Not quite twenty-eight years of age, Brooke died of blood poisoning en route to Gallipoli and was buried on the island of Skyros, Greece, home of Achilles of the ancient Homeric myths. The selection by Brooke presented here, the poem "Peace," reflects the romanticism characteristic of much prewar English poetry but also expresses Brooke's response to the war. What were his sensations as he watched the war engulf Europe? How does he characterize the spirit of pre-World War I Europe? What will awaken that spirit? Why do you think his poem suggests that Brooke would welcome death?

A remarkable Frenchman, Charles Péguy (1873–1914), wrote Source 2, "Blessed Are." Péguy was a talented poet and essayist, much of whose work expresses his nationalism as well as his concern for the poor and the cause of social justice. His writings also reflect a remarkable spiritual journey. Raised a Catholic, his dislike for the authoritarian character of the Church grew by the time he reached adulthood, and he declared himself an atheist about 1893. In 1908, however, he rediscovered a deep religious faith, though he kept his distance from the institutional

Church and probably never participated in its sacramental life. Péguy's later writings bear witness to this religiosity as well as to his continued concern for his fellow man and his French nationalism.

Péguy was forty-one when war broke out in 1914, and he therefore qualified for the army reserve, not front-line duty. Always a man of action, however, he volunteered for active service. Commissioned a lieutenant of infantry, he died leading his men in an attack on September 5, 1914. Remember the details of his life as you read "Blessed Are." What elements of Péguy's thought does the poem combine? What was his view of war? Although Péguy came from a different national and religious background than the English Protestant Brooke, what ideas did he share with Brooke? Why do you think other intellectuals also drew on the romanticism and nationalism of the late nineteenth and early twentieth centuries to welcome war?

Source 3, the "Hymn of Hate," is the work of the German poet Ernst Lissauer (1882–1937), who served as a private in the German army. Composed as the war broke out, the poem was soon set to music and became very popular in Germany. To appreciate its significance fully, you may wish to review in your textbook the sections on nineteenth-century nationalism and on the international rivalries that contributed to World War I. Which nation do the Germans see as their archenemy? Why, after consulting your textbook, do you think this country was so hated in Germany?

Novelists also drew on their wartime experiences. Henri Barbusse (1873–1935), the author of *Under Fire*, worked as a French government employee and a journalist before World War I. Politically a socialist, he was swept up by the general surge of patriotism in 1914 and volunteered for military service. He served in the French army from 1914 through the early days of the great Battle of Verdun in 1916, when he was wounded and left the service. In *Under Fire*, which was written in the trenches, he attempted to portray realistically the physical and psychological impact of modern war. The novel was recognized early as an important work and received France's most prestigious literary award, the Goncourt Prize, in 1916. The excerpt presented as Source 4 describes an attack on the Germans by veteran French infantrymen led by their trusted Corporal Bertrand. How does Barbusse describe modern warfare?

Excerpts from a second novel, *All Quiet on the Western Front* (Source 5), offer us the view of the losing side in the war. Its author, Erich Maria Remarque (1898–1970), grew up the son of a German bookbinder. Drafted at the age of eighteen, he served in the German army from 1916 to the war's end. Remarque had already begun to write before his military service, and his *All Quiet on the Western Front* represented such a realistic picture of the war that many perceived it as an attack on German patriotism. As a consequence, the novel was among the first batch of books burned by the Nazis in 1933. How does Remarque describe the experience of modern warfare? What effect did it have on the many youthful front-line soldiers like the main character, Paul Baumer? What impact did that war have on German civilians?

Two poems conclude our literary evidence on World War I. Source 6, "Dulce et Decorum Est" ("It is sweet and fitting"), is the work of Wilfred Owen (1893–1918). Owen studied briefly at the University of London before the war, intending a career in the clergy. He enlisted in the British army in 1915, aged twenty-two, and as an infantry lieutenant served in France in the great Battle of the Somme. Owen was wounded three times in 1917 and recuperated in England, where he met Siegfried Sassoon, author of the next selection, who encouraged Owen in his writing. After recovering from his wounds, Owen again served on the western front. He received the Military Cross for bravery in October 1918 and died leading his men in an attack on November 4, 1918, one week before the war's end.

Owen's battlefield experiences shaped his poetry. "Dulce et Decorum Est" is titled with a phrase from the Roman poet Horace, whose work would have been familiar to all upper-class English schoolboys of Owen's day. How would you summarize Owen's view of the war, especially his opinion of those on the home front who blindly supported it?

Siegfried Sassoon (1886–1967), author of "The General" (Source 7), was seven years older than his friend Owen, and his poetic response to the war is the reaction of one with greater experience in life and its problems. A Cambridge graduate like Rupert Brooke, he had written poetry since his boyhood. The war transformed Sassoon from an upper-class young man who enjoyed the hunt to a postwar social activist and socialist. Although he served with great bravery as a front-line officer, he experienced an increasingly bitter sense of the war's futility. Wounded in 1917, he had a long convalescence in England and went through an emotional crisis as he attempted to balance his growing pacifism with his enduring sense of duty and the comradeship he felt with those still on the front line. Sassoon's response was to throw away his Military Cross awarded for bravery and to draft a letter of protest of the war to his commanding officer. Stating that a war undertaken as one of defense had become a war of conquest, he declared, "I can no longer be a party to prolong those sufferings for ends which I believe to be evil and unjust." Such a letter from an officer in wartime would normally have resulted in court martial. Intervention of friends on his behalf led instead to Sassoon's treatment for shell shock, a common psychological problem among front-line troops. It was during his hospitalization for this treatment that Sassoon met Owen. Returning to service in 1918, Sassoon was wounded again but lived to survive the war. His poem, "The General," is very brief, but it reflects Sassoon's attitude toward the war. How does Sassoon view the general?

Participants in the war left other personal records of the conflict in the form of letters and autobiographical works. The letters in Sources 8 and 9 record such remarkable events in the midst of total war that people then, as now, tended to doubt they ever occurred. Nevertheless, the stories of these two anonymous German soldiers can be verified in the writings of their battlefield opponents. How had initial enthusiasm for the war and hatred of the enemy fared at the front? Why?

World War I was the first conflict to demand great participation from women in the war effort. Yet, oddly, few left extensive written records of the war's effect on them. Source 10, drawn from the Englishwoman Vera Brittain's (1893–1970) *The Testament of Youth,* is one of the few works we have by a woman. A student at Oxford when England declared war, Brittain left her studies shortly after for service as a nurse, and her book in part records the war from that vantage point. It also gives us a sense of the war's impact on those at the home front. What kind of warfare does Brittain describe the Germans as practicing? What was their objective in such warfare? What effect did the war have on Brittain?

Sources 11 through 15 are evidence of a nonpersonal nature, reports and statistics amassed by modern governments of the kind we have examined in earlier chapters. Nevertheless, such material will allow you to amplify your understanding of the impact of total warfare. Source

11, taken from the official record compiled by the U.S. Army's forces occupying the Rhineland area of Germany at the war's end, describes the rations for Germany's civilian population during the last days of the war in 1918. These rations reflect the effects of a British naval blockade of the ports of Germany, established to cut the country off from imported food and strategic raw materials. Because prewar Germany was not self-sufficient in food production, the effect of such a blockade was great.

In analyzing this ration information, we must, as students of history, recognize that the supplies shown here may not completely reflect the German dietary situation. Rationing presumes that producers placed all foodstuffs at their government's disposal. In practice they did not, because rationing was based on government-regulated prices that were invariably lower than free market prices in a period of shortage. The result was a lively black market trade in foodstuffs for those who could pay higher prices.

Still, the evidence here does indicate the basic ration for many Germans. Analyze this record. What dietary basics do you find lacking or in short supply? What did German civilians eat a great deal of during the war? What cumulative effect do you think such a diet, imposed by total war, had on German civilians?

The strain of warfare was not only a matter of food and other material restrictions, however. As we noted earlier, warring governments tried to gauge and influence public opinion because they knew that total warfare would become untenable if civilian spirit broke. In Source 12 you will read a report to French police officials from the area of Grenoble in southeastern France in 1917. What does that report show about public opinion? In calling millions of men for military service, total war created tremendous labor shortages and yet another strain on civilians in all countries. Who filled the jobs vacated by men in England, according to Source 13? How did governments pay for modern warfare, according to Source 15?

The ultimate cost of the war can be measured in human lives lost. Official casualty figures, however, present considerable problems of analysis. We must first understand that all such figures are approximate. Deficiencies in wartime record keeping are part of the problem, but governments manipulated figures, too. During the war security considerations led to consistent understatements of losses by each warring nation to prevent the enemy from knowing its manpower resources. At the war's end, some victorious governments allegedly inflated figures as a basis for postwar claims on their defeated enemies.

The figures for military deaths in Source 14 are taken from a recent study attempting to determine the best estimates of war losses from several sources, not just governmental records. Though we still must accept those figures as only approximations, they do allow a good sense of the relative losses of each country. Which suffered the greatest numerical losses? In which armies did a man mobilized for military service have the greatest chance of being killed? What do the high casualty rates of certain Eastern European countries tell you about those nations' capacities to wage modern warfare? Among the great powers, which nation lost the greatest portion of its population?

As you now read the evidence for this chapter, keep all these questions in mind. They should aid you in answering the central questions posed: Why was World War I different from previous wars? What impact did it have on soldiers at the front? How did it affect civilians at home?

THE EVIDENCE

THE FRONT LINES

Source 1 from Geoffrey Keynes, editor, The Poetical Works of Rupert Brooke *(London: Faber and Faber, 1960), p. 19.*

1. Rupert Brooke, "1914 Sonnet: I. Peace," 1914

Now, God be thanked Who has matched us with His hour,
   And caught our youth, and wakened us from sleeping,
With hand made sure, clear eye, and sharpened power,
   To turn, as swimmers into cleanness leaping,
Glad from a world grown old and cold and weary,
   Leave the sick hearts that honour could not move,
And half-men, and their dirty songs and dreary,
   And all the little emptiness of love!

Oh! we, who have known shame, we have found release there,
   Where there's no ill, no grief, but sleep has mending,
     Naught broken save this body, lost but breath;
Nothing to shake the laughing heart's long peace there
   But only agony, and that has ending;
     And the worst friend and enemy is but Death.

Source 2 from Charles Péguy, Basic Verities: Prose and Poetry, *translated by Ann and Julian Green (New York: Pantheon, 1943), pp. 275–277.*

2. Charles Péguy, "Blessed Are," 1914

Blessed are those who died for carnal earth
Provided it was in a just war.
Blessed are those who died for a plot of ground.
Blessed are those who died a solemn death.

Blessed are those who died in great battles,
Stretched out on the ground in the face of God.
Blessed are those who died on a final high place,
Amid all the pomp of grandiose funerals.

Blessed are those who died for carnal cities.
For they are the body of the city of God.
Blessed are those who died for their hearth and their fire,
And the lowly honors of their father's house. . . .

Blessed are those who died, for they have returned
Into primeval clay and primeval earth.
Blessed are those who died in a just war.
Blessed is the wheat that is ripe and the wheat that is gathered in sheaves.

Source 3 from Ernst Lissauer, Jugend *(1914). Translated by Barbara Henderson,* New York Times, *October 15, 1914.*

3. Ernst Lissauer, "Hymn of Hate," 1914

French and Russian they matter not,
A blow for a blow and a shot for a shot;
We love them not, we hate them not,
We hold the Weichsel and Vosges-gate,[1]
We have but one—and only hate,
We love as one, we hate as one,
We have one foe and one alone.

1. The Germans possessed defensible boundaries against the Russians and the French. In the east, they held the Vistula (*Weichsel*) River in Poland as a barrier to Russian attack. In the west, they blocked the French attack with their possession of the Vosges Mountains.

He is known to you all, he is known to you all,
He crouches behind the dark grey flood,
Full of envy, of rage, of craft, of gall,
Cut off by waves that are thicker than blood.
Come, let us stand at the Judgment place,
An oath to swear to, face to face,
An oath of bronze no wind can shake,

An oath for our sons and their sons to take.
Come, hear the word, repeat the word,
Throughout the Fatherland make it heard.
We will never forego our hate,
We have all but a single hate,
We love as one, we hate as one,
We have one foe, and one alone—

ENGLAND!

In the Captain's mess, in the banquet hall,
Sat feasting the officers, one and all,
Like a sabre-blow, like the swing of a sail,
One seized his glass held high to hail;
Sharp-snapped like the stroke of a rudder's play,
Spoke three words only: "To the Day!"[2]
Whose glass this fate?
They had all but a single hate.
Who was thus known?
They had one foe, and one alone—

ENGLAND!

Take you the folk of the Earth in pay,
With bars of gold your ramparts lay,
Bedeck the ocean with bow on bow,
Ye reckon well, but not well enough now.
French and Russian they matter not,
A blow for a blow, a shot for a shot,
We fight the battle with bronze and steel,
And the time that is coming Peace will seal.

You will hate with a lasting hate,
We will never forego our hate,
Hate by water and hate by land,
Hate of the head and hate of the hand,
Hate of the hammer and hate of the crown,

2. **To the Day!:** in German naval officers' messes before World War I, it was customary to offer a
    toast to "the Day," that is, the day England would be defeated.

Hate of seventy millions, choking down.
We love as one, we hate as one,
We have one foe, and one alone—

ENGLAND!

Source 4 from Henri Barbusse, Under Fire: The Story of a Squad, *translated by Fitzwater Wray (New York: E. P. Dutton, 1917), pp. 250–259.*

4. From Henri Barbusse, *Under Fire: The Story of a Squad,* 1916

We are ready. The men marshal themselves, still silently, their blankets cross-wise, the helmet-strap on the chin, leaning on their rifles. I look at their pale, contracted, and reflective faces. They are not soldiers, they are men. They are not adventurers, or warriors, or made for human slaughter, neither butchers nor cattle. They are laborers and artisans whom one recognizes in their uniforms. They are civilians uprooted, and they are ready. They await the signal for death or murder; but you may see, looking at their faces between the vertical gleams of their bayonets, that they are simply men.

Each one knows that he is going to take his head, his chest, his belly, his whole body, and all naked, up to the rifles pointed forward, to the shells, to the bombs piled and ready, and above all to the methodical and almost infallible machine-guns—to all that is waiting for him yonder and is now so frightfully silent—before he reaches the other soldiers that he must kill. They are not careless of their lives, like brigands, nor blinded by passion like savages. In spite of the doctrines with which they have been cultivated they are not inflamed. They are above instinctive excesses. They are not drunk, either physically or morally. It is in full consciousness, as in full health and full strength, that they are massed there to hurl themselves once more into that sort of madman's part imposed on all men by the madness of the human race. One sees the thought and the fear and the farewell that there is in their silence, their stillness, in the mask of tranquillity which unnaturally grips their faces. They are not the kind of hero one thinks of, but their sacrifice has greater worth than they who have not seen them will ever be able to understand.

They are waiting; a waiting that extends and seems eternal. Now and then one or another starts a little when a bullet, fired from the other side, skims the forward embankment that shields us and plunges into the flabby flesh of the rear wall. . . .

A man arrives running, and speaks to Bertrand, and then Bertrand turns to us—

"Up you go," he says, "it's our turn."

All move at once. We put our feet on the steps made by the sappers, raise ourselves, elbow to elbow, beyond the shelter of the trench, and climb on to the parapet.

Bertrand is out on the sloping ground. He covers us with a quick glance, and when we are all there he says, "*Allons,* forward!"[3]

Our voices have a curious resonance. The start has been made very quickly, unexpectedly almost, as in a dream. There is no whistling sound in the air. Among the vast uproar of the guns we discern very clearly this surprising silence of bullets around us—

We descend over the rough and slippery ground with involuntary gestures, helping ourselves sometimes with the rifle. . . . On all sides the slope is covered by men who, like us, are bent on the descent. On the right the outline is defined of a company that is reaching the ravine by Trench 97—an old German work in ruins. We cross our wire by openings. Still no one fires on us. Some awkward ones who have made false steps are getting up again. We form up on the farther side of the entanglements and then set ourselves to topple down the slope rather faster—there is an instinctive acceleration in the movement. Several bullets arrive at last among us. Bertrand shouts to us to reserve our bombs and wait till the last moment.

But the sound of his voice is carried away. Abruptly, across all the width of the opposite slope, lurid flames burst forth that strike the air with terrible detonations. In line from left to right fires emerge from the sky and explosions from the ground. It is a frightful curtain which divides us from the world, which divides us from the past and from the future. We stop, fixed to the ground, stupefied by the sudden host that thunders from every side; then a simultaneous effort uplifts our mass again and throws it swiftly forward. We stumble and impede each other in the great waves of smoke. With harsh crashes and whirlwinds of pulverized earth, towards the profundity into which we hurl ourselves pell-mell, we see craters opened here and there, side by side, and merging in each other. Then one knows no longer where the discharges fall. Volleys are let loose so monstrously resounding that one feels himself annihilated by the mere sound of the downpoured thunder of these great constellations of destruction that form in the sky. One sees and one feels the fragments passing close to one's head with their hiss of red-hot iron plunged in water. The blast of one explosion so burns my hands, that I let my rifle fall. I pick it up again, reeling, and set off in the tawny-gleaming tempest with lowered head, lashed by spirits of dust and soot in a crushing downpour like volcanic lava. The stridor of the bursting shells hurts your ears, beats you on the neck, goes through your temples, and you cannot endure it without a cry. The gusts of death drive us on, lift

3. **Allons:** "Let's go!"

us up, rock us to and fro. We leap, and do not know whither we go. Our eyes are blinking and weeping and obscured. The view before us is blocked by a flashing avalanche that fills space.

It is the barrage fire. We have to go through that whirlwind of fire and those fearful showers that vertically fall. We are passing through. We are through it, by chance. Here and there I have seen forms that spun round and were lifted up and laid down, illumined by a brief reflection from over yonder. I have glimpsed strange faces that uttered some sort of cry—you could see them without hearing them in the roar of annihilation. A brasier full of red and black masses huge and furious fell about me, excavating the ground, tearing it from under my feet, throwing me aside like a bouncing toy. I remember that I strode over a smoldering corpse, quite black, with a tissue of rosy blood shriveling on him; and I remember, too, that the skirts of the great-coat flying next to me had caught fire, and left a trail of smoke behind. On our right, all along Trench 97, our glances were drawn and dazzled by a rank of frightful flames, closely crowded against each other like men.

Forward!

Now, we are nearly running. I see some who fall solidly flat, face forward, and others who founder meekly, as though they would sit down on the ground. We step aside abruptly to avoid the prostrate dead, quiet and rigid, or else offensive, and also—more perilous snares!—the wounded that hook on to you, struggling.

The International Trench! We are there. The wire entanglements have been torn up into long roots and creepers, thrown afar and coiled up, swept away and piled in great drifts by the guns. Between these big bushes of rain-damped steel the ground is open and free.

The trench is not defended. The Germans have abandoned it, or else a first wave has already passed over it. Its interior bristles with rifles placed against the bank. In the bottom are scattered corpses. From the jumbled litter of the long trench, hands emerge that protrude from gray sleeves with red facings, and booted legs. In places the embankment is destroyed and its woodwork splintered—all the flank of the trench collapsed and fallen into an indescribable mixture. In other places, round pits are yawning. . . .

We have spread out in the trench. The lieutenant, who has jumped to the other side, is stooping and summoning us with signs and shouts—"Don't stay there; forward, forward!"

We climb the wall of the trench with the help of the sacks, of weapons, and of the backs that are piled up there. In the bottom of the ravine the soil is shot-churned, crowded with jetsam, swarming with prostrate bodies. Some are motionless as blocks of wood; others move slowly or convulsively. The barrage fire continues to increase its infernal discharge behind us on the ground that we have crossed. But where we are at the foot of the rise it is a dead point for the artillery.

A short and uncertain calm follows. We are less deafened and look at each other. There is fever in the eyes, and the cheek-bones are blood-red. Our breathing snores and our hearts drum in our bodies.

In haste and confusion we recognize each other, as if we had met again face to face in a nightmare on the uttermost shores of death. Some hurried words are cast upon this glade in hell—"It's you!"—"Where's Cocon?"—"Don't know."—"Have you seen the captain?"—"No."—"Going strong?"—"Yes."

The bottom of the ravine is crossed and the other slope rises opposite. We climb in Indian file by a stairway rough-hewn in the ground: "Look out!" The shout means that a soldier half-way up the steps has been struck in the loins by a shell-fragment; he falls with his arms forward, bareheaded, like the diving swimmer. We can see the shapeless silhouette of the mass as it plunges into the gulf. I can almost see the detail of his blown hair over the black profile of his face.

We debouch upon the height. A great colorless emptiness is outspread before us. At first one can see nothing but a chalky and stony plain, yellow and gray to the limit of sight. No human wave is preceding ours; in front of us there is no living soul, but the ground is peopled with dead—recent corpses that still mimic agony or sleep, and old remains already bleached and scattered to the wind, half assimilated by the earth.

As soon as our pushing and jolted file emerges, two men close to me are hit, two shadows are hurled to the ground and roll under our feet, one with a sharp cry, and the other silently, as a felled ox. Another disappears with the caper of a lunatic, as if he had been snatched away. Instinctively we close up as we hustle forward—always forward—and the wound in our line closes of its own accord. The adjutant stops, raises his sword, lets it fall, and drops to his knees. His kneeling body slopes backward in jerks, his helmet drops on his heels, and he remains there, bareheaded, face to the sky. Hurriedly the rush of the rank has split open to respect his immobility.

But we cannot see the lieutenant. No more leaders, then—— Hesitation checks the wave of humanity that begins to beat on the plateau. Above the trampling one hears the hoarse effort of our lungs. "Forward!" cries some soldier, and then all resume the onward race to perdition with increasing speed.

"Where's Bertrand?" comes the laborious complaint of one of the foremost runners. "There! Here!" He had stooped in passing over a wounded man, but he leaves him quickly, and the man extends his arms toward him and seems to sob.

It is just at the moment when he rejoins us that we hear in front of us, coming from a sort of ground swelling, the crackle of a machine-gun. It is a moment of agony—more serious even than when we were passing through the flaming earthquake of the barrage. That familiar voice speaks to us across the plain, sharp and horrible. But we no longer stop. "Go on, go on!"

Our panting becomes hoarse groaning, yet still we hurl ourselves toward the horizon.

"The Boches![4] I see them!" a man says suddenly.

"Yes—their heads, there—above the trench—it's there, the trench that line. It's close. Ah, the hogs!"

We can indeed make out little round gray caps which rise and then drop on the ground level, fifty yards away, beyond a belt of dark earth, furrowed and humped. Encouraged they spring forward, they who now form the group where I am. So near the goal, so far unscathed, shall we not reach it? Yes, we will reach it! We make great strides and no longer hear anything. Each man plunges straight ahead, fascinated by the terrible trench, bent rigidly forward, almost incapable of turning his head to right or to left. I have a notion that many of us missed their footing and fell to the ground. I jump sideways to miss the suddenly erect bayonet of a toppling rifle. Quite close to me, Farfadet jostles me with his face bleeding, throws himself on Volpatte who is beside me and clings to him. Volpatte doubles up without slackening his rush and drags him along some paces, then shakes him off without looking at him and without knowing who he is, and shouts at him in a breaking voice almost choked with exertion: "Let me go, let me go, *nom de Dieu!*[5] They'll pick you up directly—don't worry."

The other man sinks to the ground, and his face, plastered with a scarlet mask and void of all expression, turns in every direction; while Volpatte, already in the distance, automatically repeats between his teeth, "Don't worry," with a steady forward gaze on the line.

A shower of bullets spurts around me, increasing the number of those who suddenly halt, who collapse slowly, defiant and gesticulating, of those who dive forward solidly with all the body's burden, of the shouts, deep, furious, and desperate, and even of that hollow and terrible gasp when a man's life goes bodily forth in a breath. And we who are not yet stricken, we look ahead, we walk and we run, among the frolics of the death that strikes at random into our flesh.

The wire entanglements—and there is one stretch of them intact. We go along to where it has been gutted into a wide and deep opening. This is a colossal funnel-hole, formed of smaller funnels placed together, a fantastic volcanic crater, scooped there by the guns.

The sight of this convulsion is stupefying; truly it seems that it must have come from the center of the earth. Such a rending of virgin strata puts new edge on our attacking fury, and none of us can keep from shouting with a solemn shake of the head—even just now when words are but painfully torn from our throats—"Ah, Christ! Look what hell we've given 'em there! Ah, look!"

4. **Boches:** a derogatory term applied by the French to German soldiers, originating from the French *caboche,* or blockhead.

5. **nom de Dieu:** "Name of God!"

Driven as if by the wind, we mount or descend at the will of the hollows and the earthy mounds in the gigantic fissure dug and blackened and burned by furious flames. The soil clings to the feet and we tear them out angrily. The accouterments and stuffs that cover the soft soil, the linen that is scattered about from sundered knapsacks, prevent us from sticking fast in it, and we are careful to plant our feet in this débris when we jump into the holes or climb the hillocks.

Behind us voices urge us—"Forward, boys, forward, *nom de Dieu!*"

"All the regiment is behind us!" they cry. We do not turn round to see, but the assurance electrifies our rush once more.

No more caps are visible behind the embankment of the trench we are nearing. Some German dead are crumbling in front of it, in pinnacled heaps or extended lines. We are there. The parapet takes definite and sinister shape and detail; the loopholes—we are prodigiously, incredibly close!

Something falls in front of us. It is a bomb. With a kick Corporal Bertrand returns it so well that it rises and bursts just over the trench.

With that fortunate deed the squad reaches the trench.

Pépin has hurled himself flat on the ground and is involved with a corpse. He reaches the edge and plunges in—the first to enter. Fouillade, with great gestures and shouts, jumps into the pit almost at the same moment that Pépin rolls down it. Indistinctly I see—in the time of the lightning's flash—a whole row of black demons stooping and squatting for the descent, on the ridge of the embankment, on the edge of the dark ambush.

A terrible volley bursts point-blank in our faces, flinging in front of us a sudden row of flames the whole length of the earthen verge. After the stunning shock we shake ourselves and burst into devilish laughter—the discharge has passed too high. And at once, with shouts and roars of salvation, we slide and roll and fall alive into the belly of the trench!

Source 5 from Erich Maria Remarque, All Quiet on the Western Front *(New York: Fawcett Crest, 1969), pp. 167–171, 174–175.*

5. From Erich Maria Remarque, *All Quiet on the Western Front*, 1928

We have been able to bury Müller, but he is not likely to remain long undisturbed. Our lines are falling back. There are too many fresh English and American regiments over there. There's too much corned beef and white wheaten bread. Too many new guns. Too many aeroplanes.

But we are emaciated and starved. Our food is so bad and mixed up with so much substitute stuff that it makes us ill. The factory owners in Germany have grown wealthy;—dysentery dissolves our bowels. The latrine poles are always densely crowded; the people at home ought to be shown these grey, yellow, miserable, wasted faces here, these bent figures from whose bodies the colic wrings out the blood, and who with lips trembling and distorted with pain, grin at one another and say: "It is not much sense pulling up one's trousers again—"

Our artillery is fired out, it has too few shells and the barrels are so worn that they shoot uncertainly, and scatter so widely as even to fall on ourselves. We have too few horses. Our fresh troops are anæmic boys in need of rest, who cannot carry a pack, but merely know how to die. By thousands. They understand nothing about warfare, they simply go on and let themselves be shot down. A single flyer routed two companies of them for a joke, just as they came fresh from the train—before they had ever heard of such a thing as cover.

"Germany ought to be empty soon," says Kat.

We have given up hope that some day an end may come. We never think so far. A man can stop a bullet and be killed; he can get wounded, and then the hospital is his next stop. There, if they do not amputate him, he sooner or later falls into the hands of one of those staff surgeons who, with the War Service Cross in his buttonhole, says to him: "What, one leg a bit short? If you have any pluck you don't need to run at the front. The man is A1.[6] Dismiss!"

Kat tells a story that has travelled the whole length of the front from the Vosges to Flanders;—of the staff surgeon who reads the names on the list, and when a man comes before him, without looking up says: "A1. We need soldiers up there." A fellow with a wooden leg comes up before him, the staff surgeon again says A1—"And then," Kat raises his voice, "the fellow says to him: 'I already have a wooden leg, but when I go back again and they shoot off my head, then I will get a wooden head made and become a staff surgeon.'" This answer tickles us all immensely.

There may be good doctors, and there are, lots of them; all the same, every soldier some time during his hundreds of inspections falls into the clutches of one of these countless hero-grabbers who pride themselves on changing as many C3's and B3's as possible into A1's.

There are many such stories, they are mostly far more bitter. All the same, they have nothing to do with mutiny or lead-swinging. They are merely honest and call a thing by its name; for there is a very great deal of fraud, injustice, and baseness in the army.—Is it nothing that regiment after regiment returns again and again to the ever more hopeless struggle, that attack follows attack along the weakening, retreating, crumbling line?

From a mockery the tanks have become a terrible weapon. Armoured they come rolling on in long lines, and more than anything else embody for us war's horror.

6. **A1:** the highest category of physical fitness, that is, qualified for front-line duty.

We do not see the guns that bombard us; the attacking lines of the enemy infantry are men like ourselves; but these tanks are machines, their caterpillars run on as endless as the war, they are annihilation, they roll without feeling into the craters, and climb up again without stopping, a fleet of roaring, smoke-belching armour-clads, invulnerable steel beasts squashing the dead and the wounded—we shrivel up in our thin skin before them, against their colossal weight our arms are sticks of straw, and our hand-grenades matches.

Shells, gas clouds, and flotillas of tanks—shattering, starvation, death.

Dysentery, influenza, typhus—murder, burning, death.

Trenches, hospitals, the common grave—there are no other possibilities.

In one attack our company commander, Bertinck, falls. He was one of those superb front-line officers who are foremost in every hot place. He was with us for two years without being wounded, so that something had to happen in the end.

We occupy a crater and get surrounded. The stink of petroleum or oil blows across with the fumes of powder. Two fellows with a flame-thrower are seen, one carries the tin on his back, the other has the hose in his hands from which the fire spouts. If they get so near that they can reach us we are done for, we cannot retreat at the moment.

We open fire on them. But they work nearer and things begin to look bad. Bertinck is lying in the hole with us. When he sees that we cannot escape because under the sharp fire we must make the most of this cover, he takes a rifle, crawls out of the hole, and lying down propped on his elbows, he takes aim. He fires—the same moment a bullet smacks into him, they have got him. Still he lies and aims again;—once he shifts and again takes his aim; at last the rifle cracks. Bertinck lets the gun drop and says: "Good," and slips back into the hole. The hindermost of the two flame-throwers is hit, he falls, the hose slips away from the other fellow, the fires squirts about on all sides and the man burns.

Bertinck has a chest wound. After a while a fragment smashes away his chin, and the same fragment has sufficient force to tear open Leer's hip. Leer groans as he supports himself on his arm, he bleeds quickly, no one can help him. Like an emptying tube, after a couple of minutes he collapses.

What use is it to him now that he was such a good mathematician at school?

The months pass by. The summer of 1918 is the most bloody and the most terrible. The days stand like angels in gold and blue, incomprehensible, above the ring of annihilation. Every man here knows that we are losing the war. Not much is said about it, we are falling back, we will not be able to attack again after this big offensive, we have no more men and no more ammunition. . . .

There are so many airmen here, and they are so sure of themselves that they give chase to single individuals, just as though they were hares. For every one German plane there come at least five English and American. For one hungry, wretched German soldier come five of the enemy, fresh and fit.

For one German army loaf there are fifty tins of canned beef over there. We are not beaten, for as soldiers we are better and more experienced; we are simply crushed and driven back by overwhelmingly superior forces.

Behind us lie rainy weeks—grey sky, grey fluid earth, grey dying. If we go out, the rain at once soaks through our overcoat and clothing;—and we remain wet all the time we are in the line. We never get dry. Those who still wear high boots tie sand bags round the top so that the mud does not pour in so fast. The rifles are caked, the uniforms caked, everything is fluid and dissolved, the earth one dripping, soaked, oily mass in which lie the yellow pools with red spiral streams of blood and into which the dead, wounded, and survivors slowly sink down.

The storm lashes us, out of the confusion of grey and yellow the hail of splinters whips forth the childlike cries of the wounded, and in the night shattered life groans wearily to the silence.

Our hands are earth, our bodies clay and our eyes pools of rain. We do not know whether we still live. . . .

It is autumn. There are not many of the old hands left. I am the last of the seven fellows from our class.

Everyone talks of peace and armistice. All wait. If it again proves an illusion, then they will break up; hope is high, it cannot be taken away again without an upheaval. If there is not peace, then there will be revolution.

I have fourteen days' rest, because I have swallowed a bit of gas; in a little garden I sit the whole day long in the sun. The armistice is coming soon, I believe it now too. Then we will go home.

Here my thoughts stop and will not go any farther. All that meets me, all that floods over me are but feelings—greed of life, love of home, yearning of the blood, intoxication of deliverance. But no aims.

Had we returned home in 1916, out of the suffering and the strength of our experiences we might have unleashed a storm. Now if we go back we will be weary, broken, burnt out, rootless, and without hope. We will not be able to find our way any more.

And men will not understand us—for the generation that grew up before us, though it has passed these years with us here, already had a home and a calling; now it will return to its old occupations, and the war will be forgotten—and the generation that has grown up after us will be strange to us and push us aside. We will be superfluous even to ourselves, we will grow older, a few will adapt themselves, some others will merely submit, and most will be bewildered;—the years will pass by and in the end we shall fall into ruin.

But perhaps all this that I think is mere melancholy and dismay, which will fly away as the dust, when I stand once again beneath the poplars and listen to the rustling of their leaves. It cannot be that it has gone, the yearning that made our blood unquiet, the unknown, the perplexing, the oncoming things, the thousand faces of the future, the melodies from dreams and from books, the whispers and divinations of women, it cannot be that this has vanished in bombardment, in despair, in brothels.

Here the trees show gay and golden, the berries of the rowan stand red among the leaves, country roads run white out to the sky-line, and the canteens hum like beehives with rumours of peace.

I stand up.

I am very quiet. Let the months and years come, they bring me nothing more, they can bring me nothing more. I am so alone, and so without hope that I can confront them without fear. The life that has borne me through these years is still in my hands and my eyes. Whether I have subdued it, I know not. But so long as it is there it will seek its own way out, heedless of the will that is within me. . . .

He fell in October 1918, on a day that was so quiet and still on the whole front, that the army report confined itself to the single sentence: All quiet on the Western Front.

He had fallen forward and lay on the earth as though sleeping. Turning him over one saw that he could not have suffered long; his face had an expression of calm, as though almost glad the end had come.

Source 6 from C. Day Lewis, editor, The Collected Poems of Wilfred Owen *(New York: New Directions, 1964), p. 55.*

6. Wilfred Owen, "Dulce et Decorum Est," ca 1917

Bent double, like old beggars under sacks,
Knock-kneed, coughing like hags, we cursed through sludge,
Till on the haunting flares we turned our backs
And towards our distant rest began to trudge.
Men marched asleep. Many had lost their boots
But limped on, blood-shod. All went lame; all blind;
Drunk with fatigue; deaf even to the hoots
Of tired, outstripped Five-Nines[7] that dropped behind.

Gas! Gas! Quick, boys!—An ecstasy of fumbling,
Fitting the clumsy helmets just in time;

7. **Five-Nines:** one of the types of artillery used by the Germans was the 5.9-inch howitzer, which projected a very large shell in a high arc. As the barrels of such guns became worn, their accuracy was impaired.

But someone still was yelling out and stumbling
And flound'ring like a man in fire or lime . . .
Dim, through the misty panes and thick green light,
As under a green sea, I saw him drowning.

In all my dreams, before my helpless sight,
He lunges at me, guttering, choking, drowning.

If in some smothering dreams you too could pace
Behind the wagon that we flung him in,
And watch the white eyes writhing in his face,
His hanging face, like a devil's sick of sin;
If you could hear, at every jolt, the blood
Come gargling from the froth-corrupted lungs,
Obscene as cancer, bitter as the cud
Of vile, incurable sores on innocent tongues,—
My friend, you would not tell with such high zest
To children ardent for some desperate glory,
The old Lie: Dulce et decorum est
Pro patria mori.[8]

Source 7 from Siegfried Sassoon, Collected Poems, 1908–1956 *(London: Faber and Faber, 1961), p. 75.*

7. Siegfried Sassoon, "The General," ca 1917

'Good-morning; good-morning!' the General said
When we met him last week on our way to the line.
Now the soldiers he smiled at are most of 'em dead,
And we're cursing his staff for incompetent swine.
'He's a cheery old card,' grunted Harry to Jack
As they slogged up to Arras[9] with rifle and pack.

But he did for them both by his plan of attack.

8. From Horace, *Odes*, III, 2, 3: "It is sweet and fitting to die for one's country."

9. **Arras:** city of northeastern France that was the site of a major British attack in April 1917. With heavy artillery bombardment and the element of surprise, the British were able to break through German lines. Unfortunately, excessive caution on the part of British commanders in exploiting their costly initial successes permitted the Germans time to regroup and deprived the British of a sweeping victory.

Source 8 from Rudolf Hoffman, editor, Der deutscher Soldat: Briefe aus dem Weltkrieg *(Munich: 1937), pp. 297–298. Translated and quoted in Hanna Hafkesbrink,* Unknown Germany: An Inner Chronicle of the First World War Based on Letters and Diaries *(New Haven: Yale University Press, 1948), p. 141.*

8. New Year's Eve, 1914: Letter from a Former German Student Serving in France

On New Year's Eve we called across to tell each other the time and agreed to fire a salvo at 12. It was a cold night. We sang songs, and they clapped (we were only 60–70 yards apart); we played the mouth-organ and they sang and we clapped. Then I asked if they haven't got any musical instruments, and they produced some bagpipes (they are the Scots guards, with the short petticoats and bare legs) and they played some of their beautiful elegies on them, and sang, too. Then at 12 we all fired salvos into the air! . . . It was a real good "Sylvester,"[10] just like in peace-time!

Source 9 from A. F. Wedd, editor and translator, German Students' War Letters, *from the original edition by Philipp Witkop (London: Methuen, 1929), p. 36. Quoted in Hanna Hafkesbrink,* Unknown Germany: An Inner Chronicle of the First World War Based on Letters and Diaries *(New Haven: Yale University Press, 1948), pp. 141–142.*

9. Christmas Eve, 1916: Letter from a German Soldier Serving in France

There I stood for four hours in the trench on Christmas Eve, up to my ankles in water and slime, and armed with hand grenades and signal shells. My thoughts were far away, my eyes sought the silhouette of the enemy trench. Then suddenly at 12 o'clock there was a solemn pause. From our reserve position came the sound of a quartette singing Christmas carols. Singing in God's out-of-doors as in peacetime, actually only 60 meters[11] away from an embittered enemy. Was this possible? I know of no hour so uplifting and solemn as was this one. Now several Englishmen ventured to sing a lovely song. Yes, this was peace on the battlefield, peace as one had not known it for two and a half years. Neither infantry nor artillery fire disturbed this night of peace. Lost in meditation we stood in the trench and listened to the singing.

10. **Sylvester:** Roman Catholics observe December 31 as the feast of Saint Sylvester.
11. **60 meters:** 198 feet.

THE HOME FRONT

Source 10 from Vera Brittain, The Testament of Youth: An Autobiographical Study of the Years 1900–1925 *(London: Gollancz, 1981), pp. 365–366.*

10. Vera Brittain: A London Air Raid, June 13, 1917

Although three out of the four persons were gone who had made all the world that I knew,[12] the War seemed no nearer a conclusion than it had been in 1914. It was everywhere now; even before Victor was buried, the daylight air-raid of June 13th "brought it home," as the newspapers remarked, with such force that I perceived danger to be infinitely preferable when I went after it, instead of waiting for it to come after me.

I was just reaching home after a morning's shopping in Kensington High Street when the uproar began, and, looking immediately at the sky, I saw the sinister group of giant mosquitoes sweeping in close formation over London. My mother, whose temperamental fatalism had always enabled her to sleep peacefully through the usual night-time raids, was anxious to watch the show from the roof of the flats, but when I reached the doorway my father had just succeeded in hurrying her down to the basement; he did not share her belief that destiny remained unaffected by caution, and himself derived moral support in air-raids from putting on his collar and patrolling the passages.

The three of us listened glumly to the shrapnel raining down like a thunder-shower upon the park—those quiet trees which on the night of my return from Malta[13] had made death and horror seem so unbelievably remote. As soon as the banging and crashing had given way to the breathless, apprehensive silence which always followed a big raid, I made a complicated journey to the City[14] to see if my uncle had been added to the family's growing collection of casualties.

When at last, after much negociation [sic] of the crowds in Cornhill and Bishopsgate, I succeeded in getting to the National Provincial Bank, I found him safe and quite composed, but as pale as a corpse; indeed, the whole staff of men and women resembled a morose consignment of dumb spectres newly transported across the Styx.[15] The streets round the bank were terrifyingly

---

12. Vera Brittain lost her fiancée and two other male friends in World War I. The fourth person still alive in June 1917, her brother Edward, perished while serving with the British army in Italy later in 1917.

13. Brittain had served as a military nurse on the British island of Malta in the Mediterranean.

14. **the City:** the financial district of London.

15. **Styx:** in Greek mythology, the river that the souls of the dead must cross as they leave the world of the living.

quiet, and in some places so thickly covered with broken glass that I seemed to be wading ankle-deep in huge unmelted hailstones. I saw no dead nor wounded, though numerous police-supervised barricades concealed a variety of gruesome probabilities. Others were only too clearly suggested by a crimson-splashed horse lying indifferently on its side, and by several derelict tradesman's carts bloodily denuded of their drivers.

These things, I concluded, seemed less inappropriate when they happened in France, though no doubt the French thought otherwise.

Source 11 from the American Military Government of Occupied Germany, 1918–1920, Report of the Officer in Charge of Civil Affairs, Third Army and American Forces in Germany *(Washington, D.C.: U.S. Government Printing Office, 1943), pp. 155–156.*

11. German Wartime Civilian Rations, 1918

Conditions on arrival of Third Army.—When the Third Army entered its area of occupation, it found the principal foodstuffs rationed, as had been the case for several years. In brief, the situation may be outlined thus, prior to the war, the average food consumption for the German population, expressed in calories, was about 3500 calories per person per day. According to German figures, this had shrunk to 3000 calories in 1914, 2000 in 1915, 1500 in 1916, and to 1200 in the winter of 1917–1918.

All the principal foodstuffs had been rationed during the war, and, on paper at least, every resource of the Empire in the way of food was entirely under control and carefully distributed.

The ration at the beginning of the occupation was essentially as follows:

Bread	260 grams per head per day[16]
Potatoes	500 grams per head per day

The main reliance for sustenance was placed on the above two foods and, except in the large cities, where the supply was subject to much fluctuation, the amounts indicated, or more, were fairly consistently provided during the whole of the year 1919.

In addition, the following substances constituted a part of the ration in the amounts indicated:

16. To convert grams to ounces, multiply grams by 0.035. Thus the German bread ration was a little over 9 ounces per day per person, and the potato ration was 17.5 ounces per person per day.

Meat	200 grams per head per week. Frequently reduced in amount, and often not issued at all.
Fat	150–200 grams per head per week. Later became very scarce.
Butter	20 grams per head per week. Practically never issued in the ration.
Sugar	600–750 grams per head per month.
Marmalade	200 grams per head per week. Often unavailable.
Milk	Not issued at all to the population in general, on account of its scarcity. Issued only to children under 6 years of age and, on physician's certificates, to the sick, nursing mothers, pregnant women and the aged. One half to one litre per day.

Fresh vegetables, in general, were not rationed and were fairly plentiful. Additional substances, such as rice, oats, grits, margarine, sausage, "Ersatz" (substitute) coffee, eggs, and additional flour, were added to the ration from time to time when available.

Source 12 from Jean-Jacques Becker, The Great War and the French People, *translated by Arnold Pomerans (New York: St. Martin's, 1986), pp. 232–234.*

12. Report on French Public Opinion in the Department of the Isère

Grenoble, 17 June 1917

The Prefect[17] of the Department of Isère to the Minister of the Interior[18]
Office of the Sûreté Générale[19]

I have the honour to reply herewith to the questions contained in your confidential telegram circulated on *10 June inst.*:[20]

The inquiry I have myself conducted, or with the help of colleagues, to test the opinion of certain leading personages has shown that the morale of the people of Isère is far from satisfactory and that their exemplary spirit has suffered a

17. **prefect:** since the Revolution of 1789, France has been divided into departments. The chief administrative officer in each department, since the time of Napoleon, has been the prefect. The prefect, historically, has been an appointee of the central government and thus responsible to it and not to local interests.
18. **Minister of the Interior:** most police services in France are under the control of the central government's Ministry of the Interior.
19. **Sûreté Général:** the central police command charged with criminal investigations.
20. **inst.:** An archaic use of "instant" meaning "current." Here it is used to express "June 10th of the current year."

general decline during the past two months. Today there is weariness bordering on dejection, a result less of the curtailment of the public diet and supply difficulties than of the disappointment caused by the failure of our armies in April,[21] the feeling that military blunders have been made, that heavy losses have been sustained without any appreciable gains, that all further offensives will be both bloody and in vain. The inactivity of Russia, whose contribution now seems highly doubtful, has accentuated the decline in morale.[22] The remarks of soldiers coming back from the front are the major cause of this decline: these remarks, made in the trains, in the railway stations, in the cafés on the way home, and then in the villages, convey a deplorable picture of the mentality of a great number of servicemen. Each one tells of and amplifies this or that unpleasant incident, this or that error committed by his commander, this or that useless battle, this or that act of insubordination presented as so many acts of courage and determination. These remarks, listened to with a ready ear by those who are already nervous or depressed enough as it is, are then peddled about and exaggerated with the result that discontent and anxiety are increased further. Each day, incidents in public places, particularly in the large railway stations and on the trains, reflect the most deplorable attitude in the minds of servicemen.

In the countryside, the restive mood is less obvious than it is in the towns; the peasants work, but they do not hide the fact that 'it's been going on too long'; they are tired of their continuous over-exertion in the fields, of the lack of hands and of the very heavy burden of the requisitions. They are growing more and more suspicious and indifferent to the idea of collective effort and mutual solidarity, and to patriotic appeals, and can think only of their immediate interests and their own safety.

Growers increasingly complain about price rises, even though they probably suffer less than others from the cost of living and even though their produce is sold at ever higher prices.

Nevertheless, it is among the rural populations that one finds the greatest composure and resignation.

In the towns, and particularly in the industrial centres, the more impressionable and hence more excitable population—the workers, the ordinary

21. In April 1917, the French army had received a new commander, General Nivelle, who launched a massive and costly offensive to break through German lines and end the war. The offensive failed and, coming after great French losses at Verdun in 1916, provoked a mutiny in the army in which soldiers refused orders to attack until August 1917. The mutinies placed the entire French war effort at risk. Order was restored only by a new commander, General Pétain, and a new and authoritarian Prime Minister, Georges Clemenceau.

22. Russia had experienced a revolution in February 1917 that toppled Tsar Nicholas II from power and replaced him with a republic under a Provisional Government. Although the leaders of this government were committed to Russia's war against Germany, disorganization of Russian armies by the revolution prevented effective Russian action. Because the Russian collapse accompanied Germany's unrestricted submarine warfare against all shipping around England and the disastrous defeat of the Italian armies at Caporetto in October, 1917 was the great year of crisis for France and its allies.

people—are upset about the duration of the struggle, impatient with the increasing cost of living, irritated by the considerable profits being made out of the war by the big industrialists in their neighbourhood, and increasingly taken in by the propagandists of the united Socialist Party and their internationalist ideas. Under the influence of the Russian Revolution they already dream of workers' and soldiers' committees and of social revolution. These sentiments are aired frequently at workers' meetings, called ostensibly to discuss economic or union matters, and in their paper, *Le Droit du Peuple*,[23] which is waging a very skillful anti-war and internationalist campaign.

This attitude, together with the constant rise in the cost of living, has fuelled a widespread demand for wage increases which the employers have quietly met to a large degree. Unfortunately, the calm following these increases has been momentary only. The cost of living keeps rising further and it is painful to watch each wage increase being followed directly by a corresponding increase in the price of food and the cost of board and lodging. Already those workers engaged on national defence contracts are finding that the new wage scales agreed less than two months ago for Grenoble and district have become inadequate; they are presently asking for a cost-of-living allowance of 2 francs a day and have made it quite clear that if their demand is not met there will be trouble in the streets; some of them have even gone so far as to declare that they know where to find the necessary arms, alluding to the shell and explosives factories in the suburbs of Grenoble. I know perfectly well that these remarks were presumably made in order to intimidate the citizens, but it is nevertheless symptomatic that they should have been made in the first place. When they lack the courage to speak out themselves, the factory propagandists use the women working beside them who, running smaller risks, are less restrained in their threats. The demands of the reservists in the munitions factories have been forwarded to the ministry of supply and a number of agitators have been sent away—not to the front, which would have been dangerous, but to other factories in various parts of the area. Calm has therefore been restored, but there are fears that the present lull may be temporary.

If working-class militancy were to make itself felt in the munitions factories in Grenoble and in the industrial centres of the department, it would be very difficult and extremely risky to try to control it by force: the local police force would prove inadequate, even if it were reinforced by gendarmes. It is clearly necessary to strengthen the police contingent, but this can only be done through the deferment of professional policemen serving in the territorial army or the reserve. The auxiliary policemen drawn from the ranks of the retired are admittedly men of goodwill, but they are physically and mentally worn out, and their contribution and energy are inadequate. The relocation, or rather the transfer, of some gendarmerie brigades would be very useful,

23. **Le Droit du Peuple:** the *Right of the People*.

but the consequent changes in domicile would involve cumbersome formalities. . . . It would not be unhelpful if an intelligent, serving special commissioner were put in charge, with particular emphasis on the surveillance of aliens who continue to move about freely in the department and can undermine the morale of our people even as these aliens go about the business of gathering information useful to the enemy.

In conclusion, I believe that the present situation, both in respect of morale and also of social stability, while not giving cause for alarm, is far from satisfactory and that it ought to be considered serious enough to call for precautionary measures, and if necessary for energetic intervention.

What is really needed to lift flagging courage and to restore confidence in the future is a military success by our armies, a major Russian offensive, or just a German retreat.

Source 13 from Report of the War Cabinet Committee on Women in British Industry *(London: His Majesty's Stationery Office, 1919).*

13. Employment of Women in Wartime British Industry

Trades	Est. Number Females Employed in July 1914	Est. Number Females Employed in July 1918	Difference Between Numbers of Females Employed in July 1914 and July 1918	Percentage of Females to Total Number Workpeople Employed		Est. Number Females Directly Replacing Males in Jan. 1918
				July 1914	July 1918	
Metal	170,000	594,000	+424,000	9	25	195,000
Chemical	40,000	104,000	+ 64,000	20	39	35,000
Textile	863,000	827,000	− 36,000	58	67	64,000
Clothing	612,000	568,000	− 44,000	68	76	43,000
Food, drink, and tobacco	196,000	235,000	+ 39,000	35	49	60,000
Paper and printing	147,500	141,500	− 6,000	36	48	21,000
Wood	44,000	79,000	+ 35,000	15	32	23,000
China and earthenware	32,000 }					
Leather	23,100 }	197,100	+ 93,000	4	10	62,000
Other	49,000					
Government establishments	2,000	225,000	+223,000	3	47	197,000
Total	2,178,600	2,970,600	+792,000	26	37	704,000

Source 14 from J. M. Winter, The Great War and the British People (Cambridge, Mass.: Harvard University Press, 1986), p. 75.

14. Estimated Military Casualties, by Nation

Country	Total Killed or Died	Total Mobilized	Prewar Male Pop. 15–49	Total Prewar Pop.	Per 1,000 Mobilized	Total Killed	
						Per 1,000 Males 15–49	Per 1,000 People
	(in thousands)						
Britain, Ireland	723	6,147	11,540	45,221	118	63	16
Canada	61	629	2,320	8,100	97	26	8
Australia	60	413	1,370	4,900	145	44	12
New Zealand	16	129	320	1,100	124	50	15
South Africa	7	136	1,700	6,300	51	4	1
India	54	953	82,600	321,800	57	1	0
France	1,327	7,891	9,981	39,600	168	133	34
French colonies	71	449	13,200	52,700	158	5	1
Belgium	38	365	1,924	7,600	104	20	5
Italy	578	5,615	7,767	35,900	103	75	16
Portugal	7	100	1,315	6,100	70	5	1
Greece	26	353	1,235	4,900	73	21	5
Serbia	278	750	1,225	4,900	371	227	57
Rumania	250	1,000	1,900	7,600	250	132	33
Russia	1,811	15,798	40,080	167,000	115	45	11
United States	114	4,273	25,541	98,800	27	4	1
Allied Total	5,421	45,001	204,018	812,521	120	27	7
Germany	2,037	13,200	16,316	67,800	154	125	30
Austria-Hungary	1,100	9,000	12,176	58,600	122	90	19
Turkey	804	2,998	5,425	21,700	268	148	37
Bulgaria	88	400	1,100	4,700	220	80	19
Central Powers' Total	4,029	25,598	35,017	152,800	157	115	26
Total Overall	9,450	70,599	239,035	965,321	134	40	10

Source 15 from Felix Gilbert, *The End of the European Era, 1890 to the Present, 3rd ed.*
(New York: Norton, 1984), p. 161.

15. War Indebtedness to the United States, Through 1918

Great Britain	$3,696,000,000
France	1,970,000,000
Italy	1,031,000,000

QUESTIONS TO CONSIDER

Now that you have read the selections, try to consider them collectively, drawing out the effects of war on the people of Western Europe. First, consider the initial reaction to war. We saw in The Problem that war was universally greeted with patriotic enthusiasm. What forms did that enthusiasm assume in the poems of Brooke, Péguy, and Lissauer? What previous experience had these authors with modern warfare?

Next, assess the experience of front-line service as it is expressed in the literary and other sources. Why do you think the initial ardor for warfare wore off quickly? On whom or what did the writers lay the blame for the horrors of war? How radical was their discontent? Compare their literary reactions to the war with the artistic responses we examined in Chapter 10. Consider again the casualty figures in Source 14 and the descriptions of trench warfare in Sources 4 and 5. Remember that Barbusse wrote during the war and Remarque a decade later. Do their descriptions of modern warfare differ substantially? What do you think was uppermost in the minds of men subjected to such conditions?

The war inflicted unprecedented battle losses on every belligerent country, but societal groups within the warring countries did not suffer equally. In any combat situation the highest casualty rate affects noncommissioned and junior officers—the sergeants, lieutenants, and captains who lead attacks at the front of their units. What social groups does Remarque's *All Quiet on the Western Front* suggest made up the officer corps of each warring nation? What postwar effect do you think the loss of such men might have?

The front-line experience had costs for those who survived, too. Why might you conclude from the German soldiers' accounts of the holidays in 1914 and 1916 that one of the war's first casualties was patriotic devotion to its cause? As the war wore on, other reactions to combat became widespread among soldiers. Barbusse said that the war created two separate Frances, front-line and civilian. Does the character of Baumer in Remarque's novel reflect a similar division in Germany? Do you think a sense of alienation was a common reaction among veterans? How would it affect adjustment to postwar civilian life? Finally, assess the poems of Wilfred Owen and Siegfried Sassoon. How might you describe the sentiments expressed in those poems? What view of military authority does Sassoon's poem express? How old were Owen and Sassoon when they began military service? Are sentiments such as theirs usual in persons so young? What was the source for these views?

World War I affected civilian populations in ways no previous conflict had. Drawing on the German ration data, how do you think you would have found German wartime conditions? Why do you think Germans suffered nutritional deficiencies? Did such shortages also affect the German military, according to Source 5?

Every belligerent country recognized that the home front was essential to victory. The areas the Germans attacked in the London bombing described by Vera Brittain certainly lacked obvious military value. The Germans also launched long-range attacks on Paris, and one shell fell on a crowded church on Good Friday, 1918, killing or injuring 200 people. What was the goal of such attacks on targets of no military value? Recall the report to the French police on public opinion in the Grenoble area. What ideas were current among civilians? Why were French authorities so concerned about public opinion?

The war had a deep impact on women, too, Source 13 clearly shows a great spurt in the employment of Englishwomen in many industries.

In which industries especially did they find employment? How were these jobs probably related to the war effort? Women left certain jobs, too. Which did they abandon? Many of the industries they left traditionally offered low-paying employment for unskilled or semiskilled workers. How did wartime conditions allow women to improve their economic positions in England and, indeed, in all the warring nations? Do you think women's wartime contributions (remember that the nursing efforts of Vera Brittain and other women are not reflected in Source 13) would argue for improved postwar status for women?

The effects of World War I would be felt long after the armistice that ended hostilities in 1918. Refer to the table in Source 14. Notice the total numbers of men mobilized, recalling that in countries like France and Germany 80 percent of the military-age male population was in uniform. What effect do you think the absence of so many young men from their homes had on the birth rate during the years 1914–1918? What enduring impact did the deaths of many of these men have on their countries' birth rates? What implications could all these factors have in future defense considerations? Among the great powers, which country suffered the greatest proportional war losses? What do you predict the public attitudes in this country might be when war threatened again within twenty years of World War I's end? Do you think the costs of war would evoke the same response in all countries?

Finally, consider the economic costs of war. Wartime expenses outstripped tax revenues for all governments. All borrowed to pay for their war efforts. You must understand the figures in Source 15 in terms of the value of dollars during that period. Viewed in this light, the British debt represented almost five times the entire annual expenditure of the U.S. government in the years preceding the war's outbreak. From whom did the British and their allies borrow? What effect would this new creditor status have on the lender? How would such vast indebtedness affect European countries?

And what of German and Austria-Hungary, which lost the war, or Italy, which was on the winning side but failed to achieve all of its wartime goals? These countries made sacrifices comparable to those of the winning side. How would they view their war costs?

Your examination of all these issues should now allow you to answer the main questions of this chapter: Why was World War I different from previous wars? What impact did it have on the soldiers at the front? How did it affect civilians at home?

EPILOGUE

World War I permanently changed Europe and the world. As this chapter demonstrated, the conflict introduced a new kind of warfare, a total warfare that inflicted suffering on the civilian citizens of belligerent countries as well as on their men in military service. But World War I permanently changed much else, too.

The political old order of Europe expired in the trenches along with a generation of young men. The stress of modern warfare meant that no government survived politically when its war effort ended in defeat. At the war's end revolutions overthrew the old monarchies in Russia, Germany, Austria-Hungary, Bulgaria, and Turkey. The governmental change was most dramatic in Russia, where that country's wartime problems led to revolution and eventually to the world's first communist dictatorship, but everywhere defeat meant political collapse. That political collapse also contributed to numerous changes in national boundaries. The breakdown of governmental authority in many defeated countries permitted national minorities in these states to seek independence. Austria-Hungary and Turkey disappeared from the map as large, multinational empires as their subject peoples declared independence at war's end. And the Russian empire lost a large part of its western territory as Finns, Poles, Latvians, Lithuanians, Estonians, and Romanians used the moment of tsarist collapse to escape Russian rule.

World War I also facilitated the transformation of Western society. Women's labor in war industries, their work in nursing, and their participation in uniformed auxiliary services of the armed forces sustained the prewar demands of women for a political voice. In most Western countries, women gained the right to vote after World War I, a major step in attaining a status equal to that of males.

The war changed Europe economically, too. The financial needs of total warfare forced every government to borrow. The most obvious change was that the United States emerged from the war as the greatest creditor nation, but other economic changes occurred as well. As warring nations purchased raw materials and manufactured goods in the Americas and Asia during the conflict, the West's wealth began to shift out of Europe. In addition, Western European nations, particularly France, faced tremendous war-related property damage whose repair would consume funds for years to come.

Another cost of the war both in economic and human terms was found among its victims. The injured and crippled had to be treated, rehabilitated, and paid pensions. The situation of England illustrates the extent of the problem. When the government finalized its pension rolls in 1929, 2,424,000 men were receiving some sort of disability pension, about 40 percent of all the soldiers who had served in the British army in the war.

The war's unhappiest result, however, was that it did not become what U.S. President Woodrow Wilson called "a war to end all wars."

Rather, seeds for the next conflict were sown by the events and consequences of World War I. Total war created the desire for total victory, and the peace treaties reflected animosities produced by four years of bloody conflict. The Treaty of Versailles presented Germany with a settlement that would produce a desire for revision of the peace terms and even revenge. At the same time, the great losses of life in World War I engendered in many people in victorious nations a "never again" attitude that would lead them to seek to avoid another war at all costs. This attitude would in part result in efforts to appease a resurgent and vengeful Germany under Adolf Hitler (see Chapter 13) in the 1930s.

The alienation of former soldiers' from civilian life led many to search out civilian opportunities for renewing the comradeship of the front, such as veterans' groups and paramilitary organizations. Especially in the defeated countries or in those victorious countries disappointed with their gains, this impulse had dangerous consequences. In Italy and Germany, veterans enlisted in great numbers in the ranks of uniformed, right-wing organizations that became the power base for the brutal armed supporters of the dictators Mussolini and Hitler (see Chapter 13). Pledged to winning back the losses in their nations' defeats in World War I, such leaders as Hitler and Mussolini seized political power by exploiting postwar problems and resentments. Their policies were to breed a second global conflict.

CHAPTER TWELVE

FEMINISM AND THE

PEACE MOVEMENT, 1910–1990

Beginning in Britain in the 1820s, women throughout the world formed organizations that worked for demilitarization, pacifism, and, following the invention of the atomic bomb, an end to nuclear weapons. The impetus for the early-nineteenth-century peace movement was the Napoleonic Wars. English Quakers formed the London Peace Society in 1816, and soon after branches were established in many other English towns. Membership in these societies included women, and in the 1820s a few of them set up Female Auxiliary Peace Societies, the first organized women's peace groups. Swedish author Fredrika Bremer continued these efforts in continental Europe, writing against war during the Crimean War and, in 1854, forming the Women's Peace Union.

In the United States, the earliest calls for peace and disarmament came shortly after the nation's founding. In 1793, Dr. Benjamin Rush, a signer of the Declaration of Inde-

pendence, and Benjamin Bannecker, an African-American mathematician and architect, called for the establishment of a department of peace to go along with the recently established War Department. (In 1949 this branch of the government was reorganized and given the title Department of Defense; it is the largest federal department and since its establishment has received the major portion of the federal budget.) Rush's suggestion was not followed, but in the nineteenth century the Civil War became a catalyst for peace groups in the way that the Napoleonic and Crimean Wars had in Europe.

The American Civil War is often regarded as the first modern "total war," fought not only against a government or armed forces but against an opponent's economic means of existence and civilian population. It was clear to many people that future wars would bring similar devastation, and in the mid-nineteenth century a series of international peace congresses was held in Europe; these conferences called for the establishment of a congress of nations and international court of arbitration, the end of military education, and the control of arms sales. In the Western Hemisphere, the first Pan-American Congress met in 1889–90, and in 1899 one of the aims of these congresses became a reality with the establishment of the Permanent Court of Arbitration at The Hague in the Netherlands. (With the founding of the League of Nations after World War I this body became the World Court, and, with the founding of the United Nations after World War II, the International Court of Justice; its permanent seat is still in The Hague.)

The peace movement of the nineteenth century was one of many movements of social reform whose agendas and aims were linked, and in which women played major roles. Individuals and groups advocating the abolition of slavery or the restriction of alcohol often linked their goals with those of the peace movement; the largest U.S. temperance group, for example, the Women's Christian Temperance Union, believing that the violence at home caused by alcohol was connected to the international violence of war, had a department of peace. The connections between the women's rights movement and the peace movement were even stronger. The major women's suffrage organizations, the International Council of Women and the International Woman Suffrage Alliance, had platforms that supported peace and arbitration, viewing their own international cooperation as a model that nations could follow. Not all peace organizations allowed women

to be full members, inspiring some women to step up their call for equal rights in the same way that the abolition movement's exclusion of women had led female abolitionists to become stronger advocates of women's suffrage.

Despite all efforts for the peaceful arbitration of international disputes, the late nineteenth and early twentieth century saw a military build-up throughout Europe that, combined with intense nationalism and imperialistic rivalries, led to the outbreak of World War I in 1914. Though the war caused a break in the workings of the Permanent Court of Arbitration and other international bodies, it served as a spur for women's peace activities. In 1915 Aletta Jacobs, a physician from the Netherlands, and Chrystal Macmillan, a lawyer from Scotland, organized an international women's peace conference. This was held at The Hague, with over one thousand delegates from twelve nations, though the British, French, and Russian delegates were forbidden by their governments to attend. The U.S. delegation of forty-seven women included many involved with the newly formed Women's Peace Party (WPP), including its chair, the social reformer Jane Addams. The meeting sent delegations to the leaders of many countries to lobby for an end to the war, and linked peace and women's rights explicitly in its closing statement:

The International Congress of Women is convinced that one of the strongest forces for the prevention of war will be the combined influence of the women of all countries. . . . But as women can only make their influence effective if they have equal political rights with men, this Congress declares that it is the duty of the women of all countries to work with all their force for their political enfranchisement.[1]

In the United States, the two aims of the International Congress for Women—world peace and political rights for women—came into conflict. Carrie Chapman Catt, one of the founders of the Women's Peace Party and the president of the National American Woman Suffrage Association, decided to offer President Wilson the assistance of suffragists as the United States entered the war, in 1917, in return for his support of women's suffrage. This move angered Addams and other leaders of the WPP (such as Crystal Eastman), who felt that the group's pacifism should never be compromised. The split, combined with government surveillance of antiwar groups and legal restrictions on their publication or dissemination of materials, meant that the WPP was not very active during the rest of the war. Immediately afterward, both sides gained victories: women were granted the vote in 1920, and the WPP, still alive, reorganized as the U.S. branch of the Women's International League for Peace and Freedom (WILPF). With women's suffrage achieved, Catt re-turned to peace organizing, founding the National Committee on the Cause and Cure of War (NCCW), a coalition of moderate women's groups such as the YWCA, National Council of Jewish Women, Women's Christian Temperance Union, the American Association of University Women, and several women's missionary groups. (World War I caused a similar split within British suffrage groups between those who decided to support the war effort and those who opposed the war.)

Government harassment of peace activists did not end when the war ended, for the WILPF offices in Chicago were frequently raided, and Emily Green Balch, the group's secretary-treasurer, lost her position on the faculty of Wellesley College because of her peace work. Women were often charged with being Communists because of their international interests and connections; the most notorious example was the "Spider Web" conspiracy chart, which from the early 1920s linked peace groups and Communist organizations. This chart was distributed by the War Department and often included the poem: "Miss Bolshevicki has come to town/With a Russian cap and German Gown/ In Women's clubs she's sure to be found/For she's come to disarm AMERICA."[2] Balch's reputation was somewhat redeemed when she received the Nobel Peace Prize in 1946; Jane Addams received it in 1931, making them the only two U.S. women ever so honored.

1. "Program from the International Women's Congress, April 28, 29, 30, 1915," quoted in Harriet Hyman Alonso, *Peace as a Women's Issue: A History of the U.S. Movement for World Peace and Women's Rights* (Syracuse: Syracuse University Press, 1930), p. 68.

2. Quoted in Nancy Cott, *The Grounding of Modern Feminism* (New Haven: Yale University Press, 1987), p. 94.

During the 1920s and 1930s the major international peace efforts centered around establishing legislative or negotiated alternatives to war. The League of Nations was established by the peace treaties that ended World War I and was successful in preventing a number of conflicts during the 1920s. In 1928 many nations signed the Kellogg-Briand Pact calling for the use of peaceful means of resolving conflicts and condemning war as an instrument of national policy, though the lack of any measures of enforcement meant that the pact would not have much actual effect. Both WILPF and NCCW supported these moves, although some more radical women's peace groups, such as the Women's Peace Union, felt they did not go far enough, and worked for a constitutional amendment to outlaw war completely. In their efforts to achieve world peace, all of the women's groups used tactics they had developed in the suffrage campaign—parades, letter-writing campaigns, petitions, direct lobbying—and in some cases they also used tactics of nonviolent resistance developed by Gandhi in the campaign for Indian independence from the British. During this period they often worked on Latin American issues, calling, for example, for the removal of U.S. troops from Haiti, where they were stationed from 1915 to 1937.

The rise of Nazism in Germany brought an end to the League of Nations, a renewal of war, and a crisis of conscience for peace groups. Most groups and individuals eventually gave up their absolute pacifist stance

and opposed fascism, while continuing to oppose government policies that restricted freedom at home. For example, WILPF members in the United States supported conscientious objectors and opposed the internment of Japanese-Americans in camps, while those in Denmark and Norway were active in the resistance against the Nazis. After the war, WILPF was made an official non-governmental organization affiliated with the United Nations, and it pushed for the establishment of UNICEF and the UN High Commission for Refugees.

The atomic bombs that ended World War II created a new issue for peace groups—nuclear disarmament. WILPF combined with mixed-sex groups such as the National Committee for a Sane Nuclear Policy (SANE) to protest nuclear testing. In 1961, five women in Washington who were members of SANE formed Women Strike for Peace (WSP) to organize one-day actions protesting American and Soviet nuclear policies. They galvanized thousands of women who had not been active before, particularly around the issue of the contamination of milk by strontium 90, a radioactive isotope that is the chief immediate hazard in the fallout from above-ground nuclear tests. WSP was intentionally nonhierarchical with no dues or official membership; most of the women who took part in its one-day strikes across the country were white, middle-class mothers who wore white gloves and brought photographs of their children along on demonstrations. Their ladylike demeanor and middle-class status did not protect them from government investigations in this virulently anticommunist period, and in 1962 members of WSP testified before the House Un-American Activities Committee. Their testimony made the committee look ridiculous, a point captured in a Herblock cartoon in the *Washington Post* in which one congressman is shown asking another: "I came in late; which was it that was un-American—women or peace?"[3] WSP actions influenced the passage of the 1963 Test-Ban Treaty, which banned testing of atomic weapons in the atmosphere, outer space, and below water.

From 1962 to 1975, the overriding issue for U.S. peace groups was the Vietnam War, and women's groups combined with many other peace groups in actions ranging from literature distribution to nonviolent protests to mass demonstrations such as the 1969 Vietnam Moratorium. Protests against the war took place not only in the United States but throughout the world, often organized by student groups as part of the international student movement. At the same time, the civil rights movement in the United States used similar tactics and often involved the same people as the antiwar movement, in the same way that the abolitionist and peace movements of the nineteenth century had been linked. Like those in the nineteenth century, these twentieth-century movements for social change also led to a reinvigoration of the women's rights move-

ment. Though they had the right to vote and were working for social justice, women activists discovered that they were still excluded from leadership positions and that their opinions were not taken seriously. This twentieth-century women's rights movement is usually termed the *women's liberation movement,* and it eventually led to sweeping changes in women's legal rights, employment opportunities, and political power.

For women's peace organizations, this renewal of feminism often led to their making explicit connections again between the violence of war and violence against women. This became a more prominent part of women's peace activities after the end of the Vietnam War, when the attention of peace organizations in the United States and Europe was focused on the build-up of nuclear arsenals and an increase in military spending that was accompanied by cuts in social programs. New groups were formed, such as Women's Action for Nuclear Disarmament (WAND), Babies Against the Bomb, Women Opposed to the Nuclear Threat (WONT), and Women Against Military Madness (WAMM). New types of strategies were adopted, such as the establishment of permanent peace camps at missile and military production sites in Europe, the United States, Canada, and Australia, and such as the theatrical action of thousands of women encircling the Pentagon in the Women's Pentagon Actions of 1980 and 1981. Older strategies, such as marches, petition campaigns; and civil disobedience, continued as women pressured their

3. *Washington Post,* December 11, 1962.

governments to begin nuclear disarmament. In 1985 an international group of women formed Women for a Meaningful Summit and visited the diplomats involved in the disarmament talks between the United States and the Soviet Union. (There were, however, no women present as negotiators.)

The decade 1975–1985 was designated by the United Nations as the Decade for Women, bringing worldwide organizing around issues involving women's economic, political, and social roles. The decade was highlighted by three international conferences: Mexico City in 1975, Copenhagen in 1980, and Nairobi in 1985. WILPF members tried to get disarmament language into the official statements at the Mexico City conference, but they were not successful; UN organizers regarded disarmament and peace issues as "too political" and not truly "women's issues." By the Copenhagen conference, however, this attitude had changed, and by 1985 the whole conference in Nairobi was titled "Equality, Development, and Peace." Alongside the official UN conference, nongovernmental organizations had their own much larger conference that brought together over 14,000 women from around the world. Statements emerging from this conference clearly defined peace as a primary women's issue, and also pointed to the environmental and economic costs of the arms race. In the decade since Nairobi, women's peace groups have addressed issues of racism and uneven worldwide development more directly, as their

idea of "peace" has broadened from a focus on disarmament to include many issues of social justice.

Women's peace organizations that developed throughout the nineteenth and twentieth centuries were often international or had international connections, and promoted dialogue among women from diverse cultures, as well as worked toward change in the policies of specific governments. Women who were peace activists varied widely in age, level of education, and social background; some of them were also involved in groups that worked for women's rights, while others were involved in groups that included both female and male members and worked in other areas of social concern, such as civil rights or labor organizing.

Many of the women who were leaders and members of women's peace groups were also active in peace organizations for both women and men that were formed at the same time as the separate women's peace groups. Women involved in separate groups, however, had to confront an issue that did not face those involved in mixed-sex groups—why was it important or appropriate that there be separate groups for women working for peace? This was a tricky issue for many, for often they also were advocates of women's equality or greater political rights, and to stress the *differences* between men and women might have been counterproductive. Many of them have left a record of the way in which they addressed this issue in the formal position papers of the groups they founded or were involved in, or in oral interviews conducted later. In this chapter you will be using both position ·papers and interviews, along with posters and drawings made by women peace activists to answer the following questions: How did twentieth-century women involved in women's peace groups view the relationship between their being women and their advocating peace? How did they translate their ideas into actions, and how did their ideas shape the types of actions they regarded as appropriate to achieving their aims?

SOURCES AND METHOD

Traditionally, political history was thought of as the history of politics, with governmental and military leaders as the main actors, and laws, decrees, parliamentary debates, and other official documents as its primary records. These are still important, but today political history is being seen in a broader sense as the history not only of politics but of all relations involving power, and a wider range of sources is now being used to understand the power relationships in past societies and the ways in which individuals and groups who are not officially part of the government have shaped political decisions. This has meant relying on the documents produced by such individuals and groups, as well as interviews and discussions with a wide range of people. Political historians now use techniques of *oral history* first developed by anthropologists and social historians, which combine interviews with the exploration of written sources to arrive at a fuller picture of political changes and events.

Historians interested in women's lives in the recent past have also found oral history to be a valuable tool. Women's experiences and opinions are much less likely to make it into official records, both because women have been excluded from positions of political power until very recently and because groups that did include women often assumed that their views would be the same as those of the men in the group and so did not record them. Women's groups were much less likely than men's to keep formal records of their discussions, and their actions and roles have often been downplayed in newspaper and other published accounts. Thus interviews with participants are one of the few ways we can reconstruct women's involvement in groups that worked for political and social change and get some idea of their motivations and goals.

Because it allows you to come into direct contact with the history makers you wish to study, oral history is a very appealing research method, but it is most useful when written records are available for verification. Memories are not always accurate, and people may have reasons to vary their stories from what actually happened. For example, Margaret Hope

Bacon discovered while writing a biography of Mildred Scott Olmsted, who held various national offices with WILPF from 1922 to 1966, that Olmsted "had forgotten the very existence of men and women who opposed her. Even when I would show her in writing the evidence of such opposition, she continued not to remember it."[4]

Your sources for this chapter include selections from the written documents and speeches of women involved in the peace movement, position papers and posters of several peace groups, and selections from oral interviews with several women activists. They have been arranged in chronological order because it is important to keep the historical context in mind as you are reading and evaluating them. The documents come from the two key periods of the women's peace movement: the World War I era and the 1960s to the 1980s. These two periods were chosen because (1) women's peace groups were most active during these periods, and (2) these were periods of strong women's rights movements. Thus, women who were active in the peace movement during these times often felt compelled to address our first question directly, to comment about how they viewed the relationship between their being women and their advocating peace.

As you use the sources to answer the first question, you will be addressing an issue not only in political and women's history, but also in a very new area of historical investigation: *gender*. Only very recently have historians begun to study how past societies fashioned their notions of what it means to be male or female. They stress the fact that gender is not simply biological, but socially constructed and historically variable, for norms of feminine and masculine behavior change. Women peace activists were one of the few groups forced to confront the social construction of gender directly in what they were doing and thinking, as they addressed such questions as whether men were naturally more warlike than women or whether being mothers or prospective mothers made women more inclined to peace. As you read and look at the sources in this chapter, note whether they view women as somehow more peaceful than men. If they do, to what do the authors ascribe these differences: biology? education? social pressures? Do they think this inclination can or should be changed? Do they view women's peacefulness in a completely positive manner, or do they also see it as reflecting passivity? How do sources that do *not* view women as more peaceful than men explain why they feel there should be separate women's peace groups and why wars have traditionally been fought by male combatants?

Whatever their opinions about gender differences with regard to war and peace, women's peace groups carried out various actions to attempt to change government policies. Your sources discuss some of these actions. The second question in this chapter

4. Margaret Hope Bacon, *One Woman's Passion for Peace and Freedom: The Life of Mildred Scott Olmsted* (Syracuse: Syracuse University Press, 1993), p. xvii.

asks you to examine how these groups changed their ideas into actions, and how their ideas about gender differences shaped the types of actions they regarded as appropriate. As you read and look at the sources, note the types of actions that are discussed. Which of these appear to be shaped, either implicitly or explicitly, by the fact that these are *women's* peace groups? What special problems and opportunities do the women involved in these groups see as arising from their being women or from their training about acceptable female norms of behavior? Do they see any tensions between their ideas and actions, and how do they resolve these?

Along with thinking about the content of your sources for this chapter, you also need to keep in mind differences between the type of sources that you are using, as would anyone using oral interviews. How might ideas expressed in the official position papers and speeches differ from those conveyed in interviews conducted later? All of the interviews published here were conducted by women sympathetic to the peace movement. How might this have shaped their content? As you answer the questions in this chapter, you should also think about the appropriateness of each type of source. What do the oral interviews add that could not be gained from other sources? What does the information gained from all these sources add to our picture of political developments in the twentieth century?

THE EVIDENCE

Source 1 from Olive Schreiner, Woman and Labor *(New York: Frederick A. Stokes, 1911), pp. 175, 176, 178–179, 180, 185.*

1. From Olive Schreiner, *Woman and Labor,* 1911

[*Olive Schreiner (1855–1920) was a South African writer and women's rights advocate.*]

There is, perhaps, no woman, whether she have borne children, or be merely potentially a child-bearer, who could look down upon a battlefield covered with slain, but the thought would rise in her, "So many mothers' sons! So many young bodies brought into the world to lie there! So many months of weariness and pain while bones and muscles were shaped within! So many hours of anguish and struggle that breath might be! So many baby mouths drawing life at women's breasts;—all this, that men might lie with glazed eyeballs, and swollen faces, and fixed, blue, unclosed mouths, and great limbs tossed. . . .

On that day when the woman takes her place beside the man in the governance and arrangement of external affairs of her race will also be that day that heralds the death of war as a means of arranging human differences. . . .

It is not because of woman's cowardice, incapacity, nor, above all, because of her general superior virtue, that she will end war when her voice is fully and clearly heard in the governance of states—it is because, on this one point, and on this point almost alone, the knowledge of woman, simply as woman, is superior to that of man; she knows the history of human flesh; she knows its cost; he does not. . . .

Men's bodies are our woman's works of art. Given to us power to control, we will never carelessly throw them in to fill up the gaps in human relationships made by international ambitions and greeds. The thought would never come to us as women, "Cast in men's bodies; settle the thing so!" . . .

War will pass when intellectual culture and activity have made possible to the female an equal share in the control and governance of modern national life; it will probably not pass away much sooner; its extinction will not be delayed much longer.

It is especially in the domain of war that we, the bearers of men's bodies, who supply its most valuable munition, who, not amid the clamor and ardor of battle, but singly, and alone, with a three-in-the-morning courage, shed our blood and face death that the battlefield might have its food, a food more precious to us than our heart's blood; it is we especially who, in the domain of war, have our word to say, a word no man can say for us. It is our intention to enter into the domain of war and to labor there till in the course of generations we have extinguished it.

Source 2 from Maude Royden, "War and the Women's Movement," in C. R. Buxton and G. L. Dickinson, Towards a Lasting Settlement *(London: Allen and Unwin, 1915), p. 106.*

2. Maude Royden on Women and War, 1915

[*A. Maude Royden (1876–1956) was a British writer and strong supporter of women's suffrage. She edited a suffrage newspaper and became the first woman to hold a regular preaching position in the Anglican church.*]

The belief that women are innately more pacific than men has been severely shaken, if not altogether destroyed. It is now very evident that they can be as virulently militarist, as blindly partisan, not as the soldier, for in him such qualities are generally absent, but as the male non-combatant, for whom the same cannot always be said. Among women, as among men, there are extremists for war and for peace; pacifists and militarists; women who are as passionately convinced as Bernhardi[5] that war is a good thing, women who accept it as a terrible necessity, women who repudiate it altogether. All these views they share with men. There appears to be no cleavage of opinion along sex lines.

Source 3 from Jane Addams, "Account of Her Interview with the Foreign Ministers of Europe," speech published in The Survey, *New York, July 17, 1915. Quoted in Cambridge Women's Peace Collective,* My Country Is the Whole World: An Anthology of Women's Work on Peace and War *(London: Pandora Press, 1984), pp. 86–87.*

3. Jane Addams on Women and War, Carnegie Hall, New York, 1915

[*Jane Addams (1860–1935), the American social reformer and founder of Hull House (a settlement house for immigrants in Chicago), was the first president of WILPF and, in 1931, was awarded the Nobel Peace Prize.*]

Let me say just a word about the women in the various countries. The belief that a woman is against war simply and only because she is a woman and not a man, does not, of course, hold. In every country there are many, many women who believe that the War is inevitable and righteous, and that the highest possible service is being performed by their sons who go into the Army; just as there are thousands of men believing that in every country; the majority of women and men doubtless believe that.

But the women do have a sort of pang about it. Let us take the case of an artist, an artist who is in an artillery corps, let us say, and is commanded to fire upon a wonderful thing, say St Mark's at Venice, or the Duomo at Florence, or any other great architectural and beautiful thing. I am sure he would have just a little more compunction than the man who had never given himself to creating beauty and did not know the cost of it. There is certainly that deterrent on the part of the women, who have nurtured these soldiers from the time they were little things, who brought them into the world and brought them up to the age of fighting, and now see them destroyed. That curious revolt comes out again and again, even in the women who are most patriotic and who say: "I have five sons and a son-in-law in the trenches. I wish I had

5. Friedrich von Bernhardi (1849–1930) was a German general and military writer known for his strong expression of German ambitions.

more sons to give." Even those women, when they are taken off their guard, give a certain protest, a certain plaint against the whole situation which very few men I think are able to formulate.

Now, what is it that these women do in the hospitals? They nurse the men back to health and send them to the trenches, and the soldiers say to them: "You are so good to us when we are wounded, you do everything in the world to make life possible and to restore us; why do you not have a little pity for us when we are in the trenches? Why do you not put forth a little of this same effort and this same tenderness to see what might be done to pull us out of those miserable places?"

That testimony came to us, not from the nurses of one country, and not from the nurses who were taking care of the soldiers on one side, but from those who were taking care of them upon every side.

And it seems to make it quite clear that whether we are able to recognize it or not, there has grown up a generation in Europe, as there has doubtless grown up a generation in America, who have revolted against war. It is a god they know not of, that they are not willing to serve; because all of their sensibilities and their training upon which their highest ideals depend, revolt against the whole situation.

Source 4 from Crystal Eastman, "A Program for Voting Women," pamphlet of Women's Peace Party of New York, March 1918, quoted in Blanche Wiesen Cook, Crystal Eastman on Women and Revolution *(New York: Oxford University Press, 1978), pp. 266–267.*

4. Crystal Eastman on the Women's Peace Movement, 1919

[Crystal Eastman (1881–1928) was an American feminist, socialist, and labor lawyer. She was one of the founders of the Woman's Peace Party and the American Civil Liberties Union, which was originally set up to defend conscientious objectors.]

Why a *Woman's* Peace Party?, I am often asked. Is peace any more a concern of women than of men? Is it not of universal human concern? For a feminist— one who believes in breaking down sex barriers so that women and men can work and play and build the world together—it is not an easy question to answer. Yet the answer, when I finally worked it out in my own mind, convinced me that we should be proud and glad, even as feminists, to work for the Woman's Peace Party.

To begin with, there is a great and unique tradition behind our movement which would be lost if we merged our Woman's Peace Party in the general revolutionary international movement of the time. Do not forget that it was women who gathered at The Hague, a thousand strong, in the early months of the war, women from all the great belligerent and neutral countries, who conferred there together in friendship and sorrow and sanity while the mad war raged around them. Their great conference, despite its soundness and constructive statesmanship, failed of its purpose, failed of its hope. But from the beginning of the war down to the Russo–German armistice there was no world step of such daring and directness, nor of such honest, unfaltering international spirit and purpose, as the organization of the International Committee of Women for Permanent Peace at The Hague in April, 1915. This Committee has branches in twenty-two countries. The Woman's Peace Party is the American section of the Committee, and our party, organized February 1 and 2, is the New York State Branch.

When the great peace conference comes, a Congress of Women made up of groups from these twenty-two countries will meet in the same city to demand that the deliberate intelligent organization of the world for lasting peace shall be the outcome of that conference.

These established international connections make it important to keep this a woman's movement.

But there is an added reason. We women of New York State, politically speaking, have just been born. We have been born into a world at war and this fact cannot fail to color greatly the whole field of our political thinking and to determine largely the emphasis of our political action. What we hope, then, to accomplish by keeping our movement distinct is to bring thousands upon thousands of women—women of the international mind—to dedicate their new political power, not to local reforms or personal ambitions, not to discovering the difference between the Democratic and Republican parties, but to *ridding the world of war.*

Source 5 from Käthe Kollwitz, The Sacrifice (Das Opfer), Rosenwald Collection, © 1996 Board of Trustees, National Gallery of Art, Washington, 1922/23. Woodcut in black, reworked with white gouache, on japan paper. Plate 1 from "War" (Klipstein 1955 177.ii/vii (trial proof). Image: .372 × .402 cm. (14 $\frac{5}{8}$" × 15 $\frac{13}{16}$"); sheet: .415 × 437 cm. (16 $\frac{5}{16}$" × 17 $\frac{3}{16}$").

5. Käthe Kollwitz, *The Sacrifice,* 1922

[*Käthe Kollwitz (1867–1945) was a German artist and sculptor whose works were ordered removed from public view by Adolf Hitler in the 1930s because of their political and social content.*]

Sources 6 and 7 from Judith Porter Adams, Peacework: Oral Histories of Women Peace Activists *(Boston: Twayne Publishers, 1991), pp. 194–198.*

6. An Oral Interview with Dagmar Wilson, 1991

[*Dagmar Wilson (b. 1916) is a
graphic designer and children's book
illustrator who was one of the founders
of Women Strike for Peace.*]

Thirty years ago I was responsible for an action that resulted in a national peace movement which is still going strong. Women Strike for Peace. I'm not really a "political" person, although I was brought up as a pacifist. As a child growing up in the years following the "war to end wars"—World War I—I believed that nations would work out their conflicts rather than fight. Other wonderful things were happening too. Women had been liberated—my mother was a voter. I went to a progressive school for boys and girls, which in Europe, where I grew up, was not common. Socialism seemed like a wonderful experiment. I really believed that the world was moving forward in many areas, all favorable to mankind.

However, after World War II, I realized that there was something happening that was beyond politics and that affected all human beings. I felt that the question of survival on earth was not a matter of politics, nor a matter of power between governments, but was a matter of deeper concerns common to all humanity.

Many things moved me to become active step by step, but the last straw was the arrest of Bertrand Russell in 1961 in London's Trafalgar Square. He sat down with others to block traffic as a protest. He let it be known that having tried through normal channels to alert the world to the extreme danger that we were in, pitting ourselves against each other with these destructive new weapons, he felt it necessary to make a gesture. I was impressed by that. One night soon after his arrest, I was talking about his protest to some English friends who were visiting my husband and me here in the United States. They were turning me off with jokes and making cynical wisecracks. They were intelligent people distinguished in their professions, and I was distressed by their response. This was also the time of the Berlin Wall. The media had said it might mean war, and of course, war would mean nuclear war. Our administration was telling us to build fallout shelters to protect our families. I felt indignant, more than indignant. I felt insulted as a human being that responsible people, governments, were asking us to do anything so stupid, as ineffectual as this, instead of coming to grips with the problems that were causing the tensions we were facing. My husband, who knew me well enough to realize that I was getting quite tense, said, "Well, women are

very good at getting their way when they make up their minds to do something."

That phrase stayed with me. The next day I called a friend at the Committee
for a Sane Nuclear Policy in Washington, D.C., to ask if SANE was going to
respond to the Committee of 100 in support of Russell's actions. I said, "I feel
like chartering a plane and filling it with women to picket the jail." This guy
said, "Well, that's an idea for your women's movement." I said, "Women's
movement? What do you mean?" I hadn't mentioned anything of that kind; I
hadn't even thought about it. Anyway, he gave me an idea.

I stayed by the phone and thought, and thought, and thought. I said to myself, "Well, what about a women's movement?" I picked up the telephone and
started calling all my women friends from my phone book and Christmas
card list. I wanted to see what they thought. I have always been very tele-
phone-shy, so this was an unusual thing for me to do. It turned out that everybody that I spoke with had been worrying about this problem. We women
thought that the fallout shelter idea was an inane, insane, and an unsuitable
response to the world situation and spelled disaster. The response I got was
really quite enlightening. Each woman had it in the front of her mind, including a lot of women who were really not politically active.

I soon gathered together in my own living room a small group of women
out of those whom I had called. Three days later we met at my house. Six days
later, at a big meeting planned by SANE, we announced an "action." This
marked the formation of Women Strike for Peace.

What we planned was a one-day event. The women would go on strike and
leave the men "holding the baby." We said: "Now what do you think would
happen if all the women went on strike?" The whole country would stand
still. We thought it was a good way to demonstrate our own power and show
that women were an essential part of our social structure and had a right to be
heard. Six weeks from that day, there were demonstrations in sixty cities in
the United States.

We were not part of the women's liberation movement. Ours was a peace
movement activated by women. And there is a difference. We were women
working for the good of humanity. One woman in our early group who was a
very good writer wrote a statement of purpose that was powerful. One of the
strengths of the movement was that it was cliché free. We were not political
activists who were used to the old phrases. We were speaking much more
out of our everyday experiences, but we were educated and literate. This was
our statement:

> We represent a resolute stand of women in the United States against the unprece-
> dented threat to life from nuclear holocaust. We're women of all races, creeds, and
> political persuasions who are dedicated to the achievement of general and complete
> disarmament under effective international control. We cherish the right and accept
> the responsibility of the individual in democratic society to act and influence the

course of government. We demand of governments that nuclear weapons tests be banned forever, that the arms race end, and that the world abolish all weapons of destruction under United Nations safeguards. We urge immediate planning at local, state and national levels for a peacetime economy with freedom and justice for all. We urge our government to anticipate world tensions and conflicts through constructive nonmilitary actions and through the United Nations. We join with women throughout the world to challenge the right of any nation or group of nations to hold the power of life or death over the world.

That really sums up my personal beliefs; I couldn't have stated it as well.

We saw women as a vehicle for a new peace action. There were already many peace groups and individuals, but the situation was still grave. These groups had become part of the peace establishment, and we didn't think they were as effective as they once were. We were able to do things that couldn't have happened in an already existing organization. I hoped that WSP would go on as long as it was effective, but I believed that in time it would be replaced by something else.

We had learned that nuclear testing was having hazardous effects on our environment, specifically on the open fields on which cows were grazing. This was contaminating the milk supply with strontium 90. This touched us very closely. We found out that strontium 90 was replacing calcium in children's bones. When we heard voices from Capitol Hill saying, "Well, well, it's too bad; this is just one of the hazards of the nuclear age," we really began to wonder about the sanity of our nation's leaders. Women Strike for Peace was an idea whose time had come. I was the lightning conductor; it just happened to be me. The time had come when either the people of the Earth would live together or die together.

In January of WSP's second year the New York women decided to come to the White House to stage a demonstration. They filled the longest train that had ever left Pennsylvania Station in the history of the railway, all with women. That day President Kennedy was scheduled for a press conference, and we thought no one would pay any attention to our demonstration. There was an enormous rain storm that soaked all the women who were coming off the train, ruining their hats—we always made a "respectable" appearance with hats and gloves. They walked through the rain to the White House and became soaked to the skin. At the president's press conference a well-known journalist representing the *New York Post* asked, "Do you think that demonstrations at this time have any influence on you and on the public and on the direction which we take in policy?" The president replied by saying that he had seen the large numbers of women out there in the rain and that we could understand that he agreed with our message and that our message had been received. We got wonderful publicity out of that, since the press conference was televised and broadcast nationally.

Soon after we began with one-day actions all over the country. We had permanent relationships with the sixty cities that had demonstrated on the first day. We had established a phone "tree" so that we could organize actions quickly. Eventually we realized that we had to have regular meetings and we had to have a national office, and so a national movement grew from our simple beginning with a one-day action. But we never had elected representatives; we preferred a movement rather than an organization. We continued to make decisions by consensus. So many people had been penalized in the past for left-wing activities. Our structure—or lack of it—meant that it would be very, very hard for anyone to be held accountable for the whole movement.

We soon had a program researching the effects of strontium 90. We took groups of people to government offices where we found everybody very willing to give us the facts. They were not reassuring. However, getting the word out was difficult. We took the press with us wherever we could. The publications that we issued were used in universities. We were respected; we weren't just a hysterical mob of women. People recognized that we had brains, and we were sensible.

We organized a delegation of one hundred women—fifty from the United States and fifty from European countries, including the Soviet Union—to visit the 1962 eighteen-nation disarmament conference in Geneva. We lobbied all the delegations and wanted to address the plenary session. We were informed that instead of addressing the plenary session, we could meet with the Soviet and United States cochairs. A young woman—she was a Quaker—volunteered to organize us for the meeting. I learned the power of Quaker silence from her. We marched through a light rain to where the sessions were held in the suburbs of Geneva. The rain seemed to be a good omen for us; we'd always succeeded in the rain. We walked in silence, which was quite a tour de force for us chatterboxes. We waited for an hour and forty-five minutes in total silence. Finally the Soviet and American cochairmen, Valaerian Zorin and Arthur Dean, came in with their translators, secretaries, and a few press. The important thing was that they walked into a room that was totally silent; the silence was palpable. Then I got up and spoke, which I did feeling rather like a schoolmistress. We wanted them to know that we held them responsible for the future of the human race and we thought it was time they got on with the business of ending the nuclear arms race. We presented them with mountains of petitions. The press coverage in Europe of our action was excellent. That was our first really international venture.

WSP played a critical role in the 1963 Partial Test Ban Treaty's passage, but our greatest triumph was our confrontation with the House Un-American Activities Committee. They pounced on us in 1962 by subpoenaing nine WSP women. We were advised by others who had a go-around with the Committee that we "should not make a big fuss." But one of our women said, "No, this is not the way we're going to do it. If they're subpoenaing Dagmar Wilson, we should all volunteer to testify." Now that was an absolutely brilliant idea. We sent telegrams through our network saying, "Volunteer to testify. Come if you can. Hospitality offered. Bring your baby." Hundreds of women volunteered to testify. This was a new twist—most people were tempted to run a mile when the Committee pointed its magic wand at them.

I was the last one to be subpoenaed. It was a great relief to me, to be able to have my say. I had the benefit of two days of hearings before my turn came. By that time I felt quite comfortable. My testimony was summed up best by someone who said that I treated the attorney for the Committee just as though he were a rather tiresome dinner partner.

Our WSP meetings were very informal, with no protocol; we ran them like we ran our carpools. Well, that was extremely baffling to these political gentlemen. And at one point one said, "I don't understand how you get anything done at all." I answered, "Well, it puzzles us sometimes too."

The Committee was trying to find out if there was Communist influence in the peace movement. WSP was concerned about war and peace; we didn't think the world was worth blowing up over political differences. We could see ourselves marching arm in arm with Soviet mothers for the sake of our children, so we were not intimidated by the Committee's strategies. I was asked at the end of my testimony whether we would examine our books to see if we had Communist women in our midst, and I said, "Certainly not"— we would not do anything of the kind. "In fact," I said, "unless the whole human race joins us in our quest for peace, God help us."

One of the funny things about our "inquisition" before the Committee was that we were asked, in a sinister tone, if we had a mimeograph machine. It's true that we were mimeographing materials to distribute among ourselves. You know, someone's baby was always around, and we kidded ourselves that the print might appear on a child's diaper. Anybody turning a baby over might find a description of where our next meeting was going to be. So much for the sinister implication of a mimeograph machine.

We got very good press. I think that everybody was thoroughly fed up with the Committee. Congress was embarrassed by it, and the press was bored with it.

7. An Oral Interview with Madeline Duckles, 1991

[Madeline Duckles (b. 1916) joined WILPF in the 1940s and was an organizer for Women Strike for Peace. During the Vietnam War, she helped organize a program to fly napalm-burned children to the United States for treatment.]

We've made progress in civil rights, environmental issues; we've progressed on every level except for peace. Here we are, armed to the teeth when Women Strike for Peace began protesting nuclear testing when strontium 90 was appearing in children's teeth. We wanted to do something quickly. So women all over the country called a "strike" and left their work and families to protest. At that time, we had exploded two bombs and now the world has about fifty thousand nuclear weapons. So we haven't made any progress at all! And

WILPF was working hard right after women's suffrage trying to get women more involved in the political process, trying to stop war toys and get the U.S. out of Central America in 1917 and we're still there now. The problems persist.

My political education began when I went to the University of California here at Berkeley. At that time the YWCA was where the action was. There were a few remarkable women in charge of it. There were discussions of race relations, the Spanish Civil War, and labor issues. I began at the University in 1933, and this was the year of the great longshoremen's strike in San Francisco. I had never been to a union meeting before. We were gathering canned goods for the strikers. It was for me a very exciting time. All kinds of political issues were discussed.

I don't remember rejecting the values of my family, which I suppose you would call redneck, but working for peace and justice issues seemed to me natural and right and proper. When people say to me, "How do you happen to be in the peace movement?" it always seems to me the most ridiculous question because we've reached the point where this *should* be the normal thing for people to do. But still, war and preparation for war is normal, and to be in the peace movement is abnormal.

Women bring to the peace movement the best feminist qualities, which are patience, tolerance, compassion, and a hell of a lot of intelligence. We're much more loath to make judgments. We have the courage to change our minds. We're not nearly so reticent about admitting mistakes and changing course when we do wrong. Of course, there are aggressive women, but they are not the "norm" for women.

The women's movement activated a great many women, and it activated them on the issues of equality for women in jobs and the Equal Rights Amendment more than it did on the peace issues. For a long time we were trying to get to NOW to set up a peace platform. I have a speech I give on any occasion that peace is a woman's issue. My current speech, in case you would like to hear it, is that foreign policy must become a community issue, when in an administration, foreign policy is military policy. Military policy means a loss of our community services and ultimately a loss of our lives. We're in double jeopardy: if the weapons they're making are used, we'll all be dead, and meanwhile, the arms race is killing us economically. I'll stop my speech there.

Source 8 from a leaflet distributed at the Women's Pentagon Action in 1980 and published by the Women's Pentagon Action Group, Washington, D.C.

8. Unity Statement, Women's Pentagon Action, 1980

These are the frightening facts, and the hopeful ideas and feelings that are bringing women together. We invite you to read them.

We are gathering at the Pentagon on November 16 because we fear for our lives. We fear for the life of this planet, our Earth, and the life of the children who are our human future.

We are women who come in most part from the northeastern region of our United States. We are city women who know the wreckage and fear of city streets, we are country women who grieve the loss of the small farm and have lived on the poisoned earth. We are young and older, we are married, single, lesbian. We live in different kinds of households, in groups, families, alone; some are single parents.

We work at a variety of jobs. We are students-teachers-factory workers-office workers-lawyers-farmers-doctors-builders-waitresses-weavers-poets-engineers-homeworkers-electricians-artists-blacksmiths. We are all daughters and sisters.

We have come here to mourn and rage and defy the Pentagon because it is the workplace of the imperial power which threatens us all. Every day while we work, study, love, the colonels and generals who are planning our annihilation walk calmly in and out the doors of its five sides. They have accumulated over 30,000 nuclear bombs at the rate of three to six bombs every day.

They are determined to produce the billion-dollar MX missile. They are creating a technology called Stealth—the invisible, unperceivable arsenal. They have revived the cruel old killer, nerve gas. They have proclaimed Directive 59 which asks for 'small nuclear wars, prolonged but limited.' The Soviet Union works hard to keep up with United States initiatives. We can destroy each other's cities, towns, schools, children many times over. The United States has sent 'advisors,' money and arms to El Salvador and Guatamala to enable those juntas to massacre their own people.

The very same men, the same legislative committees that offer trillions of dollars to the Pentagon have brutally cut day care, children's lunches, battered women's shelters. . . .

The President has just decided to produce the neutron bomb, which kills people but leaves property intact.

There is fear among the people, and that fear, created by the industrial militarists is used as an excuse to accelerate the arms race. "We will protect you . . ." they say, but we have never been so endangered, so close to the end of human time.

We women are gathering because life on the precipice is intolerable.

We want to know what anger in these men, what fear which can only be satisfied by destruction, what coldness of heart and ambition drives their days.

We want to know because we do not want that dominance which is exploitative and murderous in international relations, and so dangerous to women and children at home—we do not want that sickness transferred by the violent society through the fathers to the sons. . . .

We want an end to the arms race. No more bombs. No more amazing inventions for death.

Sources 9 and 10 from Lynne Jones, editor, Keeping the Peace: A Women's Peace Hand-book *(London: The Women's Press, 1983), pp. 23, 24, 25–26; pp. 64–67.*

9. Nottingham Women Oppose the Nuclear Threat (WONT) on Working as a Group, 1981

Nottingham WONT started as a women's group against nuclear power. . . .

As our group has evolved, another motive for meeting as women on the nuclear issue has become important—that is, the need to develop a specifically feminist analysis of nuclear threat, and to show the links between women's oppression and nuclear technology. We feel that feminism has a particular analysis of the structures and causes of all violence (not just the "women's issues" of sexual and domestic violence), and of the changes necessary to remove it. We identify the primary source of violence as gender structure in the individual, in families, in societies, and believe that while society remains deeply sexist, no peace movement can win long-term substantial victories.

We don't think that women have a special role in the peace movement because we are "naturally" more peaceful, more protective, or more vulnerable than men. Nor do we look to women as the "Earth Mothers" who will save the planet from male aggression. Rather, we believe that it is this very role division that makes the horrors of war possible. The so-called masculine, manly qualities of toughness, dominance, not showing emotion or admitting dependence, can be seen as the driving force behind war; but they depend on women playing the opposite (but not equal) role, in which the caring qualities are associated with inferiority and powerlessness. So women's role in peacemaking should not be conciliatory but assertive, breaking out of our role, forcing men to accept women's ideas and organisation, forcing them to do their own caring. Women have for too long provided the mirrors in which men see their aggression as an heroic quality, and themselves magnified larger than life. Nuclear technology is built on the arrogance and confidence of mastery (over nature as over women) which this has fed. . . .

WONT groups are specifically feminist, so they could not by themselves constitute a broad-based mass women's anti-nuclear movement. Most of the women involved in WONT are also involved in the women's movement, and many have an "alternative life-style," living in shared households, not having a 'straight' job, etc. However, we want to reach all kinds of women, and to do this, we have tried giving talks to women's groups, running workshops, doing street theatre, etc. Our aim is to help create a broad-based women's peace movement of which WONT would be an autonomous part. . . . Our approach to actions is close to that of the nonviolent direction action wing of the national movement, and we use street theatre, striking symbolic actions, and music, rather than mass demonstrations and rallies.

WONT is a decentralised organisation. Local groups are autonomous and very varied. WONT exists nationally through national gatherings once or twice a year, regional meetings, personal contacts and an occasional newsletter. There is a national contact address, and groups take turns at answering mail. We have a telephone tree for urgent messages. Nottingham WONT meets weekly, and we often see each other during the week as many of us live or work close to each other. (This creates problems for new women joining the group who are not in that particular community.) There are no "officers" but we take turns to facilitate. This means preparing an agenda, seeing that we stick to the point in discussions, are working reasonably efficiently, and that everyone gets a chance to contribute. It's an easy job in our group, for everyone is aware of these things; so the facilitator just had to be a bit more aware, to notice the time, to sense we are nearing a decision. We reach decisions by consensus. If we cannot reach a decision, it is usually because we are all unsure, rather than because different women hold irreconcilable views. We usually approach decisions by a general discussion, and then let each woman say what she thinks to see if there is general agreement. If one woman disagrees with a generally held view, then we try to see if any accommodation can be made to satisfy her as well. We will postpone a decision to another meeting if the discussion goes on a long time without getting anywhere.

10. Tamar Swade on Nuclear Weapons, 1983

[*Tamar Swade was an English antinuclear
activist and the founder of
Babies Against the Bomb.*]

Being pregnant and in the anti-nuclear movement happened at the same time for me. I joined a study group with five other women and we gave talks on nuclear power. This led to our writing the booklet, *Nuclear Resisters.*

By then my baby had been born and the effort of demand-feeding it at the same time as researching and writing my share of the booklet was enormous. The group was wonderfully supportive, but I felt that the pressures of coping with a newborn baby—the lack of sleep, exhaustion and lack of time—clashed with the needs of an ordinary group. I wasn't free to run off and collect things or proofread as the others were, and I could no longer get out easily in the evenings when the usual anti-nuclear/peace meetings take place.

I'd suddenly become a different kind of social being and I realised I needed to start a group where everybody understood my position because they were in it too, where it was fine to go "brrm-brrm" or "whoopsy!" to a child in the middle of a sentence if necessary, or change a nappy.

I found I'd joined a separate species of two-legged, four-wheeled creatures who carry their young in push-chair pouches, who emerge from their homes during the day to swarm the parks, forage in the super-markets and disappear without trace at nightfall. Occasionally some converged for a "coffee morning" or a mother-and-baby group run by the National Childbirth Trust. Here there was much discussion about nappy rash, (not) sleeping and other problems pertaining to the day-to-day survival of mother and infant.

If only these thousands of women could inform and organise themselves, what an untapped force for peace! Why not start a mother-and-baby group whose discussions included *long-term* survival?

At first, therefore, we were called "Mother and baby anti-nuclear group." As this was rather a mouthful, we were somehow gradually shortened to "Babies against the Bomb," which stayed with us. We meet during the day, with our babies or young children. Meetings are friendly and informal and we campaign wherever and however we feel we can be most effective.

Several women who have enquired about the group have never been involved in any campaigning at all, but the fact of having a child has made them think differently about the future. Those of us who had been involved before often feel an added urgency to our desire for peace after having a child.

There are some feminists who frown upon this attitude and I would like to answer them.

There is something utterly vulnerable and loveable about a newborn baby, something wholly fascinating about this creature whose every impulse is towards survival but who is so dependent for it upon others. Its cries wrench the heart and it is agonising to think of someone so little and blameless being hurt.

I am responsible for its existence—and no amount of word-juggling can get away from this. It is my responsibility and my urgent desire to ensure its survival, to speak for its rights since it can't do so for itself.

And it's not only for my child I feel this. The same feeling now extends to all children. Through my child the immorality of this world where people needlessly starve to death, has become intolerable. With pain I could not have known before, I grieve for those women in the Third World who hear their children crying for food but who can't feed them or themselves.

I know hundreds of women who feel this. Each of them in turn probably knows hundreds of others who feel the same. Some are feminists through and through, others don't know what "feminism" means. One woman told me that the mention of nuclear war conjures up the waking nightmare of her children burning. Another pictures kissing her children goodbye for the last time. A third said her particular nightmare was that the four-minute warning would come while she was at work and she wouldn't be able to cross town in time to get to them. . . .

In fact, it seems that millions of women in numerous cultures throughout history have had similar experiences in relation to their children. Should we all feel ashamed of this deep gut-feeling? For me, feminism is about choice, about every woman's freedom to feel and act and be valued. Does it make me any less of a person if my immediate, instinctive reaction to nuclear war is in my capacity as a mother? Judging by my friends in the campaign who are mothers, certainly not! Does it mean that I suddenly care less about living my-self? Rubbish! It's more that another dimension had been added to my caring.

Our priority is peace. What does it matter how we come to want it? Let's be tolerant, supportive, sisterly. This will make us stronger and more effective; we are less likely to succeed if we are divided. If *we* can't do it, what hope is there for the rest of the world?

Source 11 from Coretta Scott King, "The Judgement of History Will Show," speech given at the International Women's Conference for Peace and Nuclear Disarmament (1984), and published in the Newsletter of the Center for Defence Information, vol. 13, no. 8.

11. Coretta Scott King on Women and the Nuclear Arms Race, 1984

[*Coretta Scott King (b. 1927), the widow of Dr. Martin Luther King, Jr., is a civil rights activist and has been an active member of WILPF since 1960. She is president of the Martin Luther King, Jr., Center for Non-Violent Social Change.*]

You can't fight poverty and discrimination, you can't provide health, security and decent housing, and you can't have a clean environment in the lengthening shadow of nuclear arsenals. The nuclear arms race creates far-reaching social problems in a number of ways. The judgement of history will show that the massive economic insecurity and the psychological numbing and alienation caused by militarization of commerce and society have had a profound effect upon our lives. The proliferation of nuclear weapons is not only the major threat to the survival of humanity; it is also the primary cause of poverty and economic stagnation around the world. The arms race is a shameful theft of funds from programs that would enrich our planet. Here in America, the cost of one bomber could pay for two fully equipped hospitals. With a serious arms control program (not just shallow treaties for show which allow weapons to continue to proliferate less noticed by the public than before), the nations of the world could apply countless billions of dollars saved to advancing social and economic progress.

The supporters of the nuclear arms race claim that peace can only be achieved through strength. Apparently, they mean an ability to destroy the world an infinite number of times. We must ask just what it is that makes the nation safe and secure. If we ruin our economy to engage in an accelerated arms race, are we really any stronger? When we demoralize and polarize millions of jobless, homeless and impoverished Americans, it seems to me that we are dangerously weak at the very fabric of our society. In this sense, the nuclear arms race breeds insecurity, not strength.

Sources 12 and 13 from Keeping the Peace, edited by Lynne Jones. First published in Great Britain by The Women's Press Ltd., 1983, 34 Great Sutton Street, London EC1V ODX, p. 125; p. 19.

12. Poster for Families Against the Bomb Rally, 1982

13. Poster for a Multigroup Demonstration in Amsterdam Against the Installation of Cruise Missiles, 1981[6]

DEMONSTRATIE

AMSTERDAM, 21 NOVEMBER
MUSEUMPLEIN, 13 UUR

GEEN NIEUWE
KERNWAPENS
IN EUROPA

6. The main text reads "Against new atomic weapons in Europe."

Families Against the Bomb
MASS LOBBY ON
CRUISE AND TRIDENT
Come and make your voice heard

House of
Commons
May 18th
1982

Our children must not be
the last generation

The lobby is being organised by Families Against the Bomb with the support of the Campaign for Nuclear Disarmament.
For more information write to FAB 124A Northview Rd London N8.
Produced by FAB London Typeset by Red Lion Setters London WC1 Printed by Spiderweb London N7

LOCAL CONTACT:

Source 14 from Ann Snitow, "Holding the Line at Greenham Common: Being Joyously Political in Dangerous Times," Mother Jones, February/March 1985.

14. Ann Snitow on Women Against Military Buildups, 1985

[*Ann Snitow (b. 1943) is an American writer who also teaches literature and women's studies.*]

Back in 1981 when I first heard about the women's peace camp at Greenham Common, I was impressed but a little worried, too. Here was a stubborn little band of squatters obstructing business as usual at a huge military base. But the early media reports celebrated these women as orderly housewives and mothers who would never make this vulgar noise just for themselves but were naturally concerned about their children, innocent animals, and growing plants.

My feminist reaction was: not *again*. I had joined the women's liberation movement in 1970 to escape this very myth of the special altruism of women, our innate peacefulness, our handy patience for repetitive tasks, our peculiar endurance—no doubt perfect for sitting numbly in the Greenham mud, babies and arms outstretched, begging men to keep our children safe from nuclear war.

We feminists had argued back then that women's work had to be done by men, too: no more "women only" when it came to emotional generosity or trips to the launderette. We did form women-only groups—an autonomous women's movement—but this was to forge a necessary solidarity for resistance, not to cordon off a magic femaleness as distorted in its way as the old reverence for motherhood. Women have a long history of allowing their own goals to be eclipsed by others, and even feminist groups have often been subsumed by other movements. Given this suspiciously unselfish past, I was uneasy with women-only groups that did not concentrate on overcoming the specific oppression of women.

And why should demilitarization be women's special task? If there's one thing in this world that *won't* discriminate in men's favor, it's a nuclear explosion. Since the army is a dense locale of male symbols, actions, and forms of association, let men sit in the drizzle, I thought; let *them* worry about the children for a change.

But even before going to Greenham I should have known better than to have trusted its media image. If the women were such nice little home birds, what were they doing out in the wild, balking at male authority, refusing to shut up or go back home? I've been to Greenham twice now in the effort to understand why many thousands of women have passed through the camps, why thousands are organized in support groups all over Britain and beyond, why thousands more can be roused to help in emergencies or show up for big actions.

What I discovered has stirred my political imagination more than any activism since that first, intense feminist surge 15 years ago. Though I still have many critical questions about Greenham, I see it as a rich source of fresh thinking about how to be joyously, effectively political in a conservative, dangerous time. . . .

The Greenham women I talked to take great pains to point out that the purpose of Greenham is not to exclude men but to include women—at last. Though a few women there might still tell you women are biologically more peaceful than men, this view has been mostly replaced by a far more complex analysis of why women need to break with our old, private complicity with public male violence. No one at Greenham seems to be arguing that the always evolving Greenham value system is inevitably female. The women recognize their continuity with the Quakers, with Gandhi, with the entire pacifist tradition, and with the anarchist critique of the state. At the same time, women, the Greenham campers believe, may have a separate statement to make about violence because we have our own specific history in relation to it. . . .

A whole activist generation is being forged at Greenham, not of age but of shared experience. These women are disobedient, disloyal to civilization, experienced in taking direct action, advanced in their ability to make a wide range of political connections. The movable hearth is their schoolroom, where they piece together a stunning if raffish political patchwork.

Before visiting Greenham, I had feared that its politics would prove simpleminded, that those absolutes, life and death, would have cast more complex social questions in the shade. How, for instance, could the old question What do women want? survive when the subject is Mutual Assured Destruction (MAD, U.S. military slang for nuclear deterrence). . . .

I wonder if women are having to learn at Greenham—with a difference—what men learn too early and carry too far: the courage to dare, to test reaction, to define oneself *against* others. Nonviolent direct action takes great courage. The big men on their horses or machines are doing as ordered—which is comfortable for them. In contrast, it can be truly terrifying to refuse to do what an angry, pushing policeman tells you to do. For women particularly, such acts are fresh and new and this cutting across the grain of feminine socialization is a favorite, daring sport of the young at the fence. Such initiations give women a revolutionary taste of conflict, lived out fully, in our own persons, with gender no longer a reliable determinant of the rules

Certainly it is no use for women to turn self-righteous, as I had found myself doing—claiming a higher moral ground than men. On that ground we are admired but ignored. As Dorothy Dinnerstein has argued in *The Mermaid and the Minotaur*, emotional women have traditionally been treated like court jesters that the king keeps around to express his own anxieties—and thus vent them harmlessly. A woman's body lying down in a road in front of a missile launcher has a very different symbolic resonance for everyone from that of a male body in the same position. Greenham's radical feminist critics wonder just what kind of peace a female lying down can bring. Won't men simply allow women to lie in the mud forever because the demonstrators themselves only underline men's concept of what is female (passivity, protest, peace) and what is male (aggression, action, war)?

Before I came to Greenham, I shared these worries. But at Greenham at its best, women's nonviolent direct action becomes not another face of female passivity but a difficult political practice with its own unique discipline. The trick—a hard one—is to skew the dynamics of the old male-female relationships toward new meanings, to interrupt the old conversation between overconfident kings and hysterical, powerless jesters. This will surely include an acknowledgment of our past complicity with men and war making and a dramatization of our new refusal to aid and assist. (I think of a delicious young woman I heard singing out to a group of also very young soldiers: "We don't find you sexy anymore, you know, with your little musket, fife, and drum.")

Perhaps some of the new meanings we need will be found buried in the old ones. If women feel powerless, we can try to share this feeling, to make individual men see that they, too, are relatively powerless in the face of a wildly escalating arms race. Naturally, this is a message men resist, but the women at Greenham are endlessly clever at dramatizing how the army shares their impotence: The army cannot prevent them from getting inside the fence or shaking it down. It cannot prevent them from blockading the gates. It cannot prevent them from returning after each eviction.

Or, rather, it could prevent all this, but only by becoming a visibly brutal force, and this would be another kind of defeat, since the British armed services and police want to maintain their image of patriarchal protectors; they do not want to appear to be batterers of nonviolent women. Greenham women expose the contradictions of gender: by being women they dramatize powerlessness but they also disarm the powerful. . . .

QUESTIONS TO CONSIDER

As you read and look at the sources, you need to keep in mind the historical context in which the women were writing, and think how this influenced their ideas and plans for action. Source 1 was written in 1911, before women in most U.S. states or any European country (except Finland) had the vote and before the outbreak of World War I. How might these factors have affected Olive Schreiner's views of what would happen when women gained a political voice? To what does she attribute gender differences in attitudes toward war?

Sources 2 and 3 both date from 1915. The outbreak of World War I was accompanied by intense nationalistic and anti-German rhetoric and demonstrations, first in England and later in the United States. How might this have shaped Maude Royden's and Jane Addams's views about whether women were "naturally" more peaceful? Both Schreiner and Addams comment on a woman's role as a mother to explain the source of women's dislike of war; what differences do you see in the two authors on this point?

Source 4 dates from 1919, just after the end of World War I and as women in the United States and England were being given the right to vote. What does Crystal Eastman hope will be the focus of women's political activities? Why does she feel the Women's Peace conference at The Hague was important? What makes the women's peace movement distinctive in her opinion? How does this differ from the ideas of Schreiner and Addams about why women are particularly interested in peace?

Source 5 is the first visual source for this chapter, a woodcut created by the German artist Käthe Kollwitz shortly after World War I. Kollwitz lost her son in that war, and though she had been a supporter of German aims at the beginning of the war, by its end she was joining antiwar demonstrations and promoting pacifism. She produced numerous images in the 1920s and 1930s that were later used by various peace groups on posters and pamphlets, including this one, entitled *The Sacrifice*. How does this fit with the ideas expressed in the written sources about mothers' response to war?

With Sources 6 and 7, we jump ahead to the 1960s and the beginnings of the women's antinuclear movement. These sources come from oral interviews with two of the women who started Women Strike for Peace, Dagmar Wilson and Madeline Duckles. Unlike Sources 1 through 4, which are speeches and position papers, Sources 6 and 7 are oral histories produced long after the events they describe. What drew these women into working for peace? What do they see as distinctive about women's involvement in peace groups? These sources refer explicitly to the types of actions WSP was involved in; how were these shaped by the fact that this was a women's peace group? How was the response these actions generated on the part of political officials shaped by the gender of those who took part? By their status as middle-class women and mothers? How do the organizational structures and methods of making decisions in WSP make it different from other political groups? How is this—at least in Wilson's eyes—related to the fact that this is a women's group? What aspects of these interviews might have been shaped by the fact that they were recorded thirty years after WSP was founded?

Sources 8 through 11 are again statements of individuals or groups, written in the early 1980s to describe their motivations, aims, and methods of action. Source 8 is the "Unity Statement" for the Women's Pentagon Action, written in 1980 by Grace Paley in consultation with many others.

What does it say has motivated women to action? Though its views on the relationship between women and peace are not expressed as explicitly as they have been in some of the other sources you have read, what implicit connection does it make? What connection does it make between the arms race and other economic issues, and how does it connect these to women? How does this compare to the way in which this was done in the oral interview with Madeline Duckles (Source 7)? Source 9 is the official statement of Women Opposed to the Nuclear Threat in Nottingham, England. What does it view as the reason for women's special role in the peace movement? What other issues does it link with a control of the arms race? What actions does Nottingham WONT undertake, and how does it view these as shaped by the gender of its members? How does its organizational structure and decision-making process compare to that of WSP? To other organizations with which you are familiar?

Source 10 is a statement from Tamar Swade, the founder of Babies Against the Bomb. How would you compare her motivation and the way this group was founded with that of Dagmar Wilson and WSP? How would you compare her views about motherhood as a motivation for peace work with those of Olive Schreiner in Source 1? Why do you feel these views led to her being criticized, and what is her answer to this criticism? Source 11 comes from a speech given by Coretta Scott King at an International Women's Conference for Peace and Nuclear Disarmament. In this, as

in the Unity Statement in Source 8, King is implicit rather than explicit in her connection between the arms race and what have traditionally been considered "women's concerns." How does she link these? Her audience for this speech is predominantly women; how might her argument have been shaped by this?

Sources 12 and 13 are posters from two demonstrations organized by women's peace groups against the installation of the Cruise and Pershing II missiles in Europe, scheduled for 1983. How do the images in the posters differ in their depiction of women responding to the nuclear threat? How do they fit with the ideas you have read of the various individuals and groups?

Source 14 is in some ways oral history in the making; that is, it is a discussion by a woman interested in peace issues about her encounter with other women involved in actions protesting military buildups. It can thus be the raw material for an oral history of the *author's* development as a peace activist, or for a history of the women's encampments at Greenham Common in England based on oral interviews. Therefore, you will need to pay attention to a variety of things at once as you read this: the actions that the women activists undertake; the reasons they give for these actions; the way in which they see these actions as shaped by the fact that they are women; the way in which the author explains the women's motivations; the interplay between the author and the women she is speaking with. As you would when evaluating any oral history (or actually any history at all), you need to think about how the author's preconceptions might have shaped her analysis. In this selection, the author is fairly explicit about this, making this issue perhaps easier to address than it is in many studies where authors do not discuss their preconceptions and point of view.

You have now read and looked at a great many sources stretched out over seventy-five years, and can return to the central questions: How did twentieth-century women involved in women's peace groups view the relationship between their being women and their advocating peace? How did they translate their ideas into actions, and how did their ideas shape the types of actions they regarded as appropriate to achieving their aims?

EPILOGUE

The collapse of the Soviet Union and the end of the Cold War arms race marked another shift in focus for women's peace groups. Some of them ceased to be active, while others turned their attention to military spending worldwide and broader economic, social, and political concerns. WILPF, for example, at an international congress in 1986 adopted as its new program, "Toward a Nuclear-Weapon and Hunger-Free Twenty-first Century." This was not a completely new direction, of course, for we have seen the connection between military expenditures and economic hardship made in the writings of peace activists from earlier decades. Noting the continuing use of rape as a means of military coercion throughout the world, WILPF started an international campaign in 1990 to confront the issue of violence against women, not limiting this to rape but working against all forms of physical, economic, and political coercion. At the moment women's peace groups are not often the chief organizers of mass demonstrations or theatrical actions, but they are part of many such actions such as those that opposed the Persian Gulf War in 1991 and those for victims of AIDS.

Other women involved in peace work have turned their attention to education, for example developing programs for kindergartners about how to resolve conflicts nonviolently and establishing peace studies programs at colleges and universities. More than two hundred campuses across the United States now have peace studies programs of some sort, and Syracuse University offers a Ph.D. in peace studies. A long-time peace activist with many groups, Rose Marciano Lucey, was one of the key forces in a citizens' lobby to establish a U.S. Peace Academy, approved by Congress in 1986. Should you wish to use this chapter as a springboard for further investigation, perhaps doing some oral history yourself, the peace studies program at your own or a nearby college or university would be a good place to start.

Just as women's peace groups are changing but still thriving, exploring gender differences in terms of peace and war remains a thriving industry.

Public opinion polls have discovered what they have labeled the "gender gap" in terms of support for military involvement; with respect to every engagement or contemplated engagement, women are consistently more opposed to war than men. Particularly during national elections, this translates into votes for the candidate perceived to be less militarily aggressive, and, because more women vote than men do, the gap in votes may be even wider than the gap in public opinion. This gap has not been wide enough, as Olive Schreiner hoped, to "herald the death of war as a means of arranging human differences," but it is something contemporary women's peace activists note they will be looking to in the future. At the same time, some feminist groups and many individual women favor an increased role for women in combat, supporting Maude Royden's words that "the belief that women are innately more pacific than men has been severely shaken." The connection between feminism and pacifism continues to be a complex and debated issue.

CHAPTER THIRTEEN

SELLING A

TOTALITARIAN SYSTEM

Hitler's dictatorship differed in one fundamental point from all its predecessors in history. His was the first dictatorship in the present period of modern technical development, a dictatorship which made complete use of all technical means for the domination of its own country.

Through technical devices like the radio and the loud-speaker, eighty million people were deprived of independent thought. It was thereby possible to subject them to the will of one man. . . .

Earlier dictators needed highly qualified assistants, even at the lowest level, men who could think and act independently. The totalitarian system in the period of modern technical development can dispense with them; the means of communication alone make it possible to mechanize the lower leadership. As a result of this there arises the new type of the uncritical recipient of orders. . . . Another result was the far-reaching supervision of the citizens of the State and the maintenance of a high degree of secrecy for criminal acts.

The nightmare of many a man that one day nations could be dominated by technical means was all but realized in Hitler's totalitarian system.[1]

This was how Albert Speer, once one of Hitler's most trusted subordinates, sought to answer the question that every student of the Nazi phenomenon must ultimately ask: "How could it have happened?"[2] Because your textbook examines the roots and de-

1. Final statement by Albert Speer to the International Military Tribunal for major war criminals at Nuremberg, 1946. Quoted in Alan Bullock, *Hitler: A Study in Tyranny*, rev. ed. (New York: Harper & Row, 1964), p. 380. An architect by training, Speer (1905–1981) first attracted Hitler's attention because of his expertise in that field and talent for orchestrating party rallies. He testified at Nuremberg, "If Hitler had had any friends, I would certainly have been one of his close friends." (*Inside the Third Reich: Memoirs by Albert Speer*, translated by Richard and Clara Winston [New York: Macmillan, 1970], p. 609). Hitler promoted Speer to Minister of Armaments during World War II, and in that capacity, Speer's efforts maintained German war production despite Allied bombing. As it became clear, however, that the war was lost and that Hitler was determined to fight on regardless of the cost to Germany, Speer made an attempt to assassinate the dictator.

2. See, for example, Richard F. Hamilton, *Who Voted for Hitler?* (Princeton, N.J.: Princeton University Press, 1982), p. 3.

velopment of Hitler's doctrines, we will not focus in this chapter on the horrific ideology of the Nazi movement. Rather, we will examine the question that Speer addressed, for in the political history of the West, the Nazi party was the first totalitarian movement to make full use of modern media to gain and maintain power.

In their use of modern media and campaign techniques to achieve power, Hitler and his followers built on a number of developments in Western politics, technology, and intellectual life. As we observed in Chapter 7, the nature of politics in the West had begun to change in the late nineteenth century. The right to vote in the more advanced European countries expanded to include all men and, after World War I, women as well. The increased electorate demanded new political techniques. No longer could gentlemen politicians gain power by winning the support of a small, male, socially privileged electorate. A mass audience had to be addressed. Although many politicians at first refused to degrade themselves by appealing for support to such an audience, we can see emerging in late-nineteenth-century campaigns the modern political objective—and the requirement—of swaying large numbers of voters.

In 1879 and 1880, the British statesman William E. Gladstone (1809–1898) won election to Parliament from Midlothian County, Scotland, following a campaign that became the model for modern ones, especially after Gladstone built his victory into his second term as prime minister. In Midlothian Gladstone delivered numerous public speeches. He presented many of these from the platform of his campaign train at a variety of locations, the first "whistle-stop campaign." Gladstone's campaign style found imitators in other democracies, although they did not always achieve his success. In the U.S. presidential campaign of 1896, the Democratic candidate, William Jennings Bryan (1860–1925), traveled about 18,000 miles and gave more than 600 speeches in an unsuccessful campaign against the Republic candidate, William McKinley (1843–1901). McKinley, who epitomized the old-style campaigner, simply received visitors from the press and public at the front porch of his Ohio home. Other candidates in many democracies would follow the example of Gladstone and Bryan.

Technological advances aided political leaders in their appeals for mass support. By the 1890s, developments like the Linotype machine, which mechanized typesetting, greatly reduced the price of newspapers and other printed materials for an increasingly literate public. Mass-circulation daily newspapers had tremendous potential for shaping public opinion. Political leaders also used other technological developments in delivering their messages. By 1920 the motion picture, photograph, radio, and microphone and public-address system all represented new media through which to influence the public.

At the same time that new media became available to political leaders, a greater understanding of how to influence public opinion was emerging in the early-twentieth-century West. During World War I, many belligerent countries employed increasingly sophisticated propaganda techniques to sustain the morale of their own citizens or to erode the will to fight among enemy populations. The lessons learned on influencing public opinion were not forgotten, as we will see.[3]

Industrial mass production required mass markets, and in the United States modern advertising techniques developed to stimulate the consumption necessary to sustain production. Advertising had political applications as well. One advertising strategy is to generate interest in a new product by creating suspense about it. When the Nazis launched a new Berlin newspaper, *Der Angriff* (*The Attack*) in 1927, a poster campaign was launched to heighten interest in it. The first posters issued simply stated, "The Attack?" The next group of posters proclaimed, "The Attack takes place on July 4!" The last set of posters was informational, alerting readers that the paper would appear on Mondays, that its motto was "For the Suppressed against the Exploiters," and that "Every German man and every German woman will read 'The Attack' and subscribe to it!"[4]

Even science, particularly psychology, contributed to the understanding of human thought essential to those who sought to shape opinion. The French social psychologist Gustave Le Bon (1841–1931), for example, affected Hitler's political technique. Le Bon's ideas, although doubted today, were highly influential in the early twentieth century. A student of mass psychology, Le Bon claimed that the mind of the crowd was most susceptible to sentiment and emotion, not reason.[5]

The rapid pace of technological development and the equally swift emergence of techniques for molding public opinion meant that, by the 1920s, there existed an incompletely understood, underused, but nonetheless formidable arsenal for the politically ambitious to employ in attaining power. Forces prepared to exploit these technological and methodological developments emerged in the politically unstable environment of much of the post–World War II West.

Rooted in defeat, frustration in World War I, or the economic debacle of the Great Depression beginning in 1929, totalitarian movements emerged in many European countries. None of these movements proved more dangerous to traditional Western values than a German party that began insignificantly in 1919 as one of a multitude of right-wing, nationalist parties founded in response to the German defeat in the Great War. The party came to be known as the National Socialist German Workers' Party (Nazi), and Adolf Hitler quickly emerged not only as its leader but as a master

3. Hitler in *Mein Kampf* (translated by Ralph Manheim [Boston: Houghton Mifflin, 1943], pp. 176–186) wrote of the lessons he had drawn from Allied porpaganda during World War I.

4. Described in Ernest K. Bramsted, *Goebbels and National Socialist Propaganda, 1925–1945* (East Lansing, Mich.: Michigan State University Press, 1965), p. 30.

5. Le Bon's great work was *The Crowd: A Study of the Popular Mind*, originally published in 1897 and available in German.

of the new style of politics, including political propaganda.

The successful propagandist must correctly identify the fears and hopes of the people he or she wishes to influence. In Germany after World War I, Nazi propaganda had a great number of fears and hopes to exploit. Most Germans rejected the Treaty of Versailles that ended the war. Humiliated by the treaty's assignment of war guilt to Germany, they were angered in turn by the huge reparations their country was forced to pay the victorious allies. German nationalists especially rejected the unilateral disarmament the treaty sought to impose on Germany. All Germans hoped for some revision of the Treaty of Versailles.

Some Germans blamed the nation's defeat on internal enemies, not on battlefield disasters. These persons, mostly conservative, identified two chief groups on which to place responsibility for the internal dissent at the war's end that had brought the overthrow of Emperor William II (Kaiser Wilhelm II) and armistice. The first groups condemned for the defeat were the parties of the left, the socialists and communists, who had participated in the Revolution of 1918 that created the Weimar Republic. To many, the communists seemed the greatest threat because that party had attempted to seize power for a Marxist state by force in the Spartacist Revolt of 1919. The communist threat, moreover, persisted after 1919. The party's voting bloc grew as the economic problems of the Great Depression intensified, and many feared that the communists might gain power through election.

The other group on whom some Germans sought to fix the blame of their defeat was the country's small Jewish minority. Such Germans drew on nineteenth-century nationalist prejudices to allege some Jewish involvement in Germany's defeat. Certain political leaders of the early German republic, the men whose government signed the Versailles Treaty, were Jews. One prominent Jewish official, Walter Rathenau (1867–1922), died at the hands of a nationalist fanatic.

The Great Depression also increased Germans' fears after 1929. The depression hit Germany particularly hard, threatening economic ruin to many. Many parties and movements identified those fears and hopes of postwar Germans and sought to address them by rejecting the Treaty of Versailles, by portraying themselves as anticommunist or anti-Semitic, and by proposing solutions to the depression. But, as we will see, it was the skill of Hitler and the Nazis in the new politics and propaganda that allowed them to exploit most effectively Germans' fears and hopes to gain power.

It was Hitler who transformed a party that essentially had been little more than a collection of malcontents in the back room of a Munich beer hall into a movement with a considerable following in the 1920s. It was Hitler who gave the party a visual identity by adopting its symbol, the swastika, and by creating its banners. It was also Hitler who exploited the alienation of many war veterans by drawing them into the S.A. (*Sturm Abteilung*), the Storm Troopers or uniformed, paramilitary branch of the party, which was prepared to use violence and intimidation against communists and socialists. And it was Hitler who launched an abortive attempt in 1923 to seize power forcibly for his party.

Hitler's failed revolution resulted in his brief imprisonment, during which he wrote *Mein Kampf* (*My Struggle*), the political statement of his movement. On his release Hitler resolved to seek power within the political system—that is, to win power through the electoral system of the German republic. To his quest for power Hitler brought the Nazi party apparatus and symbols, his excellent oratorical ability, and, most dangerously, a keen understanding of the uses of political propaganda and modern media to mold public opinion. Aiding him in presenting his party to German voters was Joseph Goebbels (1897–1945), a man whose speaking abilities, understanding of propaganda and modern media, and political unscrupulousness rivaled Hitler's own.

In his quest for power after 1923, Hitler led the Nazis through a number of electoral campaigns. The first results of Nazi appeals to German voters disappointed many of Hitler's followers. Indeed, in elections to the Reichstag, Germany's parliament, the party's vote actually declined during the 1920s. In the elections of May 1924, it captured 6.5 percent of the vote; that total declined to 3.0 percent in December 1924 and 2.6 percent in May 1928. The party's elec-

toral breakthrough of 1930, however, reversed this trend as the Nazis increased their share of the Reichstag vote to 18.3 percent. Certainly, in achieving their victory, the Nazis' extreme nationalist message capitalized on the Young Plan of 1929, which had failed to reduce the war reparation payments to the Allies so deeply resented by many Germans. The growing severity of the Great Depression after 1929 also encouraged many Germans to look to the strong leadership Hitler claimed to offer. As party membership and dues grew, and as Hitler secured some limited financial aid from a few wealthy opponents of the Young Plan such as Alfred Hugenberg,[6] for the first time the Nazis had sufficient funds to exploit the modern media thoroughly.

The Nazi share of the vote increased rapidly after 1930. The party especially demonstrated its media skills in 1932, when Hitler ran for president of Germany against the incumbent, the octogenarian war hero Field Marshal Paul von Hindenburg. Although Hindenburg won the election with 53 percent of the vote to Hitler's 36.8 percent, the campaign built momentum for the Nazis and

6. **Alfred Hugenberg** (1865–1951): leader of the Nationalist Party and a bigoted conservative ultranationalist with tremendous wealth based in industry and great influence founded on his control of a number of newspapers and Germany's largest film and newsreel firm. His newsreels, shown regularly in German theaters, and his newspapers gave the Nazis considerable coverage. Like other conservatives, Hugenberg made the mistake of classifying Hitler with other politicians. Hitler quickly excluded Hugenberg from the government once the Nazis had gained power

helped them to perfect their campaign style. In the Reichstag elections held in July 1932, the Nazis won 37.4 percent of the vote to become the largest single party in parliament, a distinction they retained despite a diminished Nazi 33.1 percent of the vote in Reichstag elections in November 1932. On the basis of these victories, which gave the Nazis control of the largest single bloc of seats in the Reichstag, conservative associates of President von Hindenburg finally convinced him to name Hitler chancellor or prime minister on January 30, 1933. The Nazis had gained control of the government, and German democracy was their first victim: by the end of the year the country was a one-party, totalitarian state.

To achieve power, the Nazis had persuaded substantial numbers of German voters to support their candidates. Certainly in the aftermath of Germany's defeat in 1918, the party's extreme nationalism attracted support, as did its anti-Semitism, which blamed the country's economic and political woes on its tiny Jewish minority. This Nazi political rhetoric of hatred ultimately became government policy when Hitler gained power. Anti-Semitism took on brutal form in the Holocaust. Extreme nationalism manifested itself in the Nazi goal of settling Germans in eastern Europe by pushing out the area's Slavic natives. But other German parties in the 1920s and early 1930s also expressed anti-Semitic and nationalistic ideas. Your objective in this chapter is to determine how Nazi use of modern media and techniques, such as propaganda for molding public opinion, allowed Hitler's party to draw the German voter's attention. As you assess the evidence that follows, you should ask yourself what kind of image the Nazis projected. Why did it appeal to German voters? How did the Nazis use media to aid their rise to power? As a result of your analysis, you should be able to answer in some form that most disturbing question, "How could it have happened?"

SOURCES AND METHOD

This chapter presents a variety of evidence: theoretical writings on Nazi political strategy, visual propaganda used by Nazis to publicize their cause, and observations on the public reception of Hitler's media campaign. Through individual and comparative study of these sources, you should be able to determine the nature of the attraction of the Nazis for German voters.

The evidence opens with two selections by Hitler on the means for gaining power. Sources 1 and 2 are taken from Hitler's *Mein Kampf,* which he wrote during his imprisonment in 1923–1924. In this work, often ignored in his early days, Hitler stated much of his future program, including his rabidly anti-Jewish and anti-Marxist policies and his plans to expand Germany eastward. In the evidence presented in this chapter, you will read Hitler's ideas on the use of propaganda and other tactics for coming to power. How were the ideas for seizing power that he expressed in 1924 to be realized within a decade? How would you assess his understanding of human psychology?

When you finish the Hitler materials, you will find an assortment of evidence selected to further your analysis of how the Nazis sought to win support for their party. You will be examining, in effect, a thoroughly modern public relations effort, complete with slogans. In Source 3, assess the nature of the Nazi propaganda effort as defined by its director, Joseph Goebbels. Why do you think Goebbels so closely controlled the party's propaganda?

Consider next the S.A., remembering, of course, that orders like that in Source 4 are not always rigidly obeyed by subordinates in any organization. Examine the pictorial evidence on the S.A. in Sources 5 and 6. The banners express Nazi slogans; the Regensburg S.A. banner proclaims, "Everything for the Fatherland." Nazi meetings always opened with solemn processions of such banners. What impression did the marching men seek to convey to their audience on the streets of Spandau?

Next read Source 7, the report of the brawl in the Pharus Hall in 1927. You should understand that this brawl was no accident; Goebbels deliberately scheduled the meeting to take place in a hall used by the Nazis' enemies, the communist and socialist political and labor groups. The hall, moreover, was in the heart of a left-wing, working-class district of Berlin. What could Goebbels have hoped to

gain from the fight that was bound to ensue from his provocative action in selecting such a meeting site?

The next evidence consists of posters produced by the Nazis. The poster, a traditional political medium, was used extensively by the Nazis. They relied especially on posters in their early days, before they secured the funds necessary to exploit more novel media. The poster in Source 8 was part of the propaganda campaign Nazi leaders organized for the spring 1924 German legislative elections. At the time of the elections, Hitler remained in prison as a result of his failed attempt to seize power in 1923, and his party nominally was outlawed. Thus party leaders entered the campaign as part of a right-wing, nationalist coalition, the "Völkischen Block" identified on the poster. The German word *Volk* is difficult to translate. Superficially, it may be translated as "people" or "nation," but for early-twentieth-century Germans the word had a much more complex meaning conveying the innate superiority of German culture, language, and people over non-German cultures and peoples. Thus its use to identify a right-wing, nationalistic political alliance was not accidental, and entirely consistent with Nazi ideology. Indeed, the Nazi origins of this poster are evident in the party's insignia, the swastika, in the lower corners of the poster. Analyze the poster to ascertain what sentiments the Nazis appealed to in post–World War I Germany and to which classes they looked for support. What group did the "String-puller" represent (notice his watch chain)? What message did his identity convey to Germans?

The second poster, Source 9, conveys much about Germany in the 1920s. Why might the Nazis address females? Of what problems did this poster, issued in the midst of the depression, remind Germans? What did it promise them? The third poster, Source 10, was the work of a skilled propaganda artist, "Mjolnir" ("Hammer"), who drew cartoons extensively for the Berlin newspaper *Der Angriff*, edited by Goebbels. Analyze the artist's message by examining the faces of the Storm Troopers. What sentiment do you find there? What sort of message does this poster convey about the party and its solutions for Germany?

Another Nazi political device was the public mass meeting designed to convey the impression of vast support for the party. It was a technique Hitler learned early while observing Social Democratic demonstrations as a youth in Vienna. He wrote in *Mein Kampf*:

> With what changed feeling I now gazed at the endless columns of a mass demonstration of Viennese workers that took place one day as they marched past four abreast! For nearly two hours I stood there watching with bated breath the gigantic human dragon slowly winding by.

As their resources increased, the Nazis perfected the mass meeting. Source 11 shows one such rally in Berlin's Sports Palace, a favored site because it seated a large audience of 12,000 persons. Events like this were always carefully staged: the aisles are lined with the party faithful, ready for the entry of the speakers, accompanied by a uniformed S.A. guard unit and party banners. Why would such an elaborate spectacle have been important to the party cause?

The Nazis also employed music as propaganda to win support. The person whose name the song bears in Source 12, Horst Wessel, was a young Nazi who wrote the words to the song as a poem. The words eventually were set to a traditional stirring tune, but Horst Wessel himself drifted away from the party in pursuit of a female prostitute. He took up residence with her and was fatally shot by her procurer, who coincidentally was a communist, in February 1930. In Goebbels's hands, Horst Wessel's misspent life was transformed into that of a hero martyred in the Nazis' cause by their communist enemies. His song became Germany's second national anthem after *Deutschland über Alles* (*Germany Above All*) in the Nazi era. In reading the song's words, identify the problems it identifies. What benefits does the song claim the party offered Germans?

Also part of Nazi political propaganda was the creation of what Goebbels himself called the "Führer (Leader) Myth." This myth, which Goebbels regarded as one of his great propaganda accomplishments, attempted to convince Germans that a strong, courageous, and brilliant Hitler personified a Germany restored from its defeat. In its more extreme manifestations, the myth almost deified Hitler, appealing to many Germans accustomed to strong rulers during the monarchy and therefore unhappy with what they believed to be the weak government of the republic. Source 13 is drawn from an elementary school textbook published shortly after the Nazis gained power, but it describes Hitler's campaign for power. What qualities did the party's propaganda apparatus wish the young to believe Hitler possessed?

The Nazis did not come to power solely through conveying a positive image for their party and leader, however. They also used propaganda to exploit fears, employed violence to intimidate voters, and used new technologies to sway the thinking of their fellow Germans. Source 14 is a pamphlet, issued, you must remember, in the midst of the economic collapse of the early 1930s. Recall the events of Germany's past as you read it, and analyze its appeal.

The violence of the Hitler movement can best be viewed on the local level. The graph in Source 15 presents the rhythm of political life in the German town of Northeim. The number of political meetings, to which the Nazis contributed more than their share, increased sharply at election times. What else increased?

Source 16 presents the political beliefs of Dr. Joseph Goebbels, a fervent Nazi and a master of political propaganda. Convinced of his own historical importance, Goebbels kept a diary from his earliest days in politics to give future generations a record of his thought and activities. He was still making entries in 1945 as the war ended. When Russian armies closed in on Berlin, Goebbels committed suicide. His diary, like any diary, must be used with caution, because most writers tend to put their own behavior and motivations in the best light. Nonetheless, it does offer an important perspective on Goebbels's propaganda work. Assess his command of his job as you read the selection. What new technologies did he employ in winning popular support for the Nazis?

The evidence in this chapter concludes with two observations on the impact of Nazi efforts to win support among Germans. The first is a report by a German Protestant leader noting membership losses from the Protestant youth movement to the Nazis. The second is by the American correspondent, William L. Shirer (1904–1993), who covered events in Germany from 1934 to 1941. A perceptive observer of the Hitler movement, Shirer was able to assess the kind of appeal it had been building in Germany during the years before he arrived. What appeal to Germans do these two very different persons note in the Nazi movement?

Now turn to the evidence. You should read it with the foregoing considerations in mind, seeking to answer the central questions of this chapter: What image did the Nazis convey to German voters? Why did they appeal to German voters? How did the Nazis use media to aid their rise to power?

FUNDAMENTAL POLITICAL STRATEGIES OF THE NAZI PARTY

Sources 1 and 2 from Adolf Hitler, Mein Kampf, *translated by Ralph Mannheim (Boston: Houghton Mifflin, 1943), pp. 178–184, 343, 582; pp. 42–44.*

1. Hitler on the Nature and Purpose of Propaganda

The goal of a political reform movement will never be reached by enlightenment work or by influencing ruling circles, but only by the achievement of political power. Every world-moving idea has not only the right, but also the duty, of securing, those means which make possible the execution of its ideas. Success is the one earthly judge concerning the right or wrong of such an effort, and under success we must not understand, as in the year 1918, the achievement of power in itself, but an exercise of that power that will benefit the nation. Thus, a coup d'état must not be regarded as successful if, as senseless state's attorneys in Germany think today, the revolutionaries have succeeded in possessing themselves of the state power, but only if, by the realization of the purposes and aims underlying such a revolutionary action, more benefit accrues to the nation than under the past régime. Something which cannot very well be claimed for the German revolution, as the gangster job of autumn, 1918, calls itself.[7] . . .

The victory of an idea will be possible the sooner, the more comprehensively propaganda has prepared people as a whole and the more exclusive, rigid, and firm the organization which carries out the fight in practice. . . .

To whom should propaganda be addressed? To the scientifically trained intelligentsia or to the less educated masses?

It must be addressed always and exclusively to the masses.

What the intelligentsia—or those who today unfortunately often go by that name—what they need is not propaganda but scientific instruction. The content of propaganda is not science any more than the object represented in a poster is art. The art of the poster lies in the designer's ability to attract the

---

7. **the gangster job of autumn 1918:** the revolution of October and November 1918 that overthrew Emperor William II and established the Weimar Republic. Hitler, like many of the German right, believed that revolution to have been the work of socialists, communists, and Jews who, by toppling the old government, had "stabbed in the back" the German army at the front in World War I and made defeat in that conflict inevitable.

attention of the crowd by form and color. A poster advertising an art exhibit must direct the attention of the public to the art being exhibited; the better it succeeds in this, the greater is the art of the poster itself. The poster should give the masses an idea of the significance of the exhibition, it should not be a substitute for the art on display. Anyone who wants to concern himself with the art itself must do more than study the poster; and it will not be enough for him just to saunter through the exhibition. We may expect him to examine and immerse himself in the individual works, and thus little by little form a fair opinion.

A similar situation prevails with what we today call propaganda.

The function of propaganda does not lie in the scientific training of the individual, but in calling the masses' attention to certain facts, processes, necessities, etc., whose significance is thus for the first time placed within their field of vision.

The whole art consists in doing this so skillfully that everyone will be convinced that the fact is real, the process necessary, the necessity correct, etc. But since propaganda is not and cannot be the necessity in itself, since its function, like the poster, consists in attracting the attention of the crowd, and not in educating those who are already educated or who are striving after education and knowledge, its effect for the most part must be aimed at the emotions and only to a very limited degree at the so-called intellect.

All propaganda must be popular and its intellectual level must be adjusted to the most limited intelligence among those it is addressed to. Consequently, the greater the mass it is intended to reach, the lower its purely intellectual level will have to be. But if, as in propaganda for sticking out a war, the aim is to influence a whole people, we must avoid excessive intellectual demands on our public, and too much caution cannot be exerted in this direction.

The more modest its intellectual ballast, the more exclusively it takes into consideration the emotions of the masses, the more effective it will be. And this is the best proof of the soundness or unsoundness of a propaganda campaign, and not success in pleasing a few scholars or young aesthetes.

The art of propaganda lies in understanding the emotional ideas of the great masses and finding, through a psychologically correct form, the way to the attention and thence to the heart of the broad masses. The fact that our bright boys do not understand this merely shows how mentally lazy and conceited they are.

Once we understand how necessary it is for propaganda to be adjusted to the broad mass, the following rule results:

It is a mistake to make propaganda many-sided, like scientific instruction, for instance.

The receptivity of the great masses is very limited, their intelligence is small, but their power of forgetting is enormous. In consequence of these facts, all effective propaganda must be limited to a very few points and must harp on these in slogans until the last member of the public understands what you want him to understand by your slogan. As soon as you sacrifice this slogan and try to be many-sided, the effect will piddle away, for the crowd can neither digest nor retain the material offered. In this way the result is weakened and in the end entirely cancelled out.

Thus we see that propaganda must follow a simple line and correspondingly the basic tactics must be psychologically sound. . . .

But the most brilliant propagandist techniques will yield no success unless one fundamental principle is borne in mind constantly and with unflagging attention. It must confine itself to a few points and repeat them over and over. Here, as so often in this world, persistence is the first and most important requirement for success.

2. Hitler on Terror in Politics

Like the woman, whose psychic state is determined less by grounds of abstract reason than by an indefinable emotional longing for a force which will complement her nature, and who, consequently, would rather bow to a strong man than dominate a weakling, likewise the masses love a commander more than a petitioner and feel inwardly more satisfied by a doctrine, tolerating no other beside itself, than by the granting of liberalistic freedom with which, as a rule, they can do little, and are prone to feel that they have been abandoned. They are equally unaware of their shameless spiritual terrorization and the hideous abuse of their human freedom, for they absolutely fail to suspect the inner insanity of the whole doctrine. All they see is the ruthless force and brutality of its calculated manifestations, to which they always submit in the end. . . .

I achieved an equal understanding of the importance of physical terror toward the individual and the masses.

Here, too, the psychological effect can be calculated with precision.

Terror at the place of employment, in the factory, in the meeting hall, and on the occasion of mass demonstrations will always be successful unless opposed by equal terror.

NAZI TECHNIQUES FOR PUBLICIZING THEIR CAUSE

Sources 3 and 4 from Jeremy Noakes and Geoffrey Pridham, editors, Documents on Nazism, 1919–1945 *(New York: Viking, 1975), pp. 103–104; pp. 163–164.*

3. Joseph Goebbels, Directives for the Presidential Campaign of 1932

(1) Reich Propaganda Department to all *Gaue*[8] and all *Gau* Propaganda Departments.

8. **Gaue:** the administrative divisions of Germany set up by the Nazi party.

. . . A striking slogan:

> Those who want everything to stay as it is vote for Hindenburg. Those who want everything changed vote for Hitler. . . .

(2) Reich Propaganda Department to all *Gaue* and all *Gau* Propaganda Departments.

. . . Hitler Poster. The Hitler poster depicts a fascinating Hitler head on a completely black background. Subtitle: white on black—"Hitler." In accordance with the Führer's wish this poster is to be put up only during the final days [of the campaign]. Since experience shows that during the final days there is a variety of coloured posters, this poster with its completely black background will contrast with all the others and will produce a tremendous effect on the masses. . . .

(3) Reich Propaganda Department
Instructions for the National Socialist Press for the election of the Reich President

1. From Easter Tuesday 29 March until Sunday 10 April inclusive, all National Socialist papers, both daily and weekly, must appear in an enlarged edition with a tripled circulation. Two-thirds of this tripled circulation must be made available, without charge, to the *Gau* leadership responsible for its area of distribution for propaganda purposes. . . .

2. From Easter Tuesday 29 March until Sunday 3 April inclusive, a special topic must be dealt with every day on the first page of all our papers in a big spread. Tuesday 29 March: Hitler as a man. Wednesday 30 March: Hitler as a fighter (gigantic achievement through his willpower, etc.). Friday 1 April: Hitler as a statesman—plenty of photos. . . .

3. On Sunday 3 April, at noon (end of an Easter truce), the great propaganda journey of the Führer through Germany will start, through which about a million people are to be reached directly through our Führer's speeches. . . . The press organization is planned so that four press centres will be set up in Germany, which in turn will pass on immediately any telephone calls to the other papers of their area, whose names have been given them.

4. S.A. Order 111 of Adolf Hitler, 1926

1. The SA will appear in public only in closed formation. This is at the same time one of the most powerful forms of propaganda. The sight of a large number of men inwardly and outwardly uniform and disciplined, whose total

commitment to fighting is clearly visible or can be sensed, makes the deepest impression on every German and speaks a more convincing and inspiring language to his heart than speech, logic, or the written word is ever capable of doing.

Calm composure and natural behaviour underline the impression of strength—the strength of marching columns and the strength of the cause for which they are marching.

The inner strength of the cause makes the German conclude instinctively that it is right: "for only what is right, honest and good can release real strength." Where whole crowds purposefully risk life and limb and their livelihood for a cause (not in the upsurge of sudden mass suggestion), the cause must be great and true!

Here lies the task of the SA from the point of view of propaganda and recruiting. The SA leaders must gear the details and forms of their appearances to a common line.

2. This instinctive "proof of truth" is not underlined but disturbed and dissipated by the addition of logical arguments and propaganda. The following should be avoided: cheers and heckling, posters about day-to-day controversies, abuse, accompanying speeches, leaflets, festivals, public amusements.

3. It is inappropriate for the SA to work in one way one day and differently the next, according to circumstances. The SA must always and on principle refrain from all actual political propaganda and agitation. This should remain the task of the political leadership alone. However, each SA man is also a member of the Party and as such of course must cooperate as much as he can in the propaganda of the political leadership. But not the SA as such. Not the SA men on duty and in uniform.

The SA man is the holy freedom fighter. The member of the Party is the clever propagandist and skilled agitator. Political propaganda tries to enlighten the opponent, to argue with him, to understand his point of view, to enter into his thoughts, to agree with him to a certain extent. But when the SA arrives on the scene, this stops. It makes no concessions. It goes all out. It only recognizes the motto (metaphorically): Kill or be killed!

4. It is forbidden for an SA to appeal to the public (or its opponents) orally or in writing, either through proclamations, announcements, leaflets, press "corrections," letters, advertisements, invitations to festivals or meetings, or in any other way.

Public consecrations of the colours and sports competitions must take place within the framework of an event organized by a local branch, which alone issues the invitations or announcements for it.

Sources 5 and 6 from Bundesarchiv, Koblenz.

5. **Banners of the Regensburg S.A.: "Everything for the Fatherland, 1923"**

6. **S.A. Propaganda Rally in Spandau, 1932**

Source 7 from Jeremy Noakes and Geoffrey Pridham, editors, Documents on Nazism, 1919–1945 *(New York: Viking, 1975), pp. 83–84.*

7. Report of a Nazi Meeting Held in a Heavily Communist Quarter of Berlin, February 1927

On the 11th of this month the Party held a public mass meeting in the "Pharus [Beer] Halls" in Wedding, the real working-class quarter, with the subject: "The Collapse of the Bourgeois Class State." Comrade Dr Goebbels was the speaker. It was quite clear to us what that meant. It had to be visibly shown that National Socialism is determined to reach the workers. We succeeded once before in getting a foothold in Wedding. There were huge crowds at the meeting. More than 1,000 people filled the hall whose political composition was four-fifths SA to one-fifth KPD.[9] But the latter had gathered their main forces in the street. When the meeting was opened by Comrade Daluege, the SA leader, there were, as was expected, provocative shouts of "On a point of order!" After the KPD members had been told that *we,* not they, decided points of order, and that they would have the right to ask questions after the talk by Comrade Dr Goebbels, the first scuffling broke out. Peace seemed to be restored until there was renewed heckling. When the chairman announced that the hecklers would be sent out if the interruptions continued, the KPD worked themselves into a frenzy. Meanwhile, the SA had gradually surrounded the centre of the disturbance, and the Communists, sensing the danger, suddenly became aggressive. What followed all happened within three or four minutes. Within seconds both sides had picked up chairs, beer mugs, even tables, and a savage fight began. The Communists were gradually pushed under the gallery which we had taken care to occupy and soon chairs and glasses came hurtling down from there also. The fight was quickly decided: the KPD left with 85 wounded, more or less: that is to say, they could not get down the stairs as fast as they had calmly and "innocently" climbed them. On our side we counted 3 badly wounded and about 10–12 slightly. When the police appeared the fight was already over. Marxist terrorism had been bloodily suppressed.

9. **Kommunistische Partei Deutschlands:** the German Communist Party.

Source 8 from Anshcläge: Ebenhausen: Langewiesche/Bradt Verlag.

8. Poster: "The String-Puller. White Collar and Manual Laborers: Vote for the Völkischen Block," 1924

9. Poster: "Women! Millions of Men Are Without Work. Millions of Children Are Without a Future. Save the German Family! Vote for Adolf Hitler!," 1932

10. Poster: "National Socialism: The Organized Will of the People," 1932

Source 11 from Bundesarchiv, Koblenz.

11. A National Socialist Rally in the Berlin Sports Palace, September 1930

Source 12 from Liederbuch der Nationalsozialistischen Deutschen Arbeiterpartei *(Munich: Zentralverlag der NSDAP, 1938). Selection translated by Julius R. Ruff.*

12. "The Horst Wessel Song,"
ca 1930

Raise high the banner! Close the serried ranks!
S.A. marches on with calm, firm stride.
Comrades killed by the Red Front and the Reaction[10]
March in spirit in our ranks.

Clear the streets for the brown battalions![11]
Clear the streets for the Storm Troopers!
The swastika gives hope to millions.
The day of freedom and bread is breaking.

10. **Red Front:** the *Rot Frontkämpfer Bund* or Red Fighters League, the communist opposition to the Storm Troopers. The more traditional right, the Nationalist Party that sought a restoration of a monarchy and is here called the **Reaction,** had an armed force, too, uniformed in green.

11. The S.A. uniform was brown.

The roll call is heard for the last time!
We all stand ready for the struggle!
Soon Hitler's banner will fly over every street
And Germany's bondage will soon end.

Source 13 from George L. Mosse, editor, Nazi Culture: Intellectual, Cultural, and Social Life in the Third Reich *(New York: Grosset and Dunlap, 1966), pp. 291–293. Selection translated by the editor.*

13. Otto Dietrich, Description of Hitler's Campaign by Airplane, 1932

On April 8, 1932, a severe storm, beyond all imagining, raged over Germany. Hail rattled down from dark clouds. Flash floods devastated fields and gardens. Muddy foam washed over streets and railroad tracks, and the hurricane uprooted even the oldest and biggest trees.

We are driving to the Mannheim Airport. Today no one would dare expose an airplane to the fury of the elements. The German Lufthansa has suspended all air traffic.

In the teeming rain stands the solid mass of the most undaunted of our followers. They want to be present, they want to see for themselves when the Führer entrusts himself to an airplane in this raging storm.

Without a moment's hesitation the Führer orders that we take off at once. We have an itinerary to keep, for in western Germany hundreds of thousands are waiting.

It is only with the greatest difficulty that the ground crew and the SA troopers, with long poles in their strong fists, manage to hold on to the wings of the plane, so that the gale does not hurl it into the air and wreck it. The giant motors begin to turn over. Impatient with its fetters, the plane begins to buck and shake, eager for the takeoff on the open runway.

One more short rearing up and our wild steed sweeps across the greensward. A few perilous jumps, one last short touch with earth, and presto we are riding through the air straight into the witches' broth.

This is no longer flying, this is a whirling dance which today we remember only as a faraway dream. Now we jump across the aerial downdrafts, now we whip our way through tattered clouds, again a whirlpool threatens to drag us down, and then it seems that a giant catapult hurls us into steep heights.

And yet, what a feeling of security is in us in the face of this fury of the elements! The Führer's absolute serenity transmits itself to all of us. In every hour of danger he is ruled by his granite-like faith in his world-historical mission, the unshakable certainty that Providence will keep him from danger for the accomplishment of his great task.

Even here he remained the pre-eminent man, who masters danger because in his innermost being he has risen far above it. In this ruthless contest between man and machine the Führer attentively follows the heroic battle of our Master Pilot Bauer as he steers straight through the gale, or quickly jumps across a whole storm field, and then again narrowly avoids a threatening cloud wall, while the radio operator on board zealously catches the signals sent by the airfields.

Source 14 from Jeremy Noakes and Geoffrey Pridham, editors, Documents on Nazism, 1919–1945 *(New York: Viking, 1975), p. 106.*

14. Nazi Pamphlet, ca 1932

Attention! Gravediggers at work!

Middle-class citizens![12] Retailers! Craftsmen! Tradesmen!

A new blow aimed at your ruin is being prepared and carried out in Hanover!

The present system enables the gigantic concern

WOOLWORTH (America)

supported by finance capital, to build a new vampire business in the centre of the city in the Georgstrasse to expose you to complete ruin. This is the wish and aim of the black-red[13] system as expressed in the following remarks of Marxist leaders.

The Marxist Engels declared in May 1890: "If capital destroys the small artisans and retailers it does a good thing. . . ."

That is the black-red system of today!

Put an end to this system and its abettors! Defend yourself, middle-class citizen! Join the mighty organization that alone is in a position to conquer your arch-enemies. Fight with us in the Section for Craftsmen and Retail Traders within the great freedom movement of Adolf Hitler!

Put an end to the system!

Mittelstand, vote for List 8![14]

12. **Middle-class citizens:** this is a rather imprecise translation of the original German *Mittelstand.* That word, difficult to translate, here describes a very specific segment of society to whom the Nazis made special appeal: small shopkeepers and craftsmen whose livelihoods increasingly were threatened by competition from large department stores and big industrial concerns.

13. Prussia was governed by a coalition of the Catholic Center Party and the Social Democrats. Because of its association with the church, the Center was labeled "Black"; the leftist Socialists were labeled "Red."

14. **Mittelstand:** middle-class shopkeepers and craftsmen.

Source 15 adapted from William Sheridan Allen, The Nazi Seizure of Power: The Experience of a Single German Town, 1922–1945, *revised ed. (New York: Franklin Watts, 1984), p. 321.*

15. Political Violence in Northeim, Germany, 1930–1932

15. Political Violence in Northeim, Germany, 1930–1932

—— Political meetings
‒‒‒ Fights (less than 20 participants)
● Major battles (more than 20 participants)

Source 16 from Joseph Goebbels, My Part in Germany's Fight, *translated by Kurt Fielder (New York: Howard Fertig, 1979), pp. 44, 47–48, 55, 66, 145–146, 214.*

16. Joseph Goebbels, *My Part in Germany's Fight*, 1934

February 29th, 1932.

Our propaganda is working at high pressure.

The clerical work is finished. Now the technical side of the fight begins. What enormous preparations are necessary to organize such a vast distribution!

Reported to the Leader (Hitler) at noon. I gave him details as to the measures we are taking. The election campaign is chiefly to be fought by means of placards and addresses. We have not much capital, but as the Party is working gratuitously a little money goes a long way.

Fifty thousand gramophone records have been made, which are so small they can be slipped into an ordinary envelope. The supporters of the Government will be astonished when they place these miniature records on the gramophone!

In Berlin everything is going well.

A film (of me) is being made and I speak a few words in it for about ten minutes. It is to be shown in all public gardens and squares of the larger cities. . . .

March 8th, 1932.

Dictate two articles and heaps of handbills. The placard war has reached its climax. Up till now we lead in the race.

Interview with the *Popolo d'Italia.*[15] I describe our methods and means of propaganda. The representative of this influential Italian paper is positively dumbfounded. "The vastest and most up-to-date propaganda of Europe." . . .

March 18th, 1932.

A critical innovation: the Leader will conduct this next campaign by plane. By this means he will be able to speak three or four times a day at various places as opportunity serves, and address about one and a half millions of people in spite of the time being so short.

April 14th, 1932.

The Leader is planning a new plane campaign for the Prussian elections. He intends to start on Sunday. His perseverance is admirable, and it is amazing how he stands the continual strain.

At work again organizing his great 'plane trips. Now we have quite a lot of experience in these matters.

An important problem is how to make use of the Leader's propaganda flights for the Press. Everything has to be minutely prepared and organized beforehand.

October 4th, 1932.

Monday: Berlin. Prepared for the Leader's meeting at Munich. Dashed off designs for seven huge placards. Things knocked off quickly and enthusiastically are always good.

It is difficult to adapt men used to editorial work to the necessities of electioneering. They are too accurate and slow. . . .

15. **Popolo d'Italia:** A newspaper founded by the Italian Fascist leader Mussolini in 1914 and edited by him until he gained political control of Italy in 1922, this journal was the official organ of the Fascist dictatorship in Italy by 1932. Indeed, until the newspaper ceased publication in 1943, Mussolini still set its general editorial direction and even contributed articles himself.

January 18th, 1933.

In the evening we go to see the film "Rebel," by Luis Trencker. A first-class production of an artistic film. Thus I could imagine the film of the future, revolutionary in character, with grand mass-scenes, composed with enormous vital energy. In one scene, in which a gigantic crucifix is carried out of a small church by the revolutionaries, the audience is deeply moved. Here you really see what can be done with the film as an artistic medium, when it is really understood. We are all much impressed.

February 10th, 1933.

The Sportpalast[16] is already packed by six o'clock in the evening. All the squares in the city swarm with people waiting to hear the Leader's speech. In the whole Reich twenty to thirty millions more are listening in to it.

Drag myself to the Sportpalast, still weak with the illness from which I have not yet fully recovered. On the platform first I address the Press, and then for twenty minutes at the microphone speak to the audience in the Sportpalast. It goes better than I had thought. It is a strange experience suddenly to be faced with an inanimate microphone when one is used to addressing a living crowd, to be uplifted by the atmosphere of it, and to read the effect of one's speech in the expression on the faces of one's hearers.

The Leader is greeted by frantic cheering. He delivers a fine address containing an outspoken declaration of war against Marxism. Towards the end he strikes a wonderful, incredibly solemn note, and closes with the word "Amen"! It is uttered so naturally that all are deeply moved and affected by it. It is filled with so much strength and belief, is so novel and courageous, that it is not to be compared to anything that has gone beforehand.

This address will be received with enthusiasm throughout Germany. The nation will be ours almost without a struggle.

The masses at the Sportpalast are beside themselves with delight. Now the German Revolution has truly begun.

'Phone calls from different parts of the country report on the fine effect the speech has made even over the Radio. As an instrument for propaganda on a large scale the efficacy of the Radio has not yet been sufficiently appreciated. In any case our adversaries did not recognize its value. All the better, we shall have to explore its possibilities.

THE IMPACT OF NAZI METHODS

Source 17 from Jeremy Noakes and Geoffrey Pridham, editors, Documents on Nazism, 1919–1945 *(New York: Viking, 1975), p. 108.*

16. **Sportpalast:** the Sports Palace, a large, indoor sports arena in Berlin.

17. Report on the Problem of Stemming the Spread of Nazi Ideas in the Protestant Youth Movement, 1931

The cause which at the moment is most closely associated with the name of National Socialism and with which, at a moderate estimate, certainly 70 per cent of our young people, often lacking knowledge of the facts, are in ardent sympathy, must be regarded, as far as our ranks are concerned, more as an ethical than a political matter. Our young people show little political interest. Secondary school students are not really much concerned with the study of Hitler's thoughts; it is simply something irrational, something infectious that makes the blood pulse through one's veins and conveys an impression that something great is under way, the roaring of a stream which one does not wish to escape: "If you can't feel it you will never grasp it. . . ."

All this must be taken into account when we see the ardour and fire of this movement reflected in our ranks. A pedantic and nagging approach seems to me useless, and so do all attempts, however well-intentioned, by the leader to refute the policy of National Socialism in detail. The majority of the young fight against this with a strange instinct. We must, in keeping with our responsibility, though it is difficult in individual cases, try first to influence the ethos, and in this we must maintain an attitude above parties. We must educate in such a way that this enthusiasm is duly tempered by deeper understanding and by disenchantment, that words like "national honour and dignity" do not become slogans but arouse individual responsibility so that no brash demagogues grow up among us.

Source 18 from William L. Shirer, Berlin Diary, The Journal of a Foreign Correspondent, *1934–1941 (New York: Knopf, 1941), pp. 18, 19, 21, 22, 23.*

18. William L. Shirer, Reactions to the Nazi Party Rally at Nuremberg, 1934

NUREMBERG, *September 5*

I'm beginning to comprehend, I think, some of the reasons for Hitler's astounding success. Borrowing a chapter from the Roman church,[17] he is restoring pageantry and colour and mysticism to the drab lives of twentieth-century Germans. This morning's opening meeting in the Luitpold Hall on the outskirts of Nuremberg was more than a gorgeous show; it also had something of the mysticism and religious fervour of an Easter or Christmas

17. **Roman church:** the Roman Catholic Church.

Mass in a great Gothic cathedral. The hall was a sea of brightly coloured flags. Even Hitler's arrival was made dramatic. The band stopped playing. There was a hush over the thirty thousand people packed in the hall. Then the band struck up the *Badenweiler March,* a very catchy tune, and used only, I'm told, when Hitler makes his big entries. Hitler appeared in the back of the auditorium, and followed by his aides, Göring, Goebbels, Hess, Himmler, and the others, he strode slowly down the long centre aisle while thirty thousand hands were raised in salute. It is a ritual, the old-timers say, which is always followed. Then an immense symphony orchestra played Beethoven's *Egmont* Overture. Great Klieg lights played on the stage, where Hitler sat surrounded by a hundred party officials and officers of the army and navy. Behind them the "blood flag," the one carried down the streets of Munich in the ill-fated putsch. Behind this, four or five hundred S.A. standards. When the music was over, Rudolf Hess, Hitler's closest confidant, rose and slowly read the names of the Nazi "martyrs"—brown-shirts who had been killed in the struggle for power—a roll-call of the dead, and the thirty thousand seemed very moved.

In such an atmosphere no wonder, then, that every word dropped by Hitler seemed like an inspired Word from on high. Man's—or at least the German's—critical faculty is swept away at such moments, and every lie pronounced is accepted as high truth itself.

NUREMBERG, *September 7*

Another great pageant tonight. Two hundred thousand party officials packed in the Zeppelin Wiese with their twenty-one thousand flags unfurled in the searchlights like a forest of weird trees. "We are strong and will get stronger," Hitler shouted at them through the microphone, his words echoing across the hushed field from the loud-speakers. And there, in the floodlit night, jammed together like sardines, in one mass formation, the little men of Germany who have made Nazism possible achieved the highest state of being the Germanic man knows: the shedding of their individual souls and minds—with the personal responsibilities and doubts and problems—until under the mystic lights and at the sound of the magic words of the Austrian they were merged completely in the Germanic herd. Later they recovered enough—fifteen thousand of them—to stage a torchlight parade through Nuremberg's ancient streets, Hitler taking the salute in front of the station across from our hotel.

NUREMBERG, *September 10*

(Later)—After seven days of almost ceaseless goose-stepping, speech-making, and pageantry, the party rally came to an end tonight. And though dead tired and rapidly developing a bad case of crowd-phobia, I'm glad I came. You have to go through one of these to understand Hitler's hold on the people, to feel the dynamic in the movement he's unleashed and the sheer, disciplined strength the Germans possess. And now—as Hitler told the correspondents yesterday in explaining his technique—the half-million men who've been here during the week will go back to their towns and villages and preach the new gospel with new fanaticism. . . .

QUESTIONS TO CONSIDER

This chapter posed three basic questions: What image did the Nazis convey to German voters? Why did they appeal to German voters? How did the Nazis use media to aid their rise to power?

First examine the image the party conveyed to Germans in the 1920s and early 1930s. Start by considering the highly visible uniformed wing of the party, the S.A. Why did the S.A. Order 111 (Source 4) place such emphasis on how the S.A. appeared in public? What was the Storm Trooper supposed to epitomize? How was that visual effect designed to build a certain image for the party? How might columns of marching men and political banners contribute to this image? Reflect, too, on the mass meetings so carefully mounted by the party. What impression might they have conveyed to the average man or woman on the street? How did the Leader myth contribute to a certain image for the party? Remember that Hitler was relatively young, forty-three years of age, when he gained power. How do you think many Germans viewed a young party leader whose use of airplanes made him seem omnipresent?

With your concept of the party's image now clearly in mind, assess the Nazi appeal to voters. You may wish to review the numerous problems facing Germany in the 1920s and early 1930s that we examined in the introduction. What did the Nazis propose as solutions to the Versailles Treaty, the threat of communist takeover, and the ills of the depression? Did the Nazis convey an image that would lead Germans to believe the party could solve the country's problems? Consider the S.A. and the Leader myth. How did they reinforce a promise to restore German power?

What groups did the Nazis specifically appeal to in our evidence, and what were their specific problems? What were the alleged conditions of the workers in Source 8, the poster of "The String-Puller"? Who was threatened by the proposed Woolworth's store in Hanover (Source 14)? How did the Nazis win support in these groups?

Beyond its proposed answers to Germany's problems and its specific appeal to certain groups, the Nazi party also had a more general appeal. Reflect for a moment on the anomie that Durkheim identified as part of modern urban life (see Chapter 10). In what ways do you think participation in mass meetings might combat this feeling? What sorts of positive feelings might it seem to provide? The twentieth century, as we saw in Chapter 10, has witnessed for many a weakening of both the ritual and authority of traditional religion. How do the photographs of the banners and rally (Sources 5 and 6) and Shirer's account (Source 18) indicate a conscious attempt by the Nazis to exploit this development? Why would you not be surprised to find German religious youth movements losing members to the Nazis? Why are you shocked but not surprised at the conclusion of Hitler's speech of February 10, 1933 (Source 16)?

Finally, consider the Nazis' techniques, their use of media and propaganda in achieving their goal of power. In this regard, consider the theoretical bases for Nazi propaganda. What was Hitler's view of the masses? According to Hitler, why would the masses submit to terror? Recall the account of the brawl in the Pharus Hall in Source 7. What effect might this event have had on Hitler's opponents? Reexamine the graph of violence in Northeim. Why did Nazi violence break out when it did? How did it affect the party's image?

Examine the party's use of media technology for propaganda. What was the response of the Italian journalist to Nazi propaganda, according to Goebbels (Source 16)? What new electronic media did the Nazis employ? What do you think the Nazis' level of success would have been without such modern technology as the microphone? What features of Nazi campaign technology have become part of modern campaigning?

As you consider these questions, you should have a better understanding of the Nazi seizure of power in Germany. The Nazis used technology and methods of political manipulation that were new to the modern world. To understand fully the magnitude of their political revolution in winning the German masses, conclude your examination by referring to Chapter 2 of this volume. Which social groups was Louis XIV of France trying to influence? What was his message? How have Western political strategies changed in the almost three centuries separating Louis XIV and Hitler?

EPILOGUE

Nazi media mastery and propaganda worked well enough by January 1933 for the party to secure the chancellorship for Hitler. In free elections, however, the Nazis never secured more than 44 percent of the vote.[18] Once

Hitler became chancellor, the task for the party and Goebbels was to use modern media and propaganda either to win the support of the majority of Germans or at least to convince them that opposition to the new political order was futile. As had been the case with the Nazi drive for

18. In the last free Reichstag elections held in March 1933, the Nazis won only 43.9 percent of the vote, despite S.A. intimidation of voters and the great political advantage accruing to the party from Hitler's position as Chancellor. The Nazis finally secured a Reichstag majority only when Hitler expelled the communist members from the Chamber.

power, implicit in this effort was the threat that force would be used against the recalcitrant. But Hitler did seem to keep his promises. The communist party was outlawed in 1933; building projects and eventually rearmament stimulated the economy and created jobs; and Germany restored its military power and defied the Treaty of Versailles. Ominously, Hitler's promises also pointed to the terrible tragedy of the Holocaust for European Jews, and to World War II. But Goebbels's propaganda machine never let Germans forget the regime's successes.

The Hitler government centralized control of all information and media in a new Ministry of Public Enlightenment and Propaganda, headed by Goebbels, which closely regulated Germany's press, film, and radio after 1933. Especially significant was Goebbels's understanding of the role of radio as a propaganda device and his use of it once in power. He said, "With the radio we have destroyed the spirit of rebellion,"[19] because the radio could bring the Nazi message into every German home. The regime saw to it that cheap radios were made available to Germans, and the number of receivers increased from 5 million in 1932 to 9.5 million in 1938. A system of government wardens notified citizens to tune in important programs and the Propaganda Ministry increased their impact still further by setting up loudspeakers in the streets and squares of Germany during key broadcasts.

Goebbels's ministry also sought to sway opinion via the medium of film. After some early crude and unpopular efforts, Goebbels's understanding of film as a propaganda device grew greatly. He wrote in 1942 of the subtle possibilities inherent in the medium:

> Even entertainment can be politically of special value, because the moment a person becomes conscious of propaganda, propaganda becomes ineffective. However, as soon as propaganda as a tendency, as a characteristic, as an attitude remains in the background and becomes apparent through human beings, then propaganda becomes effective in every respect.[20]

Armed with such methods, the Nazi regime was able to retain power, mobilize its citizens for war, and sustain their morale throughout much of World War II. There was opposition to the dictatorship, including a number of plots against Hitler himself, but the regime managed to contain such active resistance within a minority of the population. Modern media and propaganda techniques and a message that attracted many, combined with the omnipresent threat of state police power, proved to be effective devices that aided the regime in maintaining its ascendancy. Such employment of modern media and propaganda techniques, supported by the police power of the state, would characterize many later twentieth-century totalitarian regimes.

19. Quoted in Roger Manvell and Heinrich Fraenkel, *Doctor Goebbels: His Life and Death* (London: Heinemann, 1960), pp. 127–128.

20. Joseph Goebbels, *Tagebuch*, unpublished sections, in Intitut für Zeitgeschichte, Munich, entry for March 1, 1942. Quoted in David Welch, *Propaganda and the German Cinema, 1933–1945* (Oxford: Clarendon Press, 1983), p. 45.

CHAPTER FOURTEEN

THE PERILS OF PROSPERITY:

THE UNREST OF

YOUTH IN THE 1960s

THE PROBLEM

Commuters just emerging from subway exits in the university district of Paris on the evening of Friday, May 3, 1968, must have been bewildered. They stepped out into a neighborhood transformed since morning into a war zone in which police and students battled over the future of France's governmental and economic systems. These commuters witnessed a conflict in which French students, like students in many other countries in 1968, called into question a material prosperity purchased, in their view, with a loss of individual liberty in the face of the power of the modern state and giant industrial concerns.

The postwar Western world indeed was experiencing unprecedented prosperity by the late 1960s. The United States enjoyed the world's highest living standard. In Western Europe the European Economic Community (or EEC), also called the Common Market, served as a key instrument for economic recovery and growth for war-ravaged France, West Germany, Italy, Belgium, the Netherlands, and Luxembourg. Non-EEC countries, including Great Britain and the Scandinavian nations, also shared in this economic success. Even in communist Eastern Europe, war damage was repaired and the socialist economies of the region produced standards of living for their peoples substantially improved over those of the early postwar years.

Behind the façade of material success, however, were a number of problems that led to widespread unrest, especially among the young, in the 1960s. Part of the basis for this discontent may be found in the very economic success of the postwar period. Several western countries, including France and Great Britain, encouraged growth by government intervention in the economy or national ownership of industries. The economic life of Communist Eastern Europe, of course, was entirely

Chapter 14

The Perils of

Prosperity:

The Unrest of

Youth in

the 1960s

under government control. The result was a growing state economic bureaucracy in which the individual had little voice. The nature of the economic growth was unsettling, too. The West was entering a new phase of industrialization. New and sophisticated industries, such as computers and electronics, flourished; the service sector of the economy grew while older heavy industries declined in importance. The result was deep concern among many workers, who found little demand for their traditional skills and who felt powerless to avoid unemployment or underemployment. Worker dissatisfaction with the existing system only increased with economic recessions like that of 1968 in France, which added to unemployment and reduced the buying power of those who retained their jobs. Economic growth, for many, was not an unqualified success.

Many European students were dissatisfied with the system of higher education. A partial reason may be found in the West's great population growth after World War II. The postwar baby boom of 1946–1964, which affected both Europe and America, coincided with a prosperity that permitted Western democracies to provide their youth with greater educational opportunity than had been offered any earlier generation. In two decades student populations vastly increased. From 1950 to 1970, university enrollments increased from 123,000 to 651,000 in France; from 190,000 to 561,000 in Italy; from 117,000 to 410,000 in West Germany; and from 67,200 to 250,000 in Great Britain.[1] But often the quality of the educational experience declined as the system strained to cope with unprecedented enrollments. University faculty and facilities failed to grow as fast as their student bodies, producing crowded lecture halls and student-faculty ratios that went as high as 105 to 1 in Italy and rendered professors inaccessible to students.

Other problems also affected the student population. University curricula often provided a traditional education that did little to prepare a student to succeed in the new service-oriented economy. When European governments decreed half-hearted curriculum reforms to respond to economic change, they often, as in France, extended a student's course of study. The university also seemed divorced from the real problems of society, such as poverty and crime, a fact reflected in the rarity of sociology courses dealing with those problems.

These curricular problems and the impersonal nature of the modern university led to student demands for sweeping change in the educational establishment. The students wished a voice in the decisions that affected them. They increasingly demanded a say in what was taught, who taught, and how the universities were administered. As we will see, such demands also reflected the feelings of many nonstudents who bitterly felt their inability to affect the modern institutions that controlled their lives.

1. B. R. Mitchell, ed., *European Historical Statistics,* abridged ed. (New York: Columbia University Press, 1978), pp. 396–400.

Students of the 1960s were disappointed and angered by educational shortcomings, but they were even more frustrated by their inability to effect political change. The student generation of the 1960s was physically more mature than any previous generation, thanks to improved nutrition. Their sense of adulthood was heightened by the spread of techniques of birth control that freed women from the fear of pregnancy outside of marriage and fostered a youthful revolt against traditional sexual mores. That revolt could have political ramifications; a slogan frequently heard among French students in 1968 was: "Every time I make love I want to make the revolution; every time I make the revolution I want to make love." But these self-consciously mature young people could change little around them. Everywhere, those under twenty-one were eligible for military service but had no right to vote. Nor had students even a voice in their universities' governance. Typically, European governments controlled universities through centralized bureaucracies. In France, for example, such minor events as student dances had to be approved by the Ministry of Education.

Yet for all the dissatisfaction among students and workers, traditional twentieth-century political ideologies offered scant appeal. The cold war had polarized Europe for twenty years, and neither of the opposing doctrines—Russian communism or the democratic capitalism of the United States—offered real answers to student demands. Indeed, in a political sense both doctrines increas-ingly lost credibility for students. For some, the democratic ideals of the United States no longer seemed attractive because of that nation's increasingly unpopular war in Vietnam. Many found that Southeast Asia conflict, which engaged about 500,000 American servicemen by 1968, a war to uphold a favored minority in South Vietnam through military involvement. Those who looked toward a communist vision of a better world similarly were disappointed. The Soviet Union, with its regimented society, inefficient economy, and forceful crushing of dissent in its East German, Polish, and Hungarian satellites in the 1950s, was hardly the best advertisement for Marxian socialism.

Ideological disillusionment led a minority of students to radical doctrines rejecting orthodox Marxism as well as liberal democracy. The ideas of Leon Trotsky, a Marxist who rejected the need for a bureaucracy in a socialist state, attracted some. The example of Mao Zedong, the Chinese revolutionary, stirred other students to reject all authority and to attempt to rally working people to the cause of revolutionary change. Still others found attraction in nineteenth-century anarchist thought that rejected any hierarchy of control over the individual. Some also found inspiration in the revolutionary activism of Cuba's Fidel Castro and Che Guevara. Common to all was the belief that the institutions of society favored the rich, manipulated the poor, and substituted materialism bred of postwar economic growth for individual liberty and any high-minded questioning of the

Chapter 14
The Perils of
Prosperity:
The Unrest of
Youth in
the 1960s

established order. Everywhere student demands could be summed up as calls for participation by individuals in all the decisions that shaped their lives, a concept French students labeled *autogestion*.

Whatever their ideology, student radicals sought confrontation with established governmental and educational authority in the hope of garnering a mass following for change among the nonrevolutionary majority of students, workers, and others. The radicals increasingly found student followers in many countries. Unrest due to the Vietnam War was widespread on campuses in the United States from the mid-1960s. In Europe riots began in Italy in 1965 at the universities of Milan and Trento as students demanded a voice in academic policy. Italian unrest continued into the late 1960s, when student radicals combined ideas for a complete overthrow of traditional society with their demands for educational change. Incidents rooted in the desire for political change were common to German and British universities, too. In most of these countries, however, youthful radicals generated little support beyond their campuses. France was the only Western European country in which youthful unrest spread beyond students and thus threatened the existence of the government.

In 1968 France had been led for ten years by President Charles de Gaulle, the seventy-eight-year-old hero of World War II whose imperial style of government only increased the extreme state centralization traditional in that country. Signifi-

cantly, too, France was suffering an economic recession that heightened the discontent of many workers. Problems began at the new Nanterre campus of the University of Paris. Placed amid slums housing immigrant workers, this modern university center seemed to radicals a dramatic illustration of the failings of modern consumer society. Led by the anarchist Daniel Cohn-Bendit in a protest of university regulations, Nanterre students forced the closing of their campus in the spring of 1968.

Nanterre radicals next focused their attention on the main campus of the University of Paris, at the Sorbonne, after university authorities had begun disciplinary action against Cohn-Bendit and others on May 3, 1968. As police removed protesting student radicals from the Sorbonne, antipolice violence erupted among crowds of students around the university. The very appearance of the police on university grounds provoked student anger. University confines were normally beyond the jurisdiction of the police, who had last entered the Sorbonne in 1791. The crowd threw rocks and, more dangerously, the heavy cobblestones of Paris streets. Police beat students brutally in scenes broadcast on the evening television news that generated widespread support for the radicals who now demanded a change in France's government.

For the next two weeks, the university district of Paris was the scene of street fighting between police and students that drew on the traditions of a Paris that had often defied government in the past.[2] Ominously for the government, the student unrest spread to other parts of society. On May 13, 1968, unions scheduled a twenty-four-hour general strike to protest police brutality, despite the opposition of the large French Communist party, which feared the unorthodoxy of the spreading revolt. On May 14 workers began to occupy factories and to refuse to work, the young among them demanding, like the students, a voice in decisions affecting them. For other workers, improved wages were a demand. Within a week, perhaps as many as 10 million workers nationwide had seized their factories and were on strike. Even professionals in broadcasting, sports, and other fields joined the strike. The country was paralyzed and the government seemed on the brink of collapse as opposition leaders began to discuss alternative regimes.

As the government faltered, both sides in the confrontation clearly saw the significance of the growing revolt. Cohn-Bendit characterized it as "a whole generation rising against a certain sort of society—bourgeois society." A leader of the establishment, France's Prime Minister Georges Pompidou, defined the revolt as one against modern society itself. Even the authoritarian de Gaulle heard the message, con-

ceding on May 19, "Reform yes, anarchy no."[3]

Prime Mister Pompidou began to defuse the crisis by offering wage increases to the striking unions. Faced with destroying the consumer society or enjoying more of its benefits, many striking workers quickly chose the latter option. Then, on May 29, de Gaulle flew to West Germany, assured himself of the support of French army units stationed there in case of the need of force, and returned to Paris to end the crisis. Addressing the nation on radio the next day, the president refused to resign as the protesters demanded and instead dissolved the National Assembly, calling for new elections to that body. The maneuver saved the government's cause. The protesters could not call repressive a government that was willing to risk its control of the legislature in elections called ahead of schedule. Although student radicals tried to continue the revolt, most workers accepted proffered pay increases and new elections and returned to work. De Gaulle's supporters won a majority of the seats in the National Assembly on June 23, 1968, and the president retained the power to govern.

As students and workers battled police in France, equally dramatic events were moving to a climax across Europe in Czechoslovakia.

---

2. Students fought much as Parisians had in the eighteenth and nineteenth centuries, tearing up paving stones and piling them with overturned vehicles and fallen trees to create street barricades from behind which they fought police. When the student revolt ended, the government paved cobblestone streets with asphalt.

3. In the present context, *anarchy* is probably the best English word to convey briefly what de Gaulle meant. De Gaulle probably sought a certain effect by using an army colloquialism, *chien lit,* which even the French press had difficulty expressing adequately. It means making "a mess in one's own bed"; in other words, "fouling one's own nest."

Chapter 14

The Perils of

Prosperity:

The Unrest of

Youth in

the 1960s

Although unrest in democratic France and one-party Czechoslovakia displayed differences, the revolts in both countries had common roots in a rejection of highly centralized and unresponsive authority.

Czechoslovakia, an industrialized country with Western democratic traditions, experienced a coup in 1948 that established a communist government. The leaders of that regime, party First Secretaries Klement Gottwald (1948–1953) and Antonín Novotný (1953–1968) were steadfast followers of authoritarian Stalinist communism, even as the Soviet Union itself began a process of "de-Stalinization" after 1956. But by 1967 Novotný's style of communism was becoming increasingly unacceptable to Czechoslovakians in two chief regards. The most basic problem concerned the nation's two largest ethnic groups: the Czechs and the Slovaks. For a long time the Slovaks had been unhappy with Czech domination of both the Communist party and the state apparatus. The Novotný regime perpetuated this Czech domination as the Slovaks clamored for a stronger voice in national affairs.

Even more fundamental than the regime's ethnic difficulties, however, was its rigid and authoritarian Stalinist communism. Economically, this meant a managed economy, oriented toward heavy industrial goods rather than consumer items, that was hampered by centralized control, no profit motive, and low productivity. The nation had experienced serious economic problems since 1962. Politically, Novotný's government gave the country rigid control by a small party inner circle sustained by a secret police, press censorship, and extreme curbs on intellectual freedom.

A series of events led to change in Czechoslovakia through the efforts of the younger generation of party officials, intellectuals, and students. As in France, loss of support for the regime began among those who were being groomed in the educational system as future leaders, not with the materially deprived. Pressure for change in the country's highest leadership mounted as Novotný's authoritarian style of government resisted reform and economic problems persisted.

In 1963 the Slovak branch of the Communist party named a new First Secretary, the reform-minded Alexander Dubček. In a country where literature long had been politicized, writers began to desert the regime; at the Congress of Czechoslovak Writers in June 1967, they demanded an end to censorship and freedom for their craft. Other intellectuals also grew restive with the regime. But, as in France, it was young people who brought matters to a crisis point. Cries of "We want freedom, we want democracy" and "A good communist is a dead communist" punctuated traditional student May Day observances in 1966 and resulted in arrests by policemen whom the students called "Gestapo," after the Nazi security police. The government responded forcefully, expelling from the universities and drafting into the army leaders of student organizations who had called for more freedom. Nonetheless, opposition to the Novotný regime not only continued but increased, especially after the events of October 31, 1967. On that night, as on numerous previous occasions, an electrical failure left the large complex of student dormitories in Prague, the capital, without light. Students took up candles and began a procession chanting "We want light," a phrase that could indicate far more than their need for electrical power. The brutal acts of the police in confronting the students outraged public opinion, thus strengthening reform elements in the party's Central Committee sufficiently for them to gain a majority in that body. On January 5, 1968, the reformers replaced Novotný with the Slovak Alexander Dubček as first secretary of the national Communist party. On March 22, 1968, war hero Ludvik Svoboda replaced Novotný as president of the nation. A bloodless revolution had occurred in Prague.

The spring of 1968 was an exhilarating one for the people of Czechoslovakia. Dubček announced his intention to create "socialism with a human face," a socialism that would allow "a fuller assertion of the personality than any bourgeois democracy," a socialism that would be "profoundly democratic." Rigid press censorship ended, as did other controls on the individual. But Dubček soon found himself in a difficult position. Permitted freedom of expression for the first time in twenty years, Czechoslovaks demanded far more, including even a free political system with a role for noncommunist parties. Such developments, however, threatened neighboring communist dictatorships in East Germany and Poland and risked depriving the So-

viet Union of strategically located Czechoslovakia in its Warsaw Pact alliance system.

On August 21, after having watched developments in Prague for months with growing alarm, the Soviet Union acted. Troops from the Soviet Union, East Germany, Hungary, Poland, and Bulgaria entered Czechoslovakia. In the largest movement of troops in Europe since 1945, they forcibly ended the "Prague Spring" experiment.

The Soviets were met with widespread passive nationalist resistance. The majority of the population seemed to wish continuation of reform, but earlier unrest in Eastern Europe, as in the failed Hungarian revolt of 1956, had demonstrated the futility of civilians' active opposition to Soviet arms. Students again took part in resistance, however, and two, Jan Palach and Jan Zajíc, burned themselves alive in early 1969 in protest. Force prevailed, however, and Soviet pressure assured the gradual replacement of Dubček and his reform leadership with men more subservient to Moscow's wishes. Soviet party First Secretary Leonid Brezhnev announced that events in Czechoslovakia represented an expression of what came to be called the "Brezhnev Doctrine"—that is, the Soviet Union's policy to act against any threat to the stability of an East European communist regime.

Those supporting change in both France and Czechoslovakia were acutely aware of the need to sway public opinion in their favor. This task was made difficult by government controls of the media: in

Chapter 14

The Perils of

Prosperity:

The Unrest of

Youth in

the 1960s

France the radio and television systems were state controlled; in Czechoslovakia the regime controlled not only electronic media but the press as well. Your problem in this chapter is to analyze events in France and Czechoslovakia in 1968 by examining the materials issued by those who sought to rally support for change. Deprived of media controlled by the political establishment, proponents of change issued leaflets, posters, and cartoons designed to win support. What aspects of the modern state and economy provoked the events of 1968? What vision of the future did the leaders of the French and Czechoslovakian movements embrace? How did they propose to achieve it?

SOURCES AND METHOD

Modern political causes seek to mobilize support in various ways. Because posters, pamphlets, and other publications as well as simple slogans scrawled on walls all aim to energize support for a movement by publicizing its ideas, analyzing such materials provides a broad understanding of the goals and methods of any cause. In this chapter we have assembled two groups of evidence, one relating to the French disorders and the other to the Czechoslovakian reform movement of 1968.

Let us consider the French evidence first. Source 1 is a pamphlet distributed to striking workers by the March 22 Movement, a student group whose name commemorated the student upheaval at the Nanterre campus. It appeared on May 21, 1968. What were the students' goals for the future society and economy of France? What were the aims of workers in their strike? How did student leaders try to unify student and worker causes in this pamphlet? Source 2, a leaflet that appeared on May 22, 1968, was issued by a number of student and worker groups. Consider the views expressed here about President de Gaulle, the government, and the economy. Would the authors have been satisfied only with the departure of de Gaulle from the political scene? What do you deduce from their refusal of "summit negotiations" with government and management? To whom does the leaflet appeal? What vision of the future does it advocate?

You must analyze the language of Source 3 to understand the message it seeks to convey. This is a list of slogans that the student Sorbonne Occupation Committee suggested to its followers on May 16, 1968. Note the locations proposed for such slogans. The one advocating the end of bureaucrats was painted across a large mural in the Sorbonne administration building. How did this and some of the other suggested locations reflect student attitudes toward authority? Now turn to the words themselves. Slogans are important in politics; as we noted in Chapter 13, the simpler they are, the more easily they can be spread to influence large numbers of people. Each side of the 1968 confrontations sought to dismiss the validity of the other's ideas by extreme and often inaccurate name calling. In France as well as in the United States and other countries, students referred to policemen as "pigs" or "fascists." French students' chants of "CRS—SS!" likened the riot police, the CRS (*Compagnies Républicaines de Securité*) to the Nazi SS (*Schutz Staffeln* or security echelon, whose insignia resembled a sharp double *S*). The students' opponents responded in kind, often calling them "commies." What views of their opponents do the students convey in these slogans? What sort of society do they advocate? What methods do they advocate for their cause?

With the French Sources 4 through 12, you must analyze pictorial attempts to mobilize opinion. The artists conveyed these messages graphically in pictures, with a minimum of words. Here you must ascertain the nature of the message and the goals of the students and workers.

The visual evidence is of several types. In 1968 posters appeared all over the university district of Paris in defiance of long-standing laws against posters on public buildings. Often they were fairly sophisticated in execution because many advanced art students put their skills in the service of the May revolt. The political cartoon also flourished in a number of new radical publications in Paris. The cartoons presented here originated in *L'enragé* ("*The Madman*"), a publication that consisted entirely of cartoons critical of established authority in France.

Cartoons and posters often magnify the physical characteristics of public figures, sometimes to ridicule but also to make perfectly clear the subject of the message. Thus you will find the prominent nose of President de Gaulle quite exaggerated, as well as certain poses. De Gaulle often embellished his speeches by raising both arms, the same gesture he used when leading the singing of the national anthem, *La Marseillaise*, a frequent occurrence after a public address. This pose is duplicated in the cartoons and posters along with his uniform of a French general, complete with the cylindrical cap known as a *kepi*, making him instantly recognizable. Artists further identified de Gaulle by including in their pictures the Cross of Lorraine, the symbol of his World War II resistance movement, with its two transverse bars.

In analyzing the material, remember that political posters and cartoons, though based on real events, are not intended to report those occurrences accurately. They are meant instead to affect public opinion. By carefully examining the posters and cartoons, you can discover the artists' views of events and how they wished to sway public opinion. What action does each picture represent? What message is the artist trying to convey? What reaction does he or she wish to evoke in viewers? What do the pictures tell you about the participants, methods, and aspirations of the French movement?

Now let us examine the Czechoslovakian sources. The Czechoslovakian writings should be examined

[395]

Chapter 14

The Perils of

Prosperity:

The Unrest of

Youth in

the 1960s

with the same methods you applied to the French. Source 13 is a tract that circulated illegally in Czechoslovakian literary circles as early as April 1967 and was republished in a Prague student publication in March 1968. Notice first the use of language. What effect do the authors seek in condemning their opponents as "knaves"? What view does the statement as a whole express toward established ideologies, Soviet Marxist as well as U.S. capitalist? What methods for change are advocated? Did young Czechoslovakians follow the course of action recommended in the tenth commandment? Why should the intellectuals, students, and professors be the leaders in change?

Source 14 is an extract from a statement that appeared in an influential publication, *Literární Listy* (*Literary Papers*), the journal of the Czechoslovakian Writers' Union. *Literární Listy* was the chief forum in 1968 in which intellectuals expressed their views on reform. It had a large circulation (300,000 copies in June 1968), and it published the manifesto for change, "Two Thousand Words." Source 14 appeared on March 5, 1968, as one of a number of replies to the question of the nation's political future posed by the editors: "Wherefrom, with Whom, and Whither?" The answer reprinted here was made by Ivan Sviták, a philosophy professor and reform leader. Notice his choice of language. Who, in his view, was the

enemy of change? How does he characterize these people? What sort of social and political system did Czechoslovakian intellectuals seek?

Sources 15 through 20 are cartoons drawn from *Literární Listy* and its successor, *Listy*. Use the same methods of analysis here as you employed with the French posters and cartoons. You again will note exaggeration of certain physical features to clarify the cartoon's message. Alexander Dubček had a large nose, as de Gaulle did, and it was exaggerated by Czechoslovak cartoonists, just as French artists exaggerated de Gaulle's nose.

The Czechoslovakian cartoonists represented here also used symbols to illuminate their messages. The Phrygian cap worn by the woman in Source 15, for example, represents revolution and liberty. Dubček is depicted in Source 16 as Jánašík, a legendary Slovak "Robin Hood." Source 19 shows the Soviet president Leonid Brezhnev as Saint Florian. Old statues of this saint stand in many Czechoslovakian villages because he was thought to offer protection from fire.

Using the analytical methods described here, you should be able to answer the central questions of this chapter: What aspects of the modern state and economy provoked the events of 1968? What vision of the future did leaders of the French and Czechoslovakian movements embrace? How did they propose to achieve it?

THE EVIDENCE

FRANCE

Sources 1 through 3 from Vladimir Fišera, editor, Writing on the Wall, May 1968: A Documentary Anthology *(London: Allison & Busby, 1978), pp. 133–134; p. 137; pp. 125–126.*

1. The March 22 Movement, "Your Struggle Is Our Struggle," May 21, 1968

We are occupying the faculties, you are occupying the factories. Aren't we fighting for the same thing? Higher education only contains 10 percent workers' children. Are we fighting so that there will be more of them, for a democratic university reform? That would be a good thing, but it's not the most important. These workers' children would just become like other students. We are not aiming for a worker's son to be a manager. We want to wipe out segregation between workers and management.

There are students who are unable to find jobs on leaving university. Are we fighting so that they'll find jobs, for a decent graduate employment policy? It would be a good thing, but it is not vital. Psychology or sociology graduates will become the selectors, the planners and psychotechnicians who will try to organise your working conditions; mathematics graduates will become engineers, perfecting maximum-productivity machines to make your life even more unbearable. Why are we, students who are products of a middle-class life, criticising capitalist society? The son of a worker who becomes a student leaves his own class. For the son of a middle-class family, it could be his opportunity to see his class in its true light, to question the role he is destined for in society and the organisation of our society. We refuse to become scholars who are out of touch with real life. We refuse to be used for the benefit of the ruling class. We want to destroy the separation that exists between those who organise and think and those who execute their decisions. We want to form a classless society; your cause is the same as ours.

You are asking for a minimum wage of 1,000 francs in the Paris area, retirement at sixty, a 40-hour week for 48 hours' pay.

These are long-standing and just demands: nevertheless, they seem to be out of context with our aims. Yet you have gone on to occupy factories, take your managers as hostages, strike without warning. These forms of struggle have been made possible by perseverance and lengthy action in various enterprises, and because of the recent student battles.

These struggles are even more radical than our official aims, because they go further than simply seeking improvements for the worker within the

Chapter 14
The Perils of
Prosperity:
The Unrest of
Youth in
the 1960s

capitalist system, they imply the destruction of the system. They are political in the true sense of the word: you are fighting not to change the Prime Minister, but so that your boss no longer retains his power in business or society. The form that your struggle has taken offers us students the model for true socialist activity: the appropriation of the means of production and of the decision-making power by the workers.

Our struggles converge. We must destroy everything that seeks to alienate us (everyday habits, the press, etc.). We must combine our occupations in the faculties and factories.

Long live the unification of our struggles!

2. "Producers, Let Us Save Ourselves," May 22, 1968

To ten million strikers, to all workers:

No to parliamentary solutions, with de Gaulle going and the bosses staying.

No to summit negotiations which give only a new lease of life to a moribund capitalism.

No more referenda. No more spectacles.

Don't let anybody speak for us. Maintain the occupation of all workplaces.

To continue the struggle, let us put all the sectors of the economy which are hit by the strike at the service of the fighting workers.

Let us prepare today our power of tomorrow (direct food-supplies, the organisation of public services: transport, information, housing, etc.).

In the streets, in the local committees, wherever we are, workers, peasants, wage-earners, students, teachers, school students, let us organise and coordinate our struggles.

FOR THE ABOLITION OF THE EMPLOYERS, FOR WORKERS' POWER.

3. Sorbonne Occupation Committee, Slogans to Be Circulated by Any Means, May 16, 1968

(leaflets—announcements over microphones—comics—songs—painting on walls—texts daubed over the paintings in the Sorbonne—announcements in the cinema during the film, or stopping it in the middle—texts written on the posters in the underground—whenever you empty your glass in the bistro—before making love—after making love—in the lift)

Occupy the factories.

Power to the workers' councils.

Abolish class society.

Down with a society based on commodity production and the spectacle.

Abolish alienation.

An end to the university.

Mankind will not be happy until the last bureaucrat has been strung up by the guts of the last capitalist.

Death to the pigs.

Free the four people arrested for looting on 6 May.

Chapter 14

The Perils of

Prosperity:

The Unrest of

Youth in

the 1960s

THE ENEMY

Sources 4 through 8 from Bibliothèque Nationale, Les Affiches de Mai 68 ou l'imagination graphique *(Paris: Bibliothèque Nationale, 1982), p. 64; p. 15; p. 9; p. 63; p. 47.*

4. Poster, May 1968

6. Poster: "Light Salaries, Heavy Tanks," May 1968

SALAIRES LEGERS

CHARS LOURDS

5. Poster: "Let Us Smash the Old Gears!,"
May 1968

BRISONS
LES VIEUX ENGRENAGES

REVOLUTIONARY METHODS

7. Poster: "Beauty Is in the Street!," May 1968

8. Poster: "Less than 21 Years of Age: Here Is Your Ballot!," May 1968

MOINS DE 21ANS
voici votre bulletin de VOTE

LA BEAUTÉ
EST DANS LA RUE

Source 9 from Jean-Jacques Pauvert, editor, L'enragé: collection complète des 12 numéros introuvables, mai–novembre 1968 *(Paris: Jean-Jacques Pauvert, 1978).*

9. Cartoon, June 10, 1968

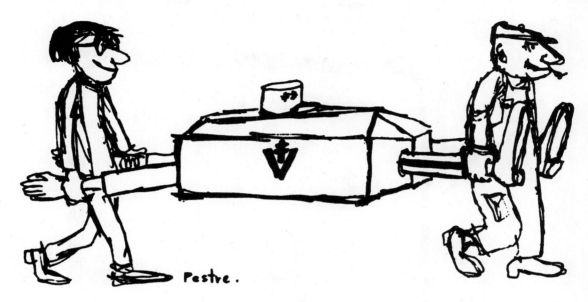

Chapter 14
The Perils of
Prosperity:
The Unrest of
Youth in
the 1960s

THE STUDENTS' VISION

Sources 10 and 11 from Bibliothèque Nationale, Les Affiches de Mai 68 ou l'imagination graphique, *p. 10; p. 24.*

10. Cartoon: "Each One of Us Is the State," May 1968

11. Cartoon: "Popular Power," May 1968

Chapter 14
The Perils of
Prosperity:
The Unrest of
Youth in
the 1960s

THE STUDENTS IN DEFEAT

Source 12 from Pauvert, L'enragé: collection complète des 12 numéros introuvables, mai–novembre 1968.

12. Cartoon, June 17, 1968

CZECHOSLOVAKIA

Sources 13 and 14 from Ivan Sviták, The Czechoslovak Experiment, 1968-1969 *(New York: Columbia University Press, 1971), pp. 17-18; p. 16.*

13. "Ten Commandments for a Young Czechoslovak Intellectual," March 1968

There are no more knaves than before; it is only that their field of activity is larger. . . . And so all of us are living in close collaboration with a few knaves.

LUDVÍK VACULÍK, in *Orientation, 1967*[4]

1. Do not collaborate with knaves. If you do, you inevitably become one of them. Engage yourself against the knaves.

2. Do not accept the responsibility forced upon you by the knaves for their own deeds. Do not believe such arguments as "we are all responsible," or the social problems touch "all of us," or "everyone has his share of guilt." Openly and clearly dissociate yourself from the deeds of the knaves and from arguments that you are responsible for them.

3. Do not believe any ideology that consists of systems of slogans and words which only speculate about your feelings. Judge people, political parties, and social systems concretely, according to the measure of freedom they give, and according to how tolerable the living conditions are. Judge them according to results, not words.

4. Do not solve only the narrow generational problems of youth; understand that the decisive problems are common to all human beings. You cannot solve them by postulating the demands of young men, but by vigorously defending the problems of all people. Do not complain about the privileges of one generation, but fight for human rights.

5. Do not consider the given social relations as constant. They are changing in your favor. Look forward. If you do not want to be wrong today, you must think from the point of view of the year 2000.

6. Do not think only as a Czech or a Slovak, but consider yourself a *European*. The world will sooner adapt to Europe (where Eastern Europe belongs) than to fourteen million Czechs and Slovaks. You live neither in America nor in the Soviet Union; you live in Europe.

---

4. **Ludvík Vaculík:** a novelist and one of the leaders of the Czechoslovakian reform movement.

Chapter 14

The Perils of

Prosperity:

The Unrest of

Youth in

the 1960s

7. Do not succumb to utopias or illusions; be dissatisfied and critical. Have the sceptical confidence of a negotiator, but have confidence in the purpose of your negotiations. The activity has its own value.

8. Do not be afraid of your task in history and be courageous in intervening in history. The social changes and transformations of man take place, no doubt, without regard to you, but to understand these changes and to influence them with the limited possibilities of an individual is far better than to accept the fatal inevitability of events.

9. Do not negotiate out of good motives alone; negotiate with sound arguments and with consideration of what you can achieve. A good deed can rise from a bad motive and vice versa. The motives are forgotten, but deeds remain.

10. Do not let yourself be *shot* in the fight between the interests of the power blocs. *Shoot* when in danger. Are you not in danger right now when you collaborate with the few knaves? Are you a knave?

14. Ivan Sviták, "Wherefrom, with Whom, and Whither?," March 5, 1968

From totalitarian dictatorship toward an open society, toward the liquidation of the power monopoly and toward the effective control of the power elite by a free press and by public opinion. From the bureaucratic management of society and culture by the "hard-line thugs" (C. Wright Mills)[5] toward the observance of fundamental human and civil rights, at least to the same extent as in the Czechoslovakia of bourgeois democracy. With the labor movement, without its *apparatchiks*;[6] with the middle classes, without their groups of willing collaborators; and with the intelligentsia in the lead. The intellectuals of this country must assert their claim to lead an open socialist society toward democracy and humanism.

5. **C. Wright Mills** (1916–1962): a Columbia University sociologist, the author of influential books including *White Collar* and *The Power Elite* and a severe critic of modern institutions.

6. **apparatchik**: a Russian word describing an individual who is part of the existing power structure.

THE PEOPLE'S VISION

Sources 15 and 16 from Literární Listy, *in Sviták,* The Czechoslovak Experiment, 1968–1969, *p. 2; p. 51.*

15. Cartoon: "If There Are No Complications the Child Should Be Born in the Ninth Month," 1968

Chapter 14
The Perils of
Prosperity:
The Unrest of
Youth in
the 1960s

16. Cartoon, 1968

THE ENEMY

Source 17 from Literární Listy, *in Robin Alison Remington, editor,* Prague in Winter: Documents on Czechoslovak Communism in Crisis *(Cambridge, Mass.: M.I.T. Press, 1969), p. 289.*

17. Cartoon, "Workers of All Countries Unite—Or I'll Shoot!," August 28, 1968

Chapter 14

The Perils of

Prosperity:

The Unrest of

Youth in

the 1960s

Sources 18 and 19 from Literární Listy, *in Sviták,* The Czechoslovak Experiment, 1968–1969, p. 196; p. 155.

18. Cartoon: "Liberté, Egalité, Freundschaft!" ("Liberty, Equality, Friendship!"), 1968

IN DEFEAT

19. Cartoon: "But There Is No Fire!," 1969

Chapter 14

The Perils of

Prosperity:

The Unrest of

Youth in

the 1960s

Source 20 from Listy, *in Remington,* Prague in Winter, *p. 373.*

20. Cartoon: "It Is Only a Matter of a Few Tactical Steps Back," January 30, 1969

JDE JENOM O NĚKOLIK
TAKTICKÝCH ÚSTUPKŮ.

Vladimír Jiránek

QUESTIONS TO CONSIDER

France and Czechoslovakia are two very different countries at opposite ends of Europe. Let us compare the events of 1968 as they unfolded in these two locations. Do they illustrate a common response to problems basic to modern life in the noncommunist and communist West?

Consider first the demands of French and Czechoslovakian protest leaders. Examine again the written and visual evidence, and consider the protesters' views on working conditions in France. What problems do they identify in Sources 1, 2, and 3? How are these problems defined graphically? Why do you think that the artist in Source 4 portrayed modern capitalism as a puppeteer? What is the significance of the puppeteer's appearance? Why did the artist show de Gaulle as part of the industrial gears of France in Source 5? Turn next to the Czechoslovakian statements on working conditions. Notice particularly Source 14 with its references to management by "hard-line thugs" and "apparatchiks." What great lie about communism (whose slogan is, "Workers of the World Unite!") do the Czechoslovakians discern in Source 17? What common theme do you find in French and

Czechoslovakian protesters' ideas on the conditions of labor in the modern economy?

Next consider the political vision of the 1968 activists. Take the French first. What sort of government did the formulators of Source 3 envision? How is that idea amplified in Sources 9, 10, and 11? These cartoons spell their messages in words, but their art contains a message, too. Look closely at Source 10. How does the artist see the individual faring against big government, industrial giants, and powerful unions? What solution does the artist propose in the caption? Which groups did the creator of Source 11 hope would seize political power? Does the same message appear in Source 9? Who is being buried? What does his body represent? Notice the clothing and grooming of the pallbearers. Can you identify the occupational groups that the artist hopes will seize power after the burial?

The Czechoslovakians also had a political vision. Review Sources 13 and 14. What political outlook do these statements express? What groups did Czechoslovakian reformers expect to lead change? Combine this message with Source 15. How do the reformers regard their chances for success? How were the political visions of the French and Czechoslovakian reformers similar?

Both movements also expressed images of their opponents and the methods to be employed in their struggles. What sort of action does the artist of Source 7 recommend to the French? What secondary message do you think underlies the portrayal of the fighter as a woman? Source 8 shows a close-up view of a Parisian paving stone. What message do you find in its accompanying statement? In Sources 6 and 12, we find some statements of the reformers' view of the opposition and its power. Why do you think the artist pictured a silhouette of a tank in Source 6? The final French selection, Source 12, is a cartoon that appeared on the cover of *L'enragé* after the defeat of the students and workers. What significance do you find in the portrayal of de Gaulle? What has crippled him? What supports him? What view of the government does the shape of his crutches convey?

The Czechoslovakian sources also characterize the reformers' opposition and their chances of success. In Source 15 what does the woman's obvious pregnancy represent? When does Dubček predict the birth? How long did the Czechoslovakian experiment in greater democracy actually last? What does Dubček's strange activity in Source 16 convey about the artist's view of the future? Sources 18 and 19 are cartoons that appeared as the Soviet Union and its Warsaw Pact allies invaded Czechoslovakia. The inspiration for Source 18 is the painting by Eugène Delacroix, *Liberty Leading the People,* in which a bare-breasted female Liberty (in a Phrygian cap) leads revolutionaries to freedom. In our cartoon the artist, however, portrays Liberty as Walter Ulbricht, the head of the East German Communist party. What is the artist's view of the friendship of this Liberty? The cartoon also employs a modified version of the motto of the French Revolution of 1789, "*Liberté,*

Chapter 14
The Perils of
Prosperity:
The Unrest of
Youth in
the 1960s

Egalité, Fraternité" ("Liberty, Equality, Brotherhood"), rendered as *"Liberté, Egalité, Freundschaft"* (German for "friendship"). Considering the preceding twenty-five years of European history, why might the artist have used French for "Liberty" and "Equality" while using German for the last word? Why is Brezhnev/ Florian in Source 19 pouring water on a house representing Czechoslovakia (CSSR: Czechoslovak Socialist Republic)? Why does Dubček object? What significance do you ascribe to the difference in the two figures' sizes?

The last cartoon, Source 20, reflects Czechoslovakia in defeat. Many alleged that making peace with the country's Russian conquerors would be simple: "It is only a matter of a few tactical steps back!" Where do the steps backward lead in this case? What does this tell us about the fate of the reform movement? What common sentiment do you detect in the French and Czechoslovakian evidence regarding the reformers' chances for meaningful success in the face of the modern state?

Answering these questions should prepare you to formulate your replies to the central questions of this chapter: What aspects of the modern state and economy provoked the events of 1968? What vision of the future did leaders of the French and Czechoslovakian movements embrace? How did they propose to achieve it?

EPILOGUE

As you continue your reading on the history of Western civilization through the events of the 1970s, 1980s, and 1990s it will become clear that the student unrest in France and other parts of Western Europe as well as events in Czechoslovakia is of enduring importance.

Perhaps in partial response to this agitation, significant political changes occurred in much of the West in the 1970s and 1980s. In most Western democracies, eighteen-year-olds won the vote. In many countries, too, at least a partial reversal of political centralization began, perhaps in some measure stemming from youthful demands for more "power to the people." This impulse to diminish state authority defied ideological labels: in France and Sweden it was begun by socialist governments, whereas in the United States it has been the work of conservative administrations. No country, however, has yet approached the French students' vision of autogestion.

In France, where student movements amassed the broadest nonstudent support, other changes occurred. His power tarnished by the events of 1968, de Gaulle resigned within a year of the student strikes over a minor issue of government reform. Universities and their curricula were radically restructured in an attempt to meet some student demands, and working conditions in the factories were improved. Even in France, however, fundamental educational and industrial policy remained firmly in the hands of government officials and corporate managers. Student political activism and bitter labor disputes, many originating in issues raised in 1968, persist.

Elsewhere, the student revolt garnered less support, produced fewer changes, and led some frustrated student radicals to turn their energies from protest to brutal political violence in the 1970s. In West Germany, some student radicals formed terrorist groups like the Baader-Meinhof gang, which lashed out violently at West German symbols of the conservative consumer society and American military installations. The Red Brigades terrorist groups in Italy had the same roots and objectives.

In the 1980s youthful discontent in Western Europe partially manifested itself in the Green movement. Especially strong in West Germany, this movement represents the continued alienation of many from the West's industrial economy and modern society. The Green movement attacks the effects of modern industry on our environment and particularly the failure of traditional governing parties effectively to address environmental issues. The Greens in West Germany also have advocated an end to their country's participation in the North Atlantic Treaty Organization (NATO). While not always well organized, Greens entered the political life of a number of countries and by 1992 had elected members to parliaments in Germany and Switzerland as well as to the European Parliament.

Eastern Europe felt the effects of Soviet actions in Czechoslovakia in 1968 for two decades, as those seeking political, economic, and social change in that region consciously confined reform within the boundaries established by the Brezhnev Doctrine. Discontent with communist rule and Soviet domination, however, grew in the 1980s led by the rise in Poland of an independent, noncommunist labor movement, Solidarity. By the late 1980s events in the Soviet Union also actually fostered change in Eastern Europe. Soviet President Mikhail Gorbachev (1985–1991) proclaimed a policy of *glasnost* (openness) and *perestroika* (restructuring) and abandoned the Brezhnev Doctrine, allowing Eastern European nations to determine their own destinies. The result was a largely peaceful revolution in 1989, when one-party communist political systems collapsed in Poland, Hungary, East Germany, Romania, and Czechoslovakia. Indeed, by the end of 1991, the ultimate result of Gorbachev's new path was the dissolution of the Soviet Union and its one-party communist political system, replaced by the Commonwealth of Independent States. Events in Czechoslovakia provide an example of the rapidity of Eastern European change in 1989 and remind us of the enduring importance of the events of 1968 in promoting that change.

In Czechoslovakia the rigid, one-party communist rule reimposed by Soviet arms in 1968 proved particularly resistant to change. The government dealt harshly with those favoring change: 500,000 dissidents lost their party memberships, hundreds of thousands of others linked with reform endured exclusion from professional employment for which they

Chapter 14

The Perils of

Prosperity:

The Unrest of

Youth in

the 1960s

were qualified, and Dubček found himself demoted to work as a mechanic. Nevertheless, opposition continued. In January 1977, a number of dissidents established Charter 77 to pressure the government to respect human rights. Its leaders included the playwright Václav Havel and the philosopher Jan Patocka. Havel spent five years in prison for his reform efforts and Patocka died after police questioning, but by the mid-1980s the success of Solidarity in Poland and the reforms of Gorbachev in the Soviet Union inspired new hope for change.

In 1988 widespread demonstrations against the communist regime began, despite the authorities' consistently forceful responses to this dissent. The year 1989 opened with a massive demonstration commemorating the twentieth anniversary of the death of the student Jan Palach protesting the loss of the Prague Spring reforms. Indeed, a demonstration by students was key in bringing down the communist government. On November 17, 1989, the authorities permitted a seemingly harmless student observance in Prague of the fiftieth anniversary of an act of student resistance to Czechoslovakia's occupation by Germany in World War II. The commemorative event quickly turned into a demonstration for greater democracy that drew 100,000 participants. Armed riot police brutally dispersed the unarmed crowd, seriously injuring 291 and arresting over 100 persons. But the brutality revolted the country, especially as unfounded rumors of a student death circulated, and opposition to the government dramatically rose. Students seized university buildings. Reformers, led by Havel, who had recently been released from prison, founded Civic Forum in the Czech lands and Public Against Violence in Slovakia to coordinate resistance. A general strike on November 27 brought the country to a virtual halt and additional demonstrations for democracy were widespread in late November and in December. Faced with great opposition, Communist party leaders finally relinquished power in late December. The country's legislature selected a new presiding officer for its deliberations, Alexander Dubček, the reformer of 1968, and a new president for the country, the playwright Václav Havel. In what has been called the "Velvet Revolution" because so little bloodshed occurred, Czechoslovakia reestablished the democratic system it had lost in the coup of 1948. The newly democratic Czechoslovakia was not safe, however, from some of the problems that had undone its former communist regime. By 1992 longstanding nationalist tensions between the country's two chief minority groups, the Czechs and the Slovaks, pushed the country toward a break into two separate nation-states. Thus, many of the issues of 1968, here, as elsewhere, still affect the West.

CHAPTER FIFTEEN

ETHNIC NATIONALISM AND

THE CHALLENGE TO THE STATE:

THE EXAMPLE OF

THE FORMER SOVIET UNION

THE PROBLEM

In the late 1980s, Western nations, especially the United States, greeted the end of the Cold War with self-congratulatory jubilation. U.S. President George Bush hoped the end of Cold War tensions would lead to a "new world order" of peace, stability, and prosperity. Some Western political leaders even spoke of a "peace dividend," in which funds previously spent for armaments could be redirected into social programs or used to reduce government deficits. Indeed, not since the end of World War II in 1945 had the West been so optimistic about a future of peace and stability.

The years since the Cold War's end, however, have not fulfilled the vision of President Bush and other statesmen. These years, instead, have brought into stark focus a growing problem that repeatedly has disrupted the stability and peace that statesmen hoped would characterize the post–Cold War era. That new problem is ethnic nationalism, and it requires some explanation.

Your study of modern Western civilization frequently has emphasized the power of nationalism to shape events, and you have seen it often as a creative force, for example, forging the unified German and Italian states in the nineteenth century. Historians and statesmen alike often have referred to such political units as Germany and Italy as "nation-states," that is, independent political units or states composed of one national or ethnic group speaking the same language and sharing the same culture. But historians and statesmen often ignored a key aspect of modern nation-state creation: in many cases the modern nation-state represented the imposition of the culture and language of a majority national group on one or more minority ethnic groups.

Chapter 15

Ethnic

Nationalism and

the Challenge

to the State:

The Example

of the Former

Soviet Union

Thus the majority created the false impression of unity in the country. In reality many minority groups retained intense devotion to their distinct cultures and languages, a form of nationalism called *ethnic nationalism.*

The second half of the twentieth century has witnessed a dramatic growth in ethnic nationalism, not in nationalism devoted to the ideal of the large nation-state. Ethnic nationalism emphasizes the role of ethnic identity in shaping an individual and claims the primary loyalty of the individual for the ethnic group. Ethnic nationalism can assume many forms. It may be expressed simply in ethnic pride and the desire to preserve national culture and language, but in its most explosive form, it is a strident and intolerant nationalism that violently demands automony within the state or independence from it, no matter how small the ethnic group.

Modern ethnic nationalism appears with particular force among ethnic groups that have not been integrated into the dominant culture of the state and that have suffered past injustices. Particularly stirring for such ethnic groups can be memories of past independence and glory. And certainly the end of the Cold War seems to have contributed to the recent upsurge of ethnic nationalism by releasing many states from the necessity of maintaining absolute unity among their citizens in the face of a common threat. Modern media also allow the wide dissemination of ethnic nationalism with the result that such nationalism is widespread throughout the late-twentieth-century world.

Ethnic tensions, often accompanied by violence, have affected established, democratic states, including Belgium, Canada, France, Great Britain, and Spain, as well as developing countries like Burundi, India, Rwanda, and Sri Lanka. Ethnic nationalism recently has led to the dissolution of modern states, too. Czechoslovakia divided peacefully into the Czech Republic and Slovakia on January 1, 1993, while Yugoslavia's ethnic groups began a bitter war in 1991 over division of that former multiethnic republic's territory. But undoubtedly the most significant result of ethnic nationalism in recent years is the dissolution of the Union of Soviet Socialist Republics (USSR), or Soviet Union, one of the superpowers of the post–World War II world. In order to understand that dissolution, we must examine the policies of the Soviet Union toward its national groups.

The communist victors in the Russian Revolution of 1917 and the subsequent civil war took control of a state composed of many national groups. Before being overthrown in 1917, the tsarist regime had built an empire stretching across eastern Europe and Asia, from Poland to the Pacific, that embraced well over two hundred language groups and adherents of many religious faiths. The nineteenth-century tsars had attempted to weld these ethnic groups into a unified state by a policy of Russification, that is, a policy that forced the empire's ethnic groups to adapt to the institutions, language, and culture of the Russians, the state's largest and most dominant national group. For much of its history, the Soviet Union practiced a policy toward its ethnic groups not far different from that of the tsars. That policy was a product of communist ideology and the practical administrative demands that confronted the successful revolutionaries.

The writings of the founders of modern communism, Karl Marx and Friedrich Engels, portrayed national identity as an increasingly outmoded phenomenon in the industrialized world, and saw human society ultimately divided along class rather than national lines:

> The working men have no country. . . . National differences are daily more and more vanishing owing to the development of the bourgeoisie, to freedom of commerce, to the world market, to uniformity in the mode of production and in the conditions of life corresponding thereto.[1]

V. I. Lenin (1870–1924), the leader of the Revolution of 1917, certainly accepted this view, but until such ethnic unity could be achieved in what Lenin optimistically called an "international culture," the unified state was essential. He wrote: "A centralized large State is an immense historic step forward from Medieval disunion to the future Socialist unity of the whole world and otherwise than through such a State. . . . there is not, nor can there be, any path to socialism."[2]

1. Karl Marx and Friedrich Engels, *The Communist Manifesto* (New York: Penguin Books, 1967), p. 102.
2. V. I. Lenin, *Sochineniya*, 3rd edition (Moscow: Publishing House of the Central Committee of the VKP(b)), vol. 17, p. 154, quoted in Robert Conquest, *Soviet Nationalities Policy in Practice* (New York: Frederick A. Praeger, 1967), p. 17.

Lenin and his colleagues, however, confronted the problem of administering a state that was in danger of disintegration in 1917–1920. Civil war raged as anticommunist "White" forces, with the aid of France, Great Britain, and the United States, battled the "Red" army of the new government. Moreover, a large number of ethnic minorities sought to realize their aspirations of national independence as the tsarist regime collapsed. The Finns, Estonians, Latvians, Lithuanians, and Poles successfully asserted their independence from Russian rule, and the Romanian population of present-day Moldova linked its homeland to Romania. Belarussians, Ukrainians, Tartars, Georgians, Armenians, Azerbaijanis, and Turkmen also sought to escape Russian rule.

Only reluctantly, in order to prevent the dissolution of Russia, did Lenin agree to restructure the country as a state organized along federal lines whose components would be defined by their ethnic composition. One week after seizing power, Lenin and his associates issued a "Declaration of the Rights of the Peoples of Russia" proclaiming new freedom for non-Russians in the hope that this concession would hold the state together. And the constitution of the Soviet Union (1924) in principle accorded autonomy and free development to all ethnic groups within a state of thirteen republics (fifteen by the collapse of the USSR). But this policy of autonomy for the national groups of the USSR never achieved practical expression in the state's history. The Soviet Union was a state

Chapter 15

Ethnic

Nationalism and

the Challenge

to the State:

The Example

of the Former

Soviet Union

with only one legal party, the Communist party, which was largely dominated by Russians; the federal system became a façade for a centralized state largely under Russian control.

Thus, in its early years, the Soviet regime forcefully opposed separatist movements despite the promise of self-determination for all ethnic groups in the "Declaration of the Rights of the Peoples of Russia" and the right of secession from the USSR contained in its constitution. Under Joseph Stalin (1879–1953), Lenin's successor as party leader and head of government, the Soviet state became increasingly committed to Russification. The state and party condemned any cultural expression of ethnic nationalism as "bourgeois," while enforcing the use of the Russian Cyrillic alphabet in place of Arabic script in Muslim parts of the Soviet Union. After 1938, the study of the Russian language became obligatory in all schools, and, although non-Russian instruction continued in non-Russian areas, it was widely available only in primary and secondary schools. Little university instruction occurred in non-Russian tongues, and non-Russian students experienced discrimination in university admissions.

The Stalinist regime employed force against non-Russian groups, too. On the eve of World War II, the Soviet Union signed the Molotov-Ribbentrop Pact (1939) with Hitler's Germany that allowed the Soviets forcibly to reincorporate into the USSR the former Russian imperial territories of eastern Poland, the Romanian territories of Bessarabia and Bukovina, and the independent Baltic states of Estonia, Latvia, and Lithuania. Non-Russians inhabited all of these areas, and in all of them the Soviets killed or exiled to Siberia anticommunist leaders. In the face of German attacks during World War II, the Stalinist regime also used terror tactics against non-Russian citizens whose loyalty it mistrusted. Thus the government forcibly relocated to Asia the Volga Germans (descendants of eighteenth-century German settlers), Crimean Tartars, Chechens, Ingushi, Kalmyks, Karachai, and Balkars under dreadful conditions that killed large numbers of people.

The seeds of the nationality problems that destroyed the USSR had been sown, and there was ethnic resistance to these Stalinist policies. For example, many of the non-Russian peoples of the western Soviet Union, especially in the Baltic states and Ukraine, initially perceived the World War II German invaders as liberators from Soviet rule and aided them. Indeed, even at the war's end, the Stalin regime had to fight for several years against an armed resistance to restored Soviet rule in Ukraine.

In 1953 Stalin's death brought some changes in Soviet policy toward non-Russian citizens. The regimes of Nikita S. Khrushchev (First Secretary of the Central Committee of the Communist party, 1953–1964) and Leonid Brezhnev (First Secretary, 1964–1992) abandoned the mass terror of the Stalinist years, but nonetheless pursued policies adversely affecting ethnic minorities. In order to maintain control of the country without Stalinist terror, both regimes increased the number of Russian party loyalists in the state and party apparatus, and Khrushchev attempted to speed up the Russification of the Soviet Union's nationalities by de-emphasizing instruction in non-Russian languages.

Other issues also challenged the Soviet leadership. During the Brezhnev regime, the economic, social, and political problems of the Soviet system became increasingly apparent. The state continued to emphasize heavy industry instead of the production of consumer goods, and the collectivized agriculture created by Stalin provided no incentive for efficient production. As a result, at a time when Soviet citizens had better incomes than ever before, they found little on which to spend their money. Chronic shortages of foodstuffs and consumer goods plagued a country rich in natural resources, and Soviet citizens spent many hours each week lined up to buy scarce essential goods.

These economic problems were the result of a rigidly centralized, state-planned economy that was unresponsive to consumer needs. This was, moreover, an economic system quite resistant to change. Brezhnev himself opposed experimentation in policy, and the complex bureaucracy of economic planning and the guaranteed employment of workers also discouraged innovation as well as efficiency. As a result, economic growth actually slowed in the later Brezhnev years.

At the same time, the Brezhnev regime also suffered from governmental problems. Top Communist party leadership was aging, and the party's structure, based on patronage for advancement, promoted a cadre of second-echelon leaders and administrators lacking vigor. As a result, the Brezhnev regime encountered increasing dissent beginning in the 1970s, despite media censorship. An underground press, the *samizdat* (self-publishing) press, flourished and urged greater attention to human rights, as did Dr. Andrei Sakharov, the country's most-honored scientist.

Much dissent also came from ethnic minorities. Soviet Jews, the victims of anti-Semitism, demonstrated for the right to emigrate to Israel. Volga Germans sought to leave the USSR for the Federal Republic of Germany. Crimean Tartars demanded to return to their homeland. In the Baltic states, sentiment for independence became increasingly public; and in the southern parts of the country, Sufi Muslim brotherhoods, the expression of a religious and philosophical movement a thousand years old, kept alive interest in a pre-Soviet Muslim past. At the same time, latter-day Islamic fundamentalists diffused a new, anti-Soviet religious ideology to a Muslim population growing more rapidly than that of the Russians of the USSR.

The Brezhnev regime responded to dissidents with imprisonment, confinement in mental institutions, and, in the case of Dr. Sakharov, internal exile in the city of Gorky. These steps did little to stifle dissent before Brezhnev's death in late 1982. Brief administrations by aging party leaders Yuri Andropov and Konstantin Chernenko from 1982 to 1985 were

Chapter 15

Ethnic

Nationalism and

the Challenge

to the State:

The Example

of the Former

Soviet Union

followed by the Communist party's selection of Mikhail Gorbachev as its new secretary.

Gorbachev vigorously attacked the problems of the Soviet Union, but faced growing challenges. At first he tried to revitalize the party by weeding out corruption and uninspired leadership. He achieved little success in this; indeed, his efforts resulted in the appointments of even more Russians to key positions. When a Russian replaced the native leader of the Kazakhstan party in 1986, there was nationalist rioting in that republic's capital of Alma Ata that cost the lives of perhaps 250 people.

Gorbachev next announced revolutionary policies of *perestroika*, or restructuring of the economy to make it more productive, and *glasnost*, a new openness in Soviet society characterized by a relaxation of censorship. Gorbachev also pursued a policy of allowing greater democracy, and in 1989 he gave up the Communist party's monopoly of the political process by allowing contested elections to a new legislature, the Congress of People's Deputies. Although 80 percent of the Communist party's candidates were elected to this body, the significance of this event was lost on few: for the first time in eight decades voters were asked to do something more than merely ratify the Communist party's candidates. These policies encouraged greater expression of dissent, as did the policies of Foreign Minister Eduard Schevardnadze, whose success in improving relations with the United States did much to diminish a Cold War seige mentality among many Soviets that had re-

strained expressions of opposition to the regime in the past. The unity of the Communist party dissolved as it divided into three major factions: conservatives wishing little or no change; Gorbachev's supporters; and democrats, led by Boris Yeltsin, who sought free elections, a free market economy, and seemed prepared to accord real self-determination to the ethnic groups of the Soviet Union. New parties proliferated as Gorbachev allowed noncommunist parties to operate in 1990 by repealing Article 6 of the USSR constitution which had accorded the Communist party the "leading role" in politics.

These reforms did little to stem ethnic unrest. In nearly every part of the USSR, nationalist agitation grew and, often, ethnic tensions mounted. Nationalist agitation began in the Baltic republics where Estonians, Latvians, and Lithuanians, recalling their brief period of modern independence from 1920 to 1940, began to organize to gain greater autonomy or even independence from the Soviet Union. These peoples feared eventually losing their national identities if they remained part of the USSR and subject to continued Russian immigration. Baltic nationalism culminated in Lithuania's declaration of independence from the USSR in March 1990. Estonia and Latvia soon followed Lithuania. Gorbachev at first tried to resist the Baltic independence movement, but soon other nationalities of the USSR also moved to control their own destinies.

In the Caucasus region of the south, ethnic nationalist sentiment rose, too. Armenians and Georgians recalled earlier periods of national independence, which they sought to resume, and Muslim thought highlighted ethnic distinctions for other peoples, like the Azerbaijanis, who had never enjoyed their own nation-state. Soon Gorbachev confronted nationalist problems in this region, too. Armed conflict between the Christian Armenians and the Muslim Azerbaijanis broke out in 1988 over the Armenian area of Nagorno-Karabakh, a part of Azerbaijan since 1921.

There even was growing nationalism in Central Asia, a region of nomadic tribes with little or no history of former national independence among its peoples when the Russians incorporated it into the tsarist empire. Much of this ethnic nationalism was rooted in Russia's treatment of Central Asia. The region historically had been administered by the Russians as almost a colony, to be exploited for its natural resources.

This ethnic nationalism presented an increasing threat to the unity of the USSR, and conservative, old-line communists and certain elements of the Red Army attempted to preserve the centralized Soviet state in a coup d'état in August 1991. The military detained Gorbachev at his vacation home while troops supporting the coup moved into Moscow to seize control of the government. The coup failed due to the resistance of Moscow's people, led by Boris Yeltsin, who had become president of the largest component of the USSR, the Russian Federation. But the coup hastened the end of the Soviet Union, the very entity its leaders had sought to maintain. One by one the republics followed their nationalist impulses and seceded from the Soviet Union. In December 1991, Russia, Belarus, and Ukraine, three former republics of the USSR with a common Slavic language heritage, took the lead in forming a new Commonwealth of Independent States to which all of the other former Soviet republics, except Estonia, Latvia, and Lithuania, ultimately adhered. On December 25, 1991, Mikhail Gorbachev resigned as president of the USSR, and that state ceased to exist.

The lot of the states that emerged from the old USSR has not been easy. The new republics of the Commonwealth were torn by violent ethnic strife. At the inception of the Commonwealth, armed conflicts included the Armenian-Azerbaijani struggle over Nagorno-Karabakh; a confused conflict in Georgia that was in part Georgian civil war and in part a Georgian conflict with other ethnic groups, including Ossetians and Abkhazians; and a struggle in Moldova between the ruling ethnic Romanians and Russian and Gagauz minorities determined to remain part of Russia. But the bloodiest ethnic conflict within a Commonwealth republic erupted in Russia itself.

Included within Russia is the oil-rich, Muslim region of Chechnya in the Caucasus Mountains. The 1.3 million Chechens have a long history of resistance to Russian domination, and in 1991 they announced their secession from the Russian Federation. Unwilling to lose this strategically important border region, and fearing that Chechen secession would encourage other ethnic groups to

Chapter 15

Ethnic

Nationalism and

the Challenge

to the State:

The Example

of the Former

Soviet Union

leave the Russian Federation, President Yeltsin ordered the Russian Army to seize the Chechen capital of Grozny. That attack began a bloody and enduring conflict between Russian forces and Chechen nationalists marked by guerilla warfare and a Chechen seizure of Russian hostages at Budyonnovsk in June 1995, which cost 140 lives. Most ominously, in 1995 the Chechens also threatened to detonate nuclear materials in Russian population centers.

The former components of the USSR experienced problems in their relations with each other, too, as they ended their old economic and military ties. The Baltic States, for example, long had been dependent on other Soviet republics for oil at low prices. Independence forced them to pay their old suppliers higher, world-level prices for their oil. Ukraine and the Russian Federation found themselves at loggerheads over ownership of the Black Sea Fleet. Both countries wanted the large fleet, but clearly Ukraine could not afford to maintain it. Disagreement between the two countries kept the fleet decaying in port for several years. These and a host of other issues mean that the dissolution of the Soviet Union will present continuing problems for its former citizens.

Your problem in this chapter is to examine modern ethnic nationalism as it manifests itself in the former Soviet Union. What were the origins of modern ethnic nationalism in the former USSR? In what forms can modern ethnic nationalism be expressed? Why does ethnic nationalism present a danger to the modern national state?

SOURCES AND METHOD

This final chapter, like all of the others in *Discovering the Western Past*, assembles a diverse body of evidence that will require you to employ several different kinds of historical analyses in its interpretation. To facilitate your analytical task, certain background information on the individual sources is essential.

Source 1, the "Declaration of the Rights of the Peoples of Russia," was issued by the communist regime of Lenin on November 15, 1917, as the new government's statement on the treatment of the national groups of the old tsarist empire. The work of a ruling party in what soon would become a one-party state confronted with dissolution along ethnic lines, this declaration must be analyzed carefully. What sort of rights did Lenin and his colleagues promise Russia's ethnic groups? How did this body of rights accord with Lenin's views on the need for a centralized state? How did this declaration influence subsequent Soviet policy toward national groups in the Union? Why would you consider this document a piece of propaganda rather than a statement of actual, or intended, government policy?

Source 2 is a political map of the former Union of Soviet Socialist Republics. Maps like this can tell us much about a country's political and ethnic structure. As we have seen, the former Soviet Union in principle was a state organized in a federal system, and the borders of its component political units were intended to coincide with the regions inhabited by the country's ethnic groups. The political division of the former USSR, which the map presents, reveals to us a veritable hierarchy of ethnic groups. The largest national groups resided in their own union republics that, in principle, were politically autonomous units with the right of secession from the union. The largest of the fifteen union republics, the Russian Soviet Federated Socialist Republic (RSFSR), was created for the Russians, the largest single ethnic group in the union. But note that the map shows other political units as well.

In principle, autonomous republics provided homelands to ethnic groups not as large as those constituting the fifteen union republics, although in practice many autonomous republics had as much or more population, territory, or industry as union republics. Clearly politics played a role in determining status. Smaller ethnic groups resided in autonomous *oblasts* (provinces), and the smallest groups possessed their own autonomous *okrugs* (districts, the basic administrative units into which the entire union was divided). There were, however, many incongruities in this arrangement, and only 53 of the 127 recognized nationalities of the union had territorial identities. Observe the map carefully. What do you note about the ethnic composition of the fifteen union republics? Why would it be difficult to divide the USSR along the lines of these fifteen republics?

In Chapter 4, you analyzed some demographic data consisting of birth and death rates that were reconstructed by historians from eighteenth-century parish registers of baptisms and burials. Sources 3, 4, and 5 in the present chapter offer the results of a modern census. This 1989 census was the last one conducted before the dissolution of the Soviet Union. Source 3 is an ethnic map of the Soviet Union showing the percentage of the total population represented by the largest ethnic group in each *oblast* of the country. Why might this map indicate potential for ethnic conflict if the largest single ethnic group in a particular area sought to enforce the use of its language on all inhabitants of its region? Source 4 is a table presenting the ethnic population of the fifteen republics that emerged from the USSR by 1991. How many of these states are ethnically homogeneous in population? What sort of ethnic tensions do the data in Source 4 lead you to predict in these republics? Calculate the number of ethnic Russians living throughout the Soviet Union and the number of them dwelling in the republics outside the RSFSR. What portion of the Union's population of 285,743,000 persons did Russians represent in 1989? Contrast the numerical position of Russians with the political role that they have played within the USSR. What political conclusions can you draw from your findings?

Next turn to Source 5, which offers birth, death, and net growth rates for the Soviet Union from 1970 to 1989. What happened to the birth rate in the western republics (Russia,

Chapter 15

Ethnic

Nationalism and

the Challenge

to the State:

The Example

of the Former

Soviet Union

Ukraine, Belorussia, Moldavia, Lithuania, Latvia, Estonia) in that period? What happened to birth rates in the southern and eastern republics (Georgia, Azerbaijan, Armenia, Kazakhstan, Uzbekistan, Kyrgyzstan, Tajikistan, and Turkmenistan)? Which republics have the highest growth rates? Consult Source 4 to determine the ethnic composition of these republics. Why could you feel confident in predicting that Russians would soon have represented only a minority in the population of the Soviet Union had it survived as a unified state? What political ramifications can you draw from your findings? How would your conclusions on the political stability of the USSR be affected when you learn that Islam is the majority religion in Azerbaijan, Kazakhstan, Kyrgyzstan, Tajikistan, and Turkmenistan? Finally, recall that death rates, and especially the infant mortality rate, are measures of how well a society is doing in providing adequate public health for its citizens. Why might you conclude that standards of public health seemed to have declined over the last two decades of the existence of the USSR? Why do you think a decline indicated institutional and economic problems in the USSR? Do you find that all the republics appear to have had equal access to health care based on infant mortality rate figures? What political conclusions might you draw from your answers to the previous two questions? Compare the infant mortality rate in the republics of the USSR in 1989 with that in Western industrialized nations (some examples for 1994 expressed in deaths per 1,000

new-borns: Finland, 5 per 1,000; Sweden, 6 per 1,000; Belgium, France, Germany, and the United Kingdom, 7 per 1,000; and the United States, 10 per 1,000). How might Soviet citizens have felt about their social and economic system by 1989 in light of these figures?

Sources 6, 7, 8, and 9 ask you to assess some of the ways in which ethnic nationalism was maintained and grew in the face of a deliberate policy of Russification of ethnic minority groups in the Soviet Union. Source 6 comes from the underground press that flourished in the last decades of the Soviet Union's existence, the *samizdat* press. Produced cheaply with mimeograph machines and other basic technologies, and distributed clandestinely to avoid government censors, *samizdat* publications were outlets for the opinions of both political and ethnic dissidents.

The *Ukrainian Herald* was one of those *samizdat* publications. It began to appear in January 1970 and came to be edited by a Ukrainian nationalist writing under the pseudonym "Maxim Sahaydak" to avoid police detection. Published in the Ukrainian language, the *Ukrainian Herald* aimed to keep that tongue alive in the face of Russification attempts by the Soviet government, but also to maintain a vision of a democratic and free Ukraine by publishing both news and Ukrainian literature. The *Ukrainian Herald* ceased publication in 1972, after six issues had been published, when a crackdown by the KGB (Secret Police) sent hundreds of Ukrainian intellectuals to labor camps, prisons, and psychiatric hospitals. It reappeared in 1974 with Issues 7 and 8, and opened with the manifesto published as Source 6. How do the Ukrainian editors believe their people had been treated in a Russian-dominated Soviet Union? What is their objective in publishing the *Herald*? What do they call on their readers to do? How could the readers help their cause?

Source 7 is from Lithuania, a heavily Catholic country where, as in Ireland, the Church is closely identified with nationalist sentiment. Thus, one of the foremost *samizdat* publications in the language of Lithuania was *The Chronicle of the Catholic Church in Lithuania*. Source 7 is a selection from an issue of this journal in 1973 recounting an event from Šiauliai, where there is a hill long covered with crosses brought by Lithuanians as expressions of their faith. Under the officially atheist government of the USSR, such placing of crosses took on political significance as acts of defiance of offical policy. Who do you think were the "atheists" who removed the crosses? Recalling that Lithuania was seized by the Soviet Union in 1940 and was invaded by Nazi Germany in 1941, what significance do you find in the "symbolic ornamentation" on the cross? Why do you think the cross bearers traveled at night? Why do you think they were able to avoid the police?

Source 8 presents a photograph of the Hill of Crosses as it appeared in 1991, shortly after Lithuanian independence. Despite the opposition of Soviet authorities, Lithuanians had placed many crosses on this hill, and in 1977 the number of crosses

reached three thousand. What effect do you think this hill had on Lithuanians during the period of Soviet rule? How do you think this symbol helped preserve Lithuanian ethnic identity?

Source 9 is a second piece of photographic evidence that reminds us that history can have political uses. The Soviet Union seized the Baltic states of Estonia, Latvia, and Lithuania under the Molotov-Ribbentrop Pact that the Soviets signed with Nazi Germany on August 23, 1939. After that seizure, the Soviets consistently maintained that the Baltic states had voluntarily joined the USSR. Source 9 presents the dramatic fiftieth-anniversary commemoration of the Molotov-Ribbentrop Pact. On August 23, 1989, some two million people formed a human chain across the three Baltic states, from the Gulf of Finland to southern Lithuania (a distance of more than 350 miles), to protest the seizure of their countries. Chanting "We want freedom!" the members of the human chain gathered in large numbers at the borders of their countries. Source 9 shows a field on the Estonian-Latvian border. The people in the foreground display the red and white flag of Latvia, and those in the background carry the blue, black, and white Estonian tricolor. How did such a demonstration contradict the official Soviet history of the events of 1939? What impact do you think peaceful demonstrations like the human chain had on the peoples of Estonia, Latvia, and Lithuania?

Source 10 is a document that presents the basic principles of the

Chapter 15

Ethnic

Nationalism and

the Challenge

to the State:

The Example

of the Former

Soviet Union

Estonian National Independence party, one of the key groups in Estonia's drive for independence. What was the opinion of Estonian nationalists on their country's annexation in 1940? What grievances did Estonians have about Soviet rule? What role did the Estonian language play in this nationalist statement? Why do you think Estonians might be concerned about limiting immigration (consult the population figures in Source 4 for assistance in answering this question)? Why do you think Estonian demands might have been echoed elsewhere? What sort of economic system did the Estonian National Independence Party seek? How was this different from that of the USSR? Although this document was drafted in 1988, before the collapse of the Soviet Union, do you find much here that would have been compatible with Estonia's membership in the Soviet Union?

Source 11 is the treaty between Belarus, the Russian Federation, and Ukraine establishing the Commonwealth of Independent States. Treaties, like this one signed in Minsk on December 8, 1991, are fundamental sources for students of history because they have the force of international law and must precisely spell out the commitments their signatories undertake. This treaty was quite significant because all of the other republics of the former Soviet Union, except Estonia, Latvia, and Lithuania, eventually became part of the Commonwealth of Independent States that it established. What became of the USSR under this treaty? What sort of ties between the former republics of the USSR did the treaty create? What abuses of the old Soviet system did the treaty seek to end? What significance do you find in the establishment of Minsk, rather than the old Soviet capital of Moscow, as the "official residence of the coordinating bodies of the Commonwealth"?

Sources 12 and 13 focus on the language laws that every former Soviet republic established. Part of a nation's identity, of course, is its distinct language, and the steps the republics took to assure the primacy of their languages tells us much about nationalist sentiments in them. The central issue in these laws is found in the provisions they made for those who spoke Russian, the language of the old central government of the USSR. This is a key issue because Russians lived in every former USSR republic; you should consult Source 4 to ascertain the size of the Russian populations in Latvia and Kyrgyzstan, the two republics of Sources 12 and 13.

Source 12 is a portion of the language law of Latvia. The law's other provisions deny Latvian citizenship to anyone who is involved in antigovernment activity, has served in the armed forces of the USSR, or has spread communist or totalitarian ideas. Also excluded from citizenship were those permanently unemployed, addicted to drugs, or possessing a criminal record. Taken together, who especially would these provisions seem designed to exclude from citizenship? The Estonian law on language was very similar to that of Latvia; after examining the population data in Source 4 for Estonia, why might you conclude that Latvian and Estonian nationalists probably feared loss of their national identities? Why would you not be surprised to learn that all three of the Baltic Republics are moving to impose immigration limits that include a tax of $22,500 to $37,500 on businesses for each foreign worker they employ?

Other republics' language laws were not as strongly anti-Russian statements as those of Latvia and Estonia, and often included provision for the continued use of Russian, as was the case in Kyrgyzstan. But even in such republics there were problems for Russians. Source 13 presents a radio editorial by Igor Tkanchik, a Russian, broadcast on the English news program in the Kyrgyz capital of Bishkek (population 625,000 in 1990). Such expressions of journalistic opinion often can highlight real problems for students of history. How widespread is Russian language use in Bishkek? Why will the new language law make it possible to exclude Russians from some employment? Although Tkanchik proclaimed his desire to remain in Kyrgyzstan, do you think many ethnic Russians might seek to return to the Russian Federation in such circumstances? Why would you not be surprised to learn that the historic Russian out-migration to the peripheries of the former empire and Soviet Union had dramatically reversed in the 1980s amidst rising ethnic nationalism?

Source 14 presents the results of a changing atmosphere for Russians in the republics with non-Russian majorities and perhaps, more importantly, the results of ethnic violence. The data presented here comes from an American group that tracks refugees worldwide, but they are based on sources in the republics of the former USSR, and you should know that all of the republics lack the resources adequately to process and count large numbers of refugees. Thus these figures must be viewed as estimates at best. Nonetheless, they give us some indication of the problems in the former Soviet Union. In the data sets, the category "former USSR" indicates citizens of the former Soviet Union of unknown ethnic origins, while the category "non–former USSR" indicates refugees from lands outside of the former Union. The largest number of refugees in the latter category are from Afghanistan, where the effects of the Soviet Union's 1979–1988 war against anticommunist insurgents are still felt. If you know that there has been armed ethnic conflict in Armenia, Azerbaijan, Georgia, and Tajikistan, what can you conclude from these refugee figures?

Your objective in this chapter is to understand the origins, force, and consequences of late-twentieth-century ethnic nationalism. As you turn to the evidence presented in this chapter, remember the chapter's central questions. What were the origins of modern ethnic nationalism in the former USSR? In what forms can modern ethnic nationalism be expressed? Why does ethnic nationalism represent a danger to the modern state?

Chapter 15

Ethnic

Nationalism and

the Challenge

to the State:

The Example

of the Former

Soviet Union

THE EVIDENCE

Source 1 from The Nation, *vol. 107, no. 2791 (December 28, 1918), p. 81.*

1. Declaration of the Rights of the Peoples of Russia, November 1917

The October[3] revolution of the workmen and peasants began under the common banner of emancipation.

The peasants are being emancipated from the power of the landowners, for there is no longer the landowner's property right in the land—it has been abolished. The soldiers and sailors are being emancipated from the power of autocratic generals, for generals will henceforth be elective and subject to recall. The workingmen are being emancipated from the whims and arbitrary will of the capitalists, for henceforth there will be established the control of the workers over mills and factories. Everything living and capable of life is being emancipated from the hateful shackles.

There remain only the peoples of Russia, who have suffered and are suffering oppression and arbitrariness, and whose emancipation must immediately be begun, whose liberation must be effected resolutely and definitely.

During the period of czarism the peoples of Russia were systematically incited against one another. The results of such a policy are known: massacres and pogroms[4] on the one hand, slavery of peoples on the other.

There can be and there must be no return to this disgraceful policy of instigation. Henceforth the policy of a voluntary and honest union of the peoples of Russia must be substituted.

In the period of imperialism, after the February revolution, when the power was transferred to the hands of the Cadet[5] bourgeoisie, the naked policy of in-

3. Russia used the Julian calendar, prescribed by Julius Caesar in 46 B.C., until February 1918. By that time, the rest of the West used the Gregorian calendar, introduced by Pope Gregory XIII in 1582. There was a difference of thirteen days between the two calendars by 1917. Thus, on the Julian calendar, the Communist seizure of power occurred on October 25, 1917, while on the Gregorian calendar it occurred on November 7, 1917.

4. **Pogroms:** riots directed against Jews in an atmosphere of growing anti-Semitism and official Russification of minorities in late nineteenth-century Russia. Authorities did little to stop those destructions of Jewish lives and property, and occasionally encouraged pogroms.

5. **Cadets:** popular name for the Constitutional Democratic Party. Founded in 1905, this party initially sought to reform the tsarist regime as a constitutional monarchy. In the Revolution of 1917, its leaders eventually agreed to establishment of a republic and dominated the first Provisional Government cabinet. But the Cadets' support for Russia's continued participation in World War I led to their loss of influence in later precommunist cabinets of 1917. As events of 1917 radicalized the Russian political scene, the Cadets increasingly represented the right in Russian politics. Many Cadets supported the "Whites" in the Russian civil war and therefore were seen by the communists as counterrevolutionaries.

stigation gave way to one of cowardly distrust of the peoples of Russia, to a policy of fault-finding and provocation, of "freedom" and "equality" of peoples. The results of such a policy are known: the growth of national enmity, the impairment of mutual trust.

An end must be put to this unworthy policy of falsehood and distrust, of fault-finding and provocation. Henceforth it must be replaced by an open and honest policy which leads to complete mutual trust of the peoples of Russia. Only as the result of such a trust can there be formed an honest and lasting union of the peoples of Russia. Only as the result of such a union can the workmen and peasants of the peoples of Russia be cemented into one revolutionary force able to resist all attempts on the part of the imperialist-annexationist bourgeoisie.

Starting with these assumptions, the first Congress of Soviets,[6] in June of this year, proclaimed the right of the peoples of Russia to free self-determination.

The second Congress of Soviets, in October of this year, reaffirmed this inalienable right of the peoples of Russia more decisively and definitely.

The united will of these Congresses, the Council of the Peoples' Commissaries, resolved to base their activity upon the question of the nationalities of Russia, as expressed in the following principles:

1. The equality and sovereignty of the peoples of Russia.

2. The right of the peoples of Russia to free self-determination, even to the point of separation and the formation of an independent state.

3. The abolition of any and all national and national-religious privileges and disabilities.

4. The free development of national minorities and ethnographic groups inhabiting the territory of Russia.

The concrete decrees which follow will be framed immediately upon the formation of a commission for the affairs of nationalities.

Source 2 from Robert J. Kaiser, The Geography of Nationalism in Russia and the USSR *(Princeton, N.J.: Princeton University Press, 1994), p. 155.*

2. Federal Structure of the Union of Soviet Socialist Republics, 1989

6. **Soviets:** locally elected councils in the hierarchy of governing bodies in revolutionary Russia and the USSR. The Congress of Soviets of June 1918 contained representatives of over 350 Soviets.

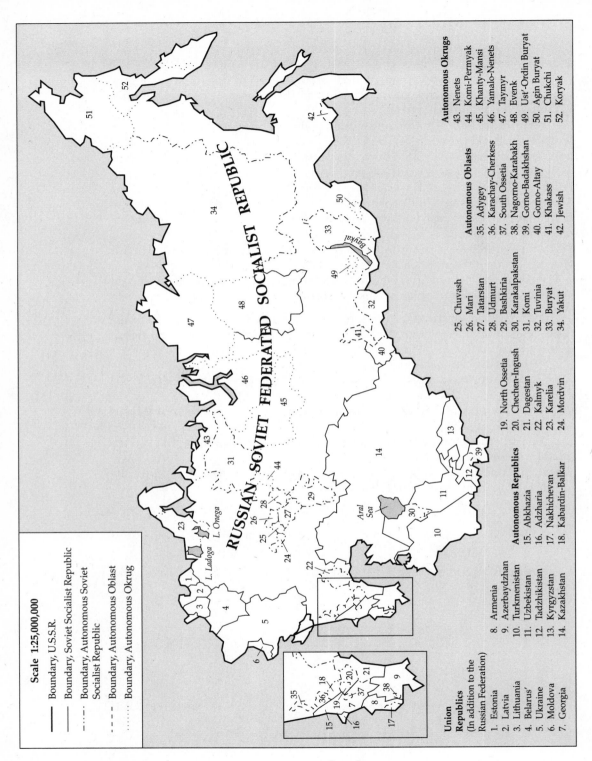

Scale 1:25,000,000

—— Boundary, U.S.S.R.

—— Boundary, Soviet Socialist Republic

—·— Boundary, Autonomous Soviet Socialist Republic

—·—·— Boundary, Autonomous Oblast

········· Boundary, Autonomous Okrug

RUSSIAN SOVIET FEDERATED SOCIALIST REPUBLIC

L. Ladoga
L. Onega
Aral Sea
L. Baykal

Union Republics
(In addition to the Russian Federation)

1. Estonia
2. Latvia
3. Lithuania
4. Belarus'
5. Ukraine
6. Moldova
7. Georgia
8. Armenia
9. Azerbaydzhan
10. Turkmenistan
11. Uzbekistan
12. Tadzhikistan
13. Kyrgyzstan
14. Kazakhstan

Autonomous Republics

15. Abkhazia
16. Adzharia
17. Nakhichevan
18. Kabardin-Balkar
19. North Ossetia
20. Chechen-Ingush
21. Dagestan
22. Kalmyk
23. Karelia
24. Mordvin
25. Chuvash
26. Mari
27. Tatarstan
28. Udmurt
29. Bashkiria
30. Karakalpakstan
31. Komi
32. Tuvinia
33. Buryat
34. Yakut

Autonomous Oblasts

35. Adygey
36. Karachay-Cherkess
37. South Ossetia
38. Nagorno-Karabakh
39. Gorno-Badakhshan
40. Gorno-Altay
41. Khakass
42. Jewish

Autonomous Okrugs

43. Nenets
44. Komi-Permyak
45. Khanty-Mansi
46. Yamalo-Nenets
47. Taymyr
48. Evenk
49. Ust'-Ordin Buryat
50. Agin Buryat
51. Chukchi
52. Koryak

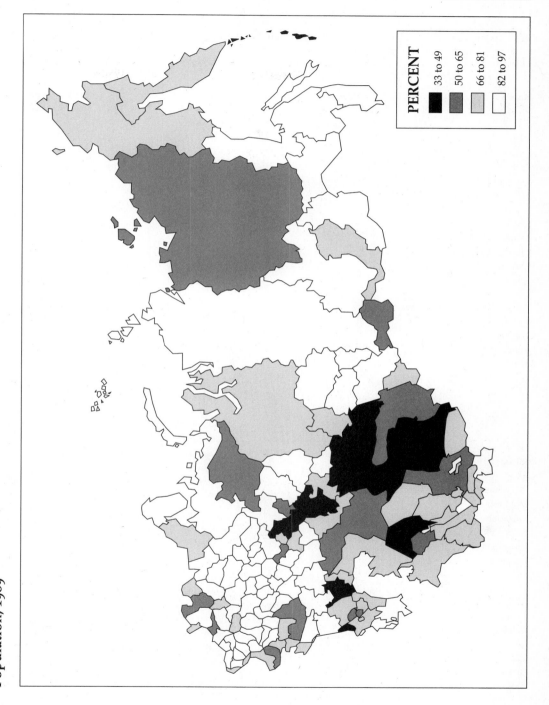

Source 3 from The FirstBook of Demographics for the Republics of the Former Soviet
Union, 1951–1990 *(Shady Side, Md: New World Demographics, L.C., 1992), map supplement.*

**3. Ethnic Diversity Within the Oblasts of the Soviet Union Shown
with the Largest Nationality Group as a Percentage of the Total
Population, 1989**

PERCENT

33 to 49
50 to 65
66 to 81
82 to 97

Source 4 from Vestnik statistiki *10-12/90. 1, 4, 6/91. Reprinted in Archie Brown, Michael Kaser, and Gerald S. Smith, editors,* The Cambridge Encyclopedia of Russia and the Former Soviet Union *(New York: Cambridge University Press, 1995), pp. 26–27.*

4. Ethnic Composition of the Successor States of the Soviet Union in the 1989 Census

Ethnic groups	Population (thousands)	Ethnic groups	Population (thousands)	Ethnic groups	Population (thousands)	Ethnic groups	Population (thousands)
Russia		Tatars	468	**Georgia**		**Lithuania**	
Russians	119,866	Karakalpaks	412	Georgians	3,787	Lithuanians	2,924
Tatars	5,522	Crimean Tatars	189	Armenians	437	Russians	344
Ukrainians	4,363	Koreans	183	Russians	341	Poles	258
Chuvash	1,774	Kyrgyz	175	Azeris	308	Belorussians	63
Bashkir	1,345	Others	846	Ossetes	164	Others	86
Belorussians	1,206			Greeks	100		
Mordva	1,073		19,810	Abkhaz	96		3,675
Chechen	899			Others	168		
Germans	842					**Turkmenistan**	
Udmurt	715	**Kazakhstan**			5,401	Turkmen	2,523
Mari	644	Kasakhs	6,535			Russians	339
Kazakhs	636	Russians	6,228	**Tajikistan**		Uzbeks	317
Avars	544	Germans	958	Tajiks	3,172	Kazakhs	88
Jews	537	Ukrainians	896	Uzbeks	1,198	Others	256
Armenians	532	Uzbeks	332	Russians	388		
Buryats	417	Tatars	328	Tatars	72		3,523
Ossetes	402	Uygurs	185	Others	263		
Kabarda	386	Belorussians	183			**Armenia**	
Yakuts	380	Koreans	103		5,093	Armenians	3,084
Others	4,939	Others	716			Azeris	85
				Moldova		Kurds	56
	147,022		16,464	Moldovans	2,795	Russians	52
				Ukrainians	600	Others	28
Ukraine		**Belarus**		Russians	562		
Ukrainians	37,419	Belorussians	7,905	Gagauz	153		3,305
Russians	11,356	Russians	1,342	Bulgarians	88		
Jews	486	Poles	418	Others	137	**Latvia**	
Belorussians	440	Ukrainians	291			Latvians	1,388
Moldovans	325	Jews	112		4,335	Russians	906
Bulgarians	234	Others	84			Belorussians	120
Poles	219					Ukrainians	92
Hungarians	163		10,152			Others	161
Romanians	135			**Kyrgyzstan**			
Others	675			Kyrgyz	2,230		2,667
				Russians	917		
	51,452	**Azerbaijan**		Uzbeks	550	**Estonia**	
		Azeris	5,805	Ukrainians	108	Estonians	963
		Russians	392	Germans	101	Russians	475
Uzbekistan		Armenians	391	Tatars	70	Ukrainians	48
Uzbeks	14,142	Lezghins	171	Others	282	Belorussians	28
Russians	1,653	Others	262			Finns	17
Tajiks	934				4,258	Others	34
Kazakhs	808		7,021				1,565

[436]

Source 5 from The FirstBook of Demographics for the Republics of the Former Soviet Union, 1951–1990 *(Shady Side, Md.: New World Demographics, L.C., 1992), p. K-2.*

5. Rates of Birth, Death, and Natural Increase or Decrease of Population in the Republics of the Former Soviet Union, 1970–1989

Area	1989 Infant Mortality per 1,000 Births	1989			1988			1985			1980			1970		
		Birth	Death	Net	Birth	Death	Net	Birth	Death	Net	Birth	Death	Net	Birth	Death	Net
USSR	22.7	17.6	10.0	7.6	18.8	10.1	8.7	19.4	10.6	8.8	18.3	10.3	8.0	17.4	8.2	9.2
Russia	17.8	14.6	10.7	3.9	16.0	10.7	5.3	16.5	11.3	5.2	15.9	11.0	4.9	14.6	8.7	5.9
Ukraine	13.0	13.3	11.6	1.7	14.5	11.7	2.8	15.0	12.1	2.9	14.8	11.4	3.4	15.2	8.8	6.4
Belorussia	11.8	15.0	10.1	4.9	16.0	10.1	5.9	16.5	10.6	5.9	16.0	9.9	6.1	16.2	7.6	8.6
Moldavia	20.4	18.9	6.6	12.3	20.9	9.7	11.2	21.9	11.2	10.7	20.0	10.2	9.8	19.4	7.4	12.0
Lithuania	10.7	15.1	10.3	4.8	15.3	10.2	5.1	16.3	10.9	5.4	15.1	10.5	4.6	17.6	8.9	8.7
Latvia	11.1	14.5	12.1	2.4	15.4	12.1	3.3	15.2	13.1	2.1	14.0	12.7	1.3	14.5	11.2	3.3
Estonia	14.7	15.4	11.7	3.7	15.9	11.8	4.1	15.4	12.6	2.8	15.0	12.3	2.7	15.8	11.1	4.7
Georgia	19.6	16.7	8.6	8.1	17.3	9.0	8.3	18.7	8.8	9.9	17.7	8.6	9.1	19.2	7.3	11.9
Azerbaydzhan	26.2	26.4	6.4	20.0	20.5	6.8	13.7	26.7	6.8	19.9	25.2	7.0	18.2	29.2	6.7	22.5
Armenia	20.4	21.6	6.0	15.6	21.6	10.3	11.3	28.8	6.5	22.3	27.5	6.8	20.7	22.1	5.1	17.0
Kazakhstan	25.9	23.0	7.6	15.4	24.6	7.7	16.9	24.9	8.0	16.9	23.8	8.0	15.8	23.4	6.0	17.4
Uzbekistan	37.7	33.3	6.3	27.0	35.1	6.8	28.3	36.8	7.4	29.4	33.8	7.8	26.0	33.6	5.5	28.1
Kirghizistan	32.2	30.4	7.2	23.2	31.2	7.4	23.8	32.0	8.1	23.9	29.6	8.4	21.2	30.5	7.4	23.1
Tadzhikistan	43.2	38.7	6.5	32.2	40.0	7.0	33.0	39.9	7.0	32.9	37.0	8.0	29.0	34.8	6.4	28.4
Turkmenistan	54.7	35.0	7.7	27.3	36.0	7.8	28.2	36.0	8.1	27.9	34.3	8.3	26.0	35.2	6.6	28.6

Chapter 15

Ethnic

Nationalism and

the Challenge

the State:

The Example

of the Former

Soviet Union

Source 6 from Maksym Sahaydk, compiler, The Ukrainian Herald Issue 7–8: Ethnocide of Ukrainians in the USSR, *translated and edited by Olena Saciuk and Bohdan Yasen (Baltimore, Paris, and Toronto: Smoloskyp Publishers, 1976), p. 15.*

6. "Word to the Reader" from the *Ukrainian Herald*

Honored Reader!

For over two years you have not had the opportunity to familiarize yourself with our journal. Possibly, the long wait caused you to lose faith. But there is no power on earth that could kill the free word of a people who refuse to submit. No repressions, however cruel, have the power to break the spirit of Freedom.

And so it is that, under the most difficult circumstances, the next consecutive issue of our journal appears. The trying times have toughened us even more and brought us closer together.

Our journal will take a clearly marked political position, the guiding direction of which will be uncompromising anticolonialism.

We will attempt to further unite around our organ all democratic, anticolonial groups in Ukraine, for it is only in this direction that we can foresee progress in broadening the national liberation struggle and the struggle for democracy.

The success of our struggle is dependent on the mass dissemination of the free press. The circumstances of work which is being done illegally do not permit the editors of our journal and those activists involved in its dissemination to try to solve this problem alone. We see two ways of disseminating the free word. 1. External—broadcasts by foreign radio stations; 2. Internal—this, Dear Reader, is your selfless, profitless, persistent task. So remember the responsibility that falls upon your shoulders. When our journal falls into your hands, do not forget to duplicate and disseminate it by all means at your disposal, keeping in mind, all the while, the rules governing conspiracy. Only under these conditions will we be able to carry out, with joined forces, the proposed assignment we have taken upon ourselves.

So, Dear Comrades,[7] let's go to work!

---

7. **Comrade:** the standard form of address under the one-party communist political system of the Soviet Union.

Source 7 from Nijolė Gražulis, editor and translator, The Chronicle of the Catholic Church in Lithuania: Underground Journal of Human Rights Violations, nos. 1–9, 1972–1974 *(Chicago: Loyola University Press and the Society for the Publication of the Chronicle of the Catholic Church in Lithuania, Inc., 1981), pp. 338–339.*

7. Excerpt from *The Chronicle of the Catholic Church in Lithuania*

ŠIAULIAI

In Lithuania there is a famous fortress hill at Meškuičiai called the Hill of Crosses. At one time it was covered with a great number of crosses erected by many Lithuanians, but atheists have desecrated this sacred place many times, tearing down the crosses and burning them. People however have continued to cart, carry, and erect both large and little crosses on this hill so dear to the heart of every Lithuanian.

The Hill of Crosses had almost recovered from the damage it suffered during the devastation of 1961. Unfortunately, at the end of April, 1973, it was grievously ravaged once more; there was no sign left that once there had been crosses here. The desolate, denuded hill seemed to be waiting for believing hands and loving hearts to once more crown its desecrated head with the symbol of the Redemption—the Cross.

At midnight on May 19, 1973, an unusual procession appeared on the outskirts of the city of Šiauliai. A small group of serious and meditative young men and women were carrying a cross. They walked quietly, pensively, saying the rosary. From time to time the cross, measuring three meters (nine feet and nine inches) and weighing forty-five kilograms (ninety-nine pounds) was transferred from the shoulders of one youth to those of another. The cross was decorated with symbolic ornamentation: a heart pierced by two swords. On the handle of one sword was a swastika, and on the other, a five-pointed star.

Lithuanian youths were carrying the cross, not in the quest of health, but in atonement for the desecration of the Cross and in reparation for the sins of our nation against the Redeemer. They carried the cross as a symbol of victory. On the night of May 19, many people knew about this procession with the cross, and they devoted an hour to prayer and the veneration of the cross. During that hour, many, with hands joined in prayer, carried the Cross of Christ in spirit. All the crossbearers had received Holy Communion the previous evening.

As preparations were being made for this procession with the cross, it was discovered that someone had informed the security police about the proposed journey. Security police agents traveled back and forth throughout the night along the proposed route from Šiauliai to the Hill of Crosses.

Chapter 15

Ethnic

Nationalism and

the Challenge

to the State:

The Example

of the Former

Soviet Union

To the crossbearers, the success of the procession seemed miraculous. At 2:30 A.M. on May 20, 1973, the Hill of Crosses was adorned with a beautiful new cross. Flowers were planted around it, and a candle was lit. Everyone knelt and prayed, "Christ our King, may your kingdom come to our country."

At 6:45 A.M. the sound of an automobile could be heard. The security police rubbed their eyes—all night they had been chasing the cross, and here it was! Evil hands uprooted the cross and hauled it off. By noontime, however, another cross stood in its place. The atheists kept destroying them, but the crosses seemed to sprout from the earth.

Source 8 from ITAR-TASS/SOVFOTO.

8. The Hill of Crosses, Šiauliai, Lithuania

Chapter 15
Ethnic
Nationalism and
the Challenge
to the State:
The Example
of the Former
Soviet Union

Source 9 from SOVFOTO/EASTFOTO.

9. **The Human Chain in the Baltic States, August 23, 1989**

Source 10 from Charles F. Furtado, Jr. and Andrea Chandler, editors, Perestroika in the Soviet Republics: Documents on the National Question *(Boulder, Colo.: Westview Press, 1992), pp. 65–68.*

10. Proposal for the Creation of the Estonian National Independence Party, January 1988

The Communist Party of Estonia has not succeeded in representing the interests of the Estonian people for nearly fifty years. Estonians are currently becoming a minority in Estonia; and the state of the economy, education, culture, and natural environment have reached a point which endangers the very existence of the Estonian people.

For this reason, there has arisen an objective need for an alternative group to represent the interests of the Estonian people. We propose the creation of the Estonian National Independence Party, whose basic goal would be the restoration of freedom and independence to the nation-state of Estonia.

If Estonian national independence had endured, all our vitally important and even minimally important problems would have been solved at Toompea, not in the Kremlin.[8] Neither deportations, forced collectivization, the sending of Estonians to war in Afghanistan,[9] nor the threat of phosphorite mining would have been possible. A nation can best represent and defend its own interests only when it is independent.

Until the independence of the Estonian nation state is regained, the Estonian National Independence Party will defend the interests of the Estonian people in the present political situation, acting as a national opposition party to the Communist Party of Estonia.

We find it necessary to include the following goals in the program of the Estonian National Independence Party:

I: The Restoration of Historic Truth

1. The disclosure and public availability of authentic materials concerning:

a) the creation of the independent Republic of Estonia and the period of independent statehood (the history of the War of Independence, the Peace Treaty of Tartu,[10] national culture, national heroes, etc.); the years 1939–1940

---

8. Toompea is the seat of Estonian government in the capital of Tallinn. The Kremlin is the walled, former residence of the Russian imperial family in Moscow that was the seat of Soviet government until 1991; since 1991 it has housed the governmental offices of the Russian Federation.

9. From 1979 until 1988 the Soviet Union fought a costly war in neighboring Afghanistan to maintain a pro-Soviet government there in the face of a rebellion chiefly led by Islamic fundamentalists. These rebels fought a guerrilla war which the Red Army proved incapable of winning.

10. **Treaty of Tartu:** signed on February 2, 1920 between Estonia and the communist regime in Russia, recognizing the independence of Estonia.

Chapter 15

Ethnic

Nationalism and

the Challenge

to the State:

The Example

of the Former

Soviet Union

and the liquidation of independence; the war years; the attempts in 1944 to restore Estonian independence.

b) the illegal acts of repression carried out against the Estonian people since 1940 (terror, imprisonment, deportations, collectivization, etc.).

II: The Struggle for the Predominance and Increased Influence of the Nationality Indigenous to the Nation-State of Estonia

1. The restoration of the prominence of the Estonian language in everyday life and official business—the adoption of the Estonian language as the official language of Estonia.

2. The enactment of a citizenship law for the Estonian Soviet Socialist Republic [ESSR] (citizenship may be granted automatically to all persons who were citizens of the Republic of Estonia prior to 6 August 1940, and to their descendants; also in certain specified instances to individuals who can speak and write the Estonian language.)

3. Estonian SSR citizenship must guarantee to the citizens of the ESSR certain precedence above other individuals. Only individuals with ESSR citizenship may work within the machinery of the state (the government and other organs of power.) Only individuals with ESSR citizenship will have the right to vote.

4. The obstruction of the large influx of migrants, and the provision for the indigenous Estonian nationality to remain a significant majority in their homeland.

III: The Struggle against the Destruction of the Natural Environment of Estonia

1. The struggle against ruinous mining and the irrational wasting of natural resources, pollution of the air as well as underground and surface waters, and destruction of farmlands.

IV: Economy

1. The reorganization of the inflexible planned economy into a free-market economy.

2. The transition of Estonia to full financial and economic autonomy.

3. The search for opportunities to develop industries with a promising long-term outlook for the twenty-first century.

4. The halting of extensive exploitation (an end to the artificial expansion of industry; and an effort to liquidate currently existing economic anomalies, for which raw materials as well as labor are imported); the development of intensive exploitation.

5. The creation of a sensible system of industry and agriculture (after first becoming acquainted with the know-how of highly developed industrial and agricultural countries), which would guarantee an increase in the standard of living, a wage for the worker, and goods for the consumer.

6. The creation of opportunities for free enterprise (including the restoration of the right to own a farm, along with giving the land for use in perpetuity), the repeal of restrictions on the activity and expansion of private enterprise.

7. The creation of normalized trade relations (on a national as well as private level) between Estonia and foreign nations.

V: *Human Rights*

1. The guarantee of all rights set forth in international agreements (the UN Universal Declaration on Human Rights; the International Pact on Economic, Social, and Cultural Rights; the Final Act of the Conference on Security and Cooperation in Europe; the declaration granting independence to colonial lands and peoples, etc.) both constitutionally and legislatively, and the unquestionable compliance therewith (the freedom of thought, conscience and religion; the right of assembly and association; the right to freedom of opinion and the free expression of those opinions, the right to leave and return to one's homeland, etc.)

2. The creation of humanly decent living conditions in prisons and places of detention. Detention and punishment must not involve the infliction of physical suffering and debasement of human dignity. Citizens of the ESSR found guilty by the courts shall serve their sentences in Estonia.

VI: *Culture and Education*

1. The improvement of primary and higher education to a level which guarantees a real education consistent with current world trends.

2. The establishment of an educational system which conforms to the special character of Estonian culture and nationality.

3. The creation of opportunities and incentives for the unrestricted advancement of Estonian culture (the release of culture from current ideological restraints; free foreign cultural exchange; unrestricted opportunities for education in a foreign country; free access to the achievements of Estonian emigre culture.)

4. The creation of new youth organizations.

5. The granting of cultural autonomy to minority nationalities (Russians, Ukrainians, Byelorussians, Jews, Finns, Germans, etc; their right to establish native language schools, cultural organizations, etc.)

VII: *Health, Social Insurance, and Social Welfare*

1. The assurance of high-quality and effective medical care. Opportunities for private practice and private clinics for doctors.

2. The abolition of social injustice regarding invalids and pensioners, the guarantee of adequate income for them.

3. The creation of decent living conditions; an end to the production of misanthropic living environments. . . .

Chapter 15

Ethnic

Nationalism and

the Challenge

to the State:

The Example

of the Former

Soviet Union

VIII: Armed Forces

1. Citizens of the ESSR will serve their military duty on Estonian soil and in the Estonian language.

2. Individuals whose conscience does not permit them to bear arms shall be given the opportunity for alternative service.

IX: Legislation and Legal Order

1. The development of an election process which guarantees the essential option of choice between several candidates (mandatory debates between candidates.) The Constitution and laws of the ESSR should not necessarily emulate those of the Union, but rather must reflect Estonian cultural tradition, and be adapted to local conditions and requirements; and their authorship must be left to the jurisdiction of the legislative organs of the ESSR. All rights set forth in the Constitution must have legislative backing. . . .

3. The endeavor to have the provisions set forth in this proposal reflected in the Constitution and other legislation of the ESSR.

X: International Representation

1. The pursuit of representation for Estonia in the United Nations Organization.

2. The restoration of Estonian representation in the International Olympic Committee and Estonian diplomatic legations in larger foreign states.

XI: The Declaration of 24 February, the Anniversary of the Establishment of the Independent Republic of Estonia, a National Holiday.

Source 11 from J. L. Black, editor, USSR Documents Annual, 1991: Disintegration of the USSR *(Gulf Breeze, Fla.: Academic International Press, 1993), vol. 2, pp. 299–301.*

11. Agreement on the Creation of a Commonwealth of Independent States, December 8, 1991

We, the Republic of Belarus, the Russian Federation (RSFSR), and Ukraine, as originator states of the USSR on the basis of the Union Treaty of 1922, and designated below as the High Contracting Parties, confirm that the USSR as a subject of international law and a geopolitical entity, now ceases to exist.

Basing ourselves on the historical association of our peoples and the links that have developed between them, taking into consideration the bilateral treaties between the High Contracting Parties, seeking to erect democratic states based in law, intending to establish their relations on the basis of mutual recognition of and respect for state sovereignty, the inalienable right to self-determination, the principle of equality and non-interference in internal affairs, a rejection of the use of force, economic or any other methods of pressure, the settlement of disputes by means of negotiation and other generally recognized principles and norms of international law, believing that further development and strengthening of relations of friendship, good-neighborliness and mutually advantageous cooperation between our states serves the fundamental national interests of their peoples and the cause of peace and security, confirming their allegiance to the goals and principles of the United Nations Charter, the Helsinki Final Act, and other documents of the CSCE,[11] promising to observe the generally recognized international norms on the rights of man and of peoples, have agreed to the following:

Art. 1. The High Contracting Parties are forming the Commonwealth of Independent States.

Art. 2. The High Contracting Parties guarantee their citizens, regardless of their nationality or other differences, equal rights and freedoms. Each of the High Contracting Parties guarantees the citizens of the other parties, and also stateless persons living on their territory, regardless of their national affiliation or other differences, civil, political, social, economic, and cultural rights and freedoms in accordance with the generally recognized international norms of human rights.

Art. 3. The High Contracting Parties, wishing to promote the expression, preservation, and development of the ethnic, cultural, linguistic, and religious distinctiveness of the national minorities living on their territory and of the unique ethno-cultural groups that have formed there, take them under their protection.

Art. 4. The High Contracting Parties will develop equal and mutually beneficial cooperation between their peoples and states in the sphere of politics, the economy, culture, education, health care, environmental protection, science, trade, and in the humanitarian and other spheres, promote a wide-scale exchange of information, and strictly observe mutual obligations.

The parties consider that it is necessary to conclude agreements on cooperation in these spheres.

Art. 5. The High Contracting Parties recognize and respect each other's territorial integrity and the inviolability of existing frontiers within the framework of the Commonwealth.

---

11. In 1975 the first meeting of the Conference on Security and Cooperation in Europe (CSCE) was held in Helsinki, Finland and brought together the United States, Canada, and every European country, except Albania. The final act of the meeting, often known as the Helsinki accords, pledged the signatories to accept post–World War II European borders and to respect such basic human rights of their citizens as those of free speech and travel. The Helsinki accords became a basis for the protest of Soviet and Eastern European dissidents in the 1980s. Subsequent meetings were held in the 1980s and 1990s, and, with the admission of the republics of the former Soviet Union, the conference now has forty-eight members.

Chapter 15

Ethnic

Nationalism and

the Challenge

to the State:

The Example

of the Former

Soviet Union

They guarantee the openness of frontiers and freedom of movement of citizens and the transfer of information within the framework of the Commonwealth.

Art. 6. The member states of the Commonwealth will cooperate in ensuring international peace and security and the realization of effective measures to reduce armaments and military expenditures. They will strive for the elimination of all nuclear weapons and for general and complete disarmament under strict international control.

The Parties will respect each other's desire to attain the status of nuclear-free zones and neutral states.

The member states of the Commonwealth will preserve and maintain under joint command a common military-strategic space, including single control over nuclear weapons, the manner of implementing which will be regulated by a special agreement.

They also jointly guarantee the requisite conditions for the stationing, functioning, and material and social well-being of the Strategic Armed Forces. The parties undertake to conduct a coordinated policy as regards the social protection and pension arrangements for military personnel and their families.

Art. 7. The High Contracting Parties acknowledge that the sphere of their joint activity, realized on an equal basis through common coordinating institutions, includes:

—coordination of foreign-policy activity;

—cooperation in the formation and development of a common economic space, of all-European and Eurasian markets, and in the sphere of customs policy;

—cooperation in the development of transport and communications systems;

—cooperation in the sphere of environmental protection, participation in the creation of an all-embracing international system of ecological safety;

—questions of migration policy;

—the fight against organized crime.

Art. 8. The Parties recognize the global nature of the Chernobyl[12] catastrophe and undertake to unite and coordinate their efforts to minimize and overcome its consequences.

For these purposes they have agreed to conclude special agreements that take account of the seriousness of the consequences of the catastrophe.

Art. 9. Disputes regarding the interpretation of the norms of the present agreement are subject to solution by means of talks between the appropriate bodies, and, when necessary, at the level of heads of government and state.

Art. 10. Each of the High Contracting Parties reserves the right to suspend the operation of the present agreement or its individual articles having noti-

12. Chernobyl was the site of a nuclear power plant in northern Ukraine. In 1986 the world's largest nuclear accident to date occurred there, spewing a large amount of radioactive material into the atmosphere. Despite considerable loss of life, the censored Soviet press at first denied the accident. Residents of Belarus and Ukraine, the most heavily affected areas, regarded the accident and the subsequent censorship as typical of the problems of the USSR.

fied the participants in the agreement a year in advance.

The provisions of the present agreement can be supplemented or changed by mutual agreement of the High Contracting Parties.

Art. 11. The application of the norms of third states, including those of the former USSR, is not permitted on the territory of the states signing this agreement from the moment of its signing.

Art. 12. The High Contracting Parties guarantee the fulfillment of the international obligations ensuing for them from the treaties and agreements of the former USSR.

Art. 13. The present agreement does not affect the obligations of the High Contracting Parties as regards third states.

The present agreement is open to accession by all member states of the former USSR, and also by other states sharing the goals and principles of the present agreement.

Art. 14. The official residence of the coordinating bodies of the Commonwealth is the city of Minsk.

The activity of agencies of the former USSR on the territory of the member states of the commonwealth ceases.

Accomplished in the city of Minsk on 8 December 1991 in three copies, each in Belarussian, Russian, and Ukrainian, the three texts having identical force.

For the Republic of Belarus	S. Shushkevich, V. Kebich
For the RSFSR	B. Yeltsin, G. Burbulis
For Ukraine	L. Kravchuk, V. Fokin

Source 12 from Yuri Amstislavsky, "Latvia: Not Everyone Wants to or Can Live There," quoted in J. L. Black, editor, Russia and Eurasia Documents Annual, 1992, *vol. 2,* CIS and Successor States *(Gulf Breeze, Fla.: Academic International Press, 1994), p. 366.*

12. Law on the Restoration of Rights of Citizens of the Latvian Republic, October 18, 1991

Persons who possessed Latvian Republic citizenship before 17 June 1940 and their successors shall be issued passports of the citizens of the Latvian Republic. Citizens of the Latvian Republic cannot simultaneously be citizens of any other country. All other residents can be regarded as Latvian Republic's citizens if they know the Latvian language (which is to be certified by a special exam), have a record of residence in Latvia of at least 16 years, have renounced their former citizenship, know the Latvian Constitution and have pledged an oath of Latvian citizenship.

Chapter 15
Ethnic
Nationalism and
the Challenge
to the State:
The Example
of the Former
Soviet Union

Source 13 from an English language broadcast on Bishkek Kyrgyz Radio, published in J. L. Black, editor, Russia and Eurasia Documents Annual, 1993, *vol. 2:* Central Eurasian States *(Gulf Breeze, Fla.: Academic International Press, 1995), pp. 178–179.*

13. Igor Tkanchik on Russians, February 3, 1993

Hello, I'm Igor Tkanchik with the English news program from Kyrgyzstan. Today I'm going to tell you about a problem that worries lots of people here in Kyrgyzstan—that's the problem of the state language and the problem of the Russian-speaking population.

Art. 5 of the draft of the new constitution of Kyrgyzstan reads: The state language of the Kyrgyz Republic is Kyrgyz. The Kyrgyz Republic provides equal and free development of the other languages that are used by the population of the republic and creates conditions for studying of these languages.

At first sight, everything seems all right. The state promises to observe equal rights for all nations and all languages. But the thing is that, according to the Law on the State Language in 1989, by 1994 all office work will be transformed into Kyrgyz. Recently, the schedule of transformation was accepted by the government. According to it, the office work will be fully transformed into the state language in 1997. In those organizations where Kyrgyz people form 70 to 80 percent of the personnel, this process already started on 15 April 1992.

Ignorance of the state language deprives a person of the right to work at a state organization or at a state enterprise. It is no secret that one third of the population of Kyrgyzstan, including a lot of Kyrgyzes, speak only Russian. Almost 80 percent of Kyrgyzes living in Bishkek, especially youngsters, regard Russian as their mother tongue. Such a law may be classified only as a violation of natural human rights. Nationalists call Russian-speaking Kyrgyzes mankurt, as a people who do not remember their history, their language, and national roots. First, the nationalists do not take into account that these people were deprived of their language by the communist bosses who were trying hard to please Moscow. And secondly, through Russian, the Kyrgyz folk became familiar with world culture and gained recognition as a people on the world scene.

But even giving Russian the status of the language of international communication will not help the problem. You can speak Russian at the market or at home, but not at a state office. The most realistically minded deputies suggested giving Russian the status of a second state language; that would alleviate the problem of the violation of human rights which under current law is present. But no one would listen to them.

There is no denying that, living in a sovereign state, you should know the state language. Believe me, people are very enthusiastic about studying Kyrgyz. But now the situation here in Kyrgyzstan is that it is much easier to learn English than Kyrgyz. It's impossible to find a Kyrgyz-Russian dictionary. The linguists seem to be busy with politics, or writing impractical major works, but not publishing a highly needed grammar textbook. It appears that somebody finds it very profitable when the Russian-speaking population does not study Kyrgyz, but rather leaves the republic.

The problem of growing animosity between natives and other nationalities frightens people. Scenes where a drunk Kyrgyz feels that the Russians should get out of my republic are starting to become a reality. Is it surprising, after all, that the Russians are seeking any opportunity to move from here to a more safe place? The people are moving to their historical motherland. But in their historical motherland they feel like aliens. Asian Russians differ much from the Russian Russians. Living here, they have acquired the oriental mentality, oriental customs, and oriental traditions. Now there are lots of mixed Kyrgyz-Russian families. That is why it is so difficult for them to acculturate to their old motherland. People move to Russian, but they miss Kyrgyzstan. There are lots of letters appearing in the press in which people say that they still have dreams about Kyrgyzstan.

I am Russian myself. I was born here in Kyrgyzstan and I consider Kyrgyzstan my motherland. All my best friends are Kyrgyzes. I love the Kyrgyz folk for their hospitality, friendliness, and kindness. Though I do not know the Kyrgyz language, I will never leave Kyrgyzstan, no matter what happens. . . .

Chapter 15

Ethnic

Nationalism and

the Challenge

to the State:

The Example

of the Former

Soviet Union

Source 14 from U.S. Committee for Refugees, World Refugee Survey, 1995 *(Washington, D.C.: Immigration and Refugee Services of America, 1995), p. 42.*

14. Refugees and Asylum Seekers in Need of Protection and/or Assistance, 1994

PERSONS SEEKING ASYLUM IN THE REPUBLICS OF THE FORMER SOVIET UNION AND THEIR ORIGINS

Armenia:	**295,800**
Azerbaijan	290,000
Georgia	5,800
Azerbaijan:	**279,000**
Armenia	229,000
Uzbekistan	50,000
Belarus:	**18,800**
Former USSR	17,000
Other	1,800
Russia:	**451,000**
Tajikistan	145,000
Georgia	101,000
Azerbaijan	84,000
Former USSR	58,000
Non-former USSR	63,000

QUESTIONS TO CONSIDER

The world of the 1990s and beyond will be a world radically changed from that of the Cold War era (1945 to 1991), and ethnic nationalism will contribute considerably in shaping the future. In this chapter we are seeking to understand ethnic nationalism by assessing its impact on the former Soviet Union. To accomplish that objective you must seek answers to three central questions of this chapter. What were the origins of modern ethnic nationalism in the for-mer USSR? In what forms can modern ethnic nationalism be expressed? Why does ethnic nationalism present a danger to the modern state?

The answers to Question 1 are intended to provide you with historical background on the roots of ethnic nationalism in the former Soviet Union. Despite the principles proclaimed by Lenin and his associates in 1917, what sort of relationship does the evidence reveal between non-Russians and Russian-dominated government in the Soviet Union? What evidence do you find that this relationship was characterized by totalitarian rule, terror, discrimination, and relegation of some non-Russians to the status of colonial subjects? Why are you not surprised that independence efforts by non-Russian peoples followed the breakdown of tsarist power in 1917 and Soviet power in 1991? Consult the population data, too. Why were non-Russians probably better able to assert their wishes in 1991 than in 1917?

Question 2 requires you to reflect on the forms in which modern ethnic nationalism is expressed. Reflecting on the experiences of Lithuanian and Ukraine, what role did cultural factors like language and religion play in advancing the nationalist cause. Successful nationalist movements realized their goals of creating inde-pendent states. But what accompanies the creation of these states? Why do the citizenship laws of Latvia and Estonia suggest that ethnic nationalism can be intolerant? Where the goal of independence has failed, as in Chechnya, in what form has nationalism been expressed?

Question 3 requires that you move beyond the former Soviet Union in your thinking. How many other states are ethnically diverse? Why do you think that even states with democratic systems of government, in contrast to that of the old USSR, might experience the disruptive effects of modern, ethnic nationalism?

EPILOGUE

The evidence in this chapter dealt with the dissolution of the Soviet Union due in large part to the ethnic nationalism of its peoples. While this chapter treated only the experience of the Soviet Union, it is clear that the force of ethnic nationalism will be felt by the West and the world for some time to come.

The future of Russia and the other states of the Commonwealth of Independent States seems far from stable. In Russia itself, a country with little background in democracy, it is unclear whether a democratic system respecting the rights of ethnic minorities will endure, especially as it confronts the growing challenge of Russian nationalism. The Pamyat Patriotic Asso-ciation, founded by Dmitri Vasilev, is a virulently anti-Semitic and nationalistic group. Vladimir V. Zhirinovsky is the foremost exponent of Russian nationalism, and an unsuccessful presidential candidate whose supporters are the second strongest party in the Russian legislature. He openly advocates the reunification of the territories of the former Russian Empire and the Soviet Union, and bitterly condemns the government of Boris Yeltsin for accepting foreign assistance. Zhirinovsky said in one speech:

> We have mutilated our country, we have made her backward. We have forced the Russian nation, the most advanced, to sink down. We have done it with force. Materially, through laws and psychologically, through pressure. And now we are being told that we can't get along

Chapter 15

Ethnic

Nationalism and

the Challenge

to the State:

The Example

of the Former

Soviet Union

without foreigners, that we cannot rely on ourselves, on the Russian people. That's terrible.[13]

Many political observers believe that pressure from Zhirinovsky and other leaders of the Russian right prompted President Yeltsin to adopt his forceful suppression of the Chechen independence movement.

The non-Russian members of the Commonwealth of Independent States also face problems. In many of the republics there are armed ethnic conflicts under way and these new states face other problems as well. In the Central Asian republics there is growing lawlessness; plants for drugs that are illegal in much of the West are major cash crops for farmers in neighboring Afghanistan, and the drugs produced from them move across the border into such Central Asian Commonwealth states as Tajikistan, Turkmenistan, and Uzbekistan. Economically, many of the new republics are ill-equipped for independence; most were treated like economic colonies by the USSR, which exploited their chief industries or crops but failed to develop the production infrastructure of modern, economically and politically independent nations. Thus, many of the new states found themselves still economically dependent on Russia, and the search for economic independence may well lead to further ethnic conflict over resources.

Democracy, usually committed to respecting the rights of minorities, has not fared well, either, in the years since 1991. All of the republics are committed to it in principle; in practice one-party regimes quickly emerged in many states. In Central Asia, for example, only Kyrgyzstan seems to have made any progress toward development of Western-style democracy, and even the Baltic states have experienced a resurgence of communist parties.

Beyond the borders of the Commonwealth of Independent States, ethnic nationalism also presents real or potential problems. In Africa, ethnic problems abound, in part because the political borders of that continent were drawn by European statesmen in a fashion reflecting European power politics rather than the zones inhabited by the continent's ethnic groups. Thus that continent probably will continue to experience the kind of ethnic conflict of the 1990s that has proven so costly in human lives in Burundi and Rwanda. In Asia, ethnic violence continues in Sri Lanka, and the potential for it exists elsewhere, most notably in the People's Republic of China with its fifty-five recognized ethnic groups.

The danger of ethnic conflict is also present in Europe. All of the democracies of Western Europe, for example, are the result of the consolidation of one ethnic group's rule over smaller ethnic groups. Thus, the United Kingdom has experienced demands for cultural autonomy from the Scots and Welsh. France has experienced similar demands from Basques, Bretons, and those influenced by the Occitan language of the south of the country. Spain confronts an often violent Basque separatist movement and a

13. Quoted in *New York Times Book Review*, August 13, 1995, p. 7.

less violent, but no less real, cultural movement among Catalans. And Belgium, in the years since World War II, has come close to collapse as a result of ethnic tensions between the majority Flemish (Dutch-speakers) and the minority Walloons (French-speakers) who long had extraordinary economic and political influence.

Nor do the problems of the West end with the issues raised by native European ethnic minority groups. Western Europe, like the United States, has become much more ethnically diverse since World War II. Immigrants from former colonies in Africa, Asia, and the Caribbean settled in Belgium, France, Great Britain, and the Netherlands. "Guest workers" from North Africa and the Middle East sought employment in Germany and other countries. Most of these immigrants found employment in low-paid positions, in what one scholar has characterized as the "unpleasant" jobs. They also encountered ethnic and social prejudice as their numbers grew. Virtually every Western European country now has nationalist political movements openly hostile to foreigners. In France the National Front of Jean-Marie Le Pen espouses a call of "France for the French," and his party won some significant local government victories in the elections of 1995. In Germany Franz Schönhuber, a former Nazi, leads the Republican party, which is committed to an antiforeigner policy. Even in the United States there has been a growing call for the adoption of English as the official language, and in the 1996 elections, there was considerable debate on closing off immigration. The result of such vocal political groups sometimes has been violence. The most widespread violence erupted in Germany where, in the late 1980s and early 1990s, neo-Nazi groups attacked foreigners.

These developments very likely will mean that few states will escape the conflicts resulting from ethnic nationalism. The modern state will define its future character in its responses to ethnic nationalism.

Text credits continued from page iv.

1984, 1979, 1970 by W. W. Norton & Company, Inc. **Pages 339–344:** Reprinted with permission of Twayne Publishers, an imprint of Simon and Schuster Macmillan, from PEACEWORK: ORAL HISTORIES OF WOMEN PEACE ACTIVISTS by Judith Porter Adams. Copyright © 1991 by G. K. Hall & Co. **Pages 347–349:** From KEEPING THE PEACE: A WOMAN'S PEACE HANDBOOK, edited by Lynne Jones, first published by The Women's Press, 1983. Source 10 reprinted by permission of Tamar Swade. **Page 349:** Coretta Scott King, "The Judgment of History Will Show," from a speech given at an International Women's Conference for Peace and Nuclear Disarmament, published in 1984 in the Newsletter of the Center for Defense Information, DEFENSE MONITOR, vol. 13, no. 8. Reprinted by permission. **Pages 351–353:** Ann Snitow, "Holding the Line at Greenham Common: Being Joyously Political in Dangerous Times," MOTHER JONES, Feb/March 1985. Reprinted with permission from MOTHER JONES magazine, © 1985. Foundation for National Progress. **Pages 367–369:** From MEIN KAMPF by Adolf Hitler, translated by Ralph Manheim. Copyright 1943 and © renewed 1971 by Houghton Mifflin Company. Reprinted by permission of Houghton Mifflin Company. All rights reserved. **Pages 369–371, 373, 375, 381–382:** Jeremy Noakes and Geoffrey Pridham, editors, DOCUMENTS ON NAZISM, 1919–1945 (New York: Viking, 1975), pp. 103–104, 163–164, 83–84, 106, 108. Copyright © 1975 by Jeremy Noakes and Geoffrey Pridham. Reprinted by permission of Sterling Lord Literistic, Inc. **Page 377:** Extract from George L. Mosse, ed., NAZI CULTURE: INTELLECTUAL, CULTURAL, AND SOCIAL LIFE IN THE THIRD REICH. Published by Grosset and Dunlap. Used by permission of George L. Mosse. **Page 379:** Adapted from THE NAZI SEIZURE OF POWER: THE EXPERIENCE OF A SINGLE GERMAN TOWN, 1922–1945, by William Sheridan Allen. Copyright © 1965, 1984 by William Sheridan Allen. Used with permission of the publisher Franklin Watts, Inc., New York. **Pages 382–384:** William L. Shirer, BERLIN DIARY, THE JOURNAL OF A FOREIGN CORRESPONDENT, 1934–1941 (New York: Knopf, 1941). Reprinted by permission of Don Congdon Associates, Inc. Copyright © 1941 renewed 1969 by William L. Shirer. **Pages 397–399:** Extracts from Vladimir Fisera's WRITING ON THE WALL are reprinted by permission of W. H. Allen Publishers. **Pages 407–408:** From THE CZECHOSLOVAK EXPERIMENT, 1968–1969 (New York: Columbia University Press, 1971), pp. 17–18; p. 16. Reprinted by permission of the author. **Pages 433–434:** Kaiser, Robert J.: THE GEOGRAPHY OF NATIONALISM IN RUSSIA AND THE USSR. Copyright © 1994 by Princeton University Press. Reprinted by permission of Princeton University Press. **Pages 435, 437:** From THE FIRSTBOOK OF DEMOGRAPHICS FOR THE REPUBLICS OF THE FORMER SOVIET UNION, 1951–1990 (Shady Side, Maryland: New Work Demographics, L.C., 1992), map supplement; p. K-2. Reprinted by permission. **Page 436:** From Soviet Census of 1989: VESTNIK STATISTIKI 10/12/90, 1,4,6/91, Reprinted in Archie Brown, Michael Kaser, and Gerald S. Smith, eds., THE CAMBRIDGE ENCYCLOPEDIA OF RUSSIA AND THE FORMER SOVIET UNION (New York: Cambridge University Press, 1995), pp. 26–27. Reprinted by permission of Cambridge University Press. **Page 438:** From Maksym Sahaydk, compiler, THE UKRAINIAN HERALD ISSUE 7-8: ETHOCIDE OF UKRAINIANS IN THE U.S.S.R. (translated and edited by Olena Saciuk and Bohdan Yasen; Baltimore, Paris and Toronto: Smoloskyp Publishers, Inc., 1976), p. 15. Reprinted by permission of Smoloskyp Publishers, Inc. **Page 439:** From Nijole Grazulism, ed. and trans., THE CHRONICLES OF THE CATHOLIC CHURCH IN LITHUANIA: UNDERGROUND JOURNAL OF HUMAN RIGHTS VIOLATIONS (Nos. 1–9, 1972–74, Chicago: Loyola University Press and the Society for the Publication of the Chronicle of the Catholic Church in Lithuania, Inc., 1981), pp. 338–39. Reprinted by permission of Loyola University Press. **Pages 443–446:** Charles F. Furtado, Jr. and Andrea Chandler, eds., PERESTROIKA IN THE SOVIET REPUBLICS: DOCUMENTS OF THE NATIONAL QUESTION (Boulder, Co.: Westview Press, 1992). Translation by Tiina Ets. Reprinted by permission of the Estonian American National Council, New York, NY. **Pages 446–449:** USSR Documents Annual 1991. Disintegration of the USSR. J. L. Black, ed. (American International Press, Gulf Breeze, Fla.), p. 299–301. Reprinted by permission. **Pages 449, 450–451:** Russian and Eurasia Documents Annual 1992. Volume 2: CIS and Successor States. J. L. Black, ed. (American International Press, Gulf Breeze, Fla.), p. 366; p. 178–179. Reprinted by permission. **Page 452:** From U.S. Committee for Refugees, WORLD REFUGEE SURVEY, 1995 (Washington, D.C.: Immigration and Refugee Services of America, 1995), p. 42. Reprinted by permission.